Karim Samji
The Qur'ān

Studies in the History and Culture of the Middle East

Volume 32

Karim Samji

The Qur'ān

A Form-Critical History

DE GRUYTER

ISBN 978-3-11-068512-1
e-ISBN (PDF) 978-3-11-058088-4
e-ISBN (EPUB) 978-3-11-058004-4
ISSN 2198-0853

Library of Congress Cataloging-in-Publication Data
A CIP catalog record for this book has been applied for at the Library of Congress.

Bibliographic information published by the Deutsche Nationalbibliothek
The Deutsche Nationalbibliothek lists this publication in the Deutsche Nationalbibliografie; detailed bibliographic data are available in the Internet at http://dnb.dnb.de.

This volume is text- and page-identical with the hardback published in 2018.
Printing: CPI books GmbH, Leck
♾ Printed on acid-free paper
Printed in Germany

www.degruyter.com

Our understanding of scripture must be the historical one.

Hermann Gunkel

Contents

Abbreviations — IX

Chapter 1: Method — 1
1.1 Introduction — **1**
1.2 Critical Approaches — **6**
1.3 Literary Genres — **27**
1.4 Summary — **34**

Chapter 2: Prayer — 36
2.1 Prayer Genre — **36**
2.2 Prayer Formulae — **37**
2.3 Prayer Setting — **44**
2.4 Prayer Forms — **54**
2.5 Summary — **82**

Chapter 3: Liturgy — 84
3.1 Liturgy Genre — **84**
3.2 Liturgy Formulae — **85**
3.3 Liturgical Setting — **97**
3.4 Liturgical Forms — **99**
3.5 Summary — **129**

Chapter 4: Wisdom — 130
4.1 Wisdom Genre — **130**
4.2 Wisdom Formulae — **131**
4.3 Wisdom Setting — **144**
4.4 Wisdom Forms — **146**
4.5 Summary — **174**

Chapter 5: Narrative — 175
5.1 Narrative Genre — **175**
5.2 Narrative Formulae — **177**
5.3 Narrative Setting — **191**
5.4 Narrative Forms — **193**
5.5 Summary — **225**

Abbreviations

ABD	*Anchor Bible Dictionary* (ed. Freedman)
AcOr	*Acta Orientalia*
BBR	*Bulletin for Biblical Research*
BCQ	*A Commentary on the Qurʾān* (Bell)
BIQ[1]	*Introduction to the Qurʾān*. 1st ed. (Bell)
BIQ[2]	*Bell's Introduction to the Qurʾān*. Rev. ed. (Bell/Watt)
BQA	*The Qurʾān*. Annotations (Bell)
BSMESB	*British Society for Middle Eastern Studies Bulletin*
BSOAS	*Bulletin of the School of Oriental and African Studies*
CBQ	*The Catholic Biblical Quarterly*
CQ	*A Concordance of the Qurʾān* (Kassis)
ChrW	*Die christliche Welt*
DBI	*Dictionary of Biblical Imagery*
DJG	*Dictionary of Jesus and the Gospels*
DLW	*Dictionary of Liturgy and Worship*
DOTWPW	*Dictionary of the Old Testament: Wisdom, Poetry & Writings*
EAC	*Encyclopedia of Ancient Christianity*
EB[9]	*Encyclopaedia Britannica*. 9th ed.
EI[1]	*Encyclopaedia of Islam*. 1st ed.
EI[2]	*Encyclopaedia of Islam*. 2nd ed.
EQ	*Encyclopaedia of the Qurʾān*
ER[2]	*Encyclopedia of Religion*. 2nd ed.
EinlPs[4]	*Einleitung in die Psalmen*. 4th ed. (Gunkel/Begrich)
ExpTim	*The Expository Times*
FOTL	*The Forms of the Old Testament Literature* (ed. Knierim/Tucker)
GdQ[2]	*Geschichte des Qorāns*. 2nd ed. (Nöldeke/Schwally)
HZ	*Historische Zeitschrift*
IJMES	*International Journal of Middle East Studies*
Isl.	*Der Islam*
JAAC	*Journal of Aesthetics and Art Criticism*
JAAR	*Journal of the American Academy of Religion*
JAOS	*Journal of the American Oriental Society*
JBL	*Journal of Biblical Literature*
JETS	*Journal of the Evangelical Theological Society*
JSS	*Journal of Semitic Studies*
JQA	*The Qurʾān*. Annotations (Jones)
JQS	*Journal of Qurʾānic Studies*
JRAS	*The Journal of the Royal Asiatic Society of Great Britain and Ireland*
KU	*Koranische Untersuchungen* (Horovitz)
Komm	*Der Koran: Kommentar und Konkordanz* (Paret)
MIO	*Mitteilungen des Instituts für Orientforschung*
MLR	*The Modern Language Review*
MSOS	*Mitteilungen des Seminars für orientalische Sprachen*
MTSR	*Method & Theory in the Study of Religion*

MThZ	*Münchener Theologische Zeitschrift*
MW	*The Muslim World*
NIB	*The New Interpreter's Bible*
NIDB	*The New Interpreter's Dictionary of the Bible*
OCA	*Orientalia Christiana Analecta*
OEBI	*Oxford Encyclopedia of Biblical Interpretation*
P&L	*Philosophy and Literature*
Q	*al-Qur'ān al-karīm*. Egyptian ed.
QS	*Qur'ānic Studies* (Wansbrough)
QSC	*The Qur'ān: Style and Contents* (ed. Rippin)
RGG¹	*Die Religion in Geschichte und Gegenwart.* 1st ed.
RGG²	*Die Religion in Geschichte und Gegenwart.* 2nd ed.
R&L	*Religion and Literature*
SI	*Studia Islamica*
SKMS²	*Studien zur Komposition der mekkanischen Suren.* 2nd ed. (Neuwirth)
SM	*Studia Missionalia*
SPMC	*Scripture, Poetry and the Making of a Community* (Neuwirth)
STCL	*Studies in 20th Century Literature*
TAPA	*Transactions and Proceedings of the American Philological Association*
TDOT	*Theological Dictionary of the Old Testament*
ThLZ	*Theologische Literaturzeitung*
ThR	*Theologische Rundschau*
VT	*Vetus Testamentum*
WMS	*Wesley and Methodist Studies*
WZKM	*Wiener Zeitschrift für die Kunde des Morgenlandes*
ZAW	*Zeitschrift für die alttestamentliche Wissenschaft*
ZThK	*Zeitschrift für Theologie und Kirche*

Acknowledgment

The English translation of Qur'ānic verses referenced in this volume principally follows *The Qur'ān*, translated by Alan Jones. Copyright © 2007 by Gibb Memorial Trust. Reproduced by permission.

Chapter 1: Method

1.1 Introduction

The present monograph examines the constructive application of genre criticism to the *corpus coranicum.*[1] Hermann Gunkel (d. 1932) established the method in response to the problems endemic to psalm criticism and extended its scope to the entire Old Testament corpus.[2] Before long his students Martin Dibelius (d. 1947) and Rudolf Bultmann (d. 1976) blazed a trail in the study of the New Testament.[3] Particularly pertinent to this discussion of method is Johann Gottfried von Herder (d. 1803), whose formative influence on Gunkel was decisive.[4]

---

1 *al-Qur'ān al-karīm* (Cairo: s.n., 1924). The English translation of Qur'ānic verses referenced in this volume principally follows *The Qur'ān*, trans. Alan Jones (Cambridge: Gibb Memorial Trust, 2007). Sigla: you^{S} (singular superscript); you^{P} (plural superscript) (ibid., 21–22). Flügel numerals converted to correspond with the Egyptian edition (see *BIQ*^{2} 202–3). The English translation of Biblical passages referenced in this volume primarily follows *The New Oxford Annotated Bible: New Revised Standard Version with the Apocrypha*, 4th rev. ed., ed. Michael D. Coogan (Oxford: Oxford University Press, 2010).

2 Hermann Gunkel, "Psalmen," in *RGG*^{2}, vol. 4, ed. idem and Leopold Zscharnack (Tübingen: Verlag von J.C.B. Mohr (Paul Siebeck), 1930), cols. 1609–27; Hans Rollmann, "Zwei Briefe Hermann Gunkels an Adolf Jülicher zur religionsgeschichtlichen und formgeschichtlichen Methode," *ZThK* 78, no. 3 (1981): 284; Gerd Lüdemann and Martin Schröder, *Die religionsgeschichtliche Schule in Göttingen: Eine Dokumentation* (Göttingen: Vandenhoeck & Ruprecht, 1987), 66–70.

3 Rollmann, "Zwei Briefe Hermann Gunkels an Adolf Jülicher," 285, fn. 18.

4 Martin J. Buss, *Biblical Form Criticism in Its Context* (Sheffield, England: Sheffield Academic Press, 1999), 216, fn. 24; Erhard S. Gerstenberger, "Psalms," in *Old Testament Form Criticism*, ed. John H. Hayes (San Antonio, Texas: Trinity University Press, 1977), 181; Johannes Hempel (d. 1964), *Die althebräische Literatur und ihr hellenistisch-jüdisches Nachleben* (Wildpark-Potsdam: Akademische Verlagsgesellschaft Athenaion, 1930), 5; Antony F. Campbell, "The Emergence of the Form-Critical and Traditio-Historical Approaches," in *Hebrew Bible / Old Testament: The History of Its Interpretation*, vol. 3, pt. 2, ed. Magne Sæbø (Göttingen: Vandenhoeck & Ruprecht, 2015), 136; John H. Hayes, *Interpreting Ancient Israelite History, Prophecy, and Law* (Eugene, Oregon: Cascade Books, 2013), 165; Johann Gottfried von Herder, *Vom Geist der ebräischen Poesie*, 2 vols. (Deßau: Verlag-Kasse, 1782–83); James Muilenburg, "Form Criticism and Beyond," *JBL* 88, no. 1 (1969): 1; Henning Graf Reventlow, *Epochen der Bibelauslegung* (München: Verlag C.H. Beck, 2001), 4:194–200, esp. 199. For the theses advanced by Hermann Samuel Reimarus (d. 1768), see idem, *Uebrige noch ungedruckte Werke des Wolfenbüttlischen Fragmentisten* (Berlin: s.n., 1787); Reventlow, *Epochen der Bibelauslegung*, 4:199; Gerald Bray, *Biblical Interpretation: Past & Present* (Downers Grove, Illinois: InterVarsity Press, 1996), 243. Significantly, Reimarus was influenced by Peter Annet (d. 1769) (Bray, *Biblical Interpretation*, 232 and 243; Peter Annet, *The Resurrection of Jesus Considered*, 3rd ed. (London: M. Cooper, 1744); idem, *The Resurrection Defenders* (London: s.n., 1745); idem, *The Free Enquirer* (London: R. Carlile, 1826 [1761])).

https://doi.org/10.1515/9783110580884-001

Dibelius positively asserts, "Herder was the pioneer of such movements in the sphere of biblical literature...he intuitively put forward many axioms, which only at a later date were to reach significance for criticism."[5] In point of fact, Herder set the stage and the tone when he endorsed the view that scripture as literature be treated historically.[6] As a result, the shape of things to come is prefigured in Herder.[7] Karl Barth (d. 1968) repeatedly stresses without exaggeration, "Without Herder, there is no Schleiermacher, no de Wette...Without Herder, there is no Erlangen school, no history of religion school."[8] Largely through Herder,

---

"Among all the ingenious gentlemen who have entered the lists against Mr. Woolston in favour of the gospel miracles, the author of the *Tryal of the Witnesses of the Resurrection of Jesus* stands foremost on the records of fame" (Annet, *The Resurrection of Jesus Considered*, 3; Thomas Woolston, *A Free-Gift to the Clergy* (London: s.n., 1722), 11; idem, *A Discourse on the Miracles of Our Saviour*, 2nd ed. (London: s.n., 1727); Thomas Sherlock, *The Trial of the Witnesses of the Resurrection of Jesus* (Hartford, Connecticut: Lincoln & Gleason, 1804 [1729]); Bray, *Biblical Interpretation*, 232–34).

5 Martin Dibelius, *Die Formgeschichte des Evangeliums*, 2nd rev. ed. (Tübingen: J.C.B. Mohr (Paul Siebeck), 1933 [1919]), 4; idem, *From Tradition to Gospel*, trans. Bertram Lee Woolf (New York: Charles Scribner's Sons, 1965), 5; idem, "Zur Formgeschichte der Evangelien," *ThR*, N.F., 1 (1929): 186; cf. Rollmann, "Zwei Briefe Hermann Gunkels an Adolf Jülicher," 283–84. Parenthetically, Dibelius acknowledges Eduard Norden (d. 1941), who coined a similar term (Eduard Norden, *Agnostos Theos: Untersuchungen zur Formengeschichte religiöser Rede* (Leipzig: Verlag B.G. Teubner, 1913); Dibelius, *Formgeschichte*, 4; cf. Buss, *Biblical Form Criticism*, 230, fn. 68).

6 Johann Gottfried von Herder, *Briefe, das Studium der Theologie betreffend*, 2nd rev. ed. (Weimar: Carl Ludolf Hoffman, 1785), 1:1; John H. Hayes and Frederick C. Prussner, *Old Testament Theology: Its History and Development* (Atlanta, Georgia: John Knox Press, 1985), 52; Hermann Gunkel, "The 'Historical Movement' in the Study of Religion," *ExpTim* 38, no. 12 (1927): 535–36; Kenton L. Sparks, "Genre Criticism," in *Methods for Exodus*, ed. Thomas B. Dozeman (Cambridge: Cambridge University Press, 2010), 57; Roy Pascal, "The 'Sturm und Drang' Movement," *MLR* 47, no. 2 (1952): 139–42. N.b. "In Old Testament studies, the term 'historical criticism' was introduced in 1794" (Martin J. Buss, *The Changing Shape of Form Criticism: A Relational Approach*, ed. Nickie M. Stipe (Sheffield, England: Sheffield Phoenix Press, 2010), 18).

7 S.v. Religionsgeschichtliche Schule, *ER*[2]; cf. Gunkel, "Historical Movement," 533; Richard N. Soulen, *Handbook of Biblical Criticism*, 2nd rev. ed. (Atlanta, Georgia: John Knox Press, 1981), 167–68; Robert A. Oden, Jr., "Historical Understanding and Understanding the Religion of Israel," in *The Bible without Theology: The Theological Tradition and Alternatives to It* (San Francisco, California: Harper & Row, 1987), 30; Werner Klatt, *Hermann Gunkel: Zu seiner Theologie der Religionsgeschichte und zur Entstehung der formgeschichtlichen Methode* (Göttingen: Vandenhoeck & Ruprecht, 1969), 25, fn. 39; Brevard S. Childs, *Biblical Theology of the Old and New Testaments: Theological Reflection on the Christian Bible* (Minneapolis, Minnesota: Fortress Press, 1993), 197–98; Rollmann, "Zwei Briefe Hermann Gunkels an Adolf Jülicher," 284.

8 Karl Barth, *Die protestantische Theologie im 19. Jahrhundert: Ihre Vorgeschichte und ihre Geschichte*, 2nd rev. ed. (Zollikon-Zürich: Evangelischer Verlag AG, 1952), 282; Charles E. Shepherd, *Theological Interpretation and Isaiah 53: A Critical Comparison of Bernhard Duhm, Brevard Childs,*

the history of religion method had deep and manifold roots in the modern classical philology of Friedrich August Wolf (d. 1824), the nascent historical discipline of Leopold von Ranke (d. 1886),[9] the emergent science of religion of Friedrich Max Müller (d. 1900),[10] and the historical-critical method of Julius Wellhausen (d. 1918).[11] For instance, the echo of Herder is heard in August Boeckh (d. 1867), who combined the philological and hermeneutical insights of Wolf and Friedrich Schleiermacher (d. 1834), respectively[12]: "The highest task of genre criticism is to investigate whether content and form...are suitable for the inner aim of a genre...."[13] Gunkel concurs that "aesthetic or literary qual-

and Alec Motyer (London: Bloomsbury T&T Clark, 2014), 9, fn. 2; Lüdemann and Schröder, *Die religionsgeschichtliche Schule, passim.* For the earlier and later periods of the *Religionsgeschichtliche Schule*, see Bray, *Biblical Interpretation*, 361–67; Alf Özen, "Die Göttinger Wurzeln der 'Religionsgeschichtlichen Schule,'" in *Die "Religionsgeschichtliche Schule": Facetten eines theologischen Umbruchs*, ed. Gerd Lüdemann (Frankfurt am Main: Peter Lang, 1996), 23–64; Reventlow, *Epochen der Bibelauslegung*, 4:325–65; Buss, *Biblical Form Criticism*, 216, fn. 24; Gerstenberger, "Psalms," 181; Konrad Hammann, *Hermann Gunkel: Eine Biographie* (Tübingen: Mohr Siebeck, 2014), 184; Erhardt Güttgemanns (d. 2008), *Offene Fragen zur Formgeschichte des Evangeliums: Eine methodologische Skizze der Grundlagenproblematik der Form- und Redaktionsgeschichte*, 2nd rev. ed. (München: Chr. Kaiser Verlag, 1971), 120; cf. Klatt, *Hermann Gunkel*, 110–11, fn. 29, and 113.

9 Oden, "Historical Understanding and Understanding the Religion of Israel," 9, 16, 22, and 27–28; Soulen, *Handbook of Biblical Criticism*, 56.

10 It is evident that Gunkel shares the same sentiments as Goethe and Müller: "He who knows one, knows none" (Friedrich Max Müller, *Einleitung in die vergleichende Religionswissenschaft* (Strassburg: Verlag von Karl J. Trübner, 1874), 13–14; Gunkel, "Historical Movement," 535; cf. Adolf von Harnack (d. 1930), *Reden und Aufsätze* (Gieszen: J. Ricker'sche Verlagsbuchhandlung, 1904), 2:168; Hans Rollmann, "Theologie und Religionsgeschichte: Zeitgenössische Stimmen zur Diskussion um die religionsgeschichtliche Methode und die Einführung religionsgeschichtlicher Lehrstühle in den theologischen Fakultäten um die Jahrhundertwende," *ZThK* 80, no. 1 (1983): 70–71; Pascal, "Sturm und Drang Movement," 147; Hayes, *Interpreting Ancient Israelite History, Prophecy, and Law*, 164–65, fn. 10; Klatt, *Hermann Gunkel*, 70–74; Hammann, *Hermann Gunkel*, 72–84; Oden, "Historical Understanding and Understanding the Religion of Israel," 34).

11 S.v. Religionsgeschichtliche Schule, *ER*²; Oden, "Historical Understanding and Understanding the Religion of Israel," 21–23.

12 Michael N. Forster, introduction to *Philosophical Writings*, by Johann Gottfried von Herder (Cambridge: Cambridge University Press, 2002), vii–viii; Oden, "Historical Understanding and Understanding the Religion of Israel," 28–29; see Hugo Greßmann, *Albert Eichhorn und Die Religionsgeschichtliche Schule* (Göttingen: Vandenhoeck & Ruprecht, 1914), 20–21.

13 August Boeckh, *Encyklopädie und Methodologie der philologischen Wissenschaften* (Leipzig: Teubner, 1877), 240–50, esp. 250; Buss, *Biblical Form Criticism*, 249–50.

ity is not merely superficial."[14] In other words, he holds that "aesthetic description can be scholarly."[15]

Turning to the critique of the eponymous Wellhausen school, Gunkel opens with a simple disclaimer: Wellhausen is above reproach.[16] Nonetheless, Gunkel asserts that an inadvertent consequence of higher criticism is the relative disregard for historical aesthetics.[17] In tandem with Herder, he lays this inopportune development at the doorstep of Enlightenment rationalism.[18] In this respect, Gunkel cites the proclivity of the Wellhausen school towards *argumentum ex silentio* and the legal dictum *quod non est in actis, non est in mundo.*[19] Yet again, without fail, he denies Wellhausen's complicity in the matter.[20] However, Gunkel takes to task historical criticism, which is premised exclusively on written rather than mixed transmission.[21] He criticizes the Wellhausen school for its failure to

---

14 Buss, *Biblical Form Criticism*, 219; Oden, "Historical Understanding and Understanding the Religion of Israel," 31.

15 Buss, *Biblical Form Criticism*, 219. What is more, Boeckh states, "the purpose of philology is purely historical" (idem, *Encyklopädie*, 18).

16 Gunkel, "Historical Movement," 532–33; James L. Crenshaw, *Gerhard von Rad* (Waco, Texas: Word Books, 1978), 166.

17 Gunkel, "Historical Movement," 534.

18 Ibid.; Pascal, "Sturm und Drang Movement," 139 and 147; cf. Joe K. Fugate, *The Psychological Basis of Herder's Aesthetics* (Paris: Mouton & Co., 1966), 234; Oden, "Historical Understanding and Understanding the Religion of Israel," 8–9 and 31; Hayden V. White, "Introduction: On History and Historicisms," in *From History to Sociology: The Transition in German Historical Thinking*, by Carlo Antoni (Detroit, Michigan: Wayne State University Press, 1959), xviii; Johann Gottfried von Herder, *Auch eine Philosophie der Geschichte zur Bildung der Menschheit* (s.l.: s.n., 1774), *passim*). For Herder's historicisms (i.e., *naturalistic*, *metaphysical*, and *aesthetic*), see White, "Introduction: On History and Historicisms," xviii–xxiii.

19 Gunkel, "Historical Movement," 534; Buss, *Biblical Form Criticism*, 210, fn. 6; cf. Klatt, *Hermann Gunkel*, 70–74; Hammann, *Hermann Gunkel*, 72–84.

20 Gunkel, "Historical Movement," 534.

21 Gunkel concludes, "The school of Wellhausen was and still is inclined, in its constructive historical work, to be too subservient to the literary documents, overlooking the fact that special precautions must be taken if the actual history is to be successfully reconstructed from the sources, however carefully these may have been sifted" (ibid., 533–34). N.b. "The words 'literary' and 'literature' refer not only to written expression, but include oral materials" (Martin J. Buss, "The Idea of *Sitz im Leben:* History and Critique," *ZAW* 90, no. 2 (1978): 158, fn. 4; cf. John Barton, *Reading the Old Testament: Method in Biblical Study*, 2nd rev. ed. (Louisville, Kentucky: Westminster John Knox Press, 1996), 29). Nevertheless, "[t]he composition of written literature, according to Gunkel, was in most cases indicative of the fact that some learned author had cut the umbilical cord of a particular genre severing its connection to its source of life" (Gerstenberger, "Psalms," 181). Herder writes on the subject of language in a similar vein (idem, *Abhandlung über den Ursprung der Sprache* (Berlin: Bey Christian Friedrich Voß, 1772), 13).

recognize the cataloguing of genres as the primary task of research.[22] As is so often the case in history, Gunkel's ideas were poorly received, and even met stern resistance.[23] It was none other than Carl Heinrich Becker (d. 1933) who promoted members of the history of religion school, and most prominently, Gunkel.[24] In concert with the "little Göttingen faculty," Gunkel promulgated his conception, in which the history of religion works hand in hand with the history of literature.[25] Henning Reventlow (d. 2010) reflects on Gunkel's place in intellectual history[26]:

> One could say that Gunkel blazed new paths in every field in which he worked, and in many cases methodologically broke new ground. Against a generation that had been represented by Wellhausen, he led scholarship to a completely altered outlook, especially in Old Testament research.

In sum, James Muilenburg (d. 1974) emphasizes, "the first and most obvious achievement of genre criticism is that it supplied a much-needed corrective to literary and historical criticism."[27] Having laid a basis for discussion, let us now turn to scholarly approaches to the Qur'ān.[28]

---

22 Hermann Gunkel, "Formen der Hymnen," *ThR* 20, nos. 10–11 (1917): 265.

23 Buss, *Biblical Form Criticism*, 218, fn. 28; cf. Klatt, *Hermann Gunkel*, 167, fn. 4.

24 Reventlow, *Epochen der Bibelauslegung*, 4:329.

25 S.v. Religionsgeschichtliche Schule, *ER*^{2}; Gerstenberger, "Psalms," 181; see Özen, "Die Göttinger Wurzeln der 'Religionsgeschichtlichen Schule,'" 44–47. According to Gunkel, "our objections, therefore, are in no way directed against criticism as such, but against the tendency to postulate an over-close relation between literary criticism and the history of religion" (idem, "Historical Movement," 533–34; idem, foreword to *Reden und Aufsätze* (Göttingen: Vandenhoeck & Ruprecht, 1913), v–vi; Mark D. Chapman, *Ernst Troeltsch and Liberal Theology: Religion and Cultural Synthesis in Wilhelmine Germany* (Oxford: Oxford University Press, 2001), 32; cf. Oden, "Historical Understanding and Understanding the Religion of Israel," 32). N.b. The publication arm of the history of religion school includes *Die Religion in Geschichte und Gegenwart* and *Theologische Rundschau* (Bray, *Biblical Interpretation*, 363; s.v. Religionsgeschichtliche Schule, *ER*^{2}; Lüdemann and Schröder, *Die religionsgeschichtliche Schule*, 13–23 and 133–36; Alf Özen, "*Die Religion in Geschichte und Gegenwart* als Beispiel für Hoch-Zeit und Niedergang der 'Religionsgeschichtlichen Schule' (*II. Teil: RGG*^{2})," in *Die "Religionsgeschichtliche Schule": Facetten eines theologischen Umbruchs*, ed. Gerd Lüdemann (Frankfurt am Main: Peter Lang, 1996), 243–98).

26 Reventlow, *Epochen der Bibelauslegung*, 4:330; idem, *History of Biblical Interpretation*, trans. Leo G. Perdue (Atlanta, Georgia: Society of Biblical Literature, 2010), 4:340.

27 Muilenburg, "Form Criticism and Beyond," 2.

28 J. Coert Rylaarsdam, foreword to *Form Criticism of the Old Testament*, by Gene M. Tucker (Philadelphia, Pennsylvania: Fortress Press, 1971), iii; Gerstenberger, "Psalms," 222.

1.2 Critical Approaches

Reception Criticism

In Theodor Nöldeke's summative article "The Koran" (1891), commentaries (sing. *tafsīr*) stand alongside scripture.[29] Otherwise, he reasonably explains, "we should still be helpless without the exegetical literature."[30] This tendency casts a long shadow over John Wansbrough's *Qur'ānic Studies: Sources and Methods of Scriptural Interpretation* (1977).[31] In fact, Wansbrough clearly states, "the manner in which the concept of authority was progressively articulated by means of these exegetical types is the formative principle and the purpose of my exposition...."[32] Reaching its zenith in the second half of the last century, this viewpoint generated a lively discussion rooted in "a stark dichotomy of method."[33] Although this set the tenor of the field to the present, the denunciation of "the priority of history" set its course.[34] In direct opposition to Ranke and Wellhausen, Wansbrough adjudges, "all such efforts at historical reconstruction (*wie es eigentlich gewesen*) tend to be reductive... ."[35] For that reason, Andrew

---

29 S.v. Mohammedanism: The Koran, *EB*[9].

30 Ibid.

31 Andrew L. Rippin, foreword to *Qur'ānic Studies: Sources and Methods of Scriptural Interpretation*, by John E. Wansbrough (Amherst, New York: Prometheus Books, 2004 [1977]), xiv; Nicolai Sinai and Angelika Neuwirth, introduction to *The Qur'ān in Context: Historical and Literary Investigations into the Qur'ānic Milieu*, ed. eadem and Michael Marx (Leiden: Brill, 2011), 3.

32 *QS* xxii.

33 Devin J. Stewart, "Reflections on the State of the Art in Western Qur'ānic Studies," in *Islam and Its Past: Jahiliyya, Late Antiquity, and the Qur'ān*, ed. Carol Bakhos and Michael Cook (Oxford: Oxford University Press, 2017), 5, fn. 1.

34 Andrew L. Rippin, "Literary Analysis of Qur'ān, Tafsīr, and Sīra: The Methodologies of John Wansbrough," in *Approaches to Islam in Religious Studies*, ed. Richard C. Martin (Tucson, Arizona: The University of Arizona Press, 1985), 163. According to Wansbrough, "historiography, like other kinds of literature, derives an important share of its momentum from the rhetorical devices upon which it depends for expression, that is, upon techniques designed, developed, or borrowed to enhance and to interpret its communication" (*QS* xxi; cf. Charles J. Adams, "Reflections on the Work of John Wansbrough," *MTSR* 9, no. 1 (1997): 80).

35 *QS* xxii; Klaus Koch, *Was ist Formgeschichte? Neue Wege der Bibelexegese*, 2nd rev. ed. (Neukirchen: Neukirchener Verlag des Erziehungsvereins, 1967), 87; Andrew L. Rippin, "Reading the Qur'ān with Richard Bell," *JAOS* 112, no. 4 (1992): 642; Leopold von Ranke, *Geschichten der romanischen und germanischen Völker von 1494 bis 1514*, 3rd ed. (Leipzig: Verlag von Duncker & Humblot, 1885), vii; Oden, "Historical Understanding and Understanding the Religion of Israel," 11; David J.A. Clines, "Contemporary Methods in Hebrew Bible Criticism," in *Hebrew Bible / Old Testament: The History of Its Interpretation*, vol. 3, pt. 2, ed. Magne Sæbø (Göttingen: Vandenhoeck & Ruprecht, 2015), 153–54.

Rippin (d. 2016) considers "the attempt at reconstructing the history of the reception of the text as the most valuable and most interesting approach."[36] Both corpora (Qurʾān and Tafsīr) are viewed as a bounded whole subject to joint analysis.[37] Furthermore, Mehdi Azaiez identifies a pair of concordant sources: the Qurʾān and the extra-qurʾānic tradition (i.e., *tafsīr, sīra-maghāzī, ḥadīth*).[38] To elaborate, as a subset of reception criticism, the history of interpretation takes a broad chronological perspective on exegetical (i.e., *tafsīr*) and quasi-exegetical (e.g., *sīra-maghāzī, ḥadīth*) literature and then narrows in on the interpretive strategies and "polyvalent readings" of commentators such as Muqātil b. Sulaymān (d. 150/767), al-Ṭabarī (d. 310/923), al-Thaʿlabī (d. 427/1035), al-Zamakhsharī (d. 538/1143), Fakhr al-Dīn al-Rāzī (d. 606/1210), al-Bayḍāwī (d. 685/1286), al-Zarkashī (d. 794/1392), and al-Suyūṭī (d. 911/1505).[39]

Then again, Mustansir Mir attests, "most of them are, in respect of their orientation, premises, and structure, works of theology rather than of literary criticism...."[40] And so, Daniel Madigan specifies, "the issues of historical context and 'original meaning' apply no less to the *tafsīr* texts than to the Qurʾān itself."[41]

---

36 Andrew L. Rippin, "The Qurʾān as Literature: Perils, Pitfalls and Prospects," *BSMESB* 10, no. 1 (1983): 44–45; idem, introduction to *Approaches to the History of the Interpretation of the Qurʾān*, ed. idem (Oxford: Clarendon Press, 1988), 3–4; Clines, "Contemporary Methods in Hebrew Bible Criticism," 3:153; Soulen, *Handbook of Biblical Criticism*, 163–64; cf. Sinai and Neuwirth, introduction, 11. The classic treatise on the subject of *tafsīr* is Ignaz Goldziher, *Die Richtungen der islamischen Koranauslegung* (Leiden: E.J. Brill, 1920); idem, *Schools of Koranic Commentators*, ed. and trans. Wolfgang H. Behn (Wiesbaden: Harrassowitz Verlag, 2006); cf. Rippin, introduction, 1–2.

37 *SKMS*^{2} 42*–43*.

38 Mehdi Azaiez, *Le contre-discours coranique* (Berlin: Walter de Gruyter, 2015), 29; Neal Robinson, *Discovering the Qurʾān: A Contemporary Approach to a Veiled Text* (London: SCM Press Ltd., 1996), 61.

39 Rippin, "Literary Analysis of Qurʾān, Tafsīr, and Sīra," 162; Gabriel Said Reynolds, "Reading the Qurʾān as Homily: The Case of Sarah's Laughter," in *The Qurʾān in Context: Historical and Literary Investigations into the Qurʾānic Milieu*, ed. Angelika Neuwirth, Nicolai Sinai, and Michael Marx (Leiden: Brill, 2011), 588; Norman Calder, "Tafsīr from Ṭabarī to Ibn Kathīr: Problems in the Description of a Genre, Illustrated with Reference to the Story of Abraham," in *Approaches to the Qurʾān*, ed. Gerald R. Hawting and Abdul-Kader A. Shareef (New York: Routledge, 1993), 103; Clines, "Contemporary Methods in Hebrew Bible Criticism," 3:156.

40 Mustansir Mir, "The Qurʾān as Literature," *R&L* 20, no. 1 (1988): 49.

41 Daniel A. Madigan, "Reflections on Some Current Directions in Qurʾānic Studies," *MW* 85, nos. 3–4 (1995): 351; idem, *The Qurʾān's Self-Image: Writing and Authority in Islam's Scripture* (Princeton, New Jersey: Princeton University Press, 2001), 81; Sinai and Neuwirth, introduction, 8, fn. 21. For Wansbrough, "the material adduced is intended to represent a cross-section of Qurʾānic commentary *prior* to the monumental work of al-Ṭabarī (d. 310/923)" (*QS* xxii; emphasis added).

Since this statement is of equal relevance to *sīra* and *maghāzī* literature, as well as to *ḥadīth*, it certainly casts serious doubt on a commonly held assumption.[42] Naturally, this brings the discussion full circle. In the meantime, the Qur'ān remains relegated to the ash heap of history.[43] Commenting on this state of affairs, Angelika Neuwirth notes that scholars in the field find themselves at a crossroads.[44] In consequence, "the Qur'ān, although seemingly at the center of the debate, has in reality been conspicuously absent from the actual exchange of arguments, becoming something of an *unreadable text* in the eyes of many scholars."[45] This impasse calls for a return to the source.[46] But as Azaiez discloses, the matter is far from resolved, especially considering the strict limits imposed by the text.[47] Thus, the aim is to discover objective linguistic criteria with which to discern the literary seams of the *corpus coranicum*, without recourse to exegetical and eisegetical *minutiae*.[48] Moreover, compounding these methodological difficulties are the theoretical ones.[49]

Form Criticism

In terms of theory, Wansbrough's work represents a watershed in the discipline. As Neuwirth explains in a striking image, the publication of *Qur'ānic Studies*

---

42 In reference to hagiographical (*sīra*) literature, see Nicolai Sinai, "The Qur'ān as Process," in *The Qur'ān in Context: Historical and Literary Investigations into the Qur'ānic Milieu*, ed. idem, Angelika Neuwirth, and Michael Marx (Leiden: Brill, 2011), 415, fn. 18. Privileging the hagiography (*sīra*), "lexical and thematic considerations" are consequently rendered "auxiliary parameters" (ibid., 416).

43 Sinai and Neuwirth, introduction, 11.

44 Angelika Neuwirth, "Vom Rezitationstext über die Liturgie zum Kanon: Zu Entstehung und Wiederauflösung der Surenkomposition im Verlauf der Entwicklung eines islamischen Kultus," in *The Qur'ān as Text*, ed. Stefan Wild (Leiden: E.J. Brill, 1996), 69.

45 Sinai and Neuwirth, introduction, 11; emphasis added.

46 Rippin, "Reading the Qur'ān with Richard Bell," 647; *EinlPs*^{4} 4; Oden, "Historical Understanding and Understanding the Religion of Israel," 36; White, "Introduction: On History and Historicisms," xxiii. In continuation: "Here it is worth remembering the motto of the Swabian exegete I.A. Bengel, which was the motto of the Nestle Greek Testament up to its twenty-fifth edition: *Te totum applica ad Textum; Rem totam applica ad te*" (Martin Hengel, *Studies in the Gospel of Mark* (Eugene, Oregon: Wipf & Stock Publishers, 2003), ix).

47 Azaiez, *Le contre-discours coranique*, 29.

48 Cf. ibid.; Richard Ettinghausen, *Antiheidnische Polemik im Koran* (Gelnhausen: F.W. Kalbfleisch, 1934), 5–7; Jack W. Corvin, "A Stylistic and Functional Study of the Prose Prayers in the Historical Narratives of the Old Testament" (PhD diss., Emory University, 1972), 239.

49 Rippin, "Reading the Qur'ān with Richard Bell," 647.

came like a bolt from the blue.[50] Important in this regard is what Wansbrough deems his "experimental method."[51] In an oft-quoted passage, he candidly assesses the status of the Qur'ān in the field: "As a document susceptible of analysis by the instruments and techniques of biblical criticism it is virtually unknown."[52] While in the case of Richard Bell (d. 1952), "there is little doubt that ideas of tendency criticism and an increasingly prominent form criticism may be seen to be playing a role," Wansbrough's method evidently traces back to the influential form-critical circle of Gunkel's New Testament students.[53] In line with Bultmann, Wansbrough postulates that scripture comprises *logia* (sing. *logion*).[54] Second is the assumption that a relative chronology of *logia* is

---

50 *SKMS*² 11*. With respect to Wansbrough, Charles Adams (d. 2011) likewise concedes that "there can be no doubt that his studies have raised questions of fundamental importance and opened new avenues of scholarship that future scholars will, in the nature of the case, be compelled to explore" (idem, "Reflections on the Work of John Wansbrough," 81).

51 *QS* xxi–xxii; Devin J. Stewart, "Wansbrough, Bultmann, and the Theory of Variant Traditions in the Qur'ān," in *Qur'ānic Studies Today*, ed. Angelika Neuwirth and Michael A. Sells (New York: Routledge, 2016), 17.

52 *QS* xxi; Stewart, "Wansbrough, Bultmann, and the Theory of Variant Traditions," 17; Adams, "Reflections on the Work of John Wansbrough," 78. Regarding Wansbrough, Adams writes that "he has drawn heavily on German biblical scholarship in developing his position; indeed, his contribution is in part to have applied methods developed in that tradition – and used first by German scholars to approach the Qur'ān – to the understanding of the Muslim scripture" (idem, "Reflections on the Work of John Wansbrough," 76). N.b. In a notable line, Mir states, "This being the case, studying the Qur'ān as literature – and purely as literature – is not unlike setting foot on new territory" (idem, "Qur'ān as Literature," 49).

53 *QS* xxi–xxii; cf. Rippin, "Reading the Qur'ān with Richard Bell," 641–42; *BQA* 1:vi–vii; Stewart, "Wansbrough, Bultmann, and the Theory of Variant Traditions," 17, 19, and 23; Rollmann, "Zwei Briefe Hermann Gunkels an Adolf Jülicher," 285, fn. 18. According to Adams, "Wansbrough's method he describes as literary...His concern is with literary forms found in the texts..." (idem, "Reflections on the Work of John Wansbrough," 78).

54 Buss, *Biblical Form Criticism*, 295; Stewart, "Wansbrough, Bultmann, and the Theory of Variant Traditions," 17 and 23–24; Erhard Blum, "Formgeschichte – A Misleading Category? Some Critical Remarks," in *The Changing Face of Form Criticism for the Twenty-first Century*, ed. Marvin A. Sweeney and Ehud Ben Zvi (Grand Rapids, Michigan: Wm. B. Eerdmans Publishing Company, 2003), 37. According to Neuwirth, "Underlying his [viz. Wansbrough's] work is Rudolf Bultmann's approach to the demythologization of scripture. Bultmann, a New Testament scholar, held that the narratives of the life of Jesus were offering theology in narrative form, where lessons were taught in the then-familiar language of myth" (eadem, "Qur'ānic Studies and Philology: Qur'ānic Textual Politics of Staging, Penetrating, and Finally Eclipsing Biblical Tradition," in *Qur'ānic Studies Today*, ed. eadem and Michael A. Sells (New York: Routledge, 2016), 181; Norman Calder, "History and Nostalgia: Reflections on John Wansbrough's *The Sectarian Milieu*," *MTSR* 9, no. 1 (1997): 58).

possible, which then entails a dubious corollary.[55] Wolfgang Richter is wary of this proposition, wherein the simple form is the original one.[56] Principally concerned with primitive literature, the objective of the form-critical approach, according to Bultmann, is to ascertain primary forms.[57] Ironically, it is upon this narrow positivist premise of early Bultmann that Wansbrough's set of imbibed assumptions rests.[58] His "reconstructive form history" is actually founded upon both postulates.[59] Ultimately, the "variant traditions hypothesis" is dependent upon Wellhausen and what Wansbrough calls "the tyranny of the 'literary critical' method."[60] It comes as no surprise that Gunkel's New Testament stu-

55 Buss, *Biblical Form Criticism*, 295; Stewart, "Wansbrough, Bultmann, and the Theory of Variant Traditions," 17; Blum, "Formgeschichte," 37. "Incidentally, Bultmann did not consider the transmission of oral materials to be fundamentally different from the history of written ones. He believed that both kinds have 'fairly fixed forms' and that 'higher' individualistic literature, too, has forms and genres" (Buss, *Biblical Form Criticism*, 295–96; Rudolf Bultmann, *Die Geschichte der synoptischen Tradition*, 3rd rev. ed. (Göttingen: Vandenhoeck & Ruprecht, 1957), 7). Bultmann also dispenses with the oral-written distinction (idem, *Geschichte der synoptischen Tradition*, 7; Franz Overbeck (d. 1905), "Über die Anfänge der patristischen Literatur," *HZ* 48, no. 3 (1882): 417–72; Blum, "Formgeschichte," 36; John S. Kloppenborg, *The Formation of Q: Trajectories in Ancient Wisdom Collections* (Philadelphia, Pennsylvania: Fortress Press, 1987), 4).

56 J.W. Rogerson, review of *Exegese als Literaturwissenschaft: Entwurf einer alttestamentlichen Literaturtheorie und Methodologie*, by Wolfgang Richter, *JSS* 20, no. 1 (1975): 119; cf. André Jolles, *Einfache Formen: Legende, Sage, Mythe, Rätsel, Spruch, Kasus, Memorabile, Märchen, Witz* (Halle: Max Niemeyer Verlag, 1930).

57 Blum, "Formgeschichte," 36; Bultmann, *Geschichte der synoptischen Tradition*, 7; Kloppenborg, *Formation of Q*, 4; Overbeck, "Über die Anfänge der patristischen Literatur," 426–44. "[T]he word 'original' (which appears in the first assumption) properly refers to a theological or philosophical rather than a historical category. It is true, 'original' can perhaps be defined as what was first said by Jesus or by a disciple in a manner resembling the surviving text. Yet Bultmann did not define it thus; rather, for him, the 'original' form can be older than Jesus, who may have presented a 'secondary' form by combining materials. Without a limit in time, an 'origin' becomes ahistorical. (In practice, Bultmann regarded the origin of many traditions to be later than Jesus)" (Buss, *Biblical Form Criticism*, 295; Blum, "Formgeschichte," 37). Kenton Sparks writes, "Form criticism's narrow focus on the Bible's small, oral units of tradition was never a necessary limitation. This limitation was an accident, which resulted from an artificial boundary that developed between literary or source criticism, which focused on the longer written sources used to compose the Bible, and form criticism, which sought to discern the nature and character of the smaller tradition units. But, in fact, all units of verbal discourse – whether large or small, oral or written – have a generic character that can be considered" (idem, "Genre Criticism," 57–58).

58 Oden, "Historical Understanding and Understanding the Religion of Israel," 26–27.

59 Buss, *Biblical Form Criticism*, 295.

60 Ibid., 297; Stewart, "Wansbrough, Bultmann, and the Theory of Variant Traditions," 25; Sinai, "Qurʾān as Process," 414; *QS* 17 and 140, fn. 2. "...Wansbrough has isolated the blurring

dents, Bultmann and Dibelius, closed ranks around this point: form criticism shoulders the heavy burden of reconstructing not only the history and development of this piecemeal material, but also its prehistory.[61] In effect, genre recedes to a vanishing point on the horizon.[62] Therefore, Gunkel's methodological critique of his wayward disciples' form criticism is a feature worthy of attention.[63]

First of all, Gunkel expressed strong reservations about the designation itself.[64] For good reason, he preferred to speak of the history of literature, which classifies materials according to genre, and not form alone.[65] Crucially, Martin Buss observes, Gunkel's New Testament students showed a blatant disregard not only for the history of religion, but also for the history of literature.[66] But, in fact, it was through his appreciation of aesthetics that Herder arrived at his concept of form.[67] Johann Wolfgang von Goethe (d. 1832), who followed on the heels of Herder, took this to its natural conclusion: "The poet is not so arbitrary with his material that the form it takes is partly determined by its own nature."[68] Gunkel draws on Goethe's insights: "Substance is visible to all...Form is secret to most."[69] For that reason, aesthetics "is a mode of grasping reality and strength-

which occurs in exegetical works between scripture and its interpretation by drawing attention to the various devices used for the separation of the two and their presence or absence" (Rippin, introduction, 5). N.b. Wansbrough cites both Richter and Mowinckel to support his critique of Wellhausen, his literary-critical school, and "the arbitrary historical method" of "higher criticism" (*QS* 126 and 140, fn. 2; Rylaarsdam, foreword, iv).

61 Dibelius, "Zur Formgeschichte der Evangelien," 187; Bultmann, *Geschichte der synoptischen Tradition*, 4. *Prima facie*, Bultmann and Dibelius pioneered the application of Gunkel's method to the New Testament. However, "on closer examination the program of Gunkel's students tends to concern itself with a narrowing instrumentalization of the genre-critical approach for specific diachronic lines of questioning, and this is exactly what the label 'form criticism' stands for" (Blum, "Formgeschichte," 36–37).

62 Blum, "Formgeschichte," 37; Sparks, "Genre Criticism," 59.

63 Rollmann, "Zwei Briefe Hermann Gunkels an Adolf Jülicher," 283–84; Blum, "Formgeschichte," 33, fn. 2; cf. Dibelius, *Formgeschichte*, 7; Boeckh, *Encyklopädie*, 250.

64 In point of fact, Gunkel "rejected the term 'form-critical' for his own work" (Blum, "Formgeschichte," 37, fn. 15).

65 Rollmann, "Zwei Briefe Hermann Gunkels an Adolf Jülicher," 283–84; Blum, "Formgeschichte," 33, fn. 2; cf. Dibelius, *Formgeschichte*, 7; Boeckh, *Encyklopädie*, 250.

66 Buss, *Biblical Form Criticism*, 286.

67 Pascal, "Sturm und Drang Movement," 146–47.

68 Ibid., 146.

69 Johann Wolfgang von Goethe, *Goethes Werke: Schriften zur Kunst, Schriften zur Literatur, Maximen und Reflexionen*, 12th rev. ed. (München: Verlag C.H. Beck, 1994), 12:471; *EinlPs*^{4} 23. "All the world's a stage" (2.7.140) (William Shakespeare, *As You Like It*, ed. Cynthia Marshall (Cambridge: Cambridge University Press, 2004), 165; Pascal, "Sturm und Drang Movement," 147; Fugate, *Psychological Basis of Herder's Aesthetics*, 205).

ening men's full participation in life," in the *Sturm und Drang* movement.[70] According to Martin Noth (d. 1968), "for Gunkel, concern was by no means merely with 'forms,' but with kinds of discourse, each of which belonged to a specific life situation (*Sitz im Leben*), which in turn had its own historical presuppositions."[71] Because of its reflexive nature, Klaus Koch succinctly states, "the regulations and needs of a particular sphere of existence determine and form the respective manners of speech and writing, just as in reverse the customary linguistic forms help to determine the face of a particular way of life."[72] It is no wonder that "Herder's delight in early poetry, in folksong, was due to his perception that this poetry was a creative element in social and personal life, the accompaniment of social tasks, battle, and work...."[73] This very fact makes it all the more clear that Gunkel's conception harks back to Herder.[74]

Important, therefore, is Bultmann's widely published statement in *Die Geschichte der synoptischen Tradition* (1921)[75]:

> Form criticism is not simply an exercise in aesthetics, nor yet simply a process of description and classification; that is to say, it does not consist of identifying the individual units of the tradition, according to their aesthetic or other characteristics, and placing them in their various categories.

---

70 Pascal, "Sturm und Drang Movement," 150.

71 Martin Noth, *Developing Lines of Theological Thought in Germany* (Virginia: Union Theological Seminary, 1963), 8; *EinlPs*[4] 10 and 22.

72 Koch, *Was ist Formgeschichte?* 34; idem, *The Growth of the Biblical Tradition: The Form-Critical Method*, trans. S.M. Cupitt (New York: Charles Scribner's Sons, 1969), 27; Stewart, "Wansbrough, Bultmann, and the Theory of Variant Traditions," 21.

73 Pascal, "Sturm und Drang Movement," 146. Therefore, "Gunkel, referring back to old and new romanticists (e.g., R. Lowth, J.G. Herder, G. Wünsch), located ancient poetry in popular activities, in various feasts and gatherings" (Gerstenberger, "Psalms," 181; Robert Lowth, *De sacra poesi Hebræorum* (Oxford: Clarendon Press, 1753)).

74 Pascal, "Sturm und Drang Movement," 146–47.

75 Bultmann, *Geschichte der synoptischen Tradition*, 4; idem, *The History of the Synoptic Tradition*, trans. John Marsh (Oxford: Basil Blackwell, 1963), 3–4. N.b. "The introduction of a historical perspective in aesthetics is usually traced back to Hegel's 1820 lectures on fine art...Hegel sets out to salvage art from its subjectivization in Kantian and romantic aesthetics, but ends up declaring that art, considered in its highest vocation, is a thing of the past. This judgment of art – that its greatness is a thing of the past – follows from Hegel's attempt to combine a notion of art's historicity with a conception of its absolute essence" (Kristin Gjesdal, "Hegel and Herder on Art, History, and Reason," *P&L* 30 (2006): 17). Against the *aesthetization of reason*, "Herder claims that mixing philosophical aesthetics and aesthetic practice easily ends in 'a monstrosity'" (ibid., 21 and 23; Johann Gottfried von Herder, "Viertes Wäldchen," in *Kritische Wälder*, ed. Heinrich Dünker (Berlin: Gustav Hempel, 1879), 408).

This in no small measure accounts for Gunkel's apprehension.[76] He objects that his students only managed to blur the lines, which he so painstakingly mapped; and he justifiably concludes, they were just grasping at straws.[77] After making a number of insightful observations, Gunkel closes on a positive note.[78] It is telling that Sigmund Mowinckel (d. 1965) – another of Gunkel's disciples who considerably advanced psalm research – also frames his cult-functional method in a similar manner[79]:

> It cannot, therefore, be our task solely to give a description of the forms and contents of the enthronement songs in the narrow sense from the point of view of genre criticism and the history of literature, but we must also seek to find the cultic situation which lies behind them, and to give a picture of this in all its ideological and liturgical complexity.

This was already appreciated by Gunkel.[80] Mowinckel takes it one step further, given that "the connection between psalm and cult is much closer than he imagined."[81] Mowinckel embraced this new avenue of research, linking literature with ritual in a way at odds with Gunkel.[82] To this appropriately styled cultic setting, Gunkel replies, though his student sees it as a logical development of his

---

76 Rollmann, "Zwei Briefe Hermann Gunkels an Adolf Jülicher," 283–85; Blum, "Formgeschichte," 33, fn. 2; cf. Hammann, *Hermann Gunkel*, 185–97; Gerd Lüdemann, "Die 'Religionsgeschichtliche Schule' und die Neutestamentliche Wissenschaft," in *Die "Religionsgeschichtliche Schule": Facetten eines theologischen Umbruchs*, ed. idem (Frankfurt am Main: Peter Lang, 1996), 9–22.

77 Ibid. On "laws of form," see Dibelius, *Formgeschichte*, 1 and 8; Bultmann, *Geschichte der synoptischen Tradition*, 7; Blum, "Formgeschichte," 37, fn. 15; cf. *EinlPs*^{4} 24; Buss, *Biblical Form Criticism*, 296.

78 Rollmann, "Zwei Briefe Hermann Gunkels an Adolf Jülicher," 285.

79 Sigmund Mowinckel, *The Psalms in Israel's Worship* [*Offersang og Sangoffer*], trans. D.R. Ap-Thomas (Oxford: Blackwell, 1962 [1951]), 1:106; idem, *Psalmenstudien II: Das Thronbesteigungsfest Jahwäs und der Ursprung der Eschatologie* (Amsterdam: Verlag P. Schippers, 1961 [1922]), *passim*; Sigurd Hjelde, *Sigmund Mowinckel und seine Zeit: Leben und Werk eines norwegischen Alttestamentlers* (Tübingen: Mohr Siebeck, 2006), 187–88. Mowinckel notes that genre criticism "has shown that each of these types has sprung up out of a definite life setting, out of its traditionally fixed function in religious life, a situation and a function, which have created the very elements of form and content, which are peculiar to the type in question" (idem, "Psalm Criticism," 15).

80 Gerstenberger, "Psalms," 181.

81 Mowinckel, *Psalms*, 1:34; Buss, "The Idea of *Sitz im Leben*," 162.

82 Corvin, "Stylistic and Functional Study of the Prose Prayers," 240; Buss, "The Idea of *Sitz im Leben*," 161–62.

own work, not all things valid in historical research are in fact sound.[83] Mowinckel subsumed quite dissimilar genres under a single rubric; thus, Gunkel faults him for failing to carefully examine the literary forms.[84] Gunkel's comments are at least partially warranted. Nonetheless, approaching the same problem from different angles, they mirror one another.[85] Since then, more recent work has been dedicated to elucidating the meaning of cult, particularly vis-à-vis its linguistic setting.[86]

In a further reassessment of Gunkel, Jack Corvin asserts that "it is only a first step to describe language and catalogue phrases," a programmatic statement which bears semblance to those of Bultmann and Mowinckel.[87] According to Corvin, form criticism requires additional refinement in light of the narrative problem in biblical criticism. Erhard Gerstenberger elaborates on Gunkel's subsequent "trimodal formulation" for ascertaining genres in the psalms[88]:

> It was he who had laid down the three necessary requirements: first, to classify the psalms by their respective life situations; second, to recognize that psalms of the same genre are governed by 'a common treasure of thoughts and moods'; and third, to analyze the linguistic and poetic structures of each psalm, because this 'form' of the literary text is a reflection of life conditions, thoughts, and moods.

However, coming face-to-face with prose prayers embedded in narratives outside the psalter, Corvin concludes that "the major premises of form history, namely,

---

83 *EinlPs*^{4} 30; John Charles Crutchfield, "Circles of Context: An Interpretation of Psalms 107–118" (PhD diss., Hebrew Union College, 2000), 3–4. Mowinckel sees in form criticism "its logical continuation in the cult-historical or cult-functional conception of the psalms" (idem, "Psalm Criticism between 1900 and 1935 (Ugarit and Psalm Exegesis)," *VT* 5, fasc. 1 (1955): 15). Moreover, Mowinckel holds that Gunkel "often stuck too much to the mere formal registration and labeling of the single elements of a psalm and did not see clearly enough that his own form-critical method demanded that it be developed into a real *cult-functional method*" (idem, *Psalms* 1:31). Ultimately, Mowinckel concedes, "Form criticism (form and genre research) is the absolutely indispensable basis of any understanding of the psalms" (idem, "Psalm Criticism," 15).
84 *EinlPs*^{4} 24.
85 Gerstenberger, "Psalms," 183.
86 Samuel E. Balentine, *Prayer in the Hebrew Bible: The Drama of Divine-Human Dialogue* (Minneapolis, Minnesota: Fortress Press, 1993), 16; cf. Crutchfield, "Circles of Context," 4–6; Gerstenberger, "Psalms," 222.
87 Corvin, "Stylistic and Functional Study of the Prose Prayers," 245.
88 Gerstenberger, "Psalms," 185; Rollmann, "Zwei Briefe Hermann Gunkels an Adolf Jülicher," 284; *EinlPs*^{4} 22–24; Buss, *Biblical Form Criticism*, 260; idem, "The Idea of *Sitz im Leben*," 15 and 159–60; Sparks, "Genre Criticism," 58–61. In the first instance, Herder's influence is palpable in Gunkel's formulation; nevertheless, "history is a necessary pre-condition to literary criticism" in the *Sturm und Drang* movement (Pascal, "Sturm und Drang Movement," 130).

life setting, a distinctive speech-form, the formative oral period, and the religious mood, were not discernable as prominent features of the narrative prayers."[89] The fact is that, as literary constructions, prose prayers are independent of life settings, but dependent on literary ones.[90] Considering their non-cultic character, Corvin decidedly parts company with Mowinckel.[91] Even more troubling is the concern that form critics approach prose prayers as though these exist in a void.[92] Sensitive to their place in literature, functional criticism therefore shifts the focus back to the text.[93] To close with, Theodor Seidl is certainly not far off the mark when he says that aspects of literary criticism appear to have experienced considerable change since Gunkel.[94]

Literary Criticism

In *Studien zur Komposition der mekkanischen Suren* (1981), Neuwirth draws substantially upon psalm criticism.[95] What is more, in direct reference to "traditional cultic formulae," Wansbrough earlier did the same.[96] In point of fact, Richter's

89 Corvin, "Stylistic and Functional Study of the Prose Prayers," 240; *EinlPs*^{4} 7.

90 Balentine, *Prayer in the Hebrew Bible*, 22.

91 Corvin, "Stylistic and Functional Study of the Prose Prayers," 244.

92 Balentine, *Prayer in the Hebrew Bible*, 18; Crutchfield, "Circles of Context," 7.

93 Balentine, *Prayer in the Hebrew Bible*, 18 and 22. To this may be added a final structural-functional refinement introduced into Qur'ān scholarship, which should not pass entirely without notice. Nicolai Sinai states, "a processual reading of the Qur'ān must treat later sūras' references to earlier ones – at least if one can reasonably attribute an interpretative function to them" (idem, "Qur'ān as Process," 431–32 and 438 (Q. 37 and Q. 51); see idem, *Fortschreibung und Auslegung: Studien zur frühen Koraninterpretation* (Wiesbaden: Harrassowitz Verlag, 2009), 21–22, fn. 62). In turn, "structural complexity" is introduced as a factor to account for "consecutive stages of textual growth" (Sinai, "Qur'ān as Process," 419, 421, and 425). Located in its past setting, this entails "reading the Qur'ānic corpus as the literary fallout of a historical process – as opposed to a 'flat' reading" (ibid., 429; idem and Neuwirth, introduction, 9; cf. Crutchfield, "Circles of Context," 1–2).

94 Theodor Seidl, "Die literaturwissenschaftliche Methode in der alttestamentlichen Exegese, Erträge – Erfahrungen – Projekte: Ein Überblick," *MThZ* 40, no. 1 (1989): 27.

95 Angelika Neuwirth, "Qur'ānic Readings of the Psalms," in *The Qur'ān in Context: Historical and Literary Investigations into the Qur'ānic Milieu*, ed. eadem, Nicolai Sinai, and Michael Marx (Leiden: Brill, 2011), 738, fn. 23; *SPMC* xix.

96 "Form criticism to which Wansbrough appeals in his approach to the documents he studies also has a historical dimension. It envisages the possibility of reconstructing the stages or steps of development through which the biblical documents may have passed in their progress from pre-literary oral pronouncements to written form...The purpose is to set out the history of the formation of a document by identifying and classifying the units of which it is composed.

Exegese als Literaturwissenschaft (1971) is lauded by Wansbrough as "a valuable and detailed exposition of the snares inherent in literary analysis...."[97] Richter argues that "form should denote the formal elements of a passage such as its structure and metre."[98] As a matter of course, Neuwirth likewise states concerning the Qur'ān, "the investigation of form analyzes the exterior form, thereby yielding a description on the levels of sentence, word, and individual phoneme."[99] However, Gerstenberger insists that "form-critical work must not content itself with an analysis of linguistic patterns...it must take into account customary life situations and their distinctive speech-forms."[100] In terms of method, Neuwirth also adopts a series of graduated steps developed for biblical exegesis.[101] Richter's comprehensive version includes textual, literary, form, genre, and redaction criticism.[102] He charges that "much that passes for sound 'literary' criticism of the Bible is in reality methodologically faulty, because it asks questions about the genre of biblical passages before a rigorous analysis of a 'literary'

When these units are put into their place in the life of the people of the time to which the document belongs (i.e., establishing their life setting) light can be thrown on the successive developments in the thinking of the community from which the document emerged...The original German name of this method, *Formgeschichte*, renders its historical aspect quite explicit" (Adams, "Reflections on the Work of John Wansbrough," 81).

97 *QS* 126, fn. 8; Wolfgang Richter, *Exegese als Literaturwissenschaft: Entwurf einer alttestamentlichen Literaturtheorie und Methodologie* (Göttingen: Vandenhoeck & Ruprecht, 1971).

98 David R. Law, *The Historical-Critical Method* (London: T&T Clark International, 2012), 141; Richter, *Exegese als Literaturwissenschaft*, 79–103 and 125–41; Blum, "Formgeschichte," 41.

99 Angelika Neuwirth, "Einige Bemerkungen zum besonderen sprachlichen und literarischen Charakter des Koran," in *Deutscher Orientalistentag*, ed. Wolfgang Voigt (Wiesbaden: Franz Steiner Verlag, 1977), 1:737; *QSC* 254; *SKMS*^{2} 37*.

100 Erhard S. Gerstenberger, *Psalms: Part I with an Introduction to Cultic Poetry, FOTL* (Grand Rapids, Michigan: Wm. B. Eerdmans Publishing Company, 1988), 14:33.

101 *SKMS*^{2} 37*; Neuwirth, "Einige Bemerkungen," 1:737; eadem, "Zum neueren Stand der Koranforschung," in *Deutscher Orientalistentag*, ed. Fritz Steppat (Wiesbaden: Franz Steiner Verlag, 1983), 187–89; Richter, *Exegese als Literaturwissenschaft*, 19; Seidl, "Die literaturwissenschaftliche Methode," 28.

102 Richter, *Exegese als Literaturwissenschaft*, 19; Barton, *Reading the Old Testament*, 23. Moreover, the prescribed order of these steps is non-negotiable (Richter, *Exegese als Literaturwissenschaft*, 21; Seidl, "Die literaturwissenschaftliche Methode," 28). John Barton comments, "...Richter may well be mistaken in any case when he says there is only one correct order for applying various methods to the text" (idem, *Reading the Old Testament*, 23). N.b. Richter and Seidl also include two additional steps: composition criticism and content analysis (Richter, *Exegese als Literaturwissenschaft*, 165–90; Seidl, "Die literaturwissenschaftliche Methode," 28; cf. Rogerson, review of *Exegese als Literaturwissenschaft*, 121).

or source-critical kind has been undertaken."[103] The crux of the matter rests on the distinction between what Richter terms form and genre criticism.[104] In a particularly telling passage, he writes that it is far from clear whether these are one and the same.[105] However, Noth rightly calls attention to the fact that a great deal is at stake in the proper definition.[106]

Canon Criticism

Written for a wider audience, Nöldeke's "The Koran" broaches a sensitive subject in scholarship.[107] "It must be owned that the first perusal leaves," he candidly states, "an impression of chaotic confusion."[108] No doubt the threads woven into the fabric are exceptionally textured, varied, and complex.[109] Nicolai Sinai observes that "such heterogeneity is certainly an easily verifiable feature of the Qur'ānic corpus."[110] As Devin Stewart explains, "formal and rhetorical fea-

---

103 On the other hand, biblical scholars "will agree that we ought not to put the cart before the horse in the way Richter disapproves of, but will claim that they never do anyway" (Barton, *Reading the Old Testament*, 23).

104 Rogerson, review of *Exegese als Literaturwissenschaft*, 118 and 121; cf. Koch, *Was ist Formgeschichte?* 6, fn. 5.

105 Richter, *Exegese als Literaturwissenschaft*, 20; Muilenburg, "Form Criticism and Beyond," 2.

106 In addition, Martin Noth early on cautioned that "the danger exists that interest will be directed no longer at the forms, but at the formulae, with the result that 'form history' will be turned into 'formula history'" (idem, *Developing Lines of Theological Thought*, 8). Noth moreover worried that "'formula history' will develop into a 'formula non-history'" (ibid.). "To understand how formulae function, how they represent 'building blocks' within literary units, how they relate to the metre of a passage, etc., is the goal of formula criticism" (Douglas Stuart, *Old Testament Exegesis*, 2nd rev. ed. (Philadelphia, Pennsylvania: The Westminster Press, 1980), 113; William R. Watters, *Formula Criticism and the Poetry of the Old Testament* (Berlin: Walter de Gruyter, 1976), 2–38). What is more, Gene M. Tucker notes, "formulas actually are short genres" (idem, *Form Criticism of the Old Testament* (Philadelphia, Pennsylvania: Fortress Press, 1971), 14). For the definition of formula, see Odil Hannes Steck (d. 2001), *Exegese des Alten Testaments: Leitfaden der Methodik*, 12th rev. ed. (Neukirchen: Neukirchener Verlag, 1989), 103; Soulen, *Handbook of Biblical Criticism*, 74.

107 S.v. Mohammedanism: The Koran, *EB*[9].

108 Ibid.; Aziz Al-Azmeh, *The Emergence of Islam in Late Antiquity: Allāh and His People* (Cambridge: Cambridge University Press, 2014), 446 and 455; Jane Dammen McAuliffe, introduction to *The Cambridge Companion to the Qur'ān*, ed. eadem (Cambridge: Cambridge University Press, 2006), 4–6.

109 Azaiez, *Le contre-discours coranique*, 29–30; Alfred-Louis de Prémare, *Aux origines du Coran* (Paris: Téraèdre, 2004), 35.

110 Sinai, "Qur'ān as Process," 408.

tures act as a much greater stumbling block."[111] Although this may smooth over certain difficulties, the *bruta facta* of "the Qur'ān's complicated literary structure" remain.[112] This has been the main point of contention since the beginning.[113] The situation is essentially unchanged as before. It has nevertheless raised a methodological issue relevant to the subject under consideration, namely, "the tendency towards atomization that predominates in recent investigation."[114] To counter this, Neuwirth has recourse to literary as well as canon criticism.[115] In line with Richter's initial step, she contends that "the literary investigation examines the text, in our case the sūra, as an isolated unit."[116] In other words, this serves as the pivot.[117] In consequence, the sūra-unit is attestable, if not manifest: "Our methodological approach of taking the sūra to be a legitimate unit, and of seeing in individual sūras – as they now stand – various

111 Devin J. Stewart, "Understanding the Qur'ān in English: Notes on Translation, Form, and Prophetic Typology," in *Diversity in Language: Contrastive Studies in English and Arabic Theoretical and Applied Linguistics*, ed. Zeinab Ibrahim, Nagwa Kassabgy, and Sabiha Aydelott (Cairo: The American University of Cairo Press, 2000), 38.

112 Sinai and Neuwirth, introduction, 15; see Hussein Abdul-Raof, "Textual Progression and Presentation Technique in Qur'ānic Discourse: An Investigation of Richard Bell's Claims of 'Disjointedness' with Especial Reference to Q. 17–20," *JQS* 7, no. 2 (2005): 36–60.

113 Raymond Farrin, *Structure and Qur'ānic Interpretation* (Ashland, Oregon: White Cloud Press, 2014), xi–xvi; Mir, "Qur'ān as Literature," 50, fn. 2. Walid A. Saleh writes, "Having accused the medieval commentators of an atomistic interpretive approach to the Qur'ān, we ourselves have failed to offer a genuine alternative. We keep hearing about the absence of thematic unity in the chapters of the Qur'ān, but we have never been able to offer an explanation, for example, as to why some are one paragraph and some are sprawling booklets. Is it possible that we have not given enough attention to their structure? Angelika Neuwirth's work has yet to be carried further..." (idem, "The Etymological Fallacy and Qur'ānic Studies: Muḥammad, Paradise, and Late Antiquity," in *The Qur'ān in Context: Historical and Literary Investigations into the Qur'ānic Milieu*, ed. Angelika Neuwirth, Nicolai Sinai, and Michael Marx (Leiden: Brill, 2011), 694; cf. David Marshall, *God, Muḥammad and the Unbelievers: A Qur'ānic Study* (Richmond, Surrey: Curzon Press, 1999), 19–20).

114 Neuwirth, "Einige Bemerkungen," 1:736; *QSC* 254; *SKMS*^{2} 38*–39*. Alluding to this tendency, Neuwirth writes, "Due to the recent privileging of Christian subtexts, the Qur'ān is now being read as a sort of Christian apocryphal work. With few exceptions, scholars no longer bother about its literary form. Instead, the text is immediately broken down into haphazard textual pieces..." (*SPMC* xx).

115 *SKMS*^{2} 40*; Issa J. Boullata, introduction to *Literary Structures of Religious Meaning in the Qur'ān*, ed. idem (New York: Routledge, 2000), x.

116 Neuwirth, "Einige Bemerkungen," 1:737; *QSC* 254; *SKMS*^{2} 37*.

117 Neuwirth, "Einige Bemerkungen," 1:736; *SKMS*^{2} 38*–39*; Mustansir Mir, "The Sūra as a Unity: A Twentieth Century Development in Qur'ān Exegesis," in *Approaches to the Qur'ān*, ed. Gerald R. Hawting and Abdul-Kader A. Shareef (New York: Routledge, 1993), 211–24, esp. 218.

realizations of a single definable genre, can be proven if distinct categories of sūras can be demonstrated."[118] Citing the composite psalms, Neuwirth draws attention to the fact that the sūra constitutes a complex genre which, as an amalgam, combines different genres, so as to forge a single cohesive unit.[119] Earlier, however, Gunkel voiced his deep concern over this admixture of genres in the psalms[120]:

> Even this relatively frequent appearance of mixed witnesses in the psalter has greatly hindered genre research to this point since, to the casual observer to whom this first jumps out, it can easily appear as if Hebrew poetry possesses no genres at all. Likewise, one may counsel anyone interested in becoming immersed in genre research, not to begin with those mixed psalms.

Caution is thrown to the wind. Evidently, in an effort to salvage the *corpus coranicum* from this perceived state of formlessness and in the face of the purported absence of hypothetical pure genres, it is claimed that the sūra had a status independent of the canon.[121] Neuwirth takes it a step further when she ventures "a sketch of the pre-canonical development of the sūra as *a literary genre*."[122] As determined by Sinai, "this implies that the 'original unit of revelation' was probably the sūra itself, and that its polythematic character is not an outcome of subsequent editing."[123]

---

118 Neuwirth, "Einige Bemerkungen," 1:736–39; *QSC* 257.

119 Neuwirth, "Einige Bemerkungen," 1:738; Gunkel, "Psalmen," col. 1626; cf. Gabriel Said Reynolds, *The Qur'ān and Its Biblical Subtext* (New York: Routledge, 2010), 244; Stewart, "Wansbrough, Bultmann, and the Theory of Variant Traditions," 44. According to Stewart, "the analogy between an individual gospel and a sermon may be fruitfully applied to the qur'ānic material, in which case it becomes an analogy between an individual sūra and a sermon" (idem, "Wansbrough, Bultmann, and the Theory of Variant Traditions," 46; cf. Bultmann, *Geschichte der synoptischen Tradition*, 400).

120 *EinlPs*[4] 29; Hermann Gunkel and Joachim Begrich, *Introduction to Psalms: The Genres of the Religious Lyric of Israel*, trans. James D. Nogalski (Macon, Georgia: Mercer University Press, 1998), 20.

121 *SKMS*[2] 37*; cf. Neuwirth, "Einige Bemerkungen," 1:737–39; *SPMC* xxi and xxiv; *EinlPs*[4] 29; Hermann Gunkel, "Die israelitische Literatur," in *Die orientalischen Literaturen*, ed. Paul Hinneberg (Leipzig: Verlag B.G. Teubner, 1906), 54; Buss, *Biblical Form Criticism*, 139, 251, and cf. 242–43; Sparks, "Genre Criticism," 59–61; Michael V. Fox, *Character and Ideology in the Book of Esther*, 2nd ed. (Grand Rapids, Michigan: Wm. B. Eerdmans Publishing Company, 2001), 142.

122 S.v. Sūra(s), *EQ*; emphasis added; Neuwirth, "Einige Bemerkungen," 1:737–39; eadem, "Structural, Linguistic, and Literary Features," in *The Cambridge Companion to the Qur'ān*, ed. Jane Dammen McAuliffe (Cambridge: Cambridge University Press, 2006), 110–11.

123 Sinai, "Qur'ān as Process," 413, fn. 16.

Biblical canon criticism sheds light on Neuwirth's claim that sūra-units "in their final forms express the consensus of the community."[124] While Brevard Childs (d. 2007) acknowledges the merits of Gunkel's scholarship, he is equally cognizant of the fact that it literally created a *crisis* in biblical theology.[125] Viewed from Childs' standpoint, canon criticism represents "the *theological response* to the challenge raised by Gunkel."[126] This post-critical method circumvents the concerns of the history of religion school.[127] Furthermore, Stewart claims, "the turn to canonical criticism has sidestepped what is perhaps the most important and direct revision of the form critics' scholarship, which came from the proponents of redaction criticism...."[128] The latter stirs up another apparently unset-

---

124 Unsurprisingly, canon criticism reaches the inevitable conclusion that "the confessing community itself is the authority" (Dale A. Brueggemann, "Brevard Childs' Canon Criticism: An Example of Post-Critical Naiveté," *JETS* 32, no. 3 (1989): 326). As a further refinement, Neuwirth states, "We may therefore consider them as mirrors of a 'canonisation from below,' a process of the successive elevation of the proclamation to the status of a canon without a political authority being involved" (*SPMC* xxiv; Neuwirth, "Referentiality and Textuality in Sūrat al-Ḥijr: Some Observations on the Qur'ānic 'Canonical Process' and the Emergence of a Community," in *Literary Structures of Religious Meaning in the Qur'ān*, ed. Issa J. Boullata (New York: Routledge, 2000), 146–47; Aleida Assmann and Jan Assmann, "Kanon und Zensur als kultursoziologische Kategorien," in *Kanon und Zensur: Beiträge zur Archäologie der literarischen Kommunikation II*, ed. eadem (München: Wilhelm Fink Verlag, 1987), 22–23 (*Kanon von oben und Kanon von unten*)).

125 Brevard S. Childs, *Introduction to the Old Testament as Scripture* (Philadelphia, Pennsylvania: Fortress Press, 1979), 510; idem, *Biblical Theology in Crisis* (Philadelphia, Pennsylvania: The Westminster Press, 1970), 99; Antonius H.J. Gunneweg (d. 1990), *Vom Verstehen des Alten Testaments: Eine Hermeneutik* (Göttingen: Vandenhoeck & Ruprecht, 1977), 73. For example, see Martin G. Klingbeil, "Off the Beaten Track: An Evangelical Reading of the Psalms without Gunkel," *BBR* 16, no. 1 (2006): 25–39.

126 Childs, *Introduction*, 511; emphasis added; Brueggemann, "Brevard Childs' Canon Criticism," 326; Gerstenberger, "Psalms," 186–87; Harry P. Nasuti, *Defining the Sacred Songs: Genre, Tradition and the Post-Critical Interpretation of the Psalms* (Sheffield, England: Sheffield Academic Press, 1999), 15.

127 According to Shepherd, "What Childs proposes, and what the history of religion school proposes, do not 'share a common understanding of history'" (idem, *Theological Interpretation*, 234–35; Childs, *The Struggle to Understand Isaiah as Christian Scripture* (Grand Rapids, Michigan: Wm. B. Eerdmans Publishing Company, 2004), 320–21).

128 Stewart, "Wansbrough, Bultmann, and the Theory of Variant Traditions," 43–46; Soulen, *Handbook of Biblical Criticism*, 101–2. Gunkel "viewed the Pentateuch as the work of a collector of old oral traditions rather than as the product of a full-fledged author. So, whereas some of his contemporaries inquired about the 'book' of Exodus, Gunkel was more interested in the origins and development of the various oral legends that stood behind the book, such as those concerning Israel's descent into Egypt, Moses, Sinai, the Wilderness, the Passover, and the Exodus event. Gunkel's method for studying the text came to be known as form criticism, so-called betling problem for Qur'ān scholarship in the person of the prophet, "by recasting him as editor of the text."[129] The great appeal of canon criticism is precisely that it "avoids this issue to some extent by presenting the editing and shaping of the text as a communal process."[130] Recognizing the limits of the canon, Neuwirth concedes, "Still, to confine the analysis to the canonical shape of the Qur'ān, neglecting both its complex referentialities and its hints to the life setting of particular text units, would render an insufficient reading."[131] Bear in mind that there are many sides to criticism, all of which are commensurable.[132] Kenton Sparks explains,[133]

---

cause it gave careful attention to the 'form' or structure of biblical traditions" (Sparks, "Genre Criticism," 57). Regarding the Deuteronomistic history, see Martin Noth, *Überlieferungsgeschichtliche Studien: Die sammelnden und bearbeitenden Geschichtswerke im Alten Testament* (Halle: Max Niemeyer Verlag, 1943), 11; s.v. Redaction Criticism: Hebrew Bible, *OEBI*; Walter Dietrich, "Historiography in the Old Testament," in *Hebrew Bible / Old Testament: The History of Its Interpretation*, vol. 3, pt. 2, ed. Magne Sæbø (Göttingen: Vandenhoeck & Ruprecht, 2015), 467–99.

129 Stewart, "Wansbrough, Bultmann, and the Theory of Variant Traditions," 45; s.v. Form Criticism: Old Testament, *ABD*; Blum, "Formgeschichte," 36, fn. 14. "The traditional historical-philological methods of analyzing the Qur'ān as pursued in scholarly circles have been oriented towards re-establishing the 'original meaning' of the text or the 'author's intention' or the 'meaning of the text to the first hearers,' however one wishes to express it...[B]y putting things in terms of what the first hearers thought, we can avoid, it is suggested, talking about the author's intention or the original meaning – both concepts which might seem to imply an active participation in the creation of the text by Muḥammad" (Rippin, introduction, 2). N.b. "For of the three elements in speech-making – speaker, subject, and person addressed – it is the last one, the hearer, that determines the speech's end and object" (Arist. *Rhet.* I.3, 1358b1, trans. Roberts (*The Complete Works of Aristotle*, rev. Oxford trans., ed. Jonathan Barnes (Princeton, New Jersey: Princeton University Press, 1984), 2:2159)).

130 Stewart, "Wansbrough, Bultmann, and the Theory of Variant Traditions," 45.

131 S.v. Sūra(s), *EQ*; Crutchfield, "Circles of Context," 6–7. N.b. "Some later writers, especially in New Testament studies since M. Dibelius, have applied the term [viz. place in life] also to the setting of a particular text, e.g., of a psalm or parable; such a usage blurs the distinctive meaning of the phrase" (Buss, "The Idea of *Sitz im Leben*," 157; idem, *Biblical Form Criticism*, 15). "As the term for typical communication situations of genres, *Sitz im Leben* should not be used for individual communication or reception situations of particular texts" (Blum, "Formgeschichte," 35).

132 Striking a conciliatory chord, Sinai notes that "a holistic or 'canonical' reading of the Qur'ānic corpus in its present shape must not necessarily be seen as conflicting with diachronic reconstructions of this corpus' textual emergence, nor as discounting the feasibility of such reconstructions" (idem, "Qur'ān as Process," 408). Cf. Rylaarsdam, foreword, iii; see David Greenwood, "Rhetorical Criticism and Formgeschichte: Some Methodological Considerations," *JBL* 89, no. 4 (1970): 421.

133 Sparks, "Genre Criticism," 66.

> Technically speaking, because all of these critical approaches involve comparison, classification, and judgments about the *kind* of text one is reading, they are best understood as legitimate aspects of genre criticism rather than as wholly discrete approaches to textual criticism.

Therefore, the validity of Childs' contention is not in question.[134] For instance, Corvin clearly sees the hand of the editor at work.[135] Then again, Gerald Wilson (d. 2005) insists that genre criticism tends to favor form over frame.[136] All the same, it is instructive to note that the question of coherency is not germane to the genre-critical study of the Qur'ān. Put otherwise, the internal coherence or incoherence of the corpus is not requisite.[137]

Genre Criticism

For the exponents of the "Qur'ān as process" movement (Nöldeke, Neuwirth, Sinai), "the textual units to be dated are thus something that is given rather than something that itself stands in need of reconstruction before dating can even begin."[138] Though a vertical reading of the Qur'ān according to sūra-unit *prima facie* simplifies matters, take the considered opinion of Albrecht Noth (d. 1999) in an analogous case.[139] Given that sūra-units are complex collections, "the useful approach is to look for points of agreement according to a 'horizontal' principle, and attempts to make distinctions between 'compilations' should be abandoned."[140] To illustrate, let us briefly examine the vertical "building

134 Childs, *Introduction*, 511. In fact, Gunkel addressed the Book of Psalms in brief (idem, "Psalterbuch," in *RGG*², vol. 4, cols. 1949–51).

135 Corvin, "Stylistic and Functional Study of the Prose Prayers," 242; C. Hassell Bullock, *Encountering the Book of Psalms: A Literary and Theological Introduction* (Grand Rapids, Michigan: Baker Academic, 2001), 57–82 ("editorial seams").

136 This is all the more relevant, since Wilson surmises, "perhaps it was his skepticism of ever bringing significant order to the Psalter as a whole which led to Gunkel's breakthrough into genre research in the Psalms" (idem, *The Editing of the Hebrew Psalter* (Chico, California: Scholars Press, 1985), 1–2).

137 Cf. *SKMS*² 40*. N.b. The form-critical method has been applied with great success to the Psalms (Gunkel et al.) as well as the Synoptic Gospels (Dibelius et al.).

138 Sinai, "Qur'ān as Process," 413, fn. 16, and 414.

139 Ibid., 413.

140 Albrecht Noth, "Der Charakter der ersten großen Sammlungen von Nachrichten zur frühen Kalifenzeit," *Isl.* 47, no. 1 (1971): 198; Martin Hinds, "Sayf ibn 'Umar's Sources on Arabia," in *Studies in Early Islamic History*, ed. Jere Bacharach, Lawrence I. Conrad, and Patricia Crone (Princeton, New Jersey: The Darwin Press, Inc., 1996), 145.

blocks" that constitute Sūrat al-Mursalāt (Q. 77): verses 1–7: oath form; verses 8–13: eschatological form; verses 14–50: litany form.[141] Since this sūra-unit is assigned to the early Meccan period, so too are its components.[142] Nevertheless, a horizontal reading calls for the grouping of these forms by genre.[143] For instance, the litany form (vv. 14–50) belongs to the liturgy genre. Before anything else, a minimal pair is required.[144] That being the case, the litany form of this sūra-unit (Q. 77) is placed side by side with the litany form of a corresponding unit (Q. 55). In light of the juxtaposition of this minimal pair, the litany form is further subdivided. In line with this typology, Q. 77.14–50 is properly speaking a litany of lament. What is more, the liturgy genre includes not only forms of litany, but also the hymn form. Therefore, in Gunkel's words,[145]

> Likewise, we ask the reader to suspend, for now, the questions of dating and literary criticism during the foundational investigation of the genres. If these questions are mixed too early with such a different type of research, then all of the effort is in vain.

That is to say, vertical sūra analysis at the synchronic stage of research hinders rather than facilitates criticism. As opposed to advancing an "atomistic view of the Qur'ān," the utility of Gunkel's method for Qur'ān criticism rests primarily in identifying literary "patterns of coherence."[146] His remarks on genre deserve careful consideration.

Gunkel laid down clear guidelines.[147] The method of genre criticism consists of two operations: form criticism and genre history.[148] On the basis of shared for-

---

141 Cf. *SKMS*^{2} 175–78, 187–201, and 216–17 (Q. 77); *JQA* 551; *BIQ*^{1} 75; s.v. Form and Structure of the Qur'ān, *EQ*; Sinai, "Qur'ān as Process," 411–12, 419, fn. 22, and cf. 420, fn. 24; Carl W. Ernst, *How to Read the Qur'ān* (Chapel Hill: University of North Carolina Press, 2011), 241, fn. 63; Gustav Richter, *Der Sprachstil des Koran* (Leipzig: Otto Harrassowitz, 1940), 1–2, 21–24, esp. 23, and 55–57.

142 Cf. *SKMS*^{2} 216–17 (Q. 77); Sinai, "Qur'ān as Process," 421 and 423 (Q. 77). According to Sinai, Q. 77 is tabulated as follows, [7+8]+[4+5+5]+[6+6+5]+5 (idem, "Qur'ān as Process," 420 and 423).

143 Cf. Claus Westermann, *Der Psalter* (Stuttgart: Calwer Verlag, 1967), 28.

144 Rogerson, review of *Exegese als Literaturwissenschaft*, 119. According to Richter, "a genre can be inferred only on the basis of a number of similar forms, so that the analysis of forms must precede the positing of genres, in practice forms have often been investigated on the basis of a prior view of the genres to which they were supposed to belong" (ibid., 118).

145 *EinlPs*^{4} 31; Gunkel and Begrich, *Introduction to Psalms*, 21.

146 Mir, "Qur'ān as Literature," 50, fns. 2–3.

147 Gunkel, "Psalmen," col. 1611.

148 "H. Gunkel, who may be regarded as the spiritual father of form criticism, did not make use of the catchword 'form criticism,' but spoke instead of the 'study of types.' The expression 'form

mal features, form criticism arranges, by category, horizontal cross-sections of discrete genres comprising compound sūras.[149] Mowinckel writes, genre criticism "has taught us to distinguish between a certain number of types, easily definable with regard to form and content, in which each individual example has been composed according to the very fixed, established rules of form and content…."[150] So the question becomes one of how to find the boundaries of pericopae.[151] As Hugo Greßmann (d. 1929) explains,[152]

> A methodological investigation must begin with the introductory and concluding formulas, since they formed the germ cells of every genre and, in the course of later development, they have also always remained characteristic signs.

In this manner, Gunkel systematically classified biblical psalm literature by its principal literary genres, e.g., lament.[153] Claus Westermann (d. 2002) states that "by means of this approach, the first and most important step toward interpreting the psalms has been taken."[154] Then it is no small matter that "most qur'ānic sūras are readily divisible into thematically and syntactically defined sections, which sometimes are also marked by changes of rhyme."[155] With reason, Greßmann concludes, "Where one encounters introductory and concluding formulas, no doubt can exist about the divisions of literary elements."[156]

As alluded to earlier, genre criticism is not simply content with identifying and classifying these units.[157] In turn, genre history determines the relative dia-

---

criticism' stems, indeed, from New Testament studies" (Noth, *Developing Lines of Theological Thought*, 8).

149 Dibelius, "Zur Formgeschichte der Evangelien," 187; cf. Noth, "Der Charakter der ersten großen Sammlungen," 198.

150 Mowinckel, "Psalm Criticism," 15.

151 Tucker, *Form Criticism of the Old Testament*, 10.

152 Hugo Greßmann, "Die literarische Analyse Deuterojesajas," *ZAW* 34, no. 4 (1914): 259; Hayes, *Interpreting Ancient Israelite History, Prophecy, and Law*, 190. A remarkably similar view is expressed by Gunkel (idem, "Psalmen," col. 1613).

153 Gunkel, "Psalmen," cols. 1613–14; *EinlPs*[4] 27.

154 Westermann, *Der Psalter*, 28; idem, *The Psalms: Structure, Content, and Message*, trans. Ralph D. Gehrke (Minneapolis, Minnesota: Augsburg Publishing House, 1980), 28.

155 Sinai, "Qur'ān as Process," 419; idem, *Fortschreibung und Auslegung*, 61–62.

156 Greßmann, "Die literarische Analyse Deuterojesajas," 259; Hayes, *Interpreting Ancient Israelite History, Prophecy, and Law*, 190.

157 Dibelius, "Zur Formgeschichte der Evangelien," 187; Bultmann, *Geschichte der synoptischen Tradition*, 4; s.v. Form and Structure of the Qur'ān, *EQ*.

chronic growth of this historical *materia prima.*[158] Gunkel writes, "Even the manner by which dating currently tends to be undertaken needs a fundamental reevaluation."[159] More to the point, Mowinckel's critique of the history of literature merits closer inspection. First of all, Herder and Georg Wilhelm Friedrich Hegel (d. 1831) exerted considerable influence on Gunkel.[160] In his later aesthetic theory, Hegel submits that genre is tied to time.[161] Similarly, Gunkel considers genres as being fixed to temporal frames of reference.[162] Herder exhibits an interest in beginnings.[163] For him, and by extension Gunkel, poetry at its dawn was still endowed with life.[164] Gunkel likewise holds that the oldest literary genres were prime and pristine.[165] In "Fundamental Problems of Hebrew Literary History," he clarifies that the history of literature is nothing short of "the history through which these types have passed."[166] However, in a statement not dissimilar to Hegel's, Gunkel also posits a disintegration of form as the eventual outcome.[167]

158 Dibelius, "Zur Formgeschichte der Evangelien," 187; Bultmann, *Geschichte der synoptischen Tradition*, 4; cf. Steck, *Exegese des Alten Testaments*, 103. Particularly relevant to the Weil–Nöldeke chronology of the Qur'ān is the fact that "in making this classification, Gunkel moved the problem of dating away from the individual psalm to the types, and sought to trace their literary history" (George W. Anderson, *A Critical Introduction to the Old Testament* (London: Gerald Duckworth & Co. Ltd., 1979), 176; Gustav Weil, *Historisch-kritische Einleitung in den Koran*, 2nd rev. ed. (Bielefeld: Verlag von Velhagen & Klasing, 1878), 63–64; *GdQ*² 1:72, fn. 1; Sinai, "Qur'ān as Process," 417 and cf. 418).

159 *EinlPs*⁴ 31; Gunkel and Begrich, *Introduction to Psalms*, 21; Gunkel, "Historical Movement," 534.

160 Buss, "The Idea of *Sitz im Leben*," 162, fn. 31; cf. idem, *Biblical Form Criticism*, 212, fn. 11; Campbell, "The Emergence of the Form-Critical and Traditio-Historical Approaches," 3:136; Boeckh, *Encyklopädie*, 528.

161 Gjesdal, "Hegel and Herder," 17 and 23.

162 *EinlPs*⁴ 29.

163 Fugate, *Psychological Basis of Herder's Aesthetics*, 264.

164 Ibid., 265; cf. *EinlPs*⁴ 27–29.

165 *EinlPs*⁴ 28; Gunkel, "Fundamental Problems of Hebrew Literary History," in *What Remains of the Old Testament and Other Essays* (New York: The Macmillan Company, 1928), 65; Gjesdal, "Hegel and Herder," 22.

166 Gunkel, "Fundamental Problems," 61.

167 *EinlPs*⁴ 29; Gunkel, "Fundamental Problems," 66; Georg Wilhelm Friedrich Hegel, *Vorlesungen über die Ästhetik II* (Frankfurt am Main: Suhrkamp, 1970), 107–26; see idem, *Vorlesungen über die Ästhetik I* (Frankfurt am Main: Suhrkamp, 1970), 486–507; cf. *SKMS*² 34*; Buss, *Biblical Form Criticism*, 212, fn. 11; Klatt, *Hermann Gunkel*, 34, fn. 27; Fugate, *Psychological Basis of Herder's Aesthetics*, 205; Theodore A. Gracyk, "Sublimity, Ugliness, and Formlessness in Kant's Aesthetic Theory," *JAAC* 45, no. 1 (1986): 52.

In the end, Gunkel's conception of literary history limits his genre history.[168] Because of this, his prudence and temper in "Die israelitische Literatur" is understandable: "The literary history of ancient Israel has as its first task the exploration of genres, their characteristics, and *if possible* their own historical development."[169] However, according to Richter, "with regard to the chronological relationship of genres to each other, and the value of genres for the purposes of historical reconstruction, not a great deal can be said with certainty...."[170] Irrespective, what is essential is rather the intellectual legacy of Gunkel.[171] Despite certain limitations, it is abundantly clear that "Gunkel located order explicitly in a 'history of literature' with two axes, the synchronic and the diachronic."[172] It follows that a literary history of scripture is predicated upon genre criticism. Ultimately, however, the historical dimension of Gunkel's method is either relegated behind literary, exegetical concerns or is altogether eclipsed.[173] So, it is to be expected when Daniel Harrington (d. 2014) carefully weighs the relative merits of form criticism.[174]

168 *EinlPs*[4] 27; Cesare Segre, *Avviamento all'analisi del testo letterario* (Torino: Giulio Einaudi, 1985), 133.
169 Gunkel, "Die israelitische Literatur," 52; idem, "The Literature of Ancient Israel," trans. Armin Siedlecki, in *Relating to the Text: Interdisciplinary and Form-Critical Insights on the Bible*, ed. Timothy J. Sandoval and Carleen Mandolfo (London: T&T Clark International, 2003), 29; emphasis added.
170 Richter draws a distinction between the history of form and that of forms; the former deals "with the relation between similar forms (i.e., individual texts), especially their chronological relationship," while the latter seeks "to ascertain the chronological relationship between groups of forms" (idem, *Exegese als Literaturwissenschaft*, 120–25; Rogerson, review of *Exegese als Literaturwissenschaft*, 117 and 119). Notable in this regard is Bultmann, who "spoke of the life setting of an individual text, while for Gunkel a life setting characterized a genre" (Buss, *Biblical Form Criticism*, 295–96; idem, *Changing Shape of Form Criticism*, 15–16, 26, and 32; cf. Rogerson, review of *Exegese als Literaturwissenschaft*, 119; Jolles, *Einfache Formen*, *passim*; Richter, *Exegese als Literaturwissenschaft*, 23; Steck, *Exegese des Alten Testaments*, 103; Wim Weren, *Windows on Jesus: Methods in Gospel Exegesis* [*Vensters op Jezus: Methoden in de uitleg van de evangeliën*], trans. John Bowden (Harrisburg, Pennsylvania: Trinity Press International, 1999), 131).
171 Blum, "Formgeschichte," 33.
172 Buss, *Biblical Form Criticism*, 227.
173 Seidl, "Die literaturwissenschaftliche Methode," 29.
174 Daniel J. Harrington, *Interpreting the New Testament* (Wilmington, Delaware: Michael Glazier, Inc., 1979), 74–75.

1.3 Literary Genres

Genre Recognition

The recognition of genres by Gunkel was not unprecedented in biblical criticism.[175] In the last quarter of the nineteenth century, Matthew Arnold (d. 1888), William Rainey Harper (d. 1906), Charles Augustus Briggs (d. 1913), Richard Moulton (d. 1924) *et alii* broke fresh ground outside Germany.[176] At the same time, Briggs recognized the originality of the theses advanced by Herder.[177] Nowhere is this more clear than in *The Literary Study of the Bible* (1896).[178] In a revealing passage, Moulton explains the title of his book[179]:

> The treatment of literary morphology: how to distinguish one literary composition from another, to say exactly where each begins and ends; to recognize epic, lyric, and other forms as they appear in their biblical dress, as well as to distinguish literary forms special to the sacred writers.

Moulton neatly sidestepped the historical questions of the Wellhausen school by defining literary study as "the discussion of *what* we have in the books of scripture."[180] It is particularly significant that he draws this dividing line on pragmatic grounds.[181] Though he acknowledges its value, Moulton launches into a thoughtful methodological critique of biblical criticism.[182] To begin with, "historic analysis, investigating dates, sometimes finds itself obliged to discriminate between different parts of the same literary composition, *and* to assign to them different periods."[183] Secondly, Moulton questions historical criticism and its

175 Barton, *Reading the Old Testament*, 8–19; Sparks, "Genre Criticism," 55.
176 Buss, *Biblical Form Criticism*, 186–208.
177 Charles Augustus Briggs, *Biblical Study: Its Principles, Methods, and History* (New York: Charles Scribner's Sons, 1883), 169 and cf. 203–4; Buss, *Biblical Form Criticism*, 193.
178 Richard G. Moulton, *The Literary Study of the Bible: An Account of the Leading Forms of Literature Represented in the Sacred Writings* (London: Isbister and Company Limited, 1896); Buss, *Biblical Form Criticism*, 189–93.
179 Moulton, *Literary Study of the Bible*, vii–viii.
180 Ibid., iv; Rylaarsdam, foreword, iv.
181 Moulton, *Literary Study of the Bible*, iv–v.
182 Ibid., iv–vii.
183 Ibid., v; emphasis added. This observation is especially pertinent to the debate over the "soundness" and "elaboration" of the *seriatim* Weil–Nöldeke chronology in Qurʾān scholarship and the Qurʾān as process movement, which calls for "a truly historical reading of the Qurʾān" by means of sūra-dating (Sinai, "Qurʾān as Process," 407, 413, and 418–29; Muhammad Khalid Masud, Brinkley Messick, and David S. Powers, "Muftis, Fatwas, and Islamic Legal Interpreta-

"almost exclusive preoccupation with subject matter, to the neglect of literary form."[184] Thus, Moulton says in plain terms, "a clear grasp of the outer literary form is an essential guide to the inner matter and spirit."[185] Elaborating on this point, Gunkel retained throughout "the distinction between the concrete, individual, particular text and the abstract, transindividual pattern of text formation, that is, the genre."[186] As a matter of consequence, "inherent in the notion of genre, of course, is that one is not dealing with a purely particular item."[187] The blurring of lines between form and genre has had detrimental effects.[188] Beyond the systematic identification of genres, developed along the lines of his aesthetic theory, the distinctive contribution of Gunkel lies chiefly in the concept of life setting (*Sitz im Leben*).[189] To this is added an appreciation of the diachronic dimension, along with the synchronic sequencing of genres.[190]

Let us now turn to the recognition of genres in Qur'ān research. In the annals of classical Islāmic scholarship, for instance, the exegete al-Rāzī already examined the oath (*qasam*) form in his monumental *al-Tafsīr al-kabīr.*[191] Moreover, according to Rosalind Ward Gwynne, in the compendious *al-Burhān fī 'ulūm al-Qur'ān*, al-Zarkashī already attended to "intricate questions of audience identification."[192] In fact, the study of qur'ānic oaths (*aqsām al-Qur'ān*) and prophetic proclamations (*mukhāṭabāt*), begun in the medieval period, continues to the present day.[193] The genres of the Qur'ān also attracted the attention of Gustav

---

tion," in *Islamic Legal Interpretation: Muftis and Their Fatwas*, ed. idem (Cambridge, Massachusetts: Harvard University Press, 1996), 4).

184 Moulton, *Literary Study of the Bible*, vi.

185 Ibid., viii and cf. x; Herder, "Shakespeare (1773)," in *Kleinere Aufsätze I* (Cambridge: Cambridge University Press, 1952), 3; Fugate, *Psychological Basis of Herder's Aesthetics*, 206. For this reason, among others, "there is reason to believe that not only Budde but also Gunkel had contact with the Anglo-American Bible as Literature movement before 1904" (Buss, *Biblical Form Criticism*, 217).

186 Blum, "Formgeschichte," 33.

187 Buss, *Biblical Form Criticism*, 15.

188 Richter, *Exegese als Literaturwissenschaft*, 46; Blum, "Formgeschichte," 33, fn. 4.

189 Buss, "The Idea of *Sitz im Leben*," 157–58 and 165; Blum, "Formgeschichte," 35, fn. 12.

190 Buss, "The Idea of *Sitz im Leben*," 157; Blum, "Formgeschichte," 33.

191 Fakhr al-Dīn al-Rāzī, *Tafsīr al-Fakhr al-Rāzī* (Beirut: Dār al-Fikr, 1981), 26:118 (Q. 37) and 28:193 (Q. 51); s.v. Fakhr al-Dīn al-Rāzī, *EI²*; Binyamin Abrahamov, "Theology," in *The Blackwell Companion to the Qur'ān*, ed. Andrew L. Rippin (Oxford: Blackwell Publishing, 2006), 429.

192 Badr al-Dīn al-Zarkashī, *al-Burhān fī 'ulūm al-Qur'ān* (Beirut: Dār al-Kutub al-'Ilmiyya, 1988), 2:237–69; Rosalind Ward Gwynne, "Patterns of Address," in *The Blackwell Companion to the Qur'ān*, ed. Andrew L. Rippin (Oxford: Blackwell Publishing, 2006), 75–76.

193 Lamya Kandil, "Die Schwüre in den mekkanischen Suren," in *The Qur'ān as Text*, ed. Stefan Wild (Leiden: E.J. Brill, 1996), 41–57; cf. *SKMS²* 187–88, 204–5 (Q. 51), and 280–81 (Q. 37);

Richter (d. 1939), whose interests lay with literary style.[194] He held that the objective of research is to define and delineate the classes of qur'ānic speech.[195] Consistent with the principles of his stylistics, Richter identified, *inter alia*, the hymnic form of speech, in addition to eschatological formulae.[196] Nearly two decades prior to the publication of Richter's study, S.D. Goitein set out in his inaugural dissertation of 1923 to consider the prayer genre and hymnic pericopae of the Qur'ānic corpus.[197] In 1926 Josef Horovitz issued his *Koranische Untersuchungen*, which explored the delimitation of narrative pericopae, in particular, punishment stories.[198] And almost a quarter century before that, Hartwig Hirschfeld published his *New Researches into the Composition and Exegesis of the Qorān* (1902), which treated numerous literary forms, most notably the parable (*mathal*).[199] Collectively, these findings establish the fact that "brief eschatological warnings, clad in opaque imagery and charged with a highly general call to recognize God's sovereignty, stand next to hymns, prayers, creeds, prophetic narratives, lengthy polemics, and detailed juridical regulations."[200] In addition, Neuwirth also discerns a handful of key components that comprise the sūra-unit, including disputations, narrations, etc.[201] Azaiez even adds denunciations for

---

Al-Azmeh, *Emergence of Islam in Late Antiquity*, 439–40, fn. 46 (*lā uqsimu bi-*). N.b. "The attention that Muslim exegetes and rhetoricians have devoted to every letter of the Qur'ān is epitomized in these systematic examinations of all possible qur'ānic formulae of designating the audience, with all their possible interpretations from the most concrete to the most speculative, excluding only the possibility of human authorship" (Gwynne, "Patterns of Address," 73–87, esp. 77).

194 Otto Spies, foreword to *Der Sprachstil des Koran*, by Gustav Richter (Leipzig: Otto Harrassowitz, 1940), v.

195 Ibid., vii.

196 Richter, *Der Sprachstil des Koran*, 1–2, 21–24, esp. 23, and 55–57; Sinai, "Qur'ān as Process," 411–12; *SKMS*² 188 and 190–95. Here again, the Weil–Nöldeke framework prevails (Spies, foreword, vi). In the present context, it is appropriate to note in passing that Weil–Nöldeke "presupposes the basic chronological framework of the *sīra* narrative" (Sinai, "Qur'ān as Process," 418).

197 Fritz Goitein, "Das Gebet im Qorān" (Diss., Universität Frankfurt am Main, 1923), i.

198 *KU* 10–32.

199 Hartwig Hirschfeld, *New Researches into the Composition and Exegesis of the Qorān* (London: Royal Asiatic Society, 1902), 84.

200 Sinai, "Qur'ān as Process," 408.

201 Neuwirth, "Structural, Linguistic, and Literary Features," 106–11; Azaiez, *Le contre-discours coranique*, 44; Ernst, *How to Read the Qur'ān*, 51–58. Neuwirth furnishes a thematic taxonomy covering the first Meccan period (*SKMS*² 187–201).

good measure.[202] In consideration of these and similar matters, it is quite apparent that the Qur'ān presents an impressive body of material.[203]

Genres of the Qur'ān

As Neuwirth specifies, the *corpus coranicum* eludes familiar categories and resists strict labels.[204] Wansbrough maintains that it is foremost a sermonary; casting a wide net, the sermon functions as the dominant literary form and vehicle in a preaching situation[205]:

> To the long and many-faceted process of *Gemeindebildung*, which culminated in the canonical text of Muslim scripture, the sermon (*khuṭba*) must have been central, as the instrument of both transmission and explication of the prophetical *logia*.

This was already appreciated by Voltaire (d. 1778), whose *Essai sur les mœurs et l'esprit des nations* insightfully reflects on the literary character of the Qur'ān as an assemblage of sermons with elements of vision, revelation, and legislation.[206] Meanwhile, Neuwirth asserts, "Above all, it is not to be understood by the term 'sermon' in the precise sense of rhetoric that expresses a truth that has already been announced and attempts to urge that truth upon the listener."[207] Be that as it may, Alfred-Louis de Prémare (d. 2006) reframes the Qur'ān as polemic.[208]

202 Azaiez, *Le contre-discours coranique*, 30 and 44–45; *SKMS*² 197–200; Robinson, *Discovering the Qur'ān*, 111–19.

203 Sinai, "Qur'ān as Process," 408; cf. *SKMS*² 9.

204 Neuwirth, "Einige Bemerkungen," 1:736.

205 *EinlPs*⁴ 13, 15, and cf. 25; *QS* 148; Stewart, "Wansbrough, Bultmann, and the Theory of Variant Traditions," 44.

206 Voltaire, *Œuvres de Voltaire*, ed. M. Beuchot (Paris: Chez Lefèvre, 1829), 15:338; Hartmut Bobzin, *Der Koran: Eine Einführung*, 7th ed. (München: Verlag C.H. Beck, 2007), 15.

207 Neuwirth, "Einige Bemerkungen," 1:736; *QSC* 253; Leo Baeck, "Griechische und jüdische Predigt," in *Aus Drei Jahrtausenden: Wissenschaftliche Untersuchungen und Abhandlungen zur Geschichte des jüdischen Glaubens* (Tübingen: Verlag von J.C.B. Mohr (Paul Siebeck), 1958), 142–43. Gabriel Said Reynolds states, "...Neuwirth pointedly denies that the Qur'ān can be considered homiletic...Neuwirth emphatically rejects the notion of Qur'ān as homily, noting that a sermon, 'expresses a truth that has already been announced and attempts to urge that truth upon the listener.' And yet this, it seems to me, is a lovely description of Qur'ānic discourse. The Qur'ān continually insists that it brings no new truth, but rather the same truth that has been proclaimed by all of the earlier prophets" (idem, *The Qur'ān and Its Biblical Subtext*, 243–44).

208 de Prémare, *Aux origines du Coran*, 44–45; Azaiez, *Le contre-discours coranique*, 30; Ettinghausen, *Antiheidnische Polemik*, 5–6.

However, Richard Ettinghausen (d. 1979) states that polemics proper develop only later.[209] Roest Crollius advances the claim that "there is perhaps no scripture that is so totally a book of prayer as is the Qur'ān."[210] He closes with the assertion that "the Qur'ān itself is prayer."[211] Then again, the pseudonymous Christoph Luxenberg's *Die syro-aramäische Lesart des Koran* (2000) reconstructs a lectionary.[212] While acknowledging its merits, de Prémare concludes to the contrary that the corpus cannot, and should not, be reduced to this.[213] But in a similar spirit, Günter Lüling (d. 2014) detects in the *Ur-Koran* a hymnal.[214] Neuwirth makes the case that "the arrangement of the qur'ānic text *grosso modo* seems to go back to the oral use of the text in the earliest community."[215] She impresses upon the reader "what it was originally conceived to be: a liturgical oration, as a text for recitation."[216] Yet again, neither is the liturgy genre all-inclusive.[217] As evident from the foregoing claims, "the Qur'ān may contain some elements of homily along with its many other elements, but it yields just as few examples of these as it yields of the catch-all categories of hymns, narratives, or legislation."[218] As an eclectic archive, the Qur'ān also preserves literary genres that fall outside the exclusive limits of sermon, polemic, prayer, and liturgy.

209 Ettinghausen, *Antiheidnische Polemik*, 5–6.

210 Ary A. Roest Crollius, "The Prayer in the Qur'ān," *SM* 24 (1975): 223; s.v. Prayer, *EQ*.

211 Crollius, "Prayer in the Qur'ān," 252.

212 Christoph Luxenberg, *Die syro-aramäische Lesart des Koran: Ein Beitrag zur Entschlüsselung der Koransprache* (Berlin: Das Arabische Buch, 2000); *SKMS*² 14*–16*; cf. Al-Azmeh, *Emergence of Islam in Late Antiquity*, 441–42.

213 de Prémare, *Aux origines du Coran*, 45–46; Neuwirth, "Qur'ānic Studies and Philology," 185.

214 Günter Lüling (d. 2014), *Über den Urkoran: Ansätze zur Rekonstruktion der vorislamisch-christlichen Strophenlieder im Koran*, 2nd ed. (Erlangen: Verlagsbuchhandlung H. Lüling, 1993); *SKMS*² 13*–14*.

215 S.v. Sūra(s), *EQ*; Angelika Neuwirth, *Der Koran als Text der Spätantike*, 3rd ed. (Berlin: Verlag der Weltreligionen, 2013 [2010]), 31. Along similar lines, see Hermann Gunkel, "The Religion of the Psalms," in *What Remains of the Old Testament and Other Essays* (New York: The Macmillan Company, 1928), 70–71.

216 Neuwirth, "Einige Bemerkungen," 1:736; *QSC* 253; de Prémare, *Aux origines du Coran*, 45; Reynolds, *The Qur'ān and Its Biblical Subtext*, 243, fn. 42.

217 Al-Azmeh, *Emergence of Islam in Late Antiquity*, 443–44. Reynolds comments, "Neuwirth's liturgical vision for the Qur'ān is not unreasonable, although her attempts to connect this to the development of a historical community, and especially her reliance on the traditional notion of Meccan and Medinan sūras, is necessarily speculative" (idem, *The Qur'ān and Its Biblical Subtext*, 244).

218 Neuwirth, "Einige Bemerkungen," 1:736; *QSC* 253.

The following chapters demonstrate the application of form criticism to the Qur'ānic corpus. In particular, the illustrative cases consider multiple genres, including prayer, liturgy, wisdom, narrative, and proclamation, along with minor genres.[219] Accordingly, chapter two presents a form-critical study of the prayer genre. The ensuing section identifies three productive cultic formulae, namely, *rabbanā* ("Our Lord"), *rabbi* ("My Lord"), and *allāhumma* ("O God"). The section thereafter addresses distinct social settings associated with the respective formulae. These situations, which gravitate toward performance in the subcult, display the full spectrum, from the private to the domestic to the corporate.[220] In light of the main functional class termed contextual prayer, the fourth section distinguishes a number of forms, namely, conversational and single response prayers.[221] This section also explores additional prayer forms, for instance, those deemed penitential, together with complaint, praise, imprecatory, and rhetorical prayers.[222] The third chapter begins by defining the liturgy genre vis-à-vis prayer in the Qur'ān. The subsequent section locates four formulae in the corpus.[223] The liturgical formula *huwa* ("He is...") represents one such case. Moreover, the doxological formula doubles as the formula of liturgical praise.[224] Prior to classifying forms of liturgy, the question of setting is decided on the basis of extant "performative markers."[225] Drawing a line between the hymn and litany forms, this chapter treats each in turn. In consideration of dominant motifs, the hymn form is subdivided into hymns to God, hymns to creation, and hymns to victory.

---

219 Gunkel, "Psalmen," col. 1618.

220 Rainer Albertz, *Persönliche Frömmigkeit und offizielle Religion: Religionsinterner Pluralismus in Israel und Babylon* (Stuttgart: Calwer Verlag, 1978), 27; *FOTL* 14:33; Balentine, *Prayer in the Hebrew Bible*, 212.

221 Corvin, "Stylistic and Functional Study of the Prose Prayers," 156 and 180; Balentine, *Prayer in the Hebrew Bible*, 19–21; Moshe Greenberg, *Biblical Prose Prayer as a Window to the Popular Religion of Ancient Israel* (Berkeley: University of California Press, 1983), 8.

222 Patrick D. Miller, *They Cried to the Lord: The Form and Theology of Biblical Prayer* (Minneapolis, Minnesota: Fortress Press, 1994), 69–70, 244, and 259–60; Greenberg, *Biblical Prose Prayer*, 22.

223 Norden, *Agnostos Theos, passim*; J.L. Lightfoot, *The Sibylline Oracles* (Oxford: Oxford University Press, 2007), 32; Laurent Pernot, "The Rhetoric of Religion," in *New Chapters in the History of Rhetoric*, ed. idem (Leiden: Brill, 2009), 332; Anton Baumstark, "Jüdischer und christlicher Gebetstypus im Koran," *Isl.* 16, no. 1 (1927): 231.

224 Baumstark, "Jüdischer und christlicher Gebetstypus im Koran," 236–37; s.v. Subḥān, *CQ*; s.v. Doxology, *DLW*; *FOTL* 14:260.

225 Anton Bierl, "Maenadism as Self-referential Chorality in Euripides' *Bacchae*," in *Choral Mediations in Greek Tragedy*, ed. Renaud Gagné and Marianne Govers Hopman (Cambridge: Cambridge University Press, 2013), 216.

Furthermore, the twofold litany form comprises litanies of praise and those of lament.

Chapter four considers the genre classified as wisdom literature. The first section identifies eleven sapiential formulae found in the Qurʾān. The following section then sheds light on wisdom contexts, particularly the adaptation of tribal ethics to teaching situations, ranging from private to small and large group instruction.[226] Even more significant, in this regard, is literally the presence of deictic formulae in the corpus.[227] Thereafter, this chapter delineates no less than ten wisdom forms. These vary between relatively short admonitions and fairly lengthy sermons.[228] Of particular relevance is the fact that the latter are delivered by means of the "conveyance command formula."[229] The fifth chapter examines the narrative genre writ large. As it so happens, *amthāl al-qurʾān* alone account for those forms termed similitudes, parables, paradigms, example stories, and controversy stories.[230] Beyond this, the chapter also surveys narrative blocks of the long saga, that is, episodes, legends, and reports.[231] The "saga-teller" con-

---

226 John Bright, "The Apodictic Prohibition: Some Observations," *JBL* 92, no. 2 (1973): 185; Erhard S. Gerstenberger, *Wesen und Herkunft des "apodiktischen Rechts"* (Neukirchen: Neukirchener Verlag des Erziehungsvereins, 1965), 110–17; cf. Albrecht Alt, *Die Ursprünge des israelitischen Rechts*, in *Kleine Schriften zur Geschichte des Volkes Israel*, 2nd rev. ed. (München: C.H. Beck'sche Verlagsbuchhandlung, 1959 [1934]), 1:278–332; Gerhard von Rad, *Weisheit in Israel* (Neukirchen: Neukirchener Verlag des Erziehungsvereins, 1970), 24; Kirsten M. Yoder Wesselhoeft, "Making Muslim Minds: Question and Answer as a Genre of Moral Reasoning in an Urban French Mosque," *JAAR* 78, no. 3 (2010): 793.

227 Cf. *QS* 19; Tahera Qutbuddin, "*Khuṭba:* The Evolution of Early Arabic Oration," in *Classical Arabic Humanities in Their Own Terms*, ed. Beatrice Gruendler (Leiden: Brill, 2008), 212–13 and 216.

228 Paul Hartog, *Polycarp and the New Testament: The Occasion, Rhetoric, Theme, and Unity of the Epistle to the Philippians and Its Allusions to New Testament Literature* (Tübingen: Mohr Siebeck, 2002), 124.

229 *QS* 16; Rolf P. Knierim and George W. Coats, *Numbers, FOTL* (Grand Rapids, Michigan: Wm. B. Eerdmans Publishing Company, 2005), 4:364.

230 S.v. Narratives, *EQ*; Adolf Jülicher, *Die Gleichnisreden Jesu* (Tübingen: Verlag von J.C.B. Mohr (Paul Siebeck), 1899), 2:vii–viii; Jeffrey T. Tucker, *Example Stories: Perspectives on Four Parables in the Gospel of Luke* (Sheffield, England: Sheffield Academic Press, 1998), 16–17; Dibelius, *Die Formgeschichte des Evangeliums*, 34–66; Boris Repschinski, *The Controversy Stories in the Gospel of Matthew: Their Redaction, Form and Relevance for the Relationship between the Matthean Community and Formative Judaism* (Göttingen: Vandenhoeck & Ruprecht, 2000), 236–45. In fact, Gunkel ends this letter to Adolf Jülicher expressing gratitude for his *The Parables of Jesus* (Rollmann, "Zwei Briefe Hermann Gunkels an Adolf Jülicher," 280).

231 Hermann Gunkel, *Die Sagen der Genesis* (Göttingen: Vandenhoeck & Ruprecht, 1901), *passim*; George W. Coats, *Genesis with an Introduction to Narrative Literature, FOTL* (Grand Rapids, Michigan: Wm. B. Eerdmans Publishing Company, 1983), 1:5–7 and 1:319; idem, *Exodus 1–18*,

structs these around motifs such as punishment and promise.[232] It is proper, therefore, that the manifold forms of narrative be located not in a single place, but rather in several settings. On the subject of saga, Gunkel states, "Frequently we are able to reconstruct an entire history of the materials used in a saga."[233] The sixth chapter, on the proclamation genre, inspects a set of vocative formulae, which occurs in the messenger situation. These prophetic speech-forms take the shape of rules and regulations linked to "the formation of community."[234] Lastly, the concluding chapter looks at the corpus through synchronic and diachronic lenses.

1.4 Summary

It should go without saying that the Qur'ān did not develop in a literary vacuum. In other words, the corpus is embedded within an intertextual matrix that emerged in late antiquity. Late Hellenistic and Arabic literary frames of reference form the coordinate plane and textual world of the Qur'ān, wherein biblical *dramatis personae*, narratives, and themes feature prominently.[235] The late antique milieu has likewise shaped its structure. For instance, "the observation that early Meccan sūras are structurally similar to the Psalms (*al-zabūr*), which equal-

---

FOTL (Grand Rapids, Michigan: Wm. B. Eerdmans Publishing Company, 1999), 2a:165–66; Burke O. Long, *2 Kings*, *FOTL* (Grand Rapids, Michigan: Wm. B. Eerdmans Publishing Company, 1991), 10:312 and 10:313–14; cf. Jolles, *Einfache Formen*, 62–90; Hirschfeld, *New Researches*, 62. On the other hand, for legend, cf. *FOTL* 1:318; *FOTL* 2a:164; *FOTL* 10:304; Jolles, *Einfache Formen*, 23–61; David Sidersky, *Les origines des légendes musulmanes dans le Coran et dans les vies des prophètes* (Paris: Librairie orientaliste Paul Geuthner, 1933), *passim*.

232 *Genesis*, trans. and comm. Hermann Gunkel, 3rd ed. (Göttingen: Vandenhoeck & Ruprecht, 1910), xxxv; *FOTL* 1:7; Claus Westermann, *Die Verheißungen an die Väter: Studien zur Vätergeschichte* (Göttingen: Vandenhoeck & Ruprecht, 1976), *passim*; Alford T. Welch, "Formulaic Features of the Punishment-Stories," in *Literary Structures of Religious Meaning in the Qur'ān*, ed. Issa J. Boullata (New York: Routledge, 2000), 77–116; cf. Roland E. Murphy, *Wisdom Literature: Job, Proverbs, Ruth, Canticles, Ecclesiastes, and Esther*, *FOTL* (Grand Rapids, Michigan: Wm. B. Eerdmans Publishing Company, 1981), 13:178 and 13:183–84.

233 Gunkel, "Die israelitische Literatur," 71; idem, "Literature of Ancient Israel," 49; Sparks, "Genre Criticism," 57; Buss, *Biblical Form Criticism*, 230 and 239–41.

234 Claus Westermann, *Grundformen prophetischer Rede* (München: Chr. Kaiser Verlag, 1960), *passim*; *QS* 148; Stewart, "Wansbrough, Bultmann, and the Theory of Variant Traditions," 44.

235 "Both formally and conceptually, Muslim scripture drew upon a traditional stock of monotheistic imagery, which may be described as schemata of revelation" (*QS* 1; Stewart, "Wansbrough, Bultmann, and the Theory of Variant Traditions," 22; cf. Al-Azmeh, *Emergence of Islam in Late Antiquity*, 488–97).

ly constitute polythematic compositions, has long been made."[236] In spite of this, the genre criticism of the Qur'ān remains a desideratum. As a codified text, it draws from a multitude of sources.[237] Each literary genre is rooted in its sphere of life. The wide range of genres is indicative of a corresponding range of situations. In terms of procedure, Gunkel states, "Since it concerns literary witnesses, the genres of this type of poetry must be substantiated."[238] Accordingly, this monograph demonstrates that the *corpus coranicum* evidences a significant number of literary genres that includes prayer, liturgy, wisdom, narrative, and proclamation. Above all, what is essential is the determined insistence of Gunkel that genre criticism is "the firm ground from which everything else must ascend."[239] Let us bring this introduction to a close and open a new critical chapter in Qur'ān scholarship with the single proviso: "To evaluate the work one must participate within its methodological presuppositions and evaluate the final results."[240]

---

236 Neuwirth, "Qur'ānic Readings of the Psalms," 734 and 738; de Prémare, *Aux origines du Coran*, 37–39 and 46; Heinrich Speyer, *Die biblischen Erzählungen im Qorān* (Darmstadt: Wissenschaftliche Buchgesellschaft, 1961), 447–49 and 497–98; Walid A. Saleh, "The Psalms in the Qur'ān and in the Islamic Religious Imagination," in *The Oxford Handbook of the Psalms*, ed. William P. Brown (Oxford: Oxford University Press, 2014), 285–87; Sinai, "Qur'ān as Process," 420–21; Robinson, *Discovering the Qur'ān*, 125–28.

237 In his "The Qur'ān as Literature," Mir argues that "the Qur'ān does not possess the literary variety of the Bible" (52). As evidence, he adduces the purported absence of a limited class of genres. He then proceeds to an exclusively "stylistic" analysis of the Qur'ān (ibid., 52–53).

238 *EinlPs*[4] 8; Gunkel and Begrich, *Introduction to Psalms*, 5.

239 Ibid.

240 Rippin, "Literary Analysis of Qur'ān, Tafsīr, and Sīra," 158.

Chapter 2: Prayer

2.1 Prayer Genre

The prayer genre abounds in the Qur'ān. Tilman Nagel also recognizes that prayer is one of the most frequently encountered genres in the corpus.[1] As Anton Baumstark (d. 1948) states in no uncertain terms, only through the Qur'ān is the earliest historical stratum of prayer recoverable.[2] In order to identify particular literary units within the Qur'ān, it is necessary to isolate the opening formulae for prayers.[3] For instance, the signature prayer form in the New Testament begins "Our Father" (*pater hēmōn*) (Matt 6:9) or "Father" (*pater*) (Luke 11:2).[4] The Qur'ān evidences a set of distinct prayer formulae, namely, *rabbanā*, *rabbi*, *allāhumma*.[5] In the absence of conspicuous closing formulae (e.g., *āmīn:* terminal "Amen"), Neuwirth astutely observes that the close of prayer building blocks is indicated by a change in the end rhyme pattern.[6] Moreover, the rhyme scheme ensures the integrity of the prayer unit. The proper identification of this qur'ānic genre also yields results in the systematic classification of prayer speech-forms.[7] "By the time we have located all the introductory and concluding formulas," Gene Tucker explains, "we will have isolated many of the original units as they were presented."[8] In turn, this will assist in situating these pericopae in their appropriate prayer settings.[9] Let us first turn to the prayer formulae in the *corpus coranicum*.

---

1 Tilman Nagel, *Der Koran: Einführung, Texte, Erläuterungen*, 4th ed. (München: C.H. Beck, 2002), 84.

2 Baumstark, "Jüdischer und christlicher Gebetstypus im Koran," 229.

3 Tucker, *Form Criticism of the Old Testament*, 10; s.v. Form and Structure of the Qur'ān, *EQ*.

4 Tucker, *Form Criticism of the Old Testament*, 10; Oscar Cullmann, *Prayer in the New Testament*, trans. John Bowden (Minneapolis, Minnesota: Fortress Press, 1995), 41–42; Merrill C. Tenney (d. 1985), *New Testament Survey*, rev. Walter M. Dunnett (Grand Rapids, Michigan: Wm. B. Eerdmans Publishing Company, 1985), 223–24; cf. Hirschfeld, *New Researches*, 89.

5 Tucker, *Form Criticism of the Old Testament*, 10 and 15; s.vv. Allāh and Rabb, *CQ*; Arthur Jeffery, *The Foreign Vocabulary of the Qur'ān* (Leiden: Brill, 2007 [1938]), 136–37 (*rabb*).

6 Tucker, *Form Criticism of the Old Testament*, 10; *SKMS*^{2} 102 (Q. 20); *BIQ*^{1} 67–69 and 73–75; s.v. Form and Structure of the Qur'ān, *EQ*.

7 Cf. Gunkel, "Psalmen," cols. 1613–15.

8 Tucker, *Form Criticism of the Old Testament*, 10. Although evidently utilizing cultic formulae (e.g., *rabbi, allāhumma*), Goitein proceeds to differentiate prayer-structures on the basis of length, that is, from simple to complex (idem, "Das Gebet im Qorān," 62–65 and 135).

9 Miller, *They Cried to the Lord*, 249.

https://doi.org/10.1515/9783110580884-002

2.2 Prayer Formulae

Rabbanā

In a general statement, Friedrich Heiler (d. 1967) rightly points out, "Every prayer opens with an invocation to the divine being."[10] Typical of the introductory formula in the text is *rabbanā* ("Our Lord").[11] Even without the explicit vocative marker, this invocation applies equally to multiple prayer types.[12] For example, Sūrat al-Mu'minūn (Q. 23.109a) furnishes an instructive case of the qur'ānic prayer form embedded in polemic[13]:

rabbanā āmannā fa-ghfir lanā wa-rḥamnā wa-anta khayru r-rāḥimīna

Our Lord,
we believe;
so forgive us, and have mercy on us.
You are the best of those who show mercy.

The narrative of the Seven Sleepers of Ephesus in Sūrat al-Kahf features another prayer of supplication (Q. 18.10a)[14]:

rabbanā ātinā min ladunka raḥmatan wa-hayyi' lanā min amrinā rashadan

Our Lord,
give us mercy from Your presence,
and prepare for us a way in our affair.

At the same time, this sūra-unit also includes a prayer-cum-creed (Q. 18.14a)[15]:

rabbunā rabbu s-samāwāti wa-l-arḍi lan nadʿuwa min dūnihī ilāhan

---

10 Friedrich Heiler, *Das Gebet: Eine religionsgeschichtliche und religionspsychologische Untersuchung*, 5th ed. (München: Verlag von Ernst Reinhardt, 1923), 58; idem, *Prayer: A Study in the History and Psychology of Religion*, trans. Samuel McComb (Oxford: Oxford University Press, 1932), 16.

11 Cullmann, *Prayer in the New Testament*, 41; Tucker, *Form Criticism of the Old Testament*, 10 and 15; see Devin J. Stewart, "The Mysterious Letters and Other Formal Features of the Qur'ān in Light of Greek and Babylonian Oracular Texts," in *New Perspectives on the Qur'ān: The Qur'ān in Its Historical Context 2*, ed. Gabriel Said Reynolds (New York: Routledge, 2011), 330 – 32.

12 Alan Jones notes, "It is quite common for there to be no particle before *rabbi* and *rabbanā*" (idem, *Arabic through the Qur'ān* (Cambridge: The Islamic Texts Society, 2005), 181).

13 *JQA* 314.

14 Ibid., 271.

15 Corvin, "Stylistic and Functional Study of the Prose Prayers," 206.

Our Lord is the Lord of the heavens and the earth.
We do not call to any god apart from Him.

At this point, it is worthwhile mentioning a pagan credal injunction interpolated in Sūrat Nūḥ (Q. 71.23):

wa-qālū lā-tadharunna ālihatakum
wa-lā tadharunna Waddan wa-lā Suwāʿan
wa-lā Yaghūtha wa-Yaʿūqa wa-Nasran

And they said:
Do not forsake your gods
and do not forsake Wadd nor Suwāʿ
nor Yaghūth nor Yaʿūq nor Nasr.

On firm ground, Alan Jones holds that "it seems unlikely that verse 23, which includes the names of five pre-Islāmic gods, could have been part of any original narrative."[16] In the words given to Noah's coevals, this pagan-prayer begins with *wa-qālū* ("And they said").[17] In fact, prayers embedded within narratives are simply introduced in this manner. On a related matter, Q. 8.35 reads,

wa-mā kāna ṣalātuhum ʿinda l-bayti illā mukāʾan wa-taṣdiyatan

Their prayer at the house is nothing but whistling and clapping of hands.

Upon closer inspection, this verse preserves important ethnographical details relating to the pagan "*actio* of prayer, that is, the way in which the prayer is spoken, the gestures are used, and the postures are adopted, which are codified through usage."[18]

Returning to the question of cultic formulae, on the basis of regular end rhyme, it is possible to locate a layered prayer composed of three units (Q. 2.286a–c)[19]:

rabbanā lā tuʾākhidhnā in nasīnā aw akhṭaʾnā

rabbanā wa-lā taḥmil ʿalaynā iṣran ka-mā ḥamaltahū ʿalā lladhīna min qablinā

---

16 *JQA* 538; cf. Abū l-Mundhir Hishām b. Muḥammad al-Kalbī, *Le livre des idoles* (*Kitāb al-aṣnām*), 2nd ed., ed. Ahmed Zeki Pacha (Cairo: Imprimerie bibliothèque egyptienne, 1924), 13.
17 Cf. Azaiez, *Le contre-discours coranique*, 8 (*yaqūlūna...fa-qul*); Neuwirth, "Structural, Linguistic, and Literary Features," 108 (*wa-yaqūlūna...fa-qul*).
18 Pernot, "The Rhetoric of Religion," 332.
19 S.v. Prayer, *ER*^{2}; Robinson, *Discovering the Qurʾān*, 223.

rabbanā wa-lā tuḥammilnā mā lā ṭāqata lanā bihī wa-'fu 'annā wa-ghfir lanā wa-rḥamnā

Our Lord,
do not take us to task if we forget or make a mistake.

Our Lord,
do not lay on us a burden
like that you laid on those who were before us.[20]

Our Lord,
do not lay on us such a burden as we are incapable of bearing.
And pardon us and forgive us and have mercy on us.

With respect to the classification of prayer, Sam Gill notes, "Such types may constitute whole prayers or they may be strung together to form a structurally more complex prayer."[21] Bell agrees that these verses conform to the prayer genre.[22] Along with the fourth and final verse of the stanza, Jones considers it a summoning of the divine presence.[23] Q. 2.286d incorporates the "essential predicate" ("You are...")[24]:

anta mawlānā fa-unṣurnā 'alā l-qawmi l-kāfirīna

You are our Protector[25]
– Give us victory over the people who are not believers.

Even so, the cultic formula (*rabbanā*) and its distinctive rhyme pattern (*-Cā*) set apart the first three lines of the final stanza of the sūra-unit. In this specific context, Heiler's observation seems particularly relevant: "An intermediate form between the prayer of the individual and that of an assembly consists of this, that on a common occasion of worship the individuals utter a prayer one after the other."[26] Apart from formal and embedded hymns, this provides a clue to the ritual logic behind serial prayers in the corpus.[27] Regardless, the pervasive and sta-

20 *BCQ* 1:61; cf. Q. 7.42 and Q. 23.62.
21 S.v. Prayer, *ER*².
22 *BCQ* 1:60; *JQA* 24.
23 *JQA* 24.
24 Norden, *Agnostos Theos*, 143–308; Pernot, "The Rhetoric of Religion," 332; Lightfoot, *The Sibylline Oracles*, 25 and 32–33.
25 Cf. Q. 22.78: *huwa mawlākum fa-ni'ma l-mawlā wa-ni'ma n-naṣīru* ("He is your Protector: how excellent a Protector; how excellent a Helper").
26 Heiler, *Das Gebet*, 57; idem, *Prayer*, 15.
27 Cf. Sidney Smith, *Isaiah Chapters XL-LV: Literary Criticism and History* (London: Oxford University Press, 1944), 8.

ble quality of the prayer form and its accompanying cultic formula *rabbanā* is well attested by internal evidence.

Rabbi

The second cultic marker that occurs throughout the corpus is *rabbi* ("My Lord"), written with defective spelling (i.e., without *mater lectionis*).[28] Take, for instance, the short consecration prayer (Q. 2.126) uttered by the "mnemohistorical" figure Abraham[29]:

> *wa-idh qāla ibrāhīmu*
> *rabbi j'al hādhā baladan āminan wa-rzuq ahlahū mina th-thamarāti man āmana minhum bi-llāhi wa-l-yawmi l-ākhiri*
>
> And when Abraham said:
> My Lord,
> make this a secure land
> and provide some of its fruits as sustenance
> for those of its people who believe in God and the Last Day.

In addition, consider the following Solomonic prayer (Q. 38.35):

> *qāla rabbi ghfir lī wa-hab lī mulkan lā yanbaghī li-aḥadin min ba'dī innaka anta l-wahhābu*
>
> He said:
> My Lord,
> Forgive me
> and give me a kingdom that no one may have after me.
> You are the Giver.

The versatile "substitution" invocation ("You are...") concludes this prayer.[30] In multiple instances, the short prayer form functions as a subscription (e.g., Q. 71.26–28). Sūrat al-Mu'minūn is a case in point; it ends with the first-person

---

28 Goitein, "Das Gebet im Qorān," 135; Carl P. Caspari, *A Grammar of the Arabic Language*, 3rd rev. ed., ed. and trans. William Wright (Cambridge: Cambridge University Press, 1896–98), 1:253 and 2:87.
29 Corvin, "Stylistic and Functional Study of the Prose Prayers," 210 and 225–28; Jan Assmann, "Mnemohistory and the Construction of Egypt," in *Moses the Egyptian: The Memory of Egypt in Western Monotheism* (Cambridge, Massachusetts: Harvard University Press, 1997), 1–22.
30 Bryan Hainsworth, *The Iliad: A Commentary* (Cambridge: Cambridge University Press, 1993), 3:15–16.

speech of the supplicant. Moreover, the closing prayer is introduced by the formula *qul* ("say, speak!").[31] Q. 23.118 reads,

wa-qul rabbi ghfir wa-rḥam wa-anta khayru r-rāḥimīna

Say:
My Lord,
forgive and have mercy,
for you are the best of those who have mercy.

Wansbrough points out, "*Qul* commonly serves to indicate liturgical instructions, frequently prayer, e.g., Q. 3.26, 10.104, 13.16, and especially sūras 112, 113, and 114."[32] Moreover, as in the biblical case, this short prayer belongs to a class of "formal prayers" that are virtually independent of their textual setting.[33]

On the other hand, consider a divinely sanctioned prayer for safe landing (v. 29) securely moored to the Noah episode (Q. 23.23–30) in the punishment saga[34]:

wa-qul rabbi anzilnī munzalan mubārakan wa-anta khayru l-munzilīna

Say:
My Lord,
cause me to land at a blessed landing place.
You are the best of those who bring people to land.

In addition, the *basmala* in its truncated form debuts as a seafarer's prayer (Q. 11.41)[35]:

---

31 Cf. *QS* 12–13. At first glance, the end-rhyme of verse 118 (-*īC*) seems to form an alternating pattern with -*ūC* (e.g., v. 117).

32 Ibid., 14.

33 Corvin, "Stylistic and Functional Study of the Prose Prayers," 203–4. In fact, "when lifted out and taken as individual, self-contained literary units, neither they nor the narratives from which they are removed suffer any perceptible loss of meaning" (Balentine, *Prayer in the Hebrew Bible*, 19–20).

34 Welch, "Formulaic Features of the Punishment-Stories," 78 and 93–96. For the saga, see Gunkel, *Die Sagen der Genesis*, *passim*; *FOTL* 1:5–7 and 1:319; *FOTL* 10:313–14; Timothy D. Finlay, "The Form-Critical Problem: Determining the Text-Type," in *The Birth Report Genre in the Hebrew Bible* (Tübingen: Mohr Siebeck, 2005), 5; Trent Butler, "Narrative Form Criticism: Dead or Alive?" in *A Biblical Itinerary: In Search of Method, Form and Content: Essays in Honor of George W. Coats*, ed. Eugene E. Carpenter (Sheffield, England: Sheffield Academic Press, 1997), 43.

35 S.v. Basmala, *EQ*. For matters related to itinerant prayer, cf. Q. 4.43, Q. 4.101, and Q. 5.6. Compare with the first stanza of "Hymn, L.M.": "Embark'd upon the mighty deep, / On Thee, my God! I cast my care; / Do Thou my vessel safely keep, / And listen to a sailor's prayer" (*The Sailors' Prayer Book* (London: John Snow, 1852), 113).

> *wa-qāla rkabū fīhā bi-smi llāhi majrāhā wa-mursāhā inna rabbī la-ghafūrun raḥīmun*
>
> He said:
> Embark in it.
> In God's name will be its course and its anchorage.
> My Lord is Forgiving and Merciful.

Bell contends that the speaker is none other than Noah.[36] In the biblical case, Balentine observes that "prayer also serves as a literary leitmotif in characterizing the sailors..." who "call out" (*qārā'*): "Please, O Lord, we pray..." (Jonah 1:14).[37] It seems that a qur'ānic analogue surfaces in Q. 10.22 with the common rhyme (*-īn*):

> *huwa lladhī yusayyirukum fī l-barri wal-baḥri ḥattā idhā kuntum fī l-fulki wa-jarayna bihim bi-rīḥin ṭayyibatin wa-fariḥū bihā jā'athā rīḥun 'āṣifun wa-jā'ahumu l-mawju min kulli makānin wa-ẓannū annahum uḥīṭa bihim da'awu llāha mukhliṣīna lahu d-dīna la-in anjaytanā min hādhihī la-nakūnanna mina sh-shākirīna*
>
> It is He who enables you to travel by land and sea;
> then, when you are in the ships,
> and they run with [the people in them] with a fair breeze
> and they rejoice in it,
> a storm-wind comes on them,
> and the waves come on them from every side
> and they think that they are engulfed.
> They call to God, being sincere to Him in their faith:
> If You deliver us from this,
> we shall be among the thankful.

But as Jones observes, the figure of Jonah is all but fleeting (v. 98) in this sūra-unit.[38]

Allāhumma

The third cultic formula is *allāhumma* ("O God"), of which there are five instances in the corpus (Q. 3.26, 5.114, 8.32, 10.10, 39.46).[39] For example, it combines with the formula *qul* in Q. 39.46 to mark the following injunction[40]:

---

36 *BCQ* 1:358.
37 Balentine, *Prayer in the Hebrew Bible*, 72.
38 *JQA* 195.
39 Goitein, "Das Gebet im Qorān," 135; s.v. Allāhumma, *CQ*; Jones, *Arabic through the Qur'ān*, 182.

quli llāhumma fāṭira s-samāwāti wa-l-arḍi ʿālima l-ghaybi wa-sh-shahādati anta taḥkumu bayna ʿibādika fī mā kānū fīhi yakhtalifūna

Say:
O God,
Creator of the heavens and earth,
Knower of the Invisible and the Witnessed,
You will judge between Your servants
concerning that about which they used to differ.

Regarding Q. 39, Jones notes that multiplicity and mixture characterize verses 4 to 66.[41] The generative cultic formula *allāhumma* ("O God") is, in point of fact, an especially productive template for extra-qurʾānic prayer.[42] Consider the optimum plea for deliverance and forgiveness (*afḍal al-istighfār*) in al-Bukhārī (d. 256/870) that combines two cultic formulae, *allāhumma* and *rabbi*[43]:

allāhumma anta rabbī lā ilāha illā anta khalaqtanī wa-ana ʿabduka wa-ana ʿalā ʿahdika wa-waʿdika mā staṭaʿtu aʿūdhu bika min sharri mā ṣanaʿtu abūʾu laka bi-niʿmatika ʿalayya wa-abūʾu laka bi-dhanbī fa-ghfir lī fa-innahu lā yaghfiru dh-dhunūba illā anta

O God, You are my Lord! None has the right to be worshipped but You. You created me and I am Your slave, and I am faithful to my covenant and my promise (to You) as much as I can. I seek refuge with You from all the evil I have done. I acknowledge before You all the blessings You have bestowed upon me, and I acknowledge before You all my sins. So I entreat You to forgive my sins, for nobody can forgive sins except You.

Parenthetically, Goitein questions the authenticity of post-qurʾānic constructions.[44]

---

40 Jones, *Arabic through the Qurʾān*, 182.
41 *JQA* 421.
42 al-Bukhārī, *Kitāb al-daʿawāt*, in *Ṣaḥīḥ al-Bukhārī* (Damascus: Dār Ibn Kathīr, 2002), 1573 – 97.
43 Ibid., 1573; al-Bukhārī, *Ṣaḥīḥ al-Bukhārī*, trans. Muhammad Muhsin Khan (Riyadh: Maktabat Dār al-Salām, 1997), 8:179, fn. 1; cf. Sharon H. Ringe, *Luke* (Louisville, Kentucky: Westminster John Knox Press, 1995), 164. For *istighfār*, see Goitein, "Das Gebet im Qorān," 20.
44 Fritz Goitein, "Das Gebet im Qorān," publ. Abstr. (Diss., Frankfurt am Main, 1923), i; idem, "Das Gebet im Qorān," 79.

2.3 Prayer Setting

Private Prayer

In terms of place in life, where *rabbi* stands alone, the first-person speech of the supplicant constitutes a specific, prayer or song of the individual.[45] By way of illustration consider the closing prayer of Sūrat Nūḥ (Q. 71.28):

> *rabbi ghfir lī wa-li-wālidayya wa-li-man dakhala baytiya mu'minan wa-li-l-mu'minīna wa-l-mu'mināti wa-lā tazidi ẓ-ẓālimīna illā tabāran*
>
> My Lord,
> forgive me and my parents
> and whoever enters my house as a believer
> and believing men and women,
> and increase the wrong-doers only in ruin.

On the problem of private prayer, Heiler introduces a new complication[46]:

> The need which impels to prayer within the primitive world is for the most part not the need of the individual, but of an entire group; therefore, in the main, it is not the individual that prays, but a group of individuals socially bound together, the family, the village community, the tribe, the clan, the league.

As a result, there emerges the problem of designating certain prayers as either private or group performances.[47] Take, for instance, Q. 21.112, which apparently ends on a talismanic note:

> *qāla rabbi ḥkum bi-l-ḥaqqi wa-rabbunā r-raḥmānu l-musta'ānu 'alā mā taṣifūna*
>
> He says,
> My Lord,
> judge with truth.
> Our Lord is the Merciful,
> Whose help can be sought against what you describe.

Since this compound prayer employs both individual (*rabbi*) and collective (*rabbanā*) cultic formulae, locating its social setting poses special problems. On the

---

45 Balentine, *Prayer in the Hebrew Bible*, 211–12; Gunkel, "Psalmen," col. 1615.
46 Heiler, *Das Gebet*, 53; idem, *Prayer*, 12.
47 Gerstenberger concedes, "it has been difficult at times to classify psalms as individual or collective poetry" (cf. *FOTL* 14:34).

one hand, verse 112 may simply represent two distinct prayer fragments joined by the coordinating conjunction (*wa-*). Then again, in light of the foregoing difficulties, it becomes necessary to look beyond the surface notion of individual authorship to communal composition.[48] Consequently, "attributions of texts will be easier, and even hybrid forms will be explainable on the basis of some overlapping of social structures."[49] This, quite reasonably, has significant explanatory power.

Domestic Prayer

According to Mowinckel, singular and plural pronouns in biblical literature allow for the tentative classification of individual and communal psalms.[50] However, citing Babylonian precedent, he argues that the singular form "is the usual and natural one, because there it is the whole and not the individual that is given reality, a *corporate personality*…."[51] As with psalmic literature (e.g., Ps 44), when singular pronouns are accompanied by "Our Lord" (*rabbanā*) in a single qur'ānic pericope, it seems to constitute a "cultic prayer," as in Q. 14.41[52]:

> *rabbanā ghfir lī wa-li-wālidayya wa-li-l-mu'minīna yawma yaqūmu l-ḥisābu*
>
> Our Lord,
> forgive me and my parents and the believers
> on the day when the reckoning comes to pass.

However, the dual private and public nature of this prayer is readily apparent.[53] This is explained by Gerstenberger, who stresses that the social locus of private

---

48 Cf. ibid.

49 Ibid.

50 Mowinckel, *Psalms*, 1:38 and cf. 1:42–80.

51 Ibid., 1:38–39; cf. Childs, *Introduction*, 519–20; David J.A. Clines, *On the Way to the Postmodern: Old Testament Essays, 1967–1998* (Sheffield, England: Sheffield Academic Press, 1998), 2:670. Taking their cue from Mowinckel, scholars such as Erhard S. Gerstenberger and Henning G. Reventlow have also taken Gunkel to task for his "neo-Romantic, Protestant preoccupation with private religion" (Balentine, *Prayer in the Hebrew Bible*, 11). For example, see Erhard S. Gerstenberger, "Individuum und Kult," in *Der bittende Mensch: Bittritual und Klagelied des Einzelnen im Alten Testament* (Neukirchen: Neukirchener Verlag, 1980), 167.

52 Mowinckel, *Psalms*, 1:38; Balentine, *Prayer in the Hebrew Bible*, 11; cf. Harm W.M. van Grol, "Psalm, Psalter, and Prayer," in *Prayer from Tobit to Qumran*, ed. Renate Egger-Wenzel and Jeremy Corley (Berlin: Walter de Gruyter, 2004), 43, fn. 4.

53 Balentine, *Prayer in the Hebrew Bible*, 11, fn. 16.

devotion is domestic.[54] In fact, Mario Puglisi goes so far as to claim that the collective is predicated upon the family.[55] In effect, as Gerstenberger astutely observes, "this primary group is seen to function as the small social unit that bridges the gap between individual and community, retaining its identity as a forum for personal piety without giving up its cultic commitments and connections."[56] In light of these considerations, a *prima facie* case of private prayer may in actual fact represent a domestic or subcult prayer performed by the head on behalf of the whole.[57]

Corporate Prayer

In terms of cultic setting, Gerstenberger also refers to constituent subgroups that form the collective.[58] He further specifies that these social spheres are mutually interdependent, as are their cultic practices.[59] For example, consider the three levels present in the ostensibly individual prayer assigned to Solomon in Sūrat an-Naml (Q. 27.19a):

> *rabbi awziʿnī an ashkura niʿmataka llatī anʿamta ʿalayya wa-ʿalā wālidayya wa-an aʿmala ṣāliḥan tarḍāhu wa-adkhilnī bi-raḥmatika fī ʿibādika ṣ-ṣāliḥīna*
>
> My Lord,
> press me to be thankful for Your blessings,
> which You bestowed on me and on my parents
> and [press me] to do a righteous thing that You approve of,
> and admit me, by Your mercy, among Your righteous servants.

54 Gerstenberger, *Der bittende Mensch*, 168; Balentine, *Prayer in the Hebrew Bible*, 11, fn. 16, and 16; Mario Puglisi, *La Preghiera* (Torino: Fratelli Bocca, 1928), 142. On the other hand, Barbara Hornig argues that "prose prayers originally were individual, free prayers that created their own form, and so they lacked the formal character which presents itself largely in the psalms" (cited in Corvin, "Stylistic and Functional Study of the Prose Prayers," 8 and 100–101; Barbara Hornig, "Das Prosagebet der nachexilischen Literatur" (Diss., Universität Leipzig, 1957), publ. Abstr., *ThLZ* 83, no. 9 (1958): cols. 644–46).

55 Puglisi, *La Preghiera*, 138.

56 Gerstenberger, *Der bittende Mensch*, 167–68; Balentine, *Prayer in the Hebrew Bible*, 11, fn. 16.

57 Albertz, *Persönliche Frömmigkeit und offizielle Religion*, 27; *FOTL* 14:33; Balentine, *Prayer in the Hebrew Bible*, 212; Claus Westermann, *What Does the Old Testament Say about God?* ed. Friedemann W. Golka (Atlanta: John Knox Press, 1979), 78; Heiler, *Das Gebet*, 54.

58 *FOTL* 14:33.

59 Ibid., 14:33–34; Balentine, *Prayer in the Hebrew Bible*, 213.

Although the cultic formula (*rabbi*) reflects personal piety, the household reference ("my parents") plainly situates it within a domestic setting. The third and final level ("among Your righteous servants") clearly reflects the fact that this prayer functions within a collective social context.[60] Therefore, "one must take seriously Gerstenberger's caution against compartmentalizing these social settings too neatly."[61]

With this in mind, the qur'ānic corporate prayer is generally indicated by the plural cultic formula, *rabbanā* ("Our Lord"). Take, for instance, verse 75a in Sūrat an-Nisā':

> *rabbanā akhrijnā min hādhihi l-qaryati ẓ-ẓālimi ahluhā wa-j'al lanā min ladunka waliyyan wa-j'al lanā min ladunka naṣīran*
>
> Our Lord,
> take us out of this settlement
> whose people are wrong-doers.
> Appoint for us from Your presence a protector.
> Appoint for us from Your presence a helper.

This collective prayer of supplication is voiced by none other than "the oppressed, men, women, and children" (*al-mustaḍ'afīna mina r-rijāli wa-n-nisā'i wa-l-wildāni*) (Q. 4.75). In the analogous biblical case, Moshe Greenberg argues that "the content of the prayers is tailored to the circumstances in which it arises; hence the prayers cannot be reused. These features distinguish the embedded petitionary prayers from institutionalized forms of worship."[62] According to Westermann, from the initial subcult emerges the collective cult.[63] Gerstenberger adds that "religious and pseudo-religious ceremonialism plays an important role" in the context of these subgroups.[64] It is here that cultic prayers undergo further development and ritual elaboration. Greenberg states, "These are the properties of experts; their details are fixed and prescribed."[65] Moreover, considering the perennial nature of the cultic calendar, members of the group gather at

---

60 As with formal prayers of consecration, "prayers of this kind are described as having been consciously composed for oral delivery in the presence of an audience..." (Corvin, "Stylistic and Functional Study of the Prose Prayers," 14 and 132–33).
61 Balentine, *Prayer in the Hebrew Bible*, 213.
62 Greenberg, *Biblical Prose Prayer*, 17.
63 Albertz, *Persönliche Frömmigkeit und offizielle Religion*, 27; Westermann, *What Does the Old Testament Say about God?* 78; Van Grol, "Psalm, Psalter, and Prayer," 43.
64 *FOTL* 14:33.
65 Greenberg, *Biblical Prose Prayer*, 17.

the sacred precinct on set occasions.[66] Therefore, Heiler appropriately notes, "Where the religious functions are in the hands of special priests, the *priest* prays in the name and by the authority of the community."[67]

Gerald Hawting states that in the *corpus coranicum* "the references to the ritual prayer are especially allusive and often consist of no more than calls for the 'establishment' (*iqāma*) of the *ṣalāt*, sometimes linked with the command to bring the *zakāt*."[68] At this point in the discussion, drawing a fine line between "prayer as subject" and "prayer as text" is thoroughly *à propos*.[69] From a comparative perspective, *ṣalāt* as subject refers to "meta-prayer, signifying thereby the communications in religious traditions about prayer."[70] Therefore, Arent Jan Wensinck (d. 1939) concludes that rendering *ṣalāt* as "prayer" is imprecise: "The translation 'prayer' simply is not accurate; the Arabic word *duʿāʾ* corresponds to the conception prayer."[71] In terms of prayer as text, Gerhard Böwering also notes that "*duʿāʾ* appears to represent the earliest layer of prayer language...."[72] He further observes that "the intersection of these two semantic fields of prayer in prophetic narratives of the Qurʾān may illustrate the assimilation of *duʿāʾ*, an early Arab way of prayer, with that of *ṣalāt*...."[73] This later conception is clearly reflected in the conjunction (*wa-*) of dual prayer pericopae in the extended Abrahamic prayer-series (Q. 14.40)[74]:

---

66 Ibid.; Albertz, *Persönliche Frömmigkeit und offizielle Religion*, 27; Westermann, *What Does the Old Testament Say about God?* 78; Van Grol, "Psalm, Psalter, and Prayer," 43.
67 Heiler, *Das Gebet*, 54; idem, *Prayer*, 13.
68 S.v. Worship, *EQ*.
69 S.v. Prayer, *ER*².
70 Ibid.
71 S.v. Ṣalāt, *EI*²; cf. Goitein, "Das Gebet im Qorān," 1 and 16–18; Jeffery, *Foreign Vocabulary of the Qur'ān*, 198–99; Toshihiko Izutsu, *God and Man in the Koran: Semantics of the Koranic Weltanschauung* (Tokyo: The Keio Institute of Cultural and Linguistic Studies, 1964), 147–48 and 193–97; Neuwirth, "Vom Rezitationstext über die Liturgie zum Kanon," 86 and 91. Fred M. Donner claims, "So the evidence seems to suggest not that the Qurʾān originated as prayer liturgy, but rather a few elements drawn from the prayer liturgy were used to embellish the Qurʾān. The implication is that the Islāmic prayer ritual and the Qurʾān text, whatever it originally was, developed independently" (idem, "The Qurʾān in Recent Scholarship: Challenges and Desiderata," in *The Qurʾān in Its Historical Context*, ed. Gabriel Said Reynolds (New York: Routledge, 2008), 35). Then again, Issa J. Boullata states, "The literary structures of the Qurʾān are not ornamental elements in it that can be dispensed with, they are part and parcel of its meaning and without them that meaning is lost" (idem, introduction, x).
72 S.v. Prayer, *EQ*; Goitein, "Das Gebet im Qorān," 1.
73 S.v. Prayer, *EQ*.
74 S.v. Worship, *EQ*.

rabbi j'alnī muqīma ṣ-ṣalāti wa-min dhurriyyatī rabbanā wa-taqabbal du'ā'i

My Lord, make me and some of my seed perform worship (*ṣalāt*),
and our Lord, receive my prayer (*du'ā'*).

It is remarkable that even texts with meta-prayer content attest to the relative fixity of the prayer genre and the cultic formulae. In the final analysis, "prayers must often be considered primarily, if not solely, as texts."[75]

Although "unrecorded prayers" remain beyond the historian's scope, the *corpus coranicum* nonetheless sheds critical light on the *actio* of prayer from a cult-functional perspective.[76] Wansbrough observes that "an interesting feature of scriptural syntax is the predominantly liturgical use of the emphatic particle *iyyā*, with pronominal suffix designating the object of worship, fear, service, etc., before the verbs: *'abada* (Q. 1.5, 34.40, 10.28, 28.63, 2.172, 16.114, 41.37, 29.56), *da'ā* (Q. 6.41), *rahiba* (Q. 2.40, 16.51), *ittaqā* (Q. 2.41), and *ista'āna* (Q. 1.5)."[77] In the context of qur'ānic polemic, the so-called partners (*shurakā'*) (e.g., Q. 10.28; Q. 28.63) will offer the following counter-testimony that incorporates *iyyā* as a specific marker singling out the cult object (Q. 10.28):

mā kuntum iyyānā ta'budūna

It was not us you worshipped.

Wheeler Thackston also notes that "*iyyā-* occurs in Koranic Arabic primarily as a pronominal carrier for pronouns that have been separated from the verb for rhetorical force."[78]

Furthermore, consider the Fātiḥa (Q. 1.1–7).[79] According to Baumstark, the *locus classicus* of qur'ānic prayer is Sūrat al-Fātiḥa.[80] Along with Hirschfeld,

---

75 S.v. Prayer, *ER*².

76 Ibid.; Mowinckel, *Psalms*, 1:31–35; Corvin, "Stylistic and Functional Study of the Prose Prayers," 26.

77 *QS* 17–18; see Goitein, "Das Gebet im Qorān," 21.

78 Wheeler M. Thackston, *An Introduction to Koranic and Classical Arabic* (Bethesda, Maryland: Ibex Publishers, 2000), 168–69.

79 Angelika Neuwirth and Karl Neuwirth, "Sūrat al-Fātiḥa – 'Eröffnung' des Text-Corpus Koran oder 'Introitus' der Gebetsliturgie?" in *Text, Methode und Grammatik: Wolfgang Richter zum 65. Geburtstag*, ed. Walter Gross, Hubert Irsigler, and Theodor Seidl (St. Ottilien: EOS Verlag, 1991), 337. Appropriate in this context is al-Zamakhsharī's Qur'ān commentary that preserves an analogous pair: *bi-smi llāt bi-smi l-'uzzā* (idem, *al-Kashshāf*, ed. W. Nassau Lees (Calcutta: W. Nassau Lees, 1856), 1:5; s.v. Basmala, *EQ*). On a related note, Ibn al-Kalbī (d. 206/821–2) also transmits the following pagan oath formula: *wa-bi-llāti wa-l-'uzzā* (idem, *Le livre des idoles* (*Kitāb al-aṣnām*), 17; Wolfdietrich Fischer, *Grammatik des klassischen Arabisch* (Wiesbaden: Otto

Jones also considers it to be “a short prayer,” while Nagel, in concert with Muslim tradition, writes that it encapsulates the essence of scripture.[81] In agreement, de Prémare says, the Fātiḥa represents the epitome of ritual.[82] In terms of content and form, Goitein places it between prayer and hymn, deeming it uniquely qur'ānic.[83] Noteworthy is Jones' observation that it is a composite sūra consisting of a pair of pericopae. He states that “in the first four verses God is spoken of in the third person; in verses 5–7 in the second person singular.”[84] What is more, Neuwirth cogently argues the following point[85]:

> In order to assign the Fātiḥa to its genuine cultic context with greater certainty, we will contextualize it with non-Islāmic liturgical texts of a similar structure. This will enable us to identify more precisely the genre to which the Fātiḥa belongs and ultimately sharpen our insight into the specific character of this most extraordinary of sūras.

For instance, in the context of *The Divine Liturgy of St. John Chrysostom*, an icon-prayer is recited in veneration of the image of Christ[86]:

Harrassowitz, 1972), 136; Caspari, *A Grammar of the Arabic Language*, 1:279 and 2:175–76; cf. *GdQ²* 1:116, fn. 3). The *basmala* in the exordium also functions as an editorial superscription for the sūra-unit in general, excluding Sūra 9 (Mahmoud Ayoub, *The Qur'ān and Its Interpreters* (Albany: State University of New York Press, 1984), 1:46; Muḥammad b. Jarīr al-Ṭabarī, *Tafsīr al-Ṭabarī: Jāmi' al-bayān 'an ta'wīl al-Qur'ān*, 2nd ed., ed. Maḥmūd Muḥammad Shākir and Aḥmad Muḥammad Shākir (Cairo: Maktabat Ibn Taymiyya, s.a.), 1:114–34; *GdQ²* 2:79–80; *JQA* 179; *BCQ* 1:291).

80 Baumstark, “Jüdischer und christlicher Gebetstypus im Koran,” 229.

81 Nagel, *Der Koran*, 84–85; *JQA* 23; Hirschfeld, *New Researches*, 71.

82 de Prémare, *Aux origines du Coran*, 35.

83 Goitein, “Das Gebet im Qorān,” publ. Abstr., ii; idem, “Das Gebet im Qorān,” 135; Baumstark, “Jüdischer und christlicher Gebetstypus im Koran,” 230, fn. 2; Norden, *Agnostos Theos*, 177–201.

84 *JQA* 23; cf. Neuwirth, “Sūrat al-Fātiḥa,” 351; *BCQ* 1:3.

85 Neuwirth, “Sūrat al-Fātiḥa,” 334; *SPMC* 166; Al-Azmeh, *Emergence of Islam in Late Antiquity*, 441.

86 *The Divine Liturgy of St. John Chrysostom*, trans. Milan G. Popovich (McKeesport and Duquesne, Pennsylvania: Sava, 1968), 44. N.b. “Icons, of course, have come to play an important role in Byzantine piety, but (apart from feasts of course) their supposed place in the liturgy cannot be documented by any liturgical text. Historically, they play no role in the ritual of the Byzantine mass and their presence on an iconostasis or elsewhere cannot be deemed essential to the celebration of the liturgy of the Great Church” (Robert F. Taft, “Icons in the Liturgy,” in *The Great Entrance: A History of the Transfer of Gifts and Other Pre-anaphoral Rites of the Liturgy of St. John Chrysostom*, *OCA*, no. 200 (Roma: Pont. Institutum Studiorum Orientalium, 1975), 416). Taft duly notes that “the two preparatory prayers said before the icons of Christ and the Theotokos are not even in the *editio princeps*. Some of the *diataxeis* have the priest kiss the icons before entering the sanctuary to vest” (ibid., 416, fn. 211). However, Thomas F. Mathews sounds a

We worship thee before thy icon and beg forgiveness of our sins. O Christ, our God; for, of thine own free will, thou wast pleased to be raised upon the cross, that thou mightest deliver thy creatures from bondage of the enemy.

Q. 1.5–7 suggests comparison with this ritual analogue:

iyyāka naʿbudu wa-iyyāka nastaʿīnu

ihdinā ṣ-ṣirāṭa l-mustaqīma

ṣirāṭa lladhīna anʿamta ʿalayhim ghayri l-maghḍūbi ʿalayhim wa-lā ḍ-ḍāllīna

You we serve;
To You we turn for help.

Guide us on the straight path –

The path of those You have blessed,
Not of those against whom there is anger
Nor of those who go astray.

According to Neuwirth, the Fātiḥa stands "at the beginning of the communal prayer rite."[87] As noted, the composite Sūrat al-Fātiḥa (Q. 1.1–7) comprises a pair of pericopae, one of which represents a "repurposed" prayer.[88] However, on the basis of form, the classification of the second pericope (Q. 1.1–4) as a prayer is altogether misleading. With its accompanying doxology and theonymic

note of caution that "the primary sources for reconstructing the appearance of the Early Byzantine liturgy are as fragmentary as the archaeological evidence...First, there are the liturgical books, properly speaking, which contain the texts and prescribe the prayers and the order of the ceremonies. Obviously, this material is extremely authoritative in describing the Byzantine liturgy; the problem is that the texts, in the form in which we have them, are all post-iconoclastic. The earliest manuscript of the liturgies of St. John Chrysostom and St. Basil the Great is the Barberini manuscript published by Brightman, which dates to around 800...These sources contain a great deal of valuable material about the liturgy of the Early Byzantine church, but it must always be used with discretion, since many changes had already taken place in the liturgy by the ninth and tenth centuries" (idem, *The Early Churches of Constantinople: Architecture and Liturgy* (University Park: The Pennsylvania State University Press, 1971), 112–13). For a "Chronological List of Manuscripts," see Taft, *Great Entrance*, 435–36 and 439–46, and idem, *A History of the Liturgy of St. John Chrysostom*, vol. 5: The Precommunion Rites, *OCA*, no. 261 (Roma: Pontificio Istituto Orientale, 2000), 527–38.

87 Neuwirth, "Sūrat al-Fātiḥa," 352; *SPMC* 177.

88 Kecia Ali, *The Lives of Muhammad* (Cambridge, Massachusetts: Harvard University Press, 2014), 3; *SPMC* xxv.

epithets, the function of verses 1–4 as an entrance-oath is readily evident within a cultic setting[89]:

bi-smi llāhi r-raḥmāni r-raḥīmi

al-ḥamdu li-llāhi rabbi l-ʿālamīna

ar-raḥmāni r-raḥīmi

māliki yawmi d-dīni

In the name of the Merciful and Compassionate God.

Praise belongs to God, the Lord of All Beings,

The Merciful, the Compassionate,

Master of the Day of Reckoning.

Wolfdietrich Fischer (d. 2013) notes that *bi-* functions as an oath formula.[90] Although "traditionally it has been construed as an invocation," since the *basmala* "has the form of an oath," it should accordingly be rendered, "By the name of the Merciful and Compassionate God," in line with *bi-llāhi* ("By God!") (e.g., Q. 4.62).[91] Moreover, "the *bi-* is held to require an implied verb expressing the intention of the one uttering the *basmala* to act or begin an action 'with the naming (glossing *ism* as *tasmiya*) of God.'"[92] Therefore, the inaudible ritual act of entering an exclusive sacred space provides the performative context for the audible entrance-oath.

89 For "Die Fātiḥa als Introitus," cf. Neuwirth, "Sūrat al-Fātiḥa," 353–56, where the author offers a comparison of the *Enarxis* (Gk. 'beginning,' 'opening') of the *The Divine Liturgy of St. John Chrysostom* and the reconstructed *Fātiḥa* (Ar. 'beginning,' 'opening') of the Muslim liturgy. For entrance-prayers in the Byzantine rite, see for example "Prayers on Entering the Church" (*The Divine Liturgy of St. John Chrysostom*, 43–44). On the oral recitation of the *basmala*, cf. Ayoub, *The Qur'ān and Its Interpreters*, 1:46. Regarding "the Entrance (Introit) Prayer," Paul Meyendorff notes, "This was the real beginning of the liturgy, everything prior being merely preparatory" (idem, introduction to *On the Divine Liturgy: St. Germanus of Constantinople*, trans. idem (Crestwood, New York: St. Vladimir's Seminary Press, 1984), 18–19).

90 Fischer, *Grammatik des klassischen Arabisch*, 136; Caspari, *A Grammar of the Arabic Language*, 2:175–76.

91 S.v. Basmala, *EQ*; Al-Azmeh, *Emergence of Islam in Late Antiquity*, 443; Fischer, *Grammatik des klassischen Arabisch*, 136.

92 S.v. Basmala, *EQ*.

Yet the brevity of the exordium has perplexed scholars.[93] Naturally, "it stands to reason that because of its extreme shortness the Fātiḥa, which forms the main content of the Islāmic congregational prayer, was repeated several times during one service."[94] As a matter of fact, Goitein's solution is mirrored in Neuwirth's amplified reconstruction of the Fātiḥa.[95] However, its place in ritual prayer or service is far from fixed.[96] The length of the entrance-oath in fact gives a clue to its function as a *sumbolon*.[97] According to Peter Struck, "the term *sumbolon* designates a particularly significant kind of authentication. It is the secret password or short, enigmatic verbal formula that verifies membership in a particular cult."[98] With regard to the Fātiḥa, Goitein makes the following observation: "On the one hand, the prayer contains the main points of Muḥammad's original preaching...On the other hand, it refrains from including any specific Islāmic tenets."[99] Reflecting on the development of the *sumbolon*, Struck observes that "the symbol marks a form of sign that brings something to light, and yet it means something that is not apparent to the uninitiated. In other words, the symbol has an esoteric or 'closing' function, as well as an exoteric or 'disclosing' one."[100] This thus explains Goitein's comment with respect to the Fātiḥa.

It is worth mentioning here that *sumbolon* "in the classical period regularly designated one of the two halves of a deliberately broken piece of material (a terracotta shard, for example) that were distributed to the two parties to an agreement in order to provide a secure authentication."[101] In this particular context, the second occurrence of the *basmala* in the Qur'ānic corpus is highly significant, as Nöldeke recognized.[102] It occurs repurposed as an epistolary formula (Q. 27.30a-31) embedded in the narrative context of the Solomon-Sheba correspondence[103]:

93 S.D. Goitein, "Prayer in Islam," in *Studies in Islamic History and Institutions* (Leiden: Brill, 2010), 82–83; cf. Neuwirth, "Sūrat al-Fātiḥa," 352.

94 Goitein, "Prayer in Islam," 83.

95 Neuwirth, "Sūrat al-Fātiḥa," 353–56.

96 Cf. ibid., 331; Al-Azmeh, *Emergence of Islam in Late Antiquity*, 443.

97 S.v. Symbol and Symbolism, *ER*².

98 Ibid.

99 Goitein, "Prayer in Islam," 83.

100 S.v. Symbol and Symbolism, *ER*².

101 Ibid.

102 *GdQ*² 1:117.

103 Ibid., 1:117 and 2:79–80; Ali, *Lives of Muhammad*, 3. Regarding the *basmala*, Bell contends that "its use in Q. 27.30 argues that by the time that sūra was revealed, the prefixing of it had become customary" (*BCQ* 1:1).

bi-smi llāhi r-raḥmāni r-raḥīmi

allā ta'lū 'alayya wa-tūnī muslimīna

By the name of the Merciful and Compassionate God.

Do not exalt yourselves against Me,
But come to Me in submission (as Muslims).

Through this *sumbolon* "the movement of humans toward the divine" is achieved.[104] Since procedure requires both halves, that is, a challenge and response, both entrance-oaths (Q. 1.1–4 and Q. 27.30a-31) function together with a shared rhyme scheme (-*īC*) to authenticate the identity of the initiated before granting access. It is worth noting that the second pericope (vv. 5–7) of the Fātiḥa also shares the same end rhyme pattern (-*īC*). Altogether, and in tandem, these constitute the ritual protocol when entering the sacred precinct.[105] Therefore, the term *fātiḥa* should be understood literally as *introitus.*[106] Now let us look beyond the exordium to the wealth of prayer forms in the *corpus coranicum.*

2.4 Prayer Forms

Conversational Prayer

In terms of biblical prayer, Corvin employs these exact terms: conversational, single-response, and unrecorded prayers.[107] In general, he names contextual prayer the principal functional class that is bound to narrative settings.[108] Literally, it comprises first and foremost embedded prayers, whose "function can be

---

104 S.v. Symbol and Symbolism, *ER*^{2}.

105 For entrance-prayers, see *The Divine Liturgy of St. John Chrysostom*, 44. According to Bell, "The suffix is, by means of *iyyā*, placed before the verb; the monotheistic attitude is thus emphasized" (*BCQ* 1:3).

106 Neuwirth, "Sūrat al-Fātiḥa," 353.

107 Corvin, "Stylistic and Functional Study of the Prose Prayers," iii–iv. Corvin claims, "if the significance of written prayers, especially those in narratives, is to be understood, they must be examined as literary creations having intentional design" (ibid., 105; Goitein, "Das Gebet im Qorān," 54–55).

108 Corvin, "Stylistic and Functional Study of the Prose Prayers," 156; Balentine, *Prayer in the Hebrew Bible*, 19–21.

understood *only within literary contexts.*"[109] Baumstark specifies, prayers of this type issue forth from the mouths of *dramatis personae* featured in narratives.[110] In other words, these emplotted prayers figure prominently in the qur'ānic text.[111] Nonetheless, Greenberg maintains that "the simplicity and manifest functionality of the patterns of speech and prayer encourage belief that in the embedded prayers we have as faithful a correspondence as we might wish to the form and practice of everyday, nonprofessional, extemporized verbal worship...."[112] In effect, embedded prayers afford a rare glimpse into normative religious practice.[113]

A subset of narrative prayers reflects the act of communication.[114] Consider the conversational prayers of the wife of ʿImrān (Q. 3.35–36) within its immediate context (Q. 3.35–37) signaled by the narrative formula *idh* ("when")[115]:

idh qālati mraʾatu ʿimrāna rabbi innī nadhartu laka mā fī baṭnī muḥarraran fa-taqabbal minnī innaka anta s-samīʿu l-ʿalīmu

fa-lammā waḍaʿathā qālat rabbi innī waḍaʿtuhā unthā wa-llāhu aʿlamu bi-mā waḍaʿat wa-laysa dh-dhakaru ka-l-unthā wa-innī sammaytuhā maryama wa-innī uʿīdhuhā bika wa-dhurriyyatahā mina sh-shayṭāni r-rajīmi

fa-taqabbalahā rabbuhā bi-qabūlin ḥasanin wa-anbatahā nabātan ḥasanan wa-kaffalahā zakariyyā kullamā dakhala ʿalayhā zakariyyā l-miḥrāba wajada ʿindahā rizqan qāla yā-maryamu annā laki hādhā qālat huwa min ʿindi llāhi inna llāha yarzuqu man yashāʾu bi-ghayri ḥisābin

When the wife of ʿImrān said:
My Lord,
I have vowed to You what is in my belly
as a dedicated [offering].
Accept it from me.
You are the Hearer and the Knower.

---

109 Greenberg, *Biblical Prose Prayer*, 8; Corvin, "Stylistic and Functional Study of the Prose Prayers," 13; emphasis added; Balentine, *Prayer in the Hebrew Bible*, 18–19 and 22.
110 Baumstark, "Jüdischer und christlicher Gebetstypus im Koran," 230.
111 Greenberg, *Biblical Prose Prayer*, 30; Balentine, *Prayer in the Hebrew Bible*, 18–19.
112 Greenberg, *Biblical Prose Prayer*, 37.
113 Ibid.
114 Corvin, "Stylistic and Functional Study of the Prose Prayers," 156.
115 Theodor Nöldeke, *Neue Beiträge zur semitischen Sprachwissenschaft* (Strassburg: Verlag von Karl J. Trübner, 1910), 17; *KU* 4; *QS* 18–19; s.v. Narratives, *EQ*. On a related prayer for expectant parents, see Q. 7.189.

When she gave birth to her, she said:
My Lord,
I have given birth to her, a female.
– And God was well aware of what she had given birth to.
The male is not like the female. –
I have called her Mary.
I seek protection with You for her
and for her offspring from the accursed Satan.

Her Lord received [the child] graciously,
and caused her to grow with fair growth;
and Zachariah took charge of her.
Whenever Zachariah went in
to the sanctuary to see her,
he found that she had provisions.
He said: O Mary, where does this come from for you?
She said: From God.
God gives provision without reckoning to those whom He wishes.

Pointing to the limits of Corvin's functional approach, Samuel Balentine reasonably argues that the inclusive definition of prayer as "all communication addressed to God in the second person...leads Corvin to include a number of texts as 'conversational prayers' that simply do not seem much like prayer," but rather "divine-human dialogue."[116] According to Corvin, conversational prayers consist of three speech elements: divine-human-divine or human-divine-human.[117] Whereas the prayers of the wife of ʿImrān are given verbatim, the divine speech element here is left unrecorded in the exercise of artistic license.[118] Irrespective, both pericopae (Q. 3.35–36) are context-bound and interwoven into the narrative fabric.[119] Furthermore, Bell observes that verse 37 "divides into three assonances in *Zakariyyā*, *rizqā(n)*, and *ḥisāb*."[120]

In fact, the shift from *-īC* to *-āC* that occurs in Q. 3.36–37 seems to facilitate a stylistic transition from one narrative to the next, with the subject Zakariyyā' as the pivot point. Let us consider the conversational prayers of Zakariyyā' (Q. 3.38–41):

116 Balentine, *Prayer in the Hebrew Bible*, 30; Corvin, "Stylistic and Functional Study of the Prose Prayers," 239; Greenberg, *Biblical Prose Prayer*, 20.
117 Corvin, "Stylistic and Functional Study of the Prose Prayers," 157.
118 Cf. ibid., 183 and 192; Balentine, *Prayer in the Hebrew Bible*, 31.
119 Balentine, *Prayer in the Hebrew Bible*, 27.
120 *BCQ* 1:71; Qutbuddin, "*Khuṭba:* The Evolution of Early Arabic Oration," 214; Welch, "Formulaic Features of the Punishment-Stories," 112, fns. 15–16; s.v. Form and Structure, *EQ*.

hunālika da'ā zakariyyā rabbahū qāla rabbi hab lī min ladunka dhurriyyatan ṭayyibatan innaka samī'u d-du'ā'i

fa-nādathu l-malā'ikatu wa-huwa qā'imun yuṣallī fī l-miḥrābi anna llāha yubashshiruka bi-yaḥyā muṣaddiqan bi-kalimatin mina llāhi wa-sayyidan wa-ḥaṣūran wa-nabiyyan mina ṣ-ṣāliḥīna

qāla rabbi annā yakūnu lī ghulāmun wa-qad balaghaniya l-kibaru wa-mra'atī 'āqirun qāla ka-dhālika llāhu yaf'alu mā yashā'u

qāla rabbi j'al lī āyatan qāla āyatuka allā tukallima n-nāsa thalāthata ayyāmin illā ramzan wa-dhkur rabbaka kathīran wa-sabbiḥ bi-l-'ashiyyi wa-l-ibkāri

Zachariah called to his Lord there, saying:

My Lord,
give me a good offspring from Yourself.
You are the Hearer of prayers (*du'ā'*).

And the angels called out to him
whilst he was standing praying in the sanctuary,
God gives you^{S} the good news of John,
confirming a word from God:
a chief and a chaste man and a prophet from among the righteous.

He said: How can I have a son,
when old age has come upon me
and my wife is barren?
He said: [It will be] so.
God does what He wishes.

He said:
My Lord,
make a sign for me.
He said: Your sign will be
that you will not be able to speak to the people for three days
except by gesture.
Remember your Lord often
and glorify [Him] in the evening and in the morning.

In line with functional criticism, let us now situate both birth narratives in Sūrat Āl 'Imrān within their wider literary setting.[121]

121 Corvin, "Stylistic and Functional Study of the Prose Prayers," 12, fn. 2.

This subsection of the sūra-unit commences with two identical formulae (*qul*). According to Bell, there is an obvious case of doubling in verses 31–32.[122] Q. 3.31–34 reads,

qul in kuntum tuḥibbūna llāha fa-ttabiʿūnī yuḥbibkumu llāhu wa-yaghfir lakum dhunūbakum wa-llāhu ghafūrun raḥīmun

qul aṭīʿū llāha wa-r-rasūla fa-in tawallaw fa-inna llāha lā yuḥibbu l-kāfirīna

inna llāha ṣṭafā ādama wa-nūḥan wa-āla ibrāhīma wa-āla ʿimrāna ʿalā l-ʿālamīna

dhurriyyatan baʿḍuhā min baʿḍin wa-llāhu samīʿun ʿalīmun

Say:
If you^{P} love God, follow me
and God will love you and forgive you your sins.
God is Forgiving and Merciful.

Say:
Obey^{P} God and the messenger.
If you turn away,
[remember that] God does not love the disbelievers.

God chose Adam and Noah and the family of Abraham
and the family of ʿImrān above all created beings,

The seed of one another.
God is the Hearer and the Knower.

Although the promise of a child is not uncommon in such supplications, Corvin notes that it is more often than not attended by considerations of a religio-political nature.[123] In particular, birth announcements gravitate toward strategies of legitimation, which privilege particular figures by placing them at the center of attention.[124] The subsequent birth announcement of Jesus and the conversational prayers of Mary (Q. 3.42–47; Q. 19.16–33; Q. 21.91) further support this claim.[125] Q. 3.42–47 reads,

---

122 *BCQ* 1:69.
123 Cf. Q. 7.189a; Corvin, "Stylistic and Functional Study of the Prose Prayers," 174–75.
124 Corvin, "Stylistic and Functional Study of the Prose Prayers," 173.
125 Bell notes that verses 42–43 "have no trace of the rhyme in *-āl*, and did not belong to the first form of the passage" (*BCQ* 1:72). He also states that verse 44 "did not belong to the original form of the story as there is no *-ā* assonance, and it interrupts the story as now carried on in

wa-idh qālati l-malā'ikatu yā-maryamu inna llāha ṣṭafāki wa-ṭahharaki wa-ṣṭafāki ʿalā nisā'i l-ʿālamīna

yā-maryamu qnutī li-rabbiki wa-sjudī wa-rkaʿī maʿa r-rākiʿīna

dhālika min anbā'i l-ghaybi nūḥīhi ilayka wa-mā kunta ladayhim idh yulqūna aqlāmahum ayyuhum yakfulu maryama wa-mā kunta ladayhim idh yakhtaṣimūna

idh qālati l-malā'ikatu yā-maryamu inna llāha yubashshiruki bi-kalimatin minhu smuhu l-masīḥu ʿīsā bnu maryama wajīhan fī d-dunyā wa-l-ākhirati wa-mina l-muqarrabīna

wa-yukallimu n-nāsa fī l-mahdi wa-kahlan wa-mina ṣ-ṣāliḥīna

qālat rabbi annā yakūnu lī waladun wa-lam yamsasnī basharun qāla ka-dhāliki llāhu yakhluqu mā yashā'u idhā qaḍā amran fa-innamā yaqūlu lahū kun fa-yakūnu

And when the angels said:
O Mary, God has chosen you and purified you
and chosen you above the [other] women [among] created beings.

O Mary, be obedient to your Lord and prostrate yourself and bow with those who bow.

That is from the tidings of the Invisible.
We reveal it to you^{S},
for you^{S} were not with them
when they threw their pens
as to which of them should be guardian of Mary,
nor were you^{S} with them when they quarreled.

When the angels said: O Mary,
God gives you good news of a word from Him,
whose name is al-Masīḥ,
Jesus, son of Mary,
illustrious in this world and the next,
and one of those brought near.

verses 45–47. It may have been inserted after verse 41 and verses 42–43 written on the back of it at a later stage" (ibid.). Bell further remarks that verses 45–51 "are very disjointed" (ibid., 1:73). He adds that "the connection of verse 46 with verse 45 is none too good as it stands..." (ibid.). Bell concludes, "Now in the first part of the passage we can detect the *-ā* assonance and if we close verses 45, 46, 47 at *ʿĪsā*, *kahlā(n)*, and *yashā'*, respectively, we get a little 'sign' story similar to that of Zachariah and Mary. This was, no doubt, the original form of the passage. The concluding parts of these verses have been added, partly to adapt the passage to the rhyme of this context, and partly to stress the importance of Jesus" (ibid.).

He will speak to the people in the cradle and in maturity,
and [he is] one of the righteous.

She said:
My Lord,
how can I have a son,
when no mortal has touched me?
He said: [It will be] so.
God creates what He wishes.
When He decides on something,
He says to it only 'Be,' and it is.

Not only does the question of authority dominate the content of the doubled frames (Q. 3.31–32) preceding the trebled birth announcement motif, it is immediately followed by an appeal to pure lineage on typological grounds.[126]

What is more, conversational prayers extend beyond the authenticating role of the birth motif. In fact, their legitimating function also extends to narrative contexts concerned with validation.[127] From the literary motley that constitutes Sūrat al-Mā'ida (*The Table*), consider the narrative pericope (Q. 5.112–15) with the rhyme scheme -*īC*[128]:

idh qāla l-ḥawāriyyūna yā-ʿīsā bna maryama hal yastaṭīʿu rabbuka an yunazzila ʿalaynā mā'idatan mina s-samā'i qāla ttaqū llāha in kuntum mu'minīna

qālū nurīdu an na'kula minhā wa-taṭma'inna qulūbunā wa-naʿlama an qad ṣadaqtanā wa-nakūna ʿalayhā mina sh-shāhidīna

qāla ʿīsā bnu maryama llāhumma rabbanā anzil ʿalaynā mā'idatan mina s-samā'i takūnu lanā ʿīdan li-awwalinā wa-ākhirinā wa-āyatan minka wa-rzuqnā wa-anta khayru r-rāziqīna

qāla llāhu innī munazziluhā ʿalaykum fa-man yakfur baʿdu minkum fa-innī uʿadhdhibuhū

---

126 See Fred M. Donner, *Narratives of Islamic Origins: The Beginnings of Islamic Historical Writing* (Princeton, New Jersey: The Darwin Press, Inc., 1998), 104–11. "[O]ne of the Qur'ān's most important rhetorical strategies: the use of the pattern of Biblical prophecies in order to comment on or serve as a model for the prophecy of Muḥammad. This strategy is in fact a sort of typology, familiar to analysts of the New Testament, whereby characters from the Hebrew Bible are taken as models for or precursors of Christ or are used to make specific arguments concerning the nature of his life and works. An understanding of this rhetorical strategy helps explain the form and content of many sūras of the Qur'ān, particularly those containing series of stories of earlier prophets" (Stewart, "Understanding the Qur'ān," 40).
127 Corvin, "Stylistic and Functional Study of the Prose Prayers," 175–77.
128 *JQA* 110.

ʿadhāban lā uʿadhdhibuhū aḥadan mina l-ʿālamīna

When the disciples said:
Jesus, son of Mary,
is your Lord able to send a table down to us from heaven?
He said: Fear God, if you are believers.

They said: We wish to eat from it,
and for our hearts to be at rest,
and [we wish] to know that you have spoken the truth to us
and to be witnesses to that.

Jesus, the son of Mary, said:
O God, Our Lord,
send a table down to us from heaven
to be a festival for us,
the first of us and the last of us,
and to be a sign from You.
Give us sustenance.
You are the best of providers.

God said: I shall send it down to you.
Those of you who do not believe afterwards,
I shall punish them with a punishment
which I do not inflict on any [other] created beings.

This confirmatory prayer (v. 114) stands out for the terminology it employs in the invocation: *allāhumma rabbanā* ("O God, Our Lord").[129]

Petitionary Prayer

An additional subset of contextual prayers consists of single response prayers.[130] These share common features with conversational prayers. Since these single transactions are "for practical and immediate assistance, there is no need for continued dialogue on the part of either the suppliant or of God."[131] In other words, brevity and urgency characterize these prayers.[132] The performative con-

129 Corvin, "Stylistic and Functional Study of the Prose Prayers," 211.
130 Ibid., 180; Balentine, *Prayer in the Hebrew Bible*, 19.
131 Corvin, "Stylistic and Functional Study of the Prose Prayers," 180.
132 Ibid.

text of the single response petition is unspecified and voiced wherever needed.[133] Petitionary prayers are composed of two principal elements at minimum: address and petition.[134] Heiler holds that this is nothing less than the primary structure of prayer.[135] Greenberg also states, "the heart of the prayer, the petition, is formulated in 'imperatives' – here, of course, expressing what the pray-er begs God to do, rather than commands him."[136] The petitionary prayer takes the literary structure: *rabbi/rabbanā...fa-* ("My Lord/Our Lord...So..."), apart from "localization."[137] Take, for example, the Noah episode (Q. 26.105–22) in the punishment saga, which begins with *rabbi* (vv. 117–18)[138]:

qāla rabbi inna qawmī kadhdhabūni

fa-ftaḥ baynī wa-baynahum fatḥan wa-najjinī wa-man maʿiya mina l-muʾminīna

He said:
My Lord,
my people have disbelieved me.

Make an opening between me and them;
and save me and those of the believers who are with me.

In this particular case, the plea is preceded "by a ground, or a motive-sentence – offering what is hoped will be a persuasive reason for God to comply."[139] Therefore, the single response petition clearly evidences a flexible literary structure.[140] The response to the prayer follows with *fa-* (vv. 119–20)[141]:

fa-anjaynāhu wa-man maʿahū fī l-fulki l-mashḥūni

thumma aghraqnā baʿdu l-bāqīna

133 Greenberg, *Biblical Prose Prayer*, 9–10.
134 Ibid., 9 and 14; Gunkel, "Psalmen," cols. 1624–25.
135 Heiler, *Das Gebet*, 51.
136 Greenberg, *Biblical Prose Prayer*, 10; Anneli Aejmelaeus, *The Traditional Prayer in the Psalms* (Berlin: Walter de Gruyter, 1986), 15–53.
137 Hainsworth, *Iliad*, 3:7–9.
138 Welch, "Formulaic Features of the Punishment-Stories," 78; *FOTL* 1:5; *FOTL* 10:313.
139 Greenberg, *Biblical Prose Prayer*, 11. Neuwirth adopts a similar division (*SKMS*^{2} 276).
140 Greenberg, *Biblical Prose Prayer*, 17.
141 Balentine, *Prayer in the Hebrew Bible*, 19.

So We saved him and those who were with him in the laden ship.

Then, afterwards, We drowned the rest.

Furthermore, consider Q. 2.250a that is seamlessly integrated by means of a shared rhyme scheme (*-īC*) into the David-Goliath narrative. The single response prayer of Saul's outnumbered soldiers (*al-junūd*) begins "they said" (*qālū*)[142]:

qālū rabbanā afrigh ʿalaynā ṣabran wa-thabbit aqdāmanā wa-unṣurnā ʿalā l-qawmi l-kāfirī-na

They said:
Our Lord,
pour out patience on us,
make firm our feet,
and give us help against the people who do not believe.

This prayer is heard and answered in the subsequent verse (Q. 2.251)[143]:

fa-hazamūhum bi-idhni llāhi wa-qatala dāwūdu jālūta wa-ātāhu llāhu l-mulka wa-l-ḥikmata wa-ʿallamahū mimmā yashāʾu wa-law-lā dafʿu llāhi n-nāsa baʿḍahum bi-baʿḍin la-fasadati l-arḍu wa-lākinna llāha dhū faḍlin ʿalā l-ʿālamīna

So by God's permission they routed them;
and David killed Goliath,
and God gave him sovereignty and wisdom
and taught him some of what He wills.
Had God not driven off some of the people by means of others,
the earth would have become corrupt.
But God is bounteous to created beings.

The function of single response prayers is fourfold. As in the case of Saul, the first is legitimation.[144] Secondly, they share an affinity with unrecorded prayers.[145] As a stylistic device, both facilitate narrative continuity.[146] Lastly, Green-

142 For the two literary strands forming the biblical David narrative, see Norman Habel, *Literary Criticism of the Old Testament* (Philadelphia: Fortress Press, 1986 [1971]), 10 – 11. Cf. Q. 3.147 and Q. 8.11; *BCQ* 1:52.
143 Balentine, *Prayer in the Hebrew Bible*, 19.
144 Corvin, "Stylistic and Functional Study of the Prose Prayers," 183 and 238.
145 Ibid., 183, fn. 1.
146 Ibid.

berg notes, "they play a part in the argument of a narrative and its depiction of character."[147]

At this point, Bell directs our attention to a prayer pericope similar in both imagery and rhyme scheme lodged within the biblical Moses-Pharaoh narrative, namely Q. 7.126.[148] Here the corporate prayer is imputed to the defeated magicians (*as-saḥara*) against Pharaoh's charges of complicity:

rabbanā afrigh ʿalaynā ṣabran wa-tawaffanā muslimīna

Our Lord,
pour out patience on us,
and take us as ones who have surrendered.

The end-rhyme (-*īC*) of line 126 does not correspond to its literary environment.[149] However, in terms of content and style, the semblance of this pair of prayer pericopae (Q. 2.250a and Q. 7.126) is unmistakable. In all likelihood, both originally functioned in tandem as a prayer-duplet.

The short Noah episode (Q. 54.9 – 17; Q. 21.76 – 77) in the punishment saga in Sūrat al-Qamar furnishes a noteworthy petitionary prayer.[150] Q. 54.9 – 17 reads[151]:

kadhdhabat qablahum qawmu nūḥin fa-kadhdhabū ʿabdanā wa-qālū majnūnun wa-zdujira

fa-daʿā rabbahū annī maghlūbun fa-ntaṣir

fa-fataḥnā abwāba s-samāʾi bi-māʾin munhamirin

wa-fajjarnā l-arḍa ʿuyūnan fa-ltaqā l-māʾu ʿalā amrin qad qudira

wa-ḥamalnāhu ʿalā dhāti alwāḥin wa-dusurin

tajrī bi-aʿyuninā jazāʾan li-man kāna kufira

wa-la-qad taraknāhā āyatan fa-hal min muddakirin

fa-kayfa kāna ʿadhābī wa-nudhuri

147 Greenberg, *Biblical Prose Prayer*, 17 – 18.
148 *BCQ* 1:52.
149 Habel, "Distinguishing Combined Reports," in *Literary Criticism of the Old Testament*, 11.
150 Welch, "Formulaic Features of the Punishment-Stories," 82 – 84 and 102 – 3; *FOTL* 1:5; *FOTL* 10:313.
151 Bell comments, "Verse 16: Note the change to first person singular, perhaps for rhyme, or perhaps the survival of an older refrain" (*BCQ* 2:325).

wa-la-qad yassarnā l-qur'āna li-dh-dhikri fa-hal min muddakirin

Before them the people of Noah denied the truth;
they denied Our servant and said, 'A man possessed,'
and he was driven away.

So he called to his Lord:
I am overcome. Help!

So We opened the doors of heaven to water that poured down,

And We made the earth gush with springs;
and the waters came together for a matter that had been decreed.

And We carried him in a vessel of planks and nails,

Which sailed before Our eyes
as a recompense for the one who was disbelieved.

And We left it as a sign,
but are there any that are reminded?

How then were My punishment and My warnings?

We have made the Recitation easy to remember
– but are there any that are reminded?

In this case, however, the narrator localizes the personal prayer in verse 10 by means of a pronominal shift. To begin with, the challenge and crisis are externalized from the prayer in order to set the scene.[152] Secondly, whereas the cultic formula *rabbi* ("My Lord") appears multiple times in Sūrat Nūḥ (Q. 71.26–28), *rabbahū* ("His Lord") here stands apart from the prayer proper, thereby functioning as a framing device. Tucker adds that "even when the introductory and concluding formulas are missing or unclear, one may still distinguish the units from one another by recognizing the conventional patterns of different genres."[153] In his incisive analysis of prose prayer, Greenberg observes that the "omission of an invocation" intimates a "familiarity" or "consciousness of being near God."[154] In the end, the deluge constitutes a total response to this prayer.[155]

152 Greenberg, *Biblical Prose Prayer*, 10.
153 Tucker, *Form Criticism of the Old Testament*, 13.
154 Greenberg, *Biblical Prose Prayer*, 11–12.
155 Corvin, "Stylistic and Functional Study of the Prose Prayers," 182.

According to Corvin, biblical prayers tend to be realized through human speech-acts.[156] However, in certain cases, initiative and resourcefulness on the part of the pray-er are also necessary to achieve the desired outcome.[157] Consider a further Noah episode (Q. 23.26–27) in the punishment saga (Q. 23.23–30)[158]:

qāla rabbi nṣurnī bi-mā kadhdhabūni

fa-awḥaynā ilayhi ani ṣnaʿi l-fulka bi-aʿyuninā wa-waḥyinā fa-idhā jāʾa amrunā wa-fāra t-tannūru fa-sluk fīhā min kullin zawjayni thnayni wa-ahlaka illā man sabaqa ʿalayhi l-qawlu minhum wa-lā tukhāṭibnī fī lladhīna ẓalamū innahum mughraqūna

He said:
My Lord,
help me,
because they believe I am lying.

So We revealed to him: Make the ship
under Our eyes and Our inspiration.
And when Our command comes and the oven boils,
put two of every kind and your family into it,
except those of them against whom the word has already preceded.
Do not address Me concerning those who have done wrong.
They will be drowned.

The construction of the ark functions here "as a catalyst designed to assure the efficacy of the prayer."[159] At this point, it is instructive to note that Noah's prayer exhibits the quality of a literary topos. In point of fact, this intruding verse (*-ūC*) reoccurs verbatim in the same sūra (Q. 23.39–41)[160]:

qāla rabbi nṣurnī bi-mā kadhdhabūni

qāla ʿammā qalīlin la-yuṣbiḥunna nādimīna

fa-akhadhathumu ṣ-ṣayḥatu bi-l-ḥaqqi fa-jaʿalnāhum ghuthāʾan fa-buʿdan li-l-qawmi ẓ-ẓālimīna

---

156 Ibid., 200–2.
157 Ibid., 200; cf. Q. 7.117.
158 Welch, "Formulaic Features of the Punishment-Stories," 93–96.
159 Corvin, "Stylistic and Functional Study of the Prose Prayers," 201.
160 *BCQ* 1:582.

He said:
My Lord,
help me,
because they believe I am lying.

He said: One morning soon they will be repentant.

So the Shout seized them justly,
and We made them wreckage.
Away with the people who do wrong.

In this particular instance, divine speech intervenes between the single response prayer and direct action.

Penitential Prayer

The expression of penitence constitutes an attested subtype of petitionary prayer.[161] Since both share the plea, the confession proper distinguishes this subset.[162] In fact, four elements combine to form the framework: optional address, confession, petition, and acknowledgement or renunciation.[163] In the biblical case, Patrick Miller specifies that the display is usually a visible act to be observed by others.[164] The qur'ānic formula begins, *rabbanā ẓalamnā anfusanā* ("Our Lord, we have wronged ourselves").[165] Take, for instance, the narrative in Sūrat al-Aʿrāf. In particular, consider verses Q. 7.22a-24 (-īC)[166]:

> *fa-lammā dhāqā sh-shajarata badat lahumā saw'ātuhumā wa-ṭafiqā yakhṣifāni ʿalayhimā min waraqi l-jannati wa-nādāhumā rabbuhumā a-lam anhakumā ʿan tilkumā sh-shajarati wa-aqul lakumā inna sh-shayṭāna lakumā ʿaduwwun mubīnun*
>
> *qālā rabbanā ẓalamnā anfusanā wa-in lam taghfir lanā wa-tarḥamnā la-nakūnanna mina l-khāsirīna*
>
> *qāla hbiṭū baʿḍukum li-baʿḍin ʿaduwwun wa-lakum fī l-arḍi mustaqarrun wa-matāʿun ilā*

161 Miller, *They Cried to the Lord*, 259–60; Greenberg, *Biblical Prose Prayer*, 22.
162 Greenberg, *Biblical Prose Prayer*, 24.
163 Ibid., 23 and 26–28.
164 Miller, *They Cried to the Lord*, 250.
165 Greenberg, *Biblical Prose Prayer*, 27.
166 *Genesis*, lvii; Gunkel, *Die Sagen der Genesis*, 6–8; *FOTL* 1:5–6; *FOTL* 2a:171; *FOTL* 4:358–59; Westermann, *Die Verheißungen an die Väter*, 47; *JQA* 147.

ḥīnin

And when they tasted the tree
their bare bodies became clear to them
and they began heaping upon themselves some of the leaves of the Garden.
And their Lord called out to them:
Did I not forbid you this tree
and tell you, 'Satan is a manifest enemy for you?'

They said:
Our Lord, we have wronged ourselves.
If You do not forgive us and have mercy on us,
we shall be among the losers.

He said: Go down, each in enmity to the other.
You will have a place to stay on earth
and enjoyment for a time.

Included in its literary structure are two additional elements. This pericope commences with an account of the infraction.[167] Then comes the customary invocatory confession, followed by the petition, and the renunciation.[168] The passage closes with a damning judgment.[169]

Certain transgressions, such as homicide, give cause for personal penitentiary prayer.[170] Although personal expressions of penitence exist in the biblical case, Miller notes, these most likely were accompanied by open displays enacted in front of the community.[171] He also points out that the recorded account draws attention to the immoral act.[172] For example, murder at the hands of Moses warrants the formulation of a personal prayer of repentance.[173] Bell writes, the guilt-ridden portrayal of Moses is one filled with deep remorse.[174] Examine this composite prayer for clemency in the narrative context of Sūrat al-Qaṣaṣ (Q. 28.14 – 15a):

---

167 Greenberg, *Biblical Prose Prayer*, 29.
168 Miller, *They Cried to the Lord*, 245.
169 Greenberg, *Biblical Prose Prayer*, 29.
170 Miller, *They Cried to the Lord*, 245 and 249; Gunkel, "Psalmen," cols. 1617 – 18; Richard J. Bautch, *Developments in Genre between Post-Exilic Penitential Prayers and the Psalms of Communal Lament* (Atlanta, Georgia: Society of Biblical Literature, 2003), *passim*.
171 Miller, *They Cried to the Lord*, 250 – 51; *FOTL* 14:141 – 42.
172 Miller, *They Cried to the Lord*, 249.
173 *SKMS*^{2} 301.
174 *BCQ* 2:45.

wa-lammā balagha ashuddahū wa-stawā ātaynāhu ḥukman wa-ʿilman wa-ka-dhālika najzī l-muḥsinīna

wa-dakhala l-madīnata ʿalā ḥīni ghaflatin min ahlihā fa-wajada fīhā rajulayni yaqtatilāni hādhā min shīʿatihī wa-hādhā min ʿaduwwihī fa-staghāthahu lladhī min shīʿatihī ʿalā lladhī min ʿaduwwihī fa-wakazahū mūsā fa-qaḍā ʿalayhi

qāla hādhā min ʿamali sh-shayṭāni innahū ʿaduwwun muḍillun mubīnun

When he reached maturity and perfection,
We gave him judgment and knowledge.
Thus We reward those who do good.

He entered the city at a time
when its people were off their guard;
and he found two men fighting there,
one from his own faction and the other from his enemies.
The one who was from his faction
sought his help against the one who was from his enemies;
so Moses struck him and finished him off.

He said:
This is of Satan's doing.
He is an enemy who clearly leads astray.

First and foremost, motive-sentences envelope the incident report.[175] The narrator at once appeals to Moses' divinely bestowed virtues. Although acknowledging the crime, Moses then himself denies personal responsibility and washes his hands of the matter entirely. The prayer (-*ī*C) follows (Q. 28.16–17)[176]:

qāla rabbi innī ẓalamtu nafsī fa-ghfir lī fa-ghafara lahū innahū huwa l-ghafūru r-raḥīmu

qāla rabbi bi-mā anʿamta ʿalayya fa-lan akūna ẓahīran li-l-mujrimīna

He said:
My Lord, I have wronged himself.
Forgive me.
So He forgave him.
He is the Forgiving, the Merciful.

He said:

175 Miller, *They Cried to the Lord*, 114–17 and 253.
176 Greenberg, *Biblical Prose Prayer*, 27.

My Lord, as You have been kind to me,
I shall never be a partisan of the sinners.

The patterned elements include the address, confession, and petition. Once the pardon is granted, Moses closes with a renunciation.[177]

Finally, the acknowledgement of wrongs committed arises in diverse scenarios.[178] Even relatively minor infractions of decorum give occasion to penitential prayer. Take, for instance, the gendered prayer (v. 44a) concluding the Solomon-Sheba narrative (Q. 27.17–44a)[179]:

qīla lahā dkhulī ṣ-ṣarḥa fa-lammā ra'athu ḥasibathu lujjatan wa-kashafat ʿan sāqayhā qāla innahū ṣarḥun mumarradun min qawārīra

qālat rabbi innī ẓalamtu nafsī wa-aslamtu maʿa sulaymāna li-llāhi rabbi l-ʿālamīna

It was said to her: Enter the hall.
When she saw it, she thought it was a pool
and she bared her legs.
He said: It is a polished hall, made of glass.

She said:
My Lord, I have wronged myself.
Together with Solomon, I surrender myself to God,
Lord of created beings.

177 On the other hand, Bell argues that "the shortness of these two verses, and the repetition of *qāla*, seem to imply that they are alternatives to the end of verse 15, and therefore to be interpreted separately. The verse thus becomes a justification of this action; as God has bestowed good, *ḥukman wa-ʿilman* above, upon him, he will not support the enemies of God, i.e., the Egyptians" (*BCQ* 2:45).
178 Miller, *They Cried to the Lord*, 245.
179 According to Bell, verse 44a "gives the conclusion, and would come as well after verse 42a as after verse 44" (*BCQ* 2:34). Jones notes, "The account of Solomon and Sheba (17–44) recalls a Jewish Aramaic account found in the Tg Esth II rather than the biblical account in 1Kgs 10 (repeated in 2Chr 9)" (*JQA* 345). The relevant selection reads, "Then Benayahu conducted her to the king, who, when he heard that she was coming, went and sat down in an apartment of glass. When the queen saw the king sitting there, she thought in her heart, and in fact said, that he was sitting in water, and she raised her dress to cross the water, when the king noticed that her foot was full of hair. He said to her, 'Thy beauty is the beauty of women, and thy hair is the hair of men; hair is becoming to a man, but to a woman it is a shame'" (*The Targum to the Five Megilloth*, ed. Bernard Grossfeld (New York: Hermon Press, 1973), 282–83).

Framed by the detailing of the *faux pas*, this penitentiary prayer moves quickly from address and confession directly to renunciation.[180] Although the prayer largely conforms to the common pattern, the absence of the petition itself is striking.[181]

Complaint Prayer

Miller calls into question the hard-and-fast divide between biblical petitionary prayer and individual lament.[182] This is borne out in the *corpus coranicum* by the divine response following laments of the individual.[183] According to Gunkel, these are composed of dual elements, the lament and the plea.[184] In a parallel text (Q. 19.2–15) that likewise treats John the Baptist alongside Zachariah, the first in a sequence of conversational prayers opens with a heartfelt lament (v. 4)[185]:

> *qāla rabbi innī wahana l-ʿaẓmu minnī wa-shtaʿala r-raʾsu shayban wa-lam akun bi-duʿāʾika rabbi shaqiyyan*
>
> He said:
> My Lord,
> My bones have become weak, and my head is aflame with hoariness.
> I have never been unblessed in my prayers (*duʿāʾ*) to You.

Zachariah's lament continues (v. 5):

> *wa-innī khiftu l-mawāliya min warāʾī wa-kānati mraʾatī ʿāqiran*
>
> [I am making supplication now, for] I fear [that I shall have no] heirs after me, because my wife is barren.

Signaled by the particle (*fa*-), the request then follows in the imperative (vv. 5a-6):

> *fa-hab lī min ladunka waliyyan*

---

180 Greenberg, *Biblical Prose Prayer*, 28.
181 Miller, *They Cried to the Lord*, 250.
182 Ibid., 69–70.
183 Ibid., 69; Gunkel, "Psalmen," cols. 1624–25.
184 Gunkel, "Psalmen," cols. 1624–25.
185 *JQA* 282; Gunkel, "Psalmen," col. 1625; Goitein, "Das Gebet im Qorān," 59–60.

yarithunī wa-yarithu min āli ya'qūba wa-j'alhu rabbi raḍiyyan

So give me, from Yourself, a successor –

Who will inherit from me and from the family of Jacob,
and make him, my Lord, well-pleasing.

The plea not only echoes Q. 3.38a above, it is expressed once again as a negative entreaty in Q. 21.89:

wa-zakariyyā idh nādā rabbahū rabbi lā tadharnī fardan wa-anta khayru l-wārithīna

And Zachariah
– when he called out to his Lord:
My Lord,
do not leave me alone,
though You are the best of inheritors.

As in Sūra 19, verse 4, the complaint proper is voiced by the distraught.[186] For example, consider the first lament of Job featured in Q. 38.41:

wa-dhkur 'abdanā ayyūba idh nādā rabbahū annī massaniya sh-shayṭānu bi-nuṣbin wa-'adhābin

Remember Our servant Job,
when he called out to his Lord:
Satan has touched me with fatigue and torment.

The indirect answer to this initial complaint prayer takes the shape of a set of prescribed actions (*-āC*) that obtains the desired effect (Q. 38.42–44)[187]:

urkuḍ bi-rijlika hadhā mughtasalun bāridun wa-sharābun

wa-wahabnā lahū ahlahū wa-mithlahum ma'ahum raḥmatan minnā wa-dhikrā li-ulī l-albābi

wa-khudh bi-yadika ḍighthan fa-ḍrib bihī wa-lā taḥnath innā wajadnāhu ṣābiran ni'ma l-'abdu innahū awwābun

'Stamp your foot.
This is a cool washing-place and a drink.'

---

186 Miller, *They Cried to the Lord*, 68–69; *FOTL* 14:246.
187 Miller, *They Cried to the Lord*, 134; Corvin, "Stylistic and Functional Study of the Prose Prayers," 200.

We gave to him his family
and the like of them with them,
as a mercy from Us and as a reminder for men of understanding:

'Take in your hand a bundle of grass,
and strike with it,
and do not break your oath.'
We found him steadfast.
How excellent a servant!
He was penitent.

The personal lament formula, *annī massaniya* ("has befallen me"), also appears in the second lament of Job (Q. 21.83)[188]:

wa-ayyūba idh nādā rabbahū annī massaniya ḍ-ḍurru wa-anta arḥamu r-rāḥimīna

And Job
– when he called out to his Lord:
Harm has touched me,
And You are the most merciful of the merciful.

This final sob of despair receives divine intervention.[189] Although it omits the optional invocation (*rabbi*/*rabbanā*), the second element (*fa-*) of this Jobian lament assumes the structure of petitionary prayer (Q. 21.84):

fa-stajabnā lahū fa-kashafnā mā bihī min ḍurrin wa-ātaynāhu ahlahū wa-mithlahum maʿa-hum raḥmatan min ʿindinā wa-dhikrā li-l-ʿābidīna

So we responded to him and removed the harm that was upon him,
and We gave him his household and their like with them,
as a mercy from Us and a reminder to those who serve.

Prayer language, therefore, "moves back and forth between plea or petition and praise or thanksgiving."[190]

188 Miller, *They Cried to the Lord*, 69; s.v. Massa, *CQ*.
189 Miller, *They Cried to the Lord*, 68.
190 Ibid., 55.

Imprecatory Prayer

With reference to the biblical lament, Gunkel astutely observes, imprecatory prayers ultimately stem from the early practice of levying severe curses against adamant adversaries.[191] As for this special class of scathing laments, consider the complex, tripartite (Q. 10.88a-c) Mosaic imprecation[192]:

wa-qāla mūsā rabbanā innaka ātayta fir'awna wa-mala'ahū zīnatan wa-amwālan fī l-ḥayāti d-dunyā

rabbanā li-yuḍillū 'an sabīlika

rabbanā ṭmis 'alā amwālihim wa-shdud 'alā qulūbihim fa-lā yu'minū ḥattā yarawu l-'adhāba l-alīma

Moses said:
Our Lord,
you have given Pharaoh and his notables adornment and wealth in the life of this world.

Our Lord,
that [enables them to] lead [men] away from your way.

Our Lord,
obliterate their wealth and harden their hearts,
so that they do not believe until they see the great torment.

In addition, Sūrat Nūḥ (Q. 71.26–28) also concludes with a pair of imprecatory prayers[193]:

wa-qāla nūḥun rabbi lā tadhar 'alā l-arḍi mina l-kāfirīna dayyāran

innaka in tadharhum yuḍillū 'ibādaka wa-lā yalidū illā fājiran kaffāran

rabbi ghfir lī wa-li-wālidayya wa-li-man dakhala baytiya mu'minan wa-li-l-mu'minīna wa-l-mu'mināti wa-lā tazidi ẓ-ẓālimīna illā tabāran

And Noah said:
My Lord,

191 Gunkel, "Psalmen," col. 1625.
192 Miller, *They Cried to the Lord*, 69. Mosaic prayers with *rabbi* include Q. 5.25; Q. 7.143, 151, 155–56; Q. 20.25–35; Q. 28.16–17, 21, 24; Goitein, "Das Gebet im Qorān," 61–62.
193 Gunkel, "Psalmen," cols. 1617 and 1625.

do not leave a single one of the disbelievers on the earth.

If You leave them, they will lead Your servants astray,
And beget only dissolute disbelievers.

My Lord,
forgive me and my parents
and whoever enters my house as a believer
and believing men and women,
and increase the wrong-doers only in ruin.

It is worthwhile to note, in the context of curse tablets, the fine line drawn between revenge prayers grounded in reason and those that are unfounded.[194] The aforementioned verses (Q. 10.88b and Q. 71.27) each furnish a rationale for the imprecation.

On the other hand, consider Sūrat al-Masad. Jakob Barth (d. 1914) initially treats Q. 111 as either a wish or curse[195]:

tabbat yadā abī lahabin wa-tabba
mā aghnā ʿanhu māluhū wa-mā kasaba
sa-yaṣlā nāran dhāta lahabin
wa-mraʾatuhū ḥammālata l-ḥaṭabi
fī jīdihā ḥablun min masadin

May the hands of Abū Lahab perish, and may he (himself) perish!
His possessions and gains will be of no avail to him.
He will roast in a flaming fire,
And his wife, the carrier of firewood,
With a rope of palm-fibre on her neck.

---

194 Angelos Chaniotis, "Ritual Performances of Divine Justice: The Epigraphy of Confession, Atonement, and Exaltation in Roman Asia Minor," in *From Hellenism to Islam: Cultural and Linguistic Change in the Roman Near East*, ed. Hannah M. Cotton, Robert G. Hoyland, Jonathan J. Price, and David J. Wasserstein (Cambridge: Cambridge University Press, 2009), 125, fn. 49; Fritz Graf, "Fluch und Segen: Ein Grabepigramm und seine Welt," in *Zona archeologica: Festschrift für Hans Peter Isler zum 60. Geburtstag*, ed. Sabrina Buzzi, Daniel Käch, Erich Kistler, Elena Mango, Marek Palaczyk, and Olympia Stefani (Bonn: Habelt, 2001), 183–91.
195 Jakob Barth, *Studien zur Kritik und Exegese des Qorans* (Strassburg: Verlag von Karl J. Trübner, 1915), 117. He "however points out that verse 2 is in the form of a statement, having the negative *mā* not *lā* and that therefore verse 1 must also be narrative past" (ibid.; *BCQ* 2:597). At the same time, Jones "sees no merit in suggestions that it dates from after the time when Abū Lahab became leader of the clan of Hāshim, thought to be in 619 CE, or that it is a factual piece dating from the time of Abū Lahab's death (after the battle of Badr)" (*JQA* 595). Cf. Q. 69.28: 'My wealth has been of no avail to me' (*mā aghnā ʿannī māliyah*).

Long held to be a curse proper, this sūra-unit in the final analysis stands out as a revenge prayer *par excellence.*[196] Moreover, a special "self-imprecation" is also attested by the indignant challenge in Q. 8.32, featuring the cultic marker *allāhumma*[197]:

> *wa-idh qālū llāhumma in kāna hādhā huwa l-ḥaqqa min ʿindika fa-amṭir ʿalaynā ḥijāratan mina s-samāʾi awi-ʾtinā bi-ʿadhābin alīmin*
>
> And when they said:
> O God,
> if this is the truth from You,
> rain stones from the sky upon us
> or bring a painful torment on us.

According to Jones, this verse in Sūrat al-Anfāl appears here as a literary flourish.[198]

Praise Prayer

In prayer language, the pendulum swings between impassioned plea and high approbation.[199] The praise prayer is composed of four elements, the praise formula, ascription of praise, grounding clause, and optional detailing.[200] The *tabāraka* formula occurs nine times in the corpus.[201] It appears no less than three times in Sūrat al-Furqān (vv. 1–2, 10, and 61–62).[202] In Q. 25.1–2 (-*īC*), "divine predication" is signaled by the definite relative pronoun[203]:

---

196 *JQA* 595. N.b. This prayer pericope omits the optional invocation. Based upon the *asbāb an-nuzūl*, Stewart argues that "it makes sense to understand sūra 111 as a retort to the curse *tabban laka* ["Perdition to you" or "Curse be upon you"], a curse responding directly to another curse" (idem, "Understanding the Qur'ān," 36–37; Uri Rubin, "Abū Lahab and Sūra CXI," *BSOAS* 42, no. 1 (1979): esp. 20).
197 Cf. s.v. šāba', §II: Oath and Curse, *TDOT.*
198 *JQA* 169.
199 Miller, *They Cried to the Lord*, 244.
200 Balentine, *Prayer in the Hebrew Bible*, 204–6; Greenberg, *Biblical Prose Prayer*, 31–32; Goitein, "Das Gebet im Qorān," 1; Corvin, "Stylistic and Functional Study of the Prose Prayers," 222.
201 Goitein, "Das Gebet im Qorān," 16; Baumstark, "Jüdischer und christlicher Gebetstypus im Koran," 231–32; s.v. Tabāraka, *CQ.*
202 Jones further notes that "verse 10 also brings in the second person singular" (*JQA* 329).
203 Norden, *Agnostos Theos, passim*; Lightfoot, *The Sibylline Oracles*, 32; Pernot, "The Rhetoric of Religion," 332; Baumstark, "Jüdischer und christlicher Gebetstypus im Koran," 231.

tabāraka lladhī nazzala l-furqāna ʿalā ʿabdihī li-yakūna li-l-ʿālamīna nadhīran

alladhī lahū mulku s-samāwāti wa-l-arḍi wa-lam yattakhidh waladan wa-lam yakun lahū sharīkun fī l-mulki wa-khalaqa kulla shayʾin fa-qaddarahū taqdīran

Blessed is He who has sent down the salvation (*al-furqān*) to His slave,
for him to be a warner to all created beings –

He to whom belongs the sovereignty of the heavens and the earth.
He has not taken to Himself a son;
nor has He any partner in sovereignty.
He has created everything and determined it precisely.

The pericope commences with the praise formula and relative ascription (*tabāraka lladhī*) followed by the grounding clause. Although detailing follows in the parallel relative clause, its direct relation to the preceding clause remains unclear. At this point it is worth considering Goitein's observation that these praise prayers function primarily as framing devices.[204] In other words, they are employed at the beginning or conclusion of the sūra-unit or pericope.[205] Q. 67.1 (-*īC*) sets the tone for Sūrat al-Mulk:

tabāraka lladhī bi-yadihi l-mulku wa-huwa ʿalā kulli shayʾin qadīrun

Blessed is He in whose hand is sovereignty
and who has power over everything –

This verse is followed by a pair of relative clauses (-*ūC*) and a conjunction (-*īC*):

alladhī khalaqa l-mawta wa-l-ḥayāta li-yabluwakum ayyukum aḥsanu ʿamalan wa-huwa l-ʿazīzu l-ghafūru

alladhī khalaqa sabʿa samāwātin ṭibāqan mā tarā fī khalqi r-raḥmāni min tafāwutin fa-rjiʿi l-baṣara hal tarā min fuṭūrin

thumma rjiʿi l-baṣara karratayni yanqalib ilayka l-baṣaru khāsiʾan wa-huwa ḥasīrun

Who created death and life that He might try you[P]
– which of you is better in conduct,
and Who is the Mighty and the Forgiving,

204 Goitein, "Das Gebet im Qorān," 16.
205 Ibid.

> Who has created seven heavens in storeys.
> You[S] cannot see any fault in the Merciful's creation.
> Look again. Do you see any cracks?
>
> Look again and again,
> and your sight will come back to you dim and weary.

Jones views this unit (Q. 67.1–4) as *magnalia dei*.[206] Bell also notes that it is "a passage evidently meant as the beginning of a chapter, extolling the perfection of creation."[207]

Moreover, even though praise prayers assume the language and form of blessing, these are not, properly speaking, acts of blessing.[208] For example, Q. 25.10 reads,

> *tabāraka lladhī in shā'a ja'ala laka khayran min dhālika jannātin tajrī min taḥtihā l-anhāru wa-yaj'al laka quṣūran*
>
> Blessed is He who, if He wishes, will assign you[S] something better than that:
> gardens, through which rivers flow,
> and will assign you[S] palaces.

Particularly important is the fact that it is presented unto God and followed by a conditional clause.[209] In the analogous biblical case, Balentine notes, "the prayer is only indirectly addressed to God. It is primarily a statement *about* God intended for the hearing of those assembled...."[210] For instance, consider Q. 25.61 that marks the beginning of a new section[211]:

> *tabāraka lladhī ja'ala fī s-samā'i burūjan wa-ja'ala fīhā sirājan wa-qamaran munīran*
>
> Blessed is He who has set constellations in the sky
> and has placed among them a lamp – a moon that gives light.

Similar in many respects is Q. 43.85:

---

206 *JQA* 528.

207 Regarding this passage, Bell states, "The name of God is ar-Raḥmān, and He is referred to in the third person" (*BCQ* 2:401). He further notes that in verse 1 "*tabāraka* does not occur in very early passages; according to Baumstark it is a Jewish prayer form" (ibid.).

208 Greenberg, *Biblical Prose Prayer*, 30; Balentine, *Prayer in the Hebrew Bible*, 205.

209 Balentine, *Prayer in the Hebrew Bible*, 206.

210 Ibid., 205.

211 Goitein, "Das Gebet im Qorān," 16.

wa-tabāraka lladhī lahū mulku s-samāwāti wa-l-arḍi wa-mā baynahumā wa-ʿindahū ʿilmu s-sāʿati wa-ilayhi turjaʿūna

Blessed is He who has sovereignty of the heavens and the earth and what is between them
and who has knowledge of the Hour
and to whom you will be returned.

The praise prayer experiences further simplification at the close of Q. 7.54:

inna rabbakumu llāhu lladhī khalaqa s-samāwāti wa-l-arḍa fī sittati ayyāmin thumma stawā ʿalā l-ʿarshi yughshī l-layla n-nahāra yaṭlubuhū ḥathīthan wa-sh-shamsa wa-l-qamara wa-n-nujūma musakhkharātin bi-amrihī alā lahu l-khalqu wa-l-amru tabāraka llāhu rabbu l-ʿālamīna

Your Lord is God
who created the heavens and the earth in six days,
then set himself on the Throne,
covering the day with the night,
which seeks it swiftly,
with the sun and the moon and the stars subject to His command.
His indeed is the creation and the command.
Blessed be God, Lord of all beings.

In this instance, the ascription to God is given full expression. Particularly pertinent here is Balentine's observation that formalized worship, in the biblical context, is generally directed at the deity who created this world.[212] On the other hand, consider the final line of Q. 23.12–14:

wa-la-qad khalaqnā l-insāna min sulālatin min ṭīnin

thumma jaʿalnāhu nuṭfatan fī qarārin makīnin

thumma khalaqnā n-nuṭfata ʿalaqatan fa-khalaqnā l-ʿalaqata muḍghatan fa-khalaqnā l-muḍghata ʿiẓāman fa-kasawnā l-ʿiẓāma laḥman thumma anshaʾnāhu khalqan ākhara fa-tabāraka llāhu aḥsanu l-khāliqīna

We created man from an extract of clay;

Then We placed him, as a drop, in a safe lodging;

Then We created from the drop a clot,
and from the clot a lump,

212 Balentine, *Prayer in the Hebrew Bible*, 212; Albertz, *Persönliche Frömmigkeit und offizielle Religion*, 37–38.

and from the lump bones;
then We clothed the bones with flesh,
and then produced another creature.
Blessed be God, the fairest of creators.

As in this case, instances of personal piety are often enough directed at the deity who created human life.[213]

Balentine notes, praise prayer becomes more formal and homogeneous in time.[214] Take, for instance, the final verse of Sūrat ar-Raḥmān (Q. 55.78):

tabāraka smu rabbika dhī l-jalāli wa-l-ikrāmi

Blessed is the name of your[S] Lord who is endowed with glory and honor.

Baumstark refers to Q. 55.78 as the closure of this long qur'ānic litany (Q. 55).[215] Therefore, this short praise prayer represents a significant transition from the language of blessing to that of liturgy, leading eventually to doxology.[216] Nowhere is this subtle shift clearer than in the juxtaposition of Q. 40.64–65:

allāhu lladhī ja'ala lakumu l-arḍa qarāran wa-s-samā'a binā'an wa-ṣawwarakum fa-aḥsana ṣuwarakum wa-razaqakum mina ṭ-ṭayyibāti dhālikumu llāhu rabbukum fa-tabāraka llāhu rabbu l-'ālamīna

huwa l-ḥayyu lā ilāha illā huwa fa-d'ūhu mukhliṣīna lahu d-dīna l-ḥamdu li-llāhi rabbi l-'ālamīna

God, who made for you[P] the earth as a dwelling place and the sky as a canopy,
and fashioned you and fashioned you well
and provided you with good things as sustenance.
Such for you is God, your Lord.
Blessed be God, Lord of created beings.

He is the Living.
There is no god save Him.
Call to Him, devoting your religion solely to Him.
Praise belongs to God, Lord of created beings.

---

213 Ibid.
214 Balentine, *Prayer in the Hebrew Bible*, 212.
215 Baumstark, "Jüdischer und christlicher Gebetstypus im Koran," 232.
216 Balentine, *Prayer in the Hebrew Bible*, 206 and 213.

While verse 64 closes with the praise formula (*tabāraka*), the subsequent verse ends with the doxological formula (*al-ḥamdu*).[217] As a result, praise prayer signifies "a movement from personal response to liturgical standardization."[218]

Rhetorical Prayer

A supplementary type of contextual prayer is purely rhetorical in nature. Q. 2.201 introduces the prescriptive corporate prayer:

> *rabbanā ātinā fī d-dunyā ḥasanatan wa-fī l-akhirati ḥasanatan wa-qinā ʿadhāba n-nāri*
>
> Our Lord,
> give us good in this world
> and good in the world to come,
> and guard us from the torment of the Fire.

Those who recite this prayer, "those will have a portion of what they have earned" (*ulāʾika lahum naṣībun mimmā kasabū wa-llāhu sarīʿu l-ḥisābi*) (Q. 2.202). However, a subtle yet sharp contrast in cultic practice is achieved by means of counterpoint. According to verse 200a, those who recite the following counter-prayer will "have no share of happiness in the world to come":

> *rabbanā ātinā fī d-dunyā*
>
> Our Lord,
> give to us in this world.

The ease with which such pseudo-prayers are derived points to the relative fixity of the prayer form. Moreover, the integrity of this prescriptive unit (Q. 2.200a-2) is borne out by the end-rhyme (-*āC*) as clearly indicated by the prior (-*īC*) and subsequent (-*ūC*) rhyme schemes.

The fixed form of the prayer-unit extends to pseudo-prayers of the individual. For instance, the rhetorical appeal at the close of Q. 63.10a is signaled by the individual cultic formula (*rabbi*):

> *fa-yaqūla rabbi lawlā akhkhartanī ilā ajalin qarībin fa-aṣṣaddaqa wa-akun mina ṣ-ṣāliḥīna*

---

217 Robinson, *Discovering the Qurʾān*, 110. Bell notes that "verse 66 also ends with *rabb l-ʿālamīn*, but is a separate declaration, not connected with the context" (*BCQ* 2:208).
218 Balentine, *Prayer in the Hebrew Bible*, 213.

And he says,
My Lord,
if only You would defer me to a near term,
that I may give alms and be one of the righteous.

This ostensibly private prayer is situated in between the moral injunction issued in a sermon addressing charity (Q. 63.9–10) and the penalty for failure to comply[219]:

yā-ayyuhā lladhīna āmanū lā tulhikum amwālukum wa-lā awlādukum ʿan dhikri llāhi wa-man yafʿal dhālika fa-ulāʾika humu l-khāsirūna

wa-anfiqū min mā razaqnākum min qabli an yaʾtiya aḥadakumu l-mawtu

O you who believe, let neither your possessions nor your children
divert you from remembrance of God.
Those who do that – those are the losers.

And spend of what We have given you as provision
before death comes to one of you.

Thereafter, the final line of this sūra (Q. 63.11) seals the fate of those who violate the divine decree, thereby answering the hypothetical prayer in the negative:

wa-lan yuʾakhkhira llāhu nafsan idhā jāʾa ajaluhā wa-llāhu khabīrun bi-mā taʿmalūna

God grants deferment to no soul when its term comes;
and God is informed of what you^{P} do.

Here again, the unity of the prayer unit (Q. 63.10a) is ensured since its rhyme scheme (-*īC*) is incongruous with that of the preceding and succeeding verses (-*ūC*).

2.5 Summary

Given that the Qurʾān "contains various prescriptions and descriptions of prayer and includes a great number of prayers, hymns, and invocations," Böwering deems "this scripture in its entirety a book of prayer."[220] Form criticism produces

219 *BCQ* 2:387; cf. Q. 2.254.
220 S.v. Prayer, *EQ*.

definite and demonstrable results in terms of identifying, classifying, and contextualizing the forms of qur'ānic prayer. In addition to determining patterned prayers, this illustrative case study has generated a systematic taxonomy, along with corresponding *termini technici.*[221] This is all the more significant in light of Adolf Deißmann's (d. 1937) weighty words, "One could compose the history of religion as the history of prayer."[222] On this note, let us turn our attention to the liturgical forms in the corpus.

221 S.v. Prayer, *ER*^{2}.
222 Gustav Adolf Deißmann, "Der Beter Jesus: Ein vergessenes Kapitel der Neutestamentlichen Theologie," *ChrW* 13 (1899): col. 702; Goitein, "Das Gebet im Qorān," i, fn. 1.

Chapter 3: Liturgy

3.1 Liturgy Genre

This chapter considers the problem of identifying speech-forms of liturgy *in statu nascendi.*[1] In particular, it will address the dual forms of hymn and litany.[2] Neuwirth states, "the fact that the qur'ānic texts are intended to be used as liturgical texts and thus – like the Psalms – to be 'performed,' i.e., to be chanted supported by a cantilena, is obvious from their composition."[3] Baumstark too recognizes the presence of discrete pieces exhibiting hymnic properties.[4] The hymn form however poses a special problem since it overlaps to a significant extent with the prayer genre. Heiler acknowledges, for all intents and purposes, the hymn is a prayer in construction.[5] Balentine is likewise attentive to the "liturgical tone" of formal prayers.[6] Although this cross-pollination blurs the lines between complex prayers and liturgical fragments, it nonetheless reflects the intrinsic relationship between these genres. Secondly, Baumstark states that the litany form belongs to "a class of liturgical texts," which he deems "stereotyped prayer."[7] In other words, litany is "prayer of a definite and fixed form."[8] As a result, liturgy and prayer share certain extrinsic features, specifically in terms of formulae.[9]

1 *SKMS*[2] 6* and 43*. Gerstenberger defines liturgy as "any text used in worship that is recited by two or more voices in a responsive fashion" (*FOTL* 14:252).
2 *SKMS*[2] 192–96.
3 Neuwirth continues, "Several sūras even point to the practice of recitation – exercised in the framework of a vigil – as the locus of the receiving of new texts. Regarding their literary shape and their function, the early qur'ānic texts are much more closely related to the Psalms than – as is usually held – to the Bible as such" (eadem, "Two Views of History and Human Future: Qur'ānic and Biblical Renderings of Divine Promises," *JQS* 10, no. 1 (2008): 2).
4 Baumstark, "Jüdischer und christlicher Gebetstypus im Koran," 229–30.
5 Heiler, *Das Gebet*, 157.
6 Balentine, *Prayer in the Hebrew Bible*, 19–20.
7 Anton Baumstark, *Liturgie comparée. Principes et Méthodes pour l'étude historique des liturgies chrétiennes*, 3rd ed. (Chevetogne, Belgique: Éditions de Chevetogne, 1953), 80; idem, *Comparative Liturgy*, trans. F.L. Cross (Westminster, Maryland: The Newman Press, 1958), 71.
8 Ibid.
9 Baumstark, *Liturgie comparée*, 80–81.

https://doi.org/10.1515/9783110580884-003

3.2 Liturgy Formulae

Rabbanā

The corporate invocation for prayers (*rabbanā:* "Our Lord") doubles as a qur'ānic liturgical formula and refrain.[10] For example, Sūrat Āl 'Imrān (Q. 3.8–9) preserves a hymnic fragment[11]:

rabbanā lā tuzigh qulūbanā ba'da idh hadaytanā wa-hab lanā min ladunka raḥmatan innaka anta l-wahhābu

rabbanā innaka jāmi'u n-nāsi li-yawmin lā rayba fīhi inna llāha lā yukhlifu l-mī'āda

Our Lord,
do not cause our hearts to deviate
after You have guided us;
and give us mercy from Yourself.
You are indeed the Giver.

Our Lord,
You are the gatherer of the people
to a day about which there is no doubt.
God will not fail to keep the tryst.

Jones advances the tentative claim that verses 1–9 are one of "three hymn-like passages," including verses 26–27 and 191–94.[12] On a related note, consider the hymn of Abraham in Q. 26.77a-82 (*-īC*)[13]:

rabbu l-'ālamīna

alladhī khalaqanī fa-huwa yahdīni

wa-lladhī huwa yuṭ'imunī wa-yasqīni

wa-idhā mariḍtu fa-huwa yashfīni

wa-lladhī yumītunī thumma yuḥyīni

---

10 *FOTL* 14:250.
11 Goitein, "Das Gebet im Qorān," publ. Abstr., ii.
12 *JQA* 64.
13 *SKMS*² 276 (vv. 78–82). This hymn is otherwise localized by means of preceding *illā* (Thackston, *Introduction*, 79).

wa-lladhī aṭmaʿu an yaghfira lī khaṭīʾatī yawma d-dīni

The Lord of all beings,

Who created me and guides me,

And Who gives me food and drink,

And Who heals me when I am sick,

And Who makes me die and then gives me life again,

And Whom I desire to forgive me my sins on the Day of Judgment.

The literary structure of this short hymn includes the opening liturgical formula (*rabb*) in combination with divine predication. What is more, a long personal prayer of Abraham follows this hymn.[14]

Allāh

The second liturgical formula is featured in a hymnic fragment (Q. 3.26–27) in the vocative: *allāhumma* ("O God").[15] In this case, it is accompanied by the "liturgical imperative" (*qul*)[16]:

> *quli llāhumma mālika l-mulki tuʾtī l-mulka man tashāʾu wa-tanziʿu l-mulka mimman tashāʾu wa-tuʿizzu man tashāʾu wa-tudhillu man tashāʾu bi-yadika l-khayru innaka ʿalā kulli shayʾin qadīrun*
>
> *tūliju l-layla fī n-nahāri wa-tūliju n-nahāra fī l-layli wa-tukhriju l-ḥayya mina l-mayyiti wa-tukhriju l-mayyita mina l-ḥayyi wa-tarzuqu man tashāʾu bi-ghayri ḥisābin*

---

14 According to Neuwirth, verses 83–89 constitute two prayers featuring dual pleas (*SKMS*[2] 276). Parenthetically, for Klaus Seybold's definition of hymns, see idem, *Die Psalmen: Eine Einführung* (Stuttgart: Verlag W. Kohlhammer, 1986), 97.

15 Jeffery, *Foreign Vocabulary*, 66–67 (*Allāh*) and 67 (*Allāhumma*).

16 Mark D. Futato, *The Book of Psalms* (Wheaton, Illinois: Tyndale House Publishers, 2009), 308–11 (Ps 96) and 319–21 (Ps 100). Bell considers Q. 3.26 a "prayer" cast in the slogan form: "the simplest form of the kind is the short statement introduced by the word 'Say.' There are about 250 of these scattered throughout the Qurʾān" (*BIQ*[1] 74).

Say:
O God,
owner of sovereignty,
You give sovereignty to those whom You wish;
You exalt those whom You wish;
And You abase those whom You wish.
In Your hand is Good.
You have power over everything.

You merge the night into the day and the day into the night.
You bring forth the living from the dead and the dead from the living.
You give sustenance to those whom You wish without reckoning.

In spite of the shift in end rhyme pattern from *-īC* to *-āC*, both the verbal pattern and reoccurring phrase (*man tashāʾu*) ensure the internal coherence of this hymnic pericope.

In addition to *allāhumma*, Sūrat al-Ghāfir exhibits three liturgical texts formulated using "relative predication" ("God, who…").[17] The first example (Q. 40.61–62) reads,

allāhu lladhī jaʿala lakumu l-layla li-taskunū fīhi wa-n-nahāra mubṣiran inna llāha la-dhū faḍlin ʿalā n-nāsi wa-lākinna akthara n-nāsi lā yashkurūna

dhālikumu llāhu rabbukum khāliqu kulli shayʾin lā ilāha illā huwa fa-annā tuʾfakūna

God, who made the night for you^{P} to rest in it
and the day to give sight.
God is possessed of bounty for the people,
but most of the people are not grateful.

Such for you^{P} is God, your Lord,
the creator of everything.
There is no God but Him.
How are you involved in lies?

Its literary structure is twofold: *allāhu lladhī…dhālikumu llāhu rabbukum.*[18] While this pericope references day and night, earth and sky are the subject of verse 64[19]:

17 Robinson, *Discovering the Qurʾān*, 109; Lightfoot, *The Sibylline Oracles*, 32.
18 Robinson, *Discovering the Qurʾān*, 110.
19 *SKMS*^{2} 310; *BCQ* 2:207.

allāhu lladhī ja'ala lakumu l-arḍa qarāran wa-s-samā'a binā'an wa-ṣawwarakum fa-aḥsana ṣuwarakum wa-razaqakum mina ṭ-ṭayyibāti dhālikumu llāhu rabbukum fa-tabāraka llāhu rabbu l-'ālamīna

God, who made for you^{P} the earth as a dwelling place and the sky as a canopy,
and fashioned you and fashioned you well
and provided you with good things as sustenance.
Such for you is God, your Lord.
Blessed be God, Lord of created beings.

The subsequent verse (v. 65) also closes on a doxology with a similar end-rhyme (*-īC*) literally accomplished by means of the rhyme-phrase (*rabb al-'ālamīn*)[20]:

huwa l-ḥayyu lā ilāha illā huwa fa-d'ūhu mukhliṣīna lahu d-dīna l-ḥamdu li-llāhi rabbi l-'ālamīna

He is the Living.
There is no god save Him.
Call^{P} to Him, devoting religion solely to Him.
Praise belongs to God, Lord of created beings.

The third and final hymnic *āyāt* (vv. 79–81) in this sūra-unit appeal to locomotive means (e.g., riding animals and sailing ships)[21]:

allāhu lladhī ja'ala lakumu l-an'āma li-tarkabū minhā wa-minhā ta'kulūna

wa-lakum fīhā manāfi'u wa-li-tablughū 'alayhā ḥājatan fī ṣudūrikum wa-'alayhā wa-'alā l-fulki tuḥmalūna

wa-yurīkum āyātihī fa-ayya āyāti llāhi tunkirūna

God, who has assigned livestock to you^{P},
for you to ride some of them and eat some of them

– You^{P} have many benefits from them –
and for you to reach on them a need that is in your breasts,
and you are carried on ships [just as] you are borne on them.

And He shows you^{P} His signs
– and which of God's signs will you deny?

20 *BCQ* 2:207.
21 *SKMS*^{2} 310; *BCQ* 2:209.

Returning to the bipartite structure, Sūrat al-Anʿām (Q. 6.101–4) preserves an instructive hymnic pericope (-*īC*)[22]:

badīʿu s-samāwāti wa-l-arḍi annā yakūnu lahū waladun wa-lam takun lahū ṣāḥibatun wa-khalaqa kulla shay'in wa-huwa bi-kulli shay'in ʿalīmun

dhālikumu llāhu rabbukum lā ilāha illā huwa khāliqu kulli shay'in fa-ʿbudūhu wa-huwa ʿalā kulli shay'in wakīlun

lā tudrikuhu l-abṣāru wa-huwa yudriku l-abṣāra wa-huwa l-laṭīfu l-khabīru

qad jā'akum baṣā'iru min rabbikum fa-man abṣara fa-li-nafsihī wa-man ʿamiya fa-ʿalayhā wa-mā ana ʿalaykum bi-ḥafīẓin

– The originator of the heavens and the earth.
How can He have a child when He has no consort,
when He created everything and is Aware of everything?

That is God, your^{P} Lord.
There is no god but Him,
the Creator of all things,
so Worship Him.
He has charge of everything.

Sight does not reach Him, but He reaches sight.
He is the Gentle and the Informed.

Clear proofs have come to you^{P} from your Lord.
Those who see clearly
– it is to their own advantage.
Those who remain blind
– it is to their disadvantage.
I am not a keeper over you.

Although it omits the initial *allāhu lladhī*, nevertheless verse 102 resumes the second part with *dhālikumu llāhu rabbukum*. A similar headless construction (-*ūC*) occurs in Q. 39.6–7[23]:

khalaqakum min nafsin wāḥidatin thumma jaʿala minhā zawjahā wa-anzala lakum mina l-anʿāmi thamāniyata azwājin yakhluqukum fī buṭūni ummahātikum khalqan min baʿdi khalqin fī ẓulumātin thalāthin dhālikumu llāhu rabbukum lahu l-mulku lā ilāha illā huwa fa-annā tuṣrafūna

22 According to Neuwirth, verses 95–99 constitute *āyāt* (*SKMS*^{2} 291).
23 *BCQ* 2:180–81; cf. *SKMS*^{2} 308. Cf. Q. 10.32 (*fa-dhālikumu llāhu rabbukumu*).

in takfurū fa-inna llāha ghaniyyun ʿankum wa-lā yarḍā li-ʿibādihi l-kufra wa-in tashkurū yarḍahu lakum wa-lā taziru wāziratun wizra ukhrā thumma ilā rabbikum marjiʿukum fa-yunabbiʾukum bi-mā kuntum taʿmalūna innahū ʿalīmun bi-dhāti ṣ-ṣudūri

He created you[P] from a single soul;
then He made its mate from it;
and He has sent down to you eight beasts, paired together.
He created you in the bellies of your mothers,
creation after creation,
in triple darkness.
That is God, your Lord.
To Him belongs the Kingdom.
There is no god but Him.
How is it that you are turned?

If you[P] are ungrateful, God is independent of you;
but He is not pleased with ingratitude on the part of His servants.
Yet if you are thankful,
He is pleased by it for you.
No laden [soul] bears the burden of another.
It is to your Lord that you will return,
and He will inform you of what you have been doing.
He knows the thoughts in men's breasts.

According to Bell, "it expresses the sublimity of God as creator and His independence of, but not indifference to, man's response to His goodness."[24] Furthermore, consider Q. 35.13, which seems to belong to an *āyāt* section[25]:

yūliju l-layla fī n-nahāri wa-yūliju n-nahāra fī l-layli wa-sakhkhara sh-shamsa wa-l-qamara kullun yajrī li-ajalin musamman dhālikumu llāhu rabbukum lahu l-mulku wa-lladhīna tadʿūna min dūnihī mā yamlikūna min qiṭmīrin

He makes the night enter into the day,
and the day into the night,
and He has subjected the sun and the moon to [your] service,
each of them running for a stated term.
That is God, your[P] Lord.
His is the Kingdom,
and those you invoke,
to His exclusion,
do not own even the skin of a date-stone.

---

24 *BCQ* 2:180.
25 Verses 9–14 (*SKMS*[2] 307; *JQA* 397; cf. *BCQ* 2:128).

Once more, appealing to day and night, this passage only produces the second member of the bipartite structure. Lastly, consider *allāh* ("God") in the following hymnic pericope (Q. 39.62):

allāhu khāliqu kulli shay'in wa-huwa 'alā kulli shay'in wakīlun

God is the creator of everything.
He is Guardian over everything.

In this hymn, *allāh* functions as a liturgical formula.[26]

Huwa

The third liturgical formula takes the form of essential predication (*huwa:* "He is…").[27] Sūrat al-Ikhlāṣ (Q. 112.1–4) begins with the liturgical imperative (-*aC*):

qul huwa llāhu aḥadun
allāhu ṣ-ṣamadu
lam yalid wa-lam yūlad
wa-lam yakun lahū kufuwan aḥadun

Say: He is God, One,
God, the Eternal,
Who has not begotten nor has been begotten.
There is no equal to Him.

According to Hirschfeld, "there is a liturgical ring about the sūra, and it was probably intended for repetition."[28] Regarding its performative setting, he states that "such a service, as simple in form as possible, perhaps only consisted in invocations and prayers, of which sūra 112 furnishes a very appropriate sample."[29]

This same liturgical formula assumes relative predication (*huwa lladhī:* "He, who…").[30] For instance, Q. 6.97–99 reads (-*ūC*):

wa-huwa lladhī ja'ala lakumu n-nujūma li-tahtadū bihā fī ẓulumāti l-barri wa-l-baḥri qad faṣṣalnā l-āyāti li-qawmin ya'lamūna

---

26 *SKMS*^{2} 309.
27 Lightfoot, *The Sibylline Oracles*, 32; Pernot, "The Rhetoric of Religion," 332.
28 *BCQ* 2:600; Hirschfeld, *New Researches*, 35; cf. *JQA* 596.
29 Hirschfeld, *New Researches*, 35.
30 Lightfoot, *The Sibylline Oracles*, 32; Pernot, "The Rhetoric of Religion," 332.

wa-huwa lladhī ansha'akum min nafsin wāḥidatin fa-mustaqarrun wa-mustawdaʿun qad faṣṣalnā l-āyāti li-qawmin yafqahūna

wa-huwa lladhī anzala mina s-samāʾi māʾan fa-akhrajnā bihī nabāta kulli shay'in fa-akhrajnā minhu khaḍiran nukhriju minhu ḥabban mutarākiban wa-mina n-nakhli min talʿihā qinwānun dāniyatun wa-jannātin min aʿnābin wa-z-zaytūna wa-r-rummāna mushtabihan wa-ghayra mutashābihin nẓurū ilā thamarihī idhā athmara wa-yanʿihī inna fī dhālikum la-āyātin li-qawmin yu'minūna

It is He who has placed the stars for you[P],
for you to be guided by them in the darknesses of land and sea.
We have expounded the signs for a people who know.

It is He who has produced you from a single soul.
[Then there is] a lodging place and a place of deposit.
We have expounded the signs for a people who understand.

It is He who has sent down water from the sky.
With it We bring forth plants of every kind.
From them We bring forth green shoots;
from them We bring forth grain in clusters;
and from the date-palm, from its spathe, clusters of dates close at hand;
and gardens of grapes and olives and pomegranates,
like one another and unlike one another.
Look[P] at their fruits when they bear fruit and at their ripening.
In that there are signs for a people who believe.

Bell keenly observes that this is "a sign passage, which has been revised by the addition of rhyme-phrases, and probably the main part of verse 99 – note the different pronoun in these parts – unless perhaps there have been two revisions, the rhyme-phrases having been added at a different time from the middle of verse 99."[31] In point of fact, verses 97a and 98a, as well as the verse-group 99a-f feature the "dynamic predicate" (e.g., "We can").[32] In the final analysis, this liturgical interpolation (vv. 99a-f) apparently represents a hymn-within-a-hymn.

Furthermore, Jones points to a "brief hymn to God at the beginning of the sūra (vv. 1–3)."[33] Neuwirth also identifies these verses as a hymnic introduction

31 *BCQ* 1:199; *SKMS*² 167 and 291 (*āyāt*).
32 Pernot, "The Rhetoric of Religion," 332; *SKMS*² 167 and cf. 175–78.
33 *JQA* 128.

with elements of polemic.[34] Sūrat al-Anʿām (Q. 6.1–3) combines the doxological formula (v. 1) with relative (v. 2) and essential predication (v. 3):

al-ḥamdu li-llāhi lladhī khalaqa s-samāwāti wa-l-arḍa wa-jaʿala ẓ-ẓulumāti wa-n-nūra thumma lladhīna kafarū bi-rabbihim yaʿdilūna

huwa lladhī khalaqakum min ṭīnin thumma qaḍā ajalan wa-ajalun musamman ʿindahū thumma antum tamtarūna

wa-huwa llāhu fī s-samāwāti wa-fī l-arḍi yaʿlamu sirrakum wa-jahrakum wa-yaʿlamu mā taksibūna

Praise belongs to God,
who has created the heavens and the earth
and made darkness and light.
Yet those who do not believe ascribe equals to their Lord.

He, who has created you[P] from clay and then fixed a term
– and [it is] a term that is stated with Him.
Yet you still doubt.

He is God in the heavens and the earth.
He knows what you keep secret and what you make public;
and He knows what you amass.

Not only is there a shared end-rhyme (-*ūC*) in both hymnic fragments (Q. 6.1–3 and Q. 6.97–99), both are directed at the congregation.[35] Together these two liturgical fragments amount to an extensive hymn.

Subḥāna

Doxologies constitute an "ascription of praise."[36] Baumstark states that *subḥāna* ("praise," "glory") is representative of a class which, according to Wansbrough, is of "obviously liturgical origin."[37] For this reason, Baumstark considers doxologies "introductory and concluding formulae in acts of worship...which accom-

34 *SKMS*[2] 290.
35 *BCQ* 1:177.
36 Baumstark, *Liturgie comparée*, 80 and 90. In its formulation, a doxology commences or incorporates the term "glory" (s.v. Doxology, *DLW*).
37 Baumstark, "Jüdischer und christlicher Gebetstypus im Koran," 236–37; *QS* 17; s.v. Subḥān, *EI*[2]; Goitein, "Das Gebet im Qorān," 14–16.

pany the different liturgical actions."[38] Additionally, the doxological formula *subḥāna* functions as the formula of liturgical praise.[39] Consider the opening of Sūrat al-Aʿlā (Q. 87.1):

sabbiḥi sma rabbika l-aʿlā

Praise^{S} the name of your^{S} Lord, the Most High!

Neuwirth notes that this first verse is a prefatory hymn of praise.[40] In the same vein as Sūra 96 (verses 1 and 3), *subḥāna* functions as a liturgical imperative.[41] She points out four similarities between these sūra-analogs (Q. 87 and Q. 96): (i) liturgical imperative, (ii) catchword (*ism rabbika*), (iii) divine predication, and (iv) resumption.[42] Consider the verse-group (Q. 87.2–5) that comprises the core hymn[43]:

alladhī khalaqa fa-sawwā

wa-lladhī qaddara fa-hadā

wa-lladhī akhraja l-marʿā

fa-jaʿalahū ghuthāʾan aḥwā

Who has created and formed,

Who has determined and guided,

Who has brought forth pasturage –

38 Baumstark, *Liturgie comparée*, 90; idem, *Comparative Liturgy*, 80.
39 Baumstark, "Jüdischer und christlicher Gebetstypus im Koran," 236–37; s.v. Subḥān, *CQ*; *FOTL* 14:260; Gunkel, "Psalmen," col. 1613.
40 *SKMS*² 225.
41 Ibid.; Robinson, *Discovering the Qur'ān*, 109; *BCQ* 2:527.
42 *SKMS*² 225; E.W. Bullinger, *Figures of Speech in the Bible, Explained and Illustrated* (London: Eyre & Spottiswoode, 1898), 206–7.
43 *SKMS*² 225; s.v. Form and Structure of the Qur'ān, *EQ*. According to Robinson: "Here, however, the hymnic atmosphere is suddenly and very effectively disrupted by the fifth *āya*, which evokes the coming judgment, in language reminiscent of Amos' description of the pastures of the shepherds morning and the top of Carmel withering as YHWH storms out of Zion (Amos 1:2)" (idem, *Discovering the Qur'ān*, 110). "This positive image of grass as sustenance for animals and the object of God's beneficent providence is numerically the smallest category in the Bible. God's judgment is often pictured as the taking away of grass...The threat eventually becomes an eschatological motif..." (s.v. Grass, *DBI*).

And then made it withered chaff.

According to Neuwirth, verses 1–8 together constitute a summons to praise God. Verses 6–8 read[44]:

sa-nuqri'uka fa-lā tansā

illā mā shā'a llāhu innahū ya'lamu l-jahra wa-mā yakhfā

wa-nuyassiruka li-l-yusrā

We shall cause you[S] to recite,
so that you do not forget

Except that which God wills.
He knows what is public and what is hidden.

We shall ease you[S] to ease.

On the one hand, Bell argues that verse 9 signals the limits of the pericope[45]:

fa-dhakkir in nafa'ati dh-dhikrā

So remind[S]
– if the Reminder is useful.

However, Neuwirth convincingly shows that the imperative (*dhakkir*) marks a new section altogether.[46]

As repurposed liturgical instructions, doxologies also assume a similar form and function to the closure of sūra-units. With reference to these framing devices, Baumstark states, these even assume the form of praise.[47] According to Jones, the "mixed peroration" of Q. 36.69–83 ends on a doxological note (v. 83)[48]:

fa-subḥāna lladhī bi-yadihī malakūtu kulli shayin wa-ilayhi turja'ūna

44 *SKMS*[2] 225; Robinson, *Discovering the Qur'ān*, 109.
45 *BCQ* 2:528.
46 *SKMS*[2] 225.
47 Baumstark, "Jüdischer und christlicher Gebetstypus im Koran," 229.
48 *JQA* 402.

Praise be to Him,
in whose hand is dominion over everything,
and to whom you are returned.

In addition, a prescriptive doxology (Q. 52.48a-49) brings to a close Sūrat aṭ-Ṭūr[49]:

wa-sabbiḥ bi-ḥamdi rabbika ḥīna taqūmu

wa-mina l-layli fa-sabbiḥhu wa-idbāra n-nujūmi

And praise^{S} your^{S} Lord by praising Him when you^{S} arise

And during the night,
And praise^{S} Him at the setting of the stars.

In a similar vein, Q. 110.3 terminates with a doxology:

fa-sabbiḥ bi-ḥamdi rabbika wa-staghfirhū innahū kāna tawwāban

Praise your^{S} Lord by praising Him and seek His forgiveness.
He is always ready to relent.

Q. 69.52 likewise concludes with an "imperative summons"[50]:

fa-sabbiḥ bi-smi rabbika l-ʿaẓīmi

So praise^{S} the name of your^{S} Lord, the Mighty.

Finally, as these formulae illustrate, the liturgy genre is a pronounced feature of the corpus.

---

49 Wansbrough states that "in qur'ānic usage both *rabb* and *allāh* (or a pronominal substitute) in combination with the verbal nouns *ḥamd* or *subḥān* (denoting gratitude or praise) generate a number of exclamatory constructions, e. g., *al-ḥamdu li-llāh, lahu l-ḥamd, bi-ḥamdi rabbika, bi-ḥamdika*, etc., or *subḥāna llāh, subḥāna lladhī, subḥāna rabbika, subḥānaka*, etc. All of these reflect an obviously liturgical origin..." (*QS* 17).
50 *FOTL* 14:245.

3.3 Liturgical Setting

Liturgical Performance

In the first place, Wansbrough notes, "*Qul* commonly serves to indicate liturgical instructions...."[51] What is more, the corpus has frequent recourse to a further performative marker in the liturgical imperative.[52] The *locus classicus* is Q. 96.1–2:

> *iqra' bi-smi rabbika lladhī khalaqa*
>
> *khalaqa l-insāna min 'alaqin*
>
> Recite^{S}!
> In the name of your Lord who created,
>
> Created man from a blood-clot (*'alaq*).

The call to commence recitation consists of a two-part ritual protocol.[53] Invoking the divine name, the presiding religious figure initiates the liturgy through a speech-act (v. 1).[54] Thereupon, "the second line, containing the praise proper, was sung or shouted as a response of the community."[55] This, then, was the cue-note for the liturgist to perform the intoned hymnic recitation or reading. These first two verses combined constitute a protocol hymn.[56]

---

51 *QS* 14; Neuwirth, "Vom Rezitationstext über die Liturgie zum Kanon," 84–85.
52 Futato, *The Book of Psalms*, 308–11 (Ps 96) and 319–21 (Ps 100); J. Clinton McCann, Jr. *The Book of Psalms: Introduction, Commentary, and Reflections, NIB* (Nashville, Tennessee: Abingdon Press, 1996), 4:1063–66 (Ps 96) and 4:1077–79 (Ps 100); Bierl, "Maenadism as Self-referential Chorality," 216. N.b. "As Toshihiko Izutsu (d. 1993) has shown, command may actually be the primary mode of all speech" (Gwynne, "Patterns of Address," 85; Toshihiko Izutsu, *Language and Magic: Studies in the Magical Function of Speech* (Tokyo: The Keio Institute of Philological Studies, 1956), 52–53).
53 Tucker, *Form Criticism of the Old Testament*, 15; Robinson, *Discovering the Qur'ān*, 100 and 109. Neuwirth considers verses 1–5 a hymn (*SKMS*^{2} 231).
54 McCann, Jr. *The Book of Psalms*, 4:1077; *FOTL* 14:245; see Bierl, "Maenadism as Self-referential Chorality," 216, fn. 23. For Baumstark's threefold typology of liturgical summons formulae, see idem, *Liturgie comparée*, 85–86.
55 *FOTL* 14:245.
56 *SKMS*^{2} 231. "Crüsemann calls this simple hymn a fundamental liturgical form. More likely, it generally served as the introductory or closing part of hymn singing and thus has been linked to other forms of praise" (*FOTL* 14:245; Frank Crüsemann, *Studien zur Formgeschichte von Hymnus und Danklied in Israel* (Neukirchen-Vluyn: Neukirchener Verlag, 1969), 19–50).

Alluding to "aural intratextuality," Jones states, "it would appear that the words *'alaq*, used to round off verse 2, and *qalam*, used to round off verse 4, are used with the sort of effect that is found in *kāhin*-style material, with catching sound but somewhat Delphic meaning."[57] The duplet (vv. 1–2) above distinctly echoes the triplet (vv. 3–5) below[58]:

iqra' wa-rabbuka l-akramu

alladhī 'allama bi-l-qalami

'allama l-insāna mā lam ya'lam

Read[S]!
For your Lord is the Most Generous,

Who taught by the pen (*qalam*),

Taught man what he did not know.

Here again, verse 3 is "voiced by an officiant" so as to elicit a communal response (vv. 4–5).[59] In fact, Neuwirth applies the same designation to both protocol hymns (vv. 1–2 and vv. 3–5).[60] Moreover, she deems this verse-group (vv. 1–5) a hymn.[61] This is significant because "many hymns of praise begin with or consist entirely of a summons."[62] For this reason, Q. 96.1–5 constitutes an "imperative hymn."[63] Bell concurs that these verses function as "an exhortation to recite or read formally in the name of the creating and revealing God."[64]

---

57 *JQA* 579; Michael Sells, "A Literary Approach to the Hymnic Sūras of the Qur'ān: Spirit, Gender, and Aural Intertextuality," in *Literary Structures of Religious Meaning in the Qur'ān*, ed. Issa J. Boullata (New York: Routledge, 2000), 4.
58 Sells, "Literary Approach to the Hymnic Sūras," 4. With respect to verse 3, Bell notes that "the rhyme changes at this verse but it is hardly likely that there was a break in composition" (*BCQ* 2:559).
59 *FOTL* 14:245.
60 *SKMS*[2] 231.
61 Ibid.
62 *FOTL* 14:245; Westermann, *Der Psalter*, 26 (Ps 150).
63 *FOTL* 14:250. Even in Westermann's narrow sense, Q. 96.1–5 qualifies as liturgical (idem, *Der Psalter*, 27 and 81–87).
64 *BCQ* 2:559.

3.4 Liturgical Forms

Hymn to God

According to Gerstenberger and Stephen Farris, hymns of praise consist of five speech elements: opening-invocation, imperative-summons, motive-sentence, praise-statement, and end-blessing.[65] In terms of the literary structure of hymns, the first and final elements are elective.[66] In view of that, the liturgist often begins the hymnic recitation directly with the imperative summons to praise.[67] In addition to the imperative hymn featuring *iqra'* (Q. 96.1–5), the cor-

---

65 *FOTL* 14:17; Stephen Farris, *The Hymns of Luke's Infancy Narratives* (Sheffield, England: JSOT Press, 1985), 70; Heiler, *Das Gebet*, 157–59; David M. Wulff, *Psychology of Religion* (New York: John Wiley & Sons, 1991), 536–37. Regarding "metrical structure," S.R. Driver notes "there are no strophes...For that the Hebrew poets, at least sometimes, grouped together a certain number of verses, and marked consciously the close of such a group, may be inferred from the *refrains* which appear from time to time in the Psalms" (idem, *An Introduction to the Literature of the Old Testament* (New York: Meridian Books, 1957), 366–67; Wulff, *Psychology of Religion*, 536; cf. Pieter van der Lugt, *Cantos and Strophes in Biblical Hebrew Poetry with Special Reference to the First Book of the Psalter* (Leiden: Brill, 2006), 1:1–68; Samuel Terrien, *The Psalms: Strophic Structure and Theological Commentary* (Grand Rapids, Michigan: Wm. B. Eerdmans Publishing Company, 2003), *passim*). Cf. David Heinrich Müller (d. 1912), "Strophenbau und Responsion im Koran," in *Die Propheten in ihrer ursprünglichen Form* (Wien: Alfred Hölder, 1896), 1:20–60; Van der Lugt, *Cantos and Strophes*, 1:22–23; Rudolf Geyer (d. 1929), "Zur Strophik des Qurāns," *WZKM* 22 (1908): 265–86; Lüling, *Über den Urkoran, passim*. Müller "sought to show that composition in strophes was characteristic of prophetic literature, in the Old Testament as well as in the Qur'ān" (*BIQ*[1] 71). In reference to Müller's hypothesis, see Theodor Nöldeke (d. 1930) and Friedrich Schwally (d. 1919) (*GdQ*[2] 1:43–44). Bell concurs that "if we are to speak of strophic form, we expect some regularity in length and arrangement of the strophes. Müller, however, failed to show that there was any such regularity. What his evidence does show is that many sūras of the Qur'ān fall into short sections or paragraphs. But these are not of fixed length, nor do they seem to follow any pattern of length. Their length is determined not by any consideration of form, but by the subject or incident treated in each" (*BIQ*[1] 71; cf. *SKMS*[2] 171 and 175).

66 *FOTL* 14:17–18. Regarding the final element of the hymn form, "the liturgical blessing," according to Westermann, "is an essential part of worship" (idem, *What Does the Old Testament Say about God?* 78). Furthermore, "an important sub-category of qur'ānic blessings are greetings, the most common of which is 'Peace!' (*salām*)" (s.v. Blessing, *EQ*; Goitein, "Das Gebet im Qorān," 24–26). Stewart adds, "Other blessings in the context of greeting are 'May God's mercy and His blessings be upon you!' (*raḥmatu llāhi wa-barakātuhū ʿalaykum*, Q. 11.73), and 'May you be well!' (*ṭibtum*, Q. 39.73)" (s.v. Blessing, *EQ*).

67 *FOTL* 14:245.

pus evidences a second protocol formula (*utlu:* "recite^{S}!" or "read^{S} aloud!"). The first instance of this appears in Q. 18.27a[68]:

> *utlu mā ūḥiya ilayka min kitābi rabbika*
>
> Read^{S} aloud what has been revealed to you of the scripture of your Lord.

The second of the minimal pair occurs in Sūrat al-ʿAnkabūt (Q. 29.45)[69]:

> *utlu mā ūḥiya ilayka mina l-kitābi wa-aqimi ṣ-ṣalāta*
>
> Read^{S} aloud what has been revealed to you of the scripture and perform worship (*ṣalāt*).

The praise of God forms the core content of this precise hymn.[70] This sūra-unit commences (Q. 59.1) with the praise formula:

> *sabbaḥa li-llāhi mā fī s-samāwāti wa-mā fī l-arḍi wa-huwa l-ʿazīzu l-ḥakīmu*
>
> All that is in the heavens and the earth praise God.
> He is the Mighty and the Wise.

What Jones identifies as "a paean to God" (Q. 59.22–24) continues[71]:

> *huwa llāhu lladhī lā ilāha illā huwa ʿālimu l-ghaybi wa-sh-shahādati huwa r-raḥmānu r-raḥīmu*
>
> *huwa llāhu lladhī lā ilāha illā huwa l-maliku l-quddūsu s-salāmu l-muʾminu l-muhayminu l-ʿazīzu l-jabbāru l-mutakabbiru subḥāna llāhi ʿammā yushrikūna*
>
> *huwa llāhu l-khāliqu l-bāriʾu l-muṣawwiru lahu l-asmāʾu l-ḥusnā yusabbiḥu lahū mā fī s-samāwāti wa-l-arḍi wa-huwa l-ʿazīzu l-ḥakīmu*
>
> He is God.
> There is no god but Him,
> Knower of the Invisible and the Witnessed.
> He is the Merciful and the Compassionate.
>
> He is God.
> There is no god but Him,

---

68 *SKMS*^{2} 268. The imperative form occurs seven times in the corpus (s.v. Talā, *CQ*).
69 *SKMS*^{2} 302.
70 *FOTL* 14:17; Gunkel, "Psalmen," col. 1613; Heiler, *Das Gebet*, 168.
71 *JQA* 509. Regarding the thanksgiving hymns, see Gunkel, "Psalmen," col. 1626; cf. Farris, *Hymns*, 70–71; *FOTL* 14:14–19; Westermann, *Der Psalter*, 25–26.

the King, the Holy, the Peace, the Faithful,
the Watcher, the Mighty, the Compelling.
Praise be to God, far above what they associate [with Him].

He is God, the Creator, the Maker, the Shaper.
To Him belong the fairest names.
All that is in the heavens and the earth praise Him.
He is the Mighty and the Wise.

Following the doxological formula, dual epithets conclude Sūrat al-Ḥasr. In a general statement, Heiler posits that the enumeration of divine epithets could well be the oldest form of praise.[72] Bell considers verses 22 through 24 to be "a hymn of praise to God."[73] Although exhibiting a distinct rhyme scheme (*-ūC*), the embedded doxology closing verse 23 does not appear to mark the end of this hymn. That is to say, the integrity of the unit (vv. 22–24) is here anchored in the opening refrain (*huwa llāhu*).[74] Returning to the hymn, Bell remarks that Q. 59.22–24 actually begins with verse 1 and progresses uninterrupted.[75]

In addition, Sūrat al-Baqara preserves a short hymn to God, which opens with the liturgical formula *allāh* (Q. 2.255)[76]:

allāhu lā ilāha illā huwa l-ḥayyu l-qayyūmu lā ta'khudhuhū sinatun wa-lā nawmun lahū mā fī s-samāwāti wa-mā fī l-arḍi man dhā lladhī yashfa'u 'indahū illā bi-idhnihī ya'lamu mā bayna aydīhim wa-mā khalfahum wa-lā yuḥīṭūna bi-shay'in min 'ilmihī illā bi-mā shā'a wasi'a kursiyyuhu s-samāwāti wa-l-arḍa wa-lā ya'ūduhū ḥifẓuhumā wa-huwa l-'aliyyu l-'aẓīmu

God.
There is no god but Him,
the Living, the Eternal.
Neither slumber nor sleep seize Him.
To Him belongs all that is in the heavens
and all that is on earth.
Who is there who intercedes with Him,
save by His permission?
He knows what is before them and what is after them,
while they encompass none of His knowledge
apart from that which He wishes.

---

72 Heiler, *Das Gebet*, 168.

73 *BCQ* 2:368.

74 This bears comparison with Q. 3.191a-94 and the internal structure of Q. 1.5 (*iyyāka*).

75 *BCQ* 2:368.

76 Exod 34:6–7 (cf. Marvin A. Sweeney, "Form and Eschatology in the Book of the Twelve Prophets," in *The Book of the Twelve and the New Form Criticism*, ed. Mark J. Boda, Michael H. Floyd, and Colin M. Toffelmire (Atlanta, Georgia: SBL Press, 2015), 152).

His throne extends over the heavens and the earth,
and He is not tired by guarding them.
He is the Exalted and the Mighty.

Bell maintains that the *āyat al-kursī* is independently situated.[77] According to Neal Robinson, "the narrative stresses God's power over life and death, thus taking up the throne verse's description of Him as 'the Living' (v. 255)."[78] He further comments that "the throne verse also stresses God's omniscience and asserts that His throne 'extends' (*wasiʿa*) over heaven and earth."[79] Accordingly, Gunkel states, the sentiment expressed in hymns is one of reverence and fear.[80]

Hymn to Creation

In addition to enumerating epithets, Gunkel identifies a number of hymnic motifs, which include God the creator and God the governor.[81] According to Westermann, hymns are characterized by descriptive as opposed to declarative praise.[82] In other words, "descriptive praise or hymns are not the result of one single deed of God."[83] On the contrary, these "praise creation and creator."[84] To illustrate, consider Sūrat an-Naḥl (Q. 16.1–17), which preserves a hymn to creation.[85] It begins with an exposition on His command (*amr*).[86] Integral to this opening verse-pair (vv. 1–2) is the variant liturgical formula (*allāh*) and the "literalized or particularized" praise formula (*subḥāna*)[87]:

---

77 *BCQ* 1:53; cf. *JQA* 24; de Prémare, *Aux origines du Coran*, 38–39; *GdQ*^{2} 1:184, fn. 2.
78 Robinson, *Discovering the Qurʾān*, 219.
79 Ibid., 218.
80 Gunkel, "Psalmen," col. 1614.
81 Ibid., cols. 1613–14; Westermann, introduction to *Ausgewählte Psalmen*, trans. and comm. idem (Göttingen: Vandenhoeck & Ruprecht, 1984), 12.
82 Westermann, *Der Psalter*, 61 and 69; Farris, *Hymns*, 71; *Ausgewählte Psalmen*, 121–90; cf. *EinlPs*^{4} 32–94; Gunkel, "Psalmen," cols. 1616–17; idem, "The Religion of the Psalms," 71–80; idem, "Formen der Hymnen," 265–304; Klatt, *Hermann Gunkel*, 241–52; Mowinckel, *Psalms*, 1:81–105; Clines, *On the Way to the Postmodern*, 2:671–73; de Prémare, *Aux origines du Coran*, 37–39; *FOTL* 14:17–18.
83 Westermann, *Der Psalter*, 26; idem, *The Psalms*, 26.
84 *FOTL* 14:249; Westermann, *Der Psalter*, 26 and 78.
85 Regarding Q. 16.3–9, Bell notes that "the passage as it stands is probably of the same date as the preceding, but as some of the rhyme-phrases are rather loosely attached the probability is that earlier material underlies it, though one cannot trace in it any prior formation" (*BCQ* 1:432).
86 *JQA* 249.
87 Balentine, *Prayer in the Hebrew Bible*, 217.

atā amru llāhi fa-lā tastaʿjilūhu subḥānahū wa-taʿālā ʿammā yushrikūna

yunazzilu l-malāʾikata bi-r-rūḥi min amrihī ʿalā man yashāʾu min ʿibādihī an andhirū annahū lā ilāha illā ana fa-ttaqūni

God's command has come;
so do[P] not seek to hasten it.
Praise be to Him,
and may He be exalted away from what they associate [with Him].

He sends down the angels with the Spirit
[that comes] from His command
upon those of His servants that He wishes,
saying, 'Give warning that there is no God but Me,
and be pious towards Me.'

Mirroring the opening summons to praise, verse 17 closes the hymn with the singular "formula of incomparability" (*a-fa-man...ka-man lā*)[88]:

a-fa-man yakhluqu ka-man lā yakhluqu a-fa-lā tadhakkarūna

Is He who creates like the one who does not create?
Will you not be reminded?

In effect, this literary device forms an enclosure around the core hymn to creation.[89] Bell observes that "verse 17 draws the lesson of the preceding passage in the form of a question. Creation is the prerogative of God and places Him far above the other gods."[90] Moreover, the rhetorical question functions as a catchword.[91] In point of fact, remembrance as a theme occurs as early as verse 13.[92] Jones holds that there is a strong underlying cohesion in the "refrain-like *in that there are signs*."[93] In other words, these signs (*āyāt*) foreground certain

88 *FOTL* 14:259–60.
89 Dirk J. Human, "Psalm 136: A Liturgy with Reference to Creation and History," in *Psalms and Liturgy*, ed. idem and Cas J.A. Vos (London: T&T Clark International, 2004), 76 and 84.
90 *BCQ* 1:434.
91 Jonathan Magonet, "On Reading Psalms as Liturgy: Psalms 96–99," in *The Shape and Shaping of the Book of Psalms: The Current State of Scholarship*, ed. Nancy L. deClaissé-Walford (Atlanta, Georgia: SBL Press, 2014), 162.
92 Cf. *JQA* 249.
93 Ibid. This refrain appears again in Q. 16, vv. 65, 67, 69, and 79.

unique traits of God the creator.[94] For that reason, this "antiphonal element" brings together the composition.[95] Verses 11 through 13 of this rural hymn read,

> *yunbitu lakum bihi z-zarʿa wa-z-zaytūna wa-n-nakhīla wa-l-aʿnāba wa-min kulli th-thamarāti inna fī dhālika la-āyatan li-qawmin yatafakkarūna*
>
> *wa-sakhkhara lakumu l-layla wa-n-nahāra wa-sh-shamsa wa-l-qamara wa-n-nujūmu mu-sakhkharātun bi-amrihī inna fī dhālika la-āyātin li-qawmin yaʿqilūna*
>
> *wa-mā dharaʾa lakum fī l-arḍi mukhtalifan alwānuhū inna fī dhālika la-āyatan li-qawmin yadhdhakkarūna*

> With it He causes crops,
> olives, palms, and vines and all kinds of fruit,
> to grow for you.
> In that there is a sign for people who reflect.
>
> He has subjected night and day and the sun and moon to your service,
> and the stars too are held subject by His command.
> In that there are signs for a people who understand.
>
> And whatever He has created for you
> in the earth in various colors;
> In that there is a sign for those who are reminded.

In addition to linkages and liturgical features, a critical element of the liturgy genre is narrative.[96] That is, a narrative leitmotif undergirds the hymn form.[97]

---

94 Robinson, *Discovering the Qurʾān*, 109.

95 S.v. Form and Structure, *EQ*; *BCQ* 1:433; Human, "Psalm 136," 78 and 86; Magonet, "On Reading Psalms as Liturgy," 162.

96 For the five elements that constitute the liturgy genre, see Magonet, "On Reading Psalms as Liturgy," 162–64. In terms of the *actio* of liturgy in Pss 96–99, Magonet notes that "the texts themselves are merely the raw material around which the liturgical event is staged" (ibid., 162–63 and 175). He further states that "it is nevertheless interesting to ask whether and how they might have functioned as liturgy" (ibid., 161). In addition, Human states, regarding Ps 136, "If this static poem is translated and transferred into a vivid and lively situation it becomes intelligible as a liturgy in the cult" (idem, "Psalm 136," 86). Finally, he concludes, "Despite all these possibilities there is no thrust for fixing the text to a single cultic setting in life in terms of the cultic tradition. To give thanks to Yahweh by means of praise, especially where his character and deeds are concerned, anticipates many cultic occasions where he could be exalted with this litany-structured liturgy. This life-bringing recitation and reenactment of Yahweh's deeds of creation and salvation should not in any way be restricted to single events" (ibid., 85).

97 Magonet, "On Reading Psalms as Liturgy," 162; Human, "Psalm 136," 76.

Alongside the primary creation story is the narration of signs (vv. 3–16) stressing the unity of God.[98] Therefore, it is only fitting that the *āyāt* sequence in this hymn to creation begins with a catchword (*khalaqa*).[99] Naturally, the account relates both the formation of the cosmos and the fashioning of man (vv. 3–4):

khalaqa s-samāwāti wa-l-arḍa bi-l-ḥaqqi taʿālā ʿammā yushrikūna

khalaqa l-insāna min nuṭfatin fa-idhā huwa khaṣīmun mubīnun

He has created the heavens and the earth in truth.
May He be exalted away from what they associate [with Him].

He has created man from a drop of sperm,
and there man is – a persuasive disputant.

In sum, the hymn to creation recounts the origin of the world as manifest in signs.[100]

Hymn to the Creator of Humanity

In addition to praising creation, the corpus preserves hymns to the creator of humankind. For example, consider Q. 53.43–49, which takes the divine predicate[101]:

wa-annahū huwa aḍḥaka wa-abkā

wa-annahū huwa amāta wa-aḥyā

wa-annahū khalaqa z-zawjayni dh-dhakara wa-l-unthā

min nuṭfatin idhā tumnā

wa-anna ʿalayhi n-nashʾata l-ukhrā

wa-annahū huwa aghnā wa-aqnā

---

98 Magonet, "On Reading Psalms as Liturgy," 162–63 and 174; *SKMS*² 300; Neuwirth, "Two Views of History and Human Future," 3.
99 Human, "Psalm 136," 76; *JQA* 249; *SKMS*² 300.
100 *BCQ* 1:434; *SKMS*² 300.
101 *SKMS*² 194.

wa-annahū huwa rabbu sh-shiʿrā

And that it is He who makes [men] laugh and makes [them] weep,

And that it is He who makes [men] die and makes [them] live,

And that He created the two pairs, male and female,

From a drop of sperm when it was ejaculated,

And that on Him rests the second growth,

And that it is He who gives wealth and riches,

And that it is He who is the Lord of Sirius.

As evident in the first line, this hymn even conveys God's special affection for His creatures.[102] In terms of motif, Neuwirth characterizes it as a hymn to His almighty powers.[103] On the one hand, the presence of this hymn form marks the height of its development in the mature corpus.[104] But, on the other hand, in terms of literary structure, Q. 53.43–49 is a headless hymn. That is to say, the opening-invocation, the imperative-summons, and motive-sentence are altogether missing.[105] Furthermore, the end-blessing is omitted as well. Barely the body of praise-statements remains intact in this fragmentary hymn.

Hymn to the Creator of the World

The corpus also includes hymns that focus on praising God the creator.[106] For instance, Sūrat Yūnus (Q. 10.3–6) preserves a hymn to the creator of the world. Jones notes that these liturgical verses constitute an *āyāt* piece fairly

---

102 Gunkel, "Psalmen," col. 1614. Jones notes, "Sirius was associated by early Arabs with very hot weather ('dog days')" (*JQA* 490, fn. 5).
103 *SKMS*[2] 194.
104 Ibid., 194 and 207–9; Westermann, *Der Psalter*, 78–80; Farris, *Hymns*, 120.
105 Farris, *Hymns*, 120. Robinson claims, "The signs section in Q. 53.43–49 also appears to be hymnic. The absence of a bidding in this instance is explained by the fact that it is part of a summary of the teaching of previous scriptures" (idem, *Discovering the Qur'ān*, 110).
106 Westermann, *Der Psalter*, 26.

brief in length.[107] The first verses (vv. 3–4) open with an iterated mixed liturgical formula (*rabb* and *allāh*) immediately followed by divine predication:

inna rabbakumu llāhu lladhī khalaqa s-samāwāti wa-l-arḍa fī sittati ayyāmin thumma stawā ʿalā l-ʿarshi yudabbiru l-amra mā min shafīʿin illā min baʿdi idhnihī dhālikumu llāhu rabbukum fa-ʿbudūhu a-fa-lā tadhakkarūna

ilayhi marjiʿukum jamīʿan waʿda llāhi ḥaqqan innahū yabdaʾu l-khalqa thumma yuʿīduhū li-yajziya lladhīna āmanū wa-ʿamilū ṣ-ṣāliḥāti bi-l-qisṭi wa-lladhīna kafarū lahum sharābun min ḥamīmin wa-ʿadhābun alīmun bi-mā kānū yakfurūna

Your[P] Lord is God,
who created the heavens and the earth in six days,
then set Himself on the Throne,
directing the affair.
There is no intercessor unless He has given His permission.
That is God, your Lord.
So serve Him.
Will you not be reminded?

To Him is the return for all of you[P]
– the promise of God is true.
He originates creation,
then causes it to return,
so that He may reward with equity
those who believe and do deeds of righteousness.
And those who disbelieve
– they will have a drink of boiling water and a painful punishment
in return for their disbelief.

Significantly, Neuwirth considers Q. 10.3–4 a hymn and verses 5 through 6 hymnical *āyāt*.[108] Verses 5 to 6 read,

huwa lladhī jaʿala sh-shamsa ḍiyāʾan wa-l-qamara nūran wa-qaddarahū manāzila li-taʿlamū ʿadada s-sinīna wa-l-ḥisāba mā khalaqa llāhu dhālika illā bi-l-ḥaqqi yufaṣṣilu l-āyāti li-qawmin yaʿlamūna

inna fī khtilāfi l-layli wa-n-nahāri wa-mā khalaqa llāhu fī s-samāwāti wa-l-arḍi la-āyātin li-qawmin yattaqūna

107 *JQA* 195.
108 *SKMS*² 294.

It is He who made the sun an illumination and the moon a light,
and decreed for it mansions,
that you^{P} might know the number of years and the reckoning [of time].
God created that only with the truth,
detailing the signs to a people who know.

In the alternation of night and day
and in what God created
in the heavens and the earth
are signs for people who fear God.

Bell notes that these verses (vv. 3–6) are altogether directed at the assembly.[109] In fact, the final rhetorical line of verse 3 and its end rhyme (*-ūC*) are identical to those found in the hymn to creation (Q. 16.17) in Sūrat an-Naḥl. Put otherwise, Q. 10.3–6 and Q. 16.1–17 "form a single, coherent liturgical unit, made up of alternating hymns."[110]

Hymn to the God of Salvation History

According to Westermann, "the praise of God's majesty divides into the praise of the creator and the praise of the lord of history."[111] In other words, hymns to the lord of salvation history developed into a prominent motif wherein "God shows His lordship and majesty."[112] In fact, it "gradually expanded and finally became an independent entity."[113] What is more, this mixed hymn form "penetrated the community laments."[114] Take, for instance, Sūrat Ṣād (Q. 38.41–44), which incorporates a familiar Jobian lament and begins with the singular imperative "remember" (*udhkur*) directed at the recitant.[115] Significantly, the refrain throughout this hymnic pericope (Q. 38.41–49) represents the elaboration of this motif.[116] Evidently, "it combined with forms of wisdom speech."[117] For example, verses 45 through 49 read,

---

109 *BCQ* 1:327.
110 Magonet, "On Reading Psalms as Liturgy," 173 and 175–76; Gunkel, "Psalmen," col. 1626.
111 Westermann, *Der Psalter*, 26; idem, *Psalms*, 26.
112 Westermann, *Der Psalter*, 26 (Ps 105) and 75; idem, *Psalms*, 90.
113 Westermann, *Der Psalter*, 26, 75–76, and 80; idem, *Psalms*, 95.
114 Westermann, *Der Psalter*, 80; idem, *Psalms*, 96.
115 Baumstark, *Liturgie comparée*, 84–85.
116 Westermann, *Der Psalter*, 80.
117 Ibid.; Westermann, *Psalms*, 96.

wa-dhkur ʿibādanā ibrāhīma wa-isḥāqa wa-yaʿqūba ulī l-aydī wa-l-abṣāri

innā akhlaṣnāhum bi-khāliṣatin dhikrā d-dāri

wa-innahum ʿindanā la-mina l-muṣṭafayna l-akhyāri

wa-dhkur ismāʿīla wa-l-yasaʿa wa-dhā l-kifli wa-kullun mina l-akhyāri

hādhā dhikrun wa-inna li-l-muttaqīna la-ḥusna maʾābin

Remember Our servants Abraham and Isaac and Jacob,
men of might and vision.

We distinguished them with a pure quality,
remembrance of the Abode.

With Us they are of the chosen, the good.

Remember Ishmael and al-Yasaʿ and Dhū l-Kifl.
Each [of them] is one of the chosen.

This is a reminder.
For those who protect themselves there is a fair resort.

Westermann says that this kind of historical discourse "is ultimately always aimed at the instruction and admonition of contemporaries."[118] Naturally, the first occurrence of the refrain (Q. 38.17) in this sūra-unit follows an itemized list of punishment stories (Q. 38.12–15) and corresponding prayer form (Q. 38.16)[119]:

kadhdhabat qablahum qawmu nūḥin wa-ʿādun wa-firʿawnu dhū l-awtādi

wa-thamūdu wa-qawmu lūṭin wa-aṣḥābu l-aykati ulāʾika l-aḥzābu

in kullun illā kadhdhaba r-rusula fa-ḥaqqa ʿiqābi

wa-mā yanẓuru hāʾulāʾi illā ṣayḥatan wāḥidatan mā lahā min fawāqin

wa-qālū rabbanā ʿajjil lanā qiṭṭanā qabla yawmi l-ḥisābi

118 Ibid.
119 *SKMS*^{2} 282.

Before them the people of Noah denied,
[as did] ʿĀd and Pharaoh,
the man with the pegs,

And Thamūd and the people of Lot
and the men of the thicket
– they were the parties.

Every one of them denied the truth of the messengers,
and My punishment was justified.

These wait only for one Shout
from which there is no respite.

They say:
Our Lord,
hasten for us our share before the Day of Reckoning.

As illustrated, hymns to the lord of salvation history assimilated prophetic motifs.[120]

Hymn to the God of Salvation

On the basis of a characteristic end rhyme (*-āC*), it is possible to locate a qur'ānic hymn composed of a liturgical summons and five serial units (Q. 3.191a-94):

rabbanā mā khalaqta hādhā bāṭilan subḥānaka fa-qinā ʿadhāba n-nāri

rabbanā innaka man tudkhili n-nāra fa-qad akhzaytahū wa-mā li-ẓ-ẓālimīna min anṣārin

rabbanā innanā samiʿnā munādiyan yunādī li-l-īmāni an āminū bi-rabbikum fa-āmannā

rabbanā fa-ghfir lanā dhunūbanā wa-kaffir ʿannā sayyiātinā wa-tawaffanā maʿa l-abrāri

rabbanā wa-ātinā mā waʿadttanā ʿalā rusulika wa-lā tukhzinā yawma l-qiyāmati innaka lā tukhlifu l-mīʿāda

Our Lord,
You did not create this in vain.

Praise be to You.

120 Westermann, *Der Psalter*, 80.

Preserve us from the torment of the Fire.

Our Lord,
those whom You cause to enter the Fire,
You have abased them.
The wrong-doers have no helpers.

Our Lord,
we have heard someone calling [us] to the faith, saying,
"Believe[P] in your Lord" and we have believed.

Our Lord,
forgive us our sins,
and acquit us of our evil deeds,
and take us with the pious.

Our Lord,
give us what You have promised us through Your messengers.
Do not shame us on the Day of Resurrection.
You will not break the tryst.

Moreover, this identification assists in drawing the structural lines between literary units. Nagel, for example, considers verses 192 through 198 as the appropriate borders of this particular unit.[121] Jones, on the other hand, correctly asserts that verses 191 to 194 demarcate the boundaries of this "hymn-like passage."[122] On the reasonable grounds that *subḥānaka* ("Praise be to You") in verse 191a functions as a doxological opening, Baumstark also argues for the compositional integrity of the cluster (Q. 3.191a-94).[123] The fact that these verses "return to the rhyme in *-ā(C)* which prevails at the beginning of the sūra" is sufficient grounds to support the supposition that this cluster constitutes a whole.[124] The presence of the introductory cultic formula, *rabbanā*, immediately preceding *subḥānaka* renders the latter an embedded and therefore localized summons.[125] In light of these formal considerations, it is evident that this hymn is comprised of five commensurable units (Q. 3.191–94). Additionally, this verse-group represents a

121 Cf. Nagel, *Der Koran*, 84–85.
122 *JQA* 64.
123 Cf. Baumstark, "Jüdischer und christlicher Gebetstypus im Koran," 239.
124 *BCQ* 1:103; cf. Hermann Gunkel, "The Close of Micah: A Prophetical Liturgy, A Study in Literary History," in *What Remains of the Old Testament and Other Essays*, trans. A.K. Dallas (New York: The Macmillan Company, 1928), 148–49.
125 Hainsworth, *Iliad*, 3:7–9.

formal hymn, since it stands out from its literary surroundings.[126] Upon Bell's suggestion, it bears a striking resemblance to the hymnic verse-pair above (Q. 3.8–9).[127] However, note the shift in pronoun usage in verse 194 and verse 9. Jones puts forward the tentative claim that verses 1–9 together form a liturgical piece.[128] The purported link between Q. 3.1–7 and the verse-pair (Q. 3.8–9) is facilitated by a partial prefatory verse (Q. 3.7a) bearing a similar end rhyme (*-āC*). It reads,

> *āmannā bihī kullun min ʿindi rabbinā wa-mā yadhdhakkaru illā ulū l-albābi*
>
> We believe in it. All is from our Lord (*rabbanā*).
> Only men of understanding are reminded.

Putting this hypothesis aside for the moment, the fact remains that the rhyme scheme *-ā(C)* between the two hymnic pericopae (Q. 3.191a-94 and Q. 3.8–9) is consistent; moreover both closing refrains – apart from localization – are virtually identical in motif, structure, and language. This all the more lends credence to Bell's observation regarding these mirrored rhyme-phrases; as a matter of fact, combined – these two pericopae constitute a substantial hymn.[129]

In terms of identifying the particular form of this hymn, Westermann recognizes "two basic modes of speaking to God, praise and petition."[130] Specifically, communal laments represent a significant variety of petition.[131] Moreover, within liturgical contexts, Gunkel relates, there is a time for everything, a time to praise and a time to lament.[132] The literary structure of these communal petitions consists of five speech elements: invocation, lament, declaration of trust, petition, and praise-vow.[133] Besides adding and subtracting elements, Westermann acknowledges the possibility of alternative constructions.[134] In this particular verse-group (Q. 3.191a-94 and Q. 3.8–9), *rabbanā* ("Our Lord") doubles as a hymnic refrain. In this formal hymn, the declaration of trust takes precedence ("You did not create this in vain"). Moreover, an embedded liturgical summons to

126 Cf. *BCQ* 1:103.
127 Cf. ibid.
128 *JQA* 64.
129 Cf. *BCQ* 1:103.
130 Claus Westermann, *Das Loben Gottes in den Psalmen*, 2nd rev. ed. (Göttingen: Vandenhoeck & Ruprecht, 1961), 28; Farris, *Hymns*, 71.
131 Farris, *Hymns*, 71.
132 Gunkel, "Psalmen," col. 1614.
133 Westermann, *Das Loben Gottes in den Psalmen*, 39; cf. Bautch, *Developments in Genre*, 36.
134 Westermann, *Das Loben Gottes in den Psalmen*, 39.

praise (v. 191b) substitutes for the praise-vow.[135] Thereafter, the petition is expressed as a double-wish.[136] Westermann explains this as "a wish or a petition that simultaneously is expressed in two directions. May God do thus to our enemies; may God do thus to us."[137] The first-part of the petition is expressed in the imperative ("preserve us"), followed by the fate of the sinners. The petition element is especially prominent in this hymn (e. g., vv. 194–95 and v. 8). There is "a tendency for the petition to expand and for the lament to disappear…."[138]

The above liturgy (Q. 3.191a-94) is a particularly instructive formal hymn. In addition, consider the compositional integrity of a hymn embedded within an Abrahamic narrative that commences (Q. 2.127):

wa-idh yarfaʿu ibrāhīmu l-qawāʿida mina l-bayti wa-ismāʿīlu

And when Abraham and Ishmael were raising the foundations of the house –

The embedded hymn immediately follows (Q. 2.127a-29):

rabbanā taqabbal minnā innaka anta s-samīʿu l-ʿalīmu

rabbanā wa-jʿalnā muslimayni laka wa-min dhurriyyatinā ummatan muslimatan laka wa-arinā manāsikanā wa-tub ʿalaynā innaka anta t-tawwābu r-raḥīmu

rabbanā wa-bʿath fīhim rasūlan minhum yatlū ʿalayhim āyātika wa-yuʿallimuhumu l-kitāba wa-l-ḥikmata wa-yuzakkīhim innaka anta l-ʿazīzu l-ḥakīmu

Our Lord,
accept [this] from us.
You are the Hearer and the Knower.

Our Lord,
make us surrender to You
and make from our seed a community that will surrender to You,
and show us Your rites,
and relent towards us.
You are the Relenting and the Merciful.

Our Lord,
raise up among them a messenger,

---

135 Ibid., 41.
136 Ibid., 39.
137 Ibid., 39, fn. 1; Claus Westermann, *Praise and Lament in the Psalms*, trans. Keith R. Crim and Richard N. Soulen (Atlanta, Georgia: John Knox Press, 1981), 52, fn. 1.
138 Westermann, *Das Loben Gottes in den Psalmen*, 39; idem, *Praise and Lament*, 55.

[who is one] of themselves,
who will recite Your signs to them
and will teach them the Scripture and the Wisdom
and will purify them.
You are the Mighty and the Wise.

These three verses constitute a hymn on two grounds: (i) the liturgical refrain (*rabbanā*) and (ii) the closing rhyme pattern (-*īC*) accomplished by means of epithets.[139] The end rhyme in fact establishes the textual progression from the opening verses of Sūrat al-Baqara to this exact hymn.[140] Verses Q. 2.1–2 read,

alif-lām-mīm

dhālika l-kitābu lā rayba fīhi hudan li-l-muttaqīna

Alif Lām Mīm

This is the Scripture
in which there is no doubt,
a guidance for those who protect themselves.

Although the shared rhyme scheme (-*īC*) appears to keep these two verses intact (as reflected in the subsequent shift in verse Q. 2.3 to -*ūC*), Bell in an analogous case, proposes that verse 1 alone, prior to the allusion to scripture (*al-kitāb*), represents the actual header for verses Q. 2.127a-29.[141] This suggestion is, however, problematic in light of Irfan Shahîd's view pertaining to the *vexata quaestio.*[142] He observes that "the 29 sūras...all, with only two exceptions, share the fact that the Qur'ān is referred to after the *fawātiḥ* at the beginning of the sūras."[143] In other words, these non-lexical vocable summonses tend to precede the mention of scripture.[144] Thus the integrity of Q 2.1–2 as an opening cueing and framing device is virtually assured.

139 See Devin J. Stewart, "Divine Epithets and the *Dibacchius: Clausulae* and Qur'ānic Rhythm," *JQS* 15, no. 2 (2013): 22–64.
140 Cf. *BCQ* 1:103.
141 Cf. ibid.
142 Irfan Shahîd, "*Fawātiḥ al-Suwar:* The Mysterious Letters of the Qur'ān," in *Literary Structures of Religious Meaning in the Qur'ān*, ed. Issa J. Boullata (New York: Routledge, 2000), 136.
143 Ibid., 139, fn. 25.
144 Ibid.; for the "*voces mysticae* and other forms of 'unintelligible' writing," see John G. Gager, introduction to *Curse Tablets and Binding Spells from the Ancient World* (Oxford: Oxford University Press, 1992), 6–7; for "theurgy," see ibid., 9 and 34, fn. 42; for the "ritual use" of letters, see

Hymn to Victory

According to Gerstenberger, biblical victory hymns fall under the rubric of praise.[145] Moreover, Westermann recognizes the difficulties faced in differentiating single-sentence declarative psalms of praise from victory hymns.[146] For example, consider the simplicity of the literalized victory hymn preserved in Sūrat al-Fatḥ (Q. 48.1)[147]:

innā fataḥnā laka fatḥan mubīnan

We have given you^{S} a clear victory.

In fact, this sentential hymn expands considerably.[148] Take, for instance, three verses that follow with a shared end-rhyme (-*Can*). In particular, note the marked shift in pronouns (vv. 2–4):

li-yaghfira laka llāhu mā taqaddama min dhanbika wa-mā ta'akhkhara wa-yutimma ni'matahū 'alayka wa-yahdiyaka ṣirāṭan mustaqīman

wa-yanṣuraka llāhu naṣran 'azīzan

huwa lladhī anzala s-sakīnata fī qulūbi l-mu'minīna li-yazdādū īmānan ma'a īmānihim wa-li-llāhi junūdu s-samāwāti wa-l-arḍi wa-kāna llāhu 'alīman ḥakīman

That God may forgive you^{S} your past sin
and your sin which is to come,
and that He may complete His blessing to you
and guide you on a straight path,

And that God may help you with mighty help.

He, who sent down the reassurance into the hearts of the believers
that they might add faith to their faith

---

ibid., 34, fn. 40. Gager states that "traditionally, these 'unintelligible' forms of speech have been treated as meaningless gibberish or nonsense. To be fair, such interpretations are not modern inventions but reach back to ancient critics...Only recently have efforts been made to reverse these effects, efforts directed at understanding the foundations of such beliefs..." (ibid., 9).

145 *FOTL* 14:257; Westermann, *Das Loben Gottes in den Psalmen*, 67.

146 Westermann, *Das Loben Gottes in den Psalmen*, 69.

147 Ibid., 67.

148 For example, Gerstenberger states, "From these primitive chants developed artistic poems narrating the course of events and extolling the heroes" (*FOTL* 14:257).

– To God belong the hosts of the heavens and the earth;
God is Knowing and Wise.

In light of that, Westermann observes, "this small variation gives an indication of the way in which a song which originally consisted of a single sentence, or rather a mere shout of joy, could gradually grow into a song."[149] As a matter of fact, this victory cry continues to grow through the incorporation of multiple speech-forms, until it constitutes an independent sūra-unit (*-Can*).

What is more, befitting its superscription, Sūrat al-Fatḥ develops a hymnic refrain functioning in tandem with a variable rhyme-phrase.[150] Mirroring the close of verse 4, the double-refrain appears again (v. 7):

wa-li-llāhi junūdu s-samāwāti wa-l-arḍi wa-kāna llāhu ʿazīzan ḥakīman

– To God belong the hosts of the heavens and the earth.
God is Mighty and Wise.

This is all the more reason to consider at least the initial outgrowth of the first verse a short victory hymn (vv. 1–7). Furthermore, this is supported by the reversion (v. 8) to the first-person plural pronoun. In terms of its life setting, Westermann informs us that these victory hymns were transmitted "as a part of the celebration in a service of worship after the overcoming of the foe."[151] Nonetheless, this is a headless and tailless hymn, since it opens without an invocation and summons, and it closes on a refrain. Although standing alone, it is noteworthy in the present context that this exact rhyme-phrase (*wa-kāna llāhu ʿazīzan ḥakīman*) reappears in verse 19.[152] Conforming to the same end rhyme pattern (*-Can*), the conjoining hymnic fragment (vv. 18–20) reads,

la-qad raḍiya llāhu ʿani l-muʾminīna idh yubāyiʿūnaka taḥta sh-shajarati fa-ʿalima mā fī qulūbihim fa-anzala s-sakīnata ʿalayhim wa-athābahum fatḥan qarīban

wa-maghānima kathīratan yaʾkhudhūnahā wa-kāna llāhu ʿazīzan ḥakīman

wa ʿadakumu llāhu maghānima kathīratan taʾkhudhūnahā fa-ʿajjala lakum hādhihī wa-kaffa aydiya n-nāsi ʿankum wa-li-takūna āyatan li-l-muʾminīna wa-yahdiyakum ṣirāṭan mustaqī-

149 Westermann, *Das Loben Gottes in den Psalmen*, 67; idem, *Praise and Lament*, 90.
150 *BIQ*[1] 69–71.
151 Westermann, *Das Loben Gottes in den Psalmen*, 68; idem, *Praise and Lament*, 91.
152 *BIQ*[1] 70. In fact, the corpus evidences twenty-five occurrences of this particular oral-formula (s.v. ʿAzīz, *CQ*).

man

God was pleased with the believers
when they swore allegiance to you^{S} under the tree,
and He knew what was in their hearts.
And so He sent down reassurance to them
and rewarded them with a victory near at hand,

And numerous spoils to take.
God is Mighty and Wise.

God has promised you^{P} numerous spoils to take,
and has hastened these to you,
and has restrained the hands of the people from you.
[This is] so that it may be a sign to the believers
and that He may guide you on a straight path.

This second fragment also reflects prevalent victory hymn motifs; in particular, the reference to spoils of war (*maghānim*), victory (*fatḥ*), and most subtly, hands (*aydiya*).[153] The latter figure of speech reoccurs in verse 24:

wa-huwa lladhī kaffa aydiyahum ʿankum wa-aydiyakum ʿanhum bi-baṭni makkata min baʿdi an aẓfarakum ʿalayhim wa-kāna llāhu bi-mā taʿmalūna baṣīran

He, who has restrained their hands from you^{P}
and your hands from them in the valley of Mecca,
after He had made you victors over them.
God is observer of what you do.

Significantly, Bell notes that this verse addresses a conquest, "had fighting taken place."[154] Therefore, the short formulaic expression (*kaffa aydiya-... ʿan-*) tends to be associated with the eschatological victory song.[155] For example, in verses 18–20 there is "the promise that there will be a *fatḥ*, a 'clearing up,' or 'victory'

153 Cf. Westermann, *Das Loben Gottes in den Psalmen*, 67 (Judg 16:23–24) and 68–69. This figure of speech occurs in Q. 48.20.
154 *BCQ* 2:285.
155 In fact, the third and last occurrence of this short phrase (perf. act.) occurs in Q. 5.11 in conjunction with a "threatened attack" (ibid., 1:151; s.v. Kaffa, *CQ*; Westermann, *Das Loben Gottes in den Psalmen*, 68–69; Gerhard von Rad, *Der Heilige Krieg im alten Israel*, 4th ed. (Göttingen: Vandenhoeck & Ruprecht, 1965), 7–9; cf. A.S. Kapelrud, review of *The Divine Warrior in Early Israel*, by P.D. Miller, Jr., *JSS* 20, no. 1 (1975): 116–17; Crenshaw, *Gerhard von Rad*, 169–70).

in the near future, and plenty of spoil."[156] In addition, Sūrat al-Fatḥ features a subsequent fragment (v. 27):

la-qad ṣadaqa llāhu rasūlahu r-ru'yā bi-l-ḥaqqi la-tadkhulunna l-masjida l-ḥarāma in shā'a llāhu āminīna muḥalliqīna ru'ūsakum wa-muqaṣṣirīna lā takhāfūna fa-ʿalima mā lam taʿlamū fa-jaʿala min dūni dhālika fatḥan qarīban

God has fulfilled in truth the vision he gave to His messenger:
you[P] will enter the sacred mosque,
if God wills, in security,
your heads shaven, your hair cut short, not fearing.
He knew what you did not know;
and He has appointed before that a victory near at hand.

Since it likewise alludes to *fatḥan qarīban*, these hymns were composed "for the future victory feast."[157] Having discussed at length multiple hymn forms, let us now turn our attention to the litany form of liturgy.

Litany of Praise

Litanies are classed according to a twofold typology that includes litany of praise and litany of lament.[158] For instance, consider Sūrat ar-Raḥmān, which constitutes a litany of praise.[159] The pervasive refrain is perhaps the most distinctive feature of this *locus classicus*.[160] Q. 55.13 reads,

156 *BCQ* 2:284.

157 Westermann, *Das Loben Gottes in den Psalmen*, 68, fn. 43 (Ps 149); idem, *Praise and Lament*, 92, fn. 43.

158 Litany of petition constitutes a third form (Human, "Psalm 136," 73).

159 Angelika Neuwirth, "Qur'ānic Literary Structure Revisited: Sūrat ar-Raḥmān between Mythic Account and Decodation of Myth," in *Story-Telling in the Framework of Non-fictional Arabic Literature*, ed. Stefan Leder (Wiesbaden: Harrassowitz Verlag, 1998), 392.

160 Goitein, "Das Gebet im Qorān," 93–97. "The refrain is much less frequent in sūras 37 and 54" (Neuwirth, "Qur'ānic Literary Structure Revisited," 396, fn. 34). Bell notes, "This refrain has the pronoun in the dual throughout, the sūra being understood as addressed to men and *jinn*" (*BQA* 2:548; *JQA* 494, fn. 2). Rudi Paret (d. 1983) also posits, "Es ist nicht ersichtlich, warum er gerade in Vers 13 einsetzt, und nicht schon früher" (*Komm* 466). Moreover, Jones comments that "it is unlike most other refrains in the Qur'ān, as it is essentially external to the structure of the sūra: a viable piece remains if the refrains are ignored" (*JQA* 494). Likewise, Bell "further suggests that the refrain might have been added later" (Muhammad Abdel Haleem, "Context and Internal Relationships: Keys to Qur'ānic Exegesis: A Study of Sūrat al-Raḥmān," in *Approaches to the Qur'ān*, ed. Gerald R. Hawting and Abdul-Kader A. Shareef (London: Routledge, 1993), 80). However, "Bell does not support his suggestion that the material was at one time used without

fa-bi-ayyi ālā'i rabbikumā tukadhdhibāni

So which of your Lord's bounties will you both deny?

"By virtue of the refrain that pervades the entire text," Neuwirth concludes, "the sūra takes on the aspect of an integral liturgical text."[161] Moreover, Tucker remarks that generic considerations factor in determining how it takes shape in literature and where it is situated in life.[162] The literary structure of the litany form consists of a "series of brief acts of prayer and praise with a fixed response."[163] Therefore, Q. 55 is "a text to be recited *by* the community who evoke for themselves the divine acts of creation and His promise of paradise in a kind of litany, i.e., an antiphonal text based on repeated structural elements."[164] In point of fact, Wansbrough considers the refrain to be "the response formula of a litany."[165]

This litany of mercy, accordingly, begins *ar-raḥmān* (Q. 55.1), which "indicates the one who actively issues mercy, i.e., who extends benefits and favor."[166] This is significant since the first pericope constitutes a hymn.[167] In

the refrain" (ibid.; *BQA* 2:548–52). N.b. "Abdel Haleem's approach," according to Neuwirth, "rests on the canonized codex, the *muṣḥaf*" (eadem, "Two Views of History and Human Future," 8). Neuwirth's "historical-critical approach," on the other hand, "relies on the qur'ānic communication process, *qur'ān*" (ibid.).

161 Neuwirth, "Two Views of History and Human Future," 10. Furthermore, Neuwirth refers to Q. 55 as "a nearly pure hymn" (eadem, "Qur'ānic Literary Structure Revisited," 394). For the "rereading of a hymn," see Albert Gelin, "La question des 'relectures' bibliques à l'intérieur d'une tradition vivante," in *Sacra Pagina*, ed. Joseph Coppens, Albert Descamps, and Édouard Massaux (Gembloux, Belgium: J. Duculot, 1959), 1:303–15; Clines, *On the Way to the Postmodern*, 2:680–82; Neuwirth, "Qur'ānic Readings of the Psalms," 746–75 (Ps 136 and Q. 55); de Prémare, *Aux origines du Coran*, 38 (Ps 136 and Q. 55).

162 Regarding Ps 136, see Tucker, *Form Criticism of the Old Testament*, 16.

163 Evelyn Underhill, *Worship* (New York: Harper & Brothers Publishers, 1957 [1936]), 100; Heiler, *Das Gebet*, 55; cf. Baumstark, *Liturgie comparée*, 83.

164 Neuwirth, "Two Views of History and Human Future," 11.

165 Neuwirth, "Qur'ānic Literary Structure Revisited," 393; cf. Abdel Haleem, "Context and Internal Relationships," 80 and 93. In a well-known passage, Wansbrough states, "I should like here to insist upon the term litany rather than refrain. The role of the latter in the Qur'ān and elsewhere, is that of concluding formula, which does not adequately describe employment of the device in this passage" (*QS* 25–26).

166 Abdel Haleem, "Context and Internal Relationships," 96–97; Neuwirth, "Qur'ānic Literary Structure Revisited," 393, fn. 23, and 408, fn. 57.

167 *SKMS*[2] 209; Neuwirth, "Two Views of History and Human Future," 3; eadem, "Symmetrie und Paarbildung in der koranischen Eschatologie: Philologisch-Stilistisches zu Sūrat ar-Raḥmān," in *Mélanges de l'Université Saint-Joseph* 50 (1984): 457.

point of fact, Q. 55.1–16 conforms to the literary structure of hymns.[168] A literalized liturgical summons (vv. 2–4) – echoing the imperative hymn (Q. 96.1–5) – immediately follows the opening invocation (v. 1).[169] The anacrusis (Q. 55.1–4) reads[170]:

ar-raḥmānu

ʻallama l-qurʾāna

khalaqa l-insāna

ʻallamahu l-bayāna

The Merciful

He has taught the Recitation,

Created man,

Taught him exposition.

Thereafter come the motive clauses (vv. 5–6):

ash-shamsu wa-l-qamaru bi-ḥusbānin

wa-n-najmu wa-sh-shajaru yasjudāni

The sun and moon are in a reckoning.

The stars and the trees bow down.

Addressing celestial and terrestrial phenomena, Neuwirth considers these to be a verse-pair.[171] Then follows a series of intensifying praise statements; these hymnical *āyāt* (vv. 7–12) read,

---

168 Cf. *SKMS*² 209; Neuwirth, "Two Views of History and Human Future," 3–4; eadem, "Qurʾānic Literary Structure Revisited," 400–405.
169 Neuwirth concurs that "verses 1–4 resound Q. 96.1–4" (eadem, "Qurʾānic Literary Structure Revisited," 394, fn. 24); cf. Robinson, *Discovering the Qurʾān*, 110.
170 *SKMS*² 209.
171 Ibid. N.b. "The stars": "Or shrubs" (*JQA* 494, fn. 1).

wa-s-samāʾa rafaʿahā wa-waḍaʿa l-mīzāna

allā taṭghaw fī l-mīzāni

wa-aqīmū l-wazna bi-l-qisṭi wa-lā tukhsirū l-mīzāna

wa-l-arḍa waḍaʿahā li-l-anāmi

fīhā fākihatun wa-n-nakhlu dhātu l-akmāmi

wa-l-ḥabbu dhū l-ʿaṣfi wa-r-rayḥānu

He has raised up the Heaven, and He has set the balance,

That you[P] may not transgress in the balance.

Perform[P] weighing with justice
and do not skimp in the balance.

He has put down the earth for all creatures;

In it there are fruit and palm trees bearing blossoms,

Husked grain and fragrant herbs.

Upon establishing the progressive litanic refrain in verse 13, the hymn continues with a doublet that assumes dynamic predication (vv. 14–15)[172]:

khalaqa l-insāna min ṣalṣālin ka-l-fakhkhāri

wa-khalaqa l-jānna min mārijin min nārin

He created man from clay like potter's clay,

And He created the *Jinn* from smokeless fire.

However, rather than presently closing the hymnic piece with an end blessing, the second refrain (v. 16) functions as a transition from hymn to litany.[173] None-

172 Neuwirth, "Two Views of History and Human Future," 8; cf. *SKMS*[2] 209.
173 Human, "Psalm 136," 79. Neuwirth considers verses 14–28 a second "hymn to God" (eadem, "Two Views of History and Human Future," 4); cf. *SKMS*[2] 209 (vv. 14–35).

theless, the long liturgy (Q. 55) ultimately concludes with a short doxology. Directed straight at the audience, verse 78 reads[174]:

> *tabāraka smu rabbika dhī l-jalāli wa-l-ikrāmi*
>
> Blessed is the name of your[S] Lord who is endowed with glory and honor.

Baumstark also explicitly refers to Q. 55.78 as the close of Sūrat ar-Raḥmān.[175] Therefore, the fifth and final liturgical element following the last refrain (v. 77) ends the litany.[176]

Concerning God's mighty works, the central litany of praise (vv. 17–32) opens with a doubled liturgical formula (*rabb*).[177] Verse 17 reads,

> *rabbu l-mashriqayni wa-rabbu l-maghribayni*
>
> The Lord of the two easts and the Lord of the two wests.

In terms of symmetry and structure, Muhammad Abdel Haleem observes, "Only when a pair is completed do we have the concluding refrain."[178] Thus verse 18 iterates the litanic refrain: "So which of your Lord's bounties will you both deny?"[179] The core litany (vv. 19–32) continues in this manner until Q. 55.33–35 introduces a new speech-form with the vocative particle (*yā-*). Verse 33 reads[180]:

> *yā-maʿshara l-jinni wa-l-insi ini staṭaʿtum an tanfudhū min aqṭāri s-samāwāti wa-l-arḍi fa-nfudhū lā tanfudhūna illā bi-sulṭānin*
>
> O company of *Jinn* and men,
> if you are able to penetrate any of the regions of the heavens and the earth,
> penetrate them.
> You will not do so without authority.

---

174 Abdel Haleem, "Context and Internal Relationships," 93.
175 Baumstark, "Jüdischer und christlicher Gebetstypus im Koran," 232.
176 *SKMS*[2] 210.
177 Ibid., 209 (vv. 14–35); Neuwirth, "Two Views of History and Human Future," 4–5. "The change here, *iltifāt*, from 'His,' third person pronoun, to the noun 'your Lord' is significant..." (Abdel Haleem, "Context and Internal Relationships," 79; Human, "Psalm 136," 83).
178 Abdel Haleem, "Context and Internal Relationships," 81 and 87; Neuwirth, "Symmetrie und Paarbildung in der koranischen Eschatologie," *passim*. Equally, Bell states, regarding sūra-units, "Their length is determined not by any consideration of form, but by the subject or incident treated in each" (*BIQ*[1] 71).
179 Human, "Psalm 136," 84.
180 Robinson, *Discovering the Qurʾān*, 118.

It cautions against the evils of transgression.[181] Once again, the litanic refrain (v. 36) facilitates a transition from warning to response. "Eschatological scenarios" begin with "preludes which catalogue the cosmic catastrophes which precede the Judgment."[182] The eschatological formula in verse 37 reads *fa-idhā:* "So when...."[183] What is more, these preludes even allude to building cases against offenders.[184] Q. 55.37–41 reads,

fa-idhā nshaqqati s-samāʾu fa-kānat wardatan ka-d-dihāni

fa-bi-ayyi ālāʾi rabbikumā tukadhdhibāni

fa-yawmaʾidhin lā yusʾalu ʿan dhanbihī insun wa-lā jānnun

fa-bi-ayyi ālāʾi rabbikumā tukadhdhibāni

yuʿrafu l-mujrimūna bi-sīmāhum fa-yuʾkhadhu bi-n-nawāṣī wa-l-aqdāmi

So when the heaven is split and turns crimson like red leather,

– So which of your Lord's bounties will you two deny?

On that day (*fa-yawmaʾidhin*)[185] neither man nor *Jinn* will be questioned about his sin.

– So which of your Lord's bounties will you two deny?

The sinners will be known by their marks,
and they will be seized by their feet and forelocks.

On this point, Neuwirth notes, with the exception of verses 37 to 44, the structure presents no difficulty.[186] The refrain (v. 42) segues into eschatology proper (vv. 43–44) with the formulaic *hādhihī jahannamu llatī* ("This is hell, which")[187]:

hādhihī jahannamu llatī yukadhdhibu bihā l-mujrimūna

181 Cf. ibid. (vv. 31–35).
182 Ibid., 103–5; Neuwirth, "Two Views of History and Human Future," 5.
183 Robinson, *Discovering the Qurʾān*, 104; *SKMS*² 191 and 210.
184 Robinson, *Discovering the Qurʾān*, 104.
185 Cf. *SKMS*² 191.
186 Ibid., 210.
187 Minimal pair (*hādhihī jahannamu llatī*): Q. 36.63 and Q. 55.43.

yaṭūfūna baynahā wa-bayna ḥamīmin ānin

This is hell, which the sinners deny;

They will circle between it and boiling hot water.

Abdel Haleem explains that "the pairing structure is maintained throughout... There is no refrain between 43 and 44 because the pair has not been completed."[188] Following the refrain (v. 45), the motif shifts to soteriology (vv. 46–76) with the formulaic *man khāfa maqāma rabbihī* ("the one who has feared the time when he will stand before his Lord").[189] The second member of the antithetic parallelism frames the extended diptych that follows.[190] Q. 55.46 reads,

wa-li-man khāfa maqāma rabbihī jannatāni

But for the one who fears the time when he will stand before his Lord
there are two gardens.

On a final note, Abdel Haleem observes that "verse 1, verse 27, and this final verse 78 fuse the whole sūra into one solid unit."[191] Significantly, verses 26 and 27 read[192]:

kullu man 'alayhā fānin

wa-yabqā wajhu rabbika dhū l-jalāli wa-l-ikrāmi

Everyone on it perishes,

But the face of your^{S} Lord, which is full of glory and honor, endures.

188 Abdel Haleem, "Context and Internal Relationships," 87.
189 Minimal pair (*man khāfa maqāma rabbihī*): Q. 55.46 and Q. 79.40.
190 Westermann, *Der Psalter*, 22; Heiler, *Das Gebet*, 158–59. "In Sūra 56, the positive panel of the diptych is further divided, thus implying a distinction between two levels of blessedness... This may also be the implication of the two pairs of gardens which feature in the previous sūra (Q. 55.46–60, 62–76)" (Robinson, *Discovering the Qur'ān*, 105–6 (*fa-man...wa-man...*); Neuwirth, "Two Views of History and Human Future," 6–7).
191 Abdel Haleem, "Context and Internal Relationships," 94.
192 "On earth" (*JQA* 495, fn. 3).

Once again, firmly directed at the listener in the responsive audience, this central verse (v. 27) resonates with the dominant motif defining this litany of praise.[193] Likewise, "the sūra closes with a final statement, a liturgical *motto*, alluding again to the *two* aspects of divinity, majesty and generosity – both of them amply demonstrated in the preceding parts of the text."[194]

Litany of Lament

Whereas the litany of mercy (Q. 55) addresses the lot of the blessed, that of the wicked falls squarely on the litany of woes.[195] The form, which belongs to the wisdom genre, is constructed on the basis of the woe formula (*waylun*).[196] Gerstenberger states, "The normal prophetic woe form contains general and timeless indictments of historically unspecified evildoers."[197] The literary structure of genuine woe-speech is twofold (*waylun li-...alladhī:* "Woe to those who..."), and tends to be accompanied by *yawm* or *yawmaʾidhin* ("on that day").[198] The litany of lament (Q. 77.14–50) in this sūra-unit features the tenfold woe-refrain beginning with verse 15[199]:

> *waylun yawmaʾidhin li-l-mukadhdhibīna*
>
> Woe on that day to those who deny the truth.

According to Jones, "this seems to be one of the earliest examples in the Qurʾān of a verse being used as a refrain."[200] The woe-litany begins with a question and continues from there.[201] Notably, this opening verse employs the didactic formu-

---

193 Cf. Neuwirth, "Qurʾānic Literary Structure Revisited," 408.
194 Ibid., 407.
195 Ibid., 393; *BCQ* 2:477.
196 Gunkel, "Psalmen," col. 1618; cf. Westermann, *Grundformen prophetischer Rede*, 136–42.
197 Erhard S. Gerstenberger, "The Woe-Oracles of the Prophets," *JBL* 81, no. 3 (1962): 252; cf. John L. McLaughlin, *The Marzēaḥ in the Prophetic Literature: References and Allusions in Light of the Extra-Biblical Evidence* (Leiden: Brill, 2001), 92.
198 *SKMS*² 197–98; Robinson, *Discovering the Qurʾān*, 116.
199 Goitein, "Das Gebet im Qorān," 89–91; *Komm* 498; cf. Gerstenberger, "Woe-Oracles of the Prophets," 250, fn. 7, and 253.
200 *JQA* 551; Robinson, *Discovering the Qurʾān*, 116.
201 *BQA* 2:626–27; cf. *SKMS*² 216; *BCQ* 2:475.

la (*wa-mā adrāka mā:* "And what can give you^{S} an idea of what") characteristic of the wisdom genre.[202] Verse 14 reads,

wa-mā adrāka mā yawmu l-faṣli

And what can give you^{S} an idea of what the day of decision is?

What makes this initial verse significant is the fact that the final verse (50) similarly ends with a question, thereby creating an interrogatory framework[203]:

fa-bi-ayyi ḥadīthin ba'dahū yu'minūna

In what statement will they believe after this?

It is noticeable that the "woe cry" both succeeds the first verse and at the same time precedes the final one.[204]

What is more, a series of negative-interrogatives (*a-lam:* "Did not...") follow thrice in the wake of the initial "interjection or exclamation."[205] The first is an *ubi sunt* grouping (vv. 16–18)[206]:

a-lam nuhliki l-awwalīna

thumma nutbi'uhumu l-ākhirīna

ka-dhālika naf'alu bi-l-mujrimīna

Did not We destroy the ancients,

Then cause the later ones to follow them?

Thus we deal with the sinners.

---

202 Gerstenberger, "The Woe-Oracles of the Prophets," 261; Sinai, "Qur'ān as Process," 426, fn. 30.
203 Cf. *SKMS*^{2} 200–1 and 217.
204 Gerstenberger, "Woe-Oracles of the Prophets," 250.
205 Ibid.
206 *QS* 7; Carl H. Becker, "Ubi sunt qui ante nos in mundo fuere," in *Aufsätze zur Kultur- und Sprachgeschichte vornehmlich des Orients: Ernst Kuhn zum 70. Geburtstage am 7. Februar 1916 gewidmet von Freunden und Schülern* (Breslau: Verlag von M. & H. Marcus, 1916), 87–105; Mark Lidzbarski, "Ubi sunt qui ante nos in mundo fuere," *Isl.* 8, nos. 3–4 (1918): 300; Stewart, "Wansbrough, Bultmann, and the Theory of Variant Traditions," 29–30; *FOTL* 13:183–84.

The second rhetorical question in the litany shifts to the hymnic motif addressing the creation of humankind (vv. 20–23)[207]:

a-lam nakhluqkum min mā'in mahīnin

fa-ja'alnāhu fī qarārin makīnin

ilā qadarin ma'lūmin

fa-qadarnā fa-ni'ma l-qādirūna

Did We not create you^{P} from a base fluid,

Which We placed in a safe abode,

For a known term.

We determined
– We are excellent determiners.

Naturally, the interrogative cluster turns to the related subject of creation (vv. 25–27)[208]:

a-lam naj'ali l-arḍa kifātan

aḥyā'an wa-amwātan

wa-ja'alnā fīhā rawāsiya shāmikhātin wa-asqaynākum mā'an furātan

Did we not make the earth a housing

For the living and the dead,

And set in it lofty mountains
and provided you^{P} with fresh water?

After this preliminary *āyāt* section comes one featuring paradise and its infernal counterpart.[209]

207 *SKMS*^{2} 217.
208 Ibid.
209 *JQA* 551.

Accordingly, the fate of the deniers takes precedence over that of the God-fearing in this litany of lament.[210] Of particular interest is the fact that this double image is achieved through a series of imperative statements.[211] In reference to hell-fire, the doubled imperatives read (vv. 29–33):

inṭaliqū ilā mā kuntum bihī tukadhdhibūna

inṭaliqū ilā ẓillin dhī thalāthi shuʿabin

lā ẓalīlin wa-lā yughnī mina l-lahabi

innahā tarmī bi-shararin ka-l-qaṣri

ka-annahū jimālatun ṣufrun

Depart^{P} to that which you used to deny.

Depart^{P} to the shadow with three branches,

Which gives no shade
and is of no avail against the flame.

It throws out sparks like castles

As if they were light-colored she-camels.

On the other side, dual imperatives also characterize the paradisical verses (vv. 41–44):

inna l-muttaqīna fī ẓilālin wa-ʿuyūnin

wa-fawākiha mimmā yashtahūna

kulū wa-shrabū hanīʾan bi-mā kuntum taʿmalūna

innā ka-dhālika najzī l-muḥsinīna

The God-fearing are among shade and springs,

And such fruits as they desire.

210 *SKMS*^{2} 217.
211 Namely, verses 29–30, 39, 43, and 46.

'Eat^{P} and drink^{P} with relish
in return for what you have been doing.'

Thus We recompense those who do good.

In reference to the following verse (v. 46), Bell holds that the sinful are safe for the moment, whereas Neuwirth sees the irony[212]:

kulū wa-tamattaʿū qalīlan innakum mujrimūna

'Eat and enjoy yourselves a little. You are sinners.'

In either case, the litany of lament ends on a cautionary note.[213]

3.5 Summary

The form-critical method has discerned dual forms of the liturgy genre in the *corpus coranicum*. First and foremost, this chapter laid bare the literary structure of hymns of praise. In particular, after identifying a group of liturgical formulae, it further classified multiple hymn forms according to motifs. In addition, it explored the generative properties of the imperative formula in terms of liturgical setting. Secondly, this chapter substantiated on formal grounds the presence of the litany form. Moreover, it discussed several forms, including the litany of praise and that of lament. In the end, these findings lend substance to Neuwirth's statement regarding "the emergence of an oral canon which was tangible within live recitation and whose *Sitz im Leben* was the community's service…."[214] Lastly, Dibelius remarks that "the bounds of the category cannot be always strictly maintained, for the style of a sermon, of a prayer, and of a hymn may touch one another closely."[215] At this point, let us turn to the sermon in the wisdom genre.

---

212 *BCQ* 2:478; *SKMS*[2] 217.

213 *JQA* 551.

214 Neuwirth, "Vom Rezitationstext über die Liturgie zum Kanon," 78; *SPMC* 141.

215 Martin Dibelius, *A Fresh Approach to the New Testament and Early Christian Literature* (New York: Charles Scribner's Sons, 1936), 253.

Chapter 4: Wisdom

4.1 Wisdom Genre

To begin with, this chapter examines sapiential speech-forms in the Qur'ān.[1] According to Bernhard Anderson (d. 2007), this genre comprises proverbial and dialogic wisdom.[2] In addition to tutoring the youth, Roland Murphy (d. 2002) observes, wisdom enshrines social norms and mores.[3] As a result, the length of pericopae ranges from terse truths to prolific words of wisdom.[4] Furthermore, in an oft-discussed line, Dibelius writes, "In the beginning was the sermon."[5] It is a matter of consequence for Wansbrough that "the paraenetic *khuṭba* or sermon form was a primary mode in which the prophetic *logia* were conveyed…."[6] There-

1 Westermann, *Der Psalter*, 80; David E. Aune, *Prophecy in Early Christianity and the Ancient Mediterranean World* (Grand Rapids, Michigan: Wm. B. Eerdmans Publishing Company, 1983), 107; cf. Walter Baumgartner, "Die literarischen Gattungen in der Weisheit des Jesus Sirach," *ZAW* 34, no. 3 (1914): 186–87; Bultmann, *Geschichte der synoptischen Tradition*, 73.

2 Bernhard W. Anderson, *Understanding the Old Testament*, 4th ed. (Englewood Cliffs, New Jersey: Prentice-Hall, 1986), 569; Corvin, "Stylistic and Functional Study of the Prose Prayers," 53–54.

3 *FOTL* 13:177; see Walter T. Wilson, *The Mysteries of Righteousness: The Literary Composition and Genre of the Sentences of Pseudo-Phocylides* (Tübingen: Verlag von J.C.B. Mohr (Paul Siebeck), 1994), 33–39.

4 Corvin, "Stylistic and Functional Study of the Prose Prayers," 53; Peter H. Davids, *The Epistle of James: A Commentary on the Greek Text* (Grand Rapids, Michigan: Wm. B. Eerdmans Publishing Company, 1982), 24; *FOTL* 13:177; cf. Albrecht Noth, *Quellenkritische Studien zu Themen, Formen und Tendenzen frühislamischer Geschichtsüberlieferung*, vol. 1: Themen und Formen (Bonn: Selbstverlag des Orientalischen Seminars der Universität Bonn, 1973), 85; Qutbuddin, "*Khuṭba:* The Evolution of Early Arabic Oration," 179.

5 Martin Dibelius, "Die alttestamentlichen Motive in der Leidensgeschichte des Petrus- und des Johannes-Evangeliums," in *Abhandlungen zur semitischen Religionskunde und Sprachwissenschaft*, ed. Wilhelm Frankenberg and Friedrich Küchler (Giessen: Verlag von Alfred Töpelmann, 1918), 146; James Louis Martyn, *History and Theology in the Fourth Gospel*, 3rd rev. ed. (Louisville, Kentucky: Westminster John Knox Press, 2003), 147.

6 *QS* 148; cf. Stewart, "Wansbrough, Bultmann, and the Theory of Variant Traditions," 44; Pernot, "The Rhetoric of Religion," 329; Qutbuddin, "*Khuṭba:* The Evolution of Early Arabic Oration," 190; Arist. *Rhet.* I.3, 1358b1–1359a30 (*The Complete Works of Aristotle*, 2:2159–61). N.b. Although she "pointedly denies that the Qur'ān can be considered homiletic," Neuwirth nonetheless presents *mathal* under the rubric of homiletic devices (Reynolds, *The Qur'ān and Its Biblical Subtext*, 243; Neuwirth, "Einige Bemerkungen," 1:736; eadem, *Der Koran als Text der Spätantike*, 498–509).

https://doi.org/10.1515/9783110580884-004

fore, it is significant that *kērygma* ("object of preaching") and *katēchēsis* ("elementary instruction") are two sides of the same coin.[7]

4.2 Wisdom Formulae

Yā-ayyuhā n-nās

The formula for admonition is closely related to the vocative formula (*qul yā-ayyuhā n-nās:* "Say: O people") that introduces qur'ānic "messenger-speech."[8] To illustrate, consider the sermon fragment in Q. 2.21–22 (-*ūC*)[9]:

> *yā-ayyuhā n-nāsu 'budū rabbakumu lladhī khalaqakum wa-lladhīna min qablikum la'allakum tattaqūna*
>
> *alladhī ja'ala lakumu l-arḍa firāshan wa-s-samā'a binā'an wa-anzala mina s-samā'i mā'an fa-akhraja bihī mina th-thamarāti rizqan lakum fa-lā taj'alū li-llāhi andādan wa-antum ta'lamūna*

> O people!
> Serve your Lord,
> who created you and those who were before you,
> so that you may protect yourselves,
>
> [God] who made the earth a resting-place for you
> and the sky a canopy,
> and who sent down water from the sky,
> and through it brought forth a provision of fruits for you.
> Do not set up rivals to God when you know better.

---

7 S.v. Catechesis, *EAC*; Carl E. Braaten, *History and Hermeneutics* (Philadelphia, Pennsylvania: The Westminster Press, 1966), 78–79. The Qur'ān, Lawrence I. Conrad claims, "is profoundly colored by later Islāmic *kērygma*" (idem, "Qur'ānic Studies: A Historian's Perspective," in *Results of Contemporary Research on the Qur'ān: The Question of a Historio-Critical Text of the Qur'ān*, ed. Manfred S. Kropp (Beirut: Orient-Institut, 2007), 9). Also see James I.H. McDonald, *Kerygma and Didache: The Articulation and Structure of the Earliest Christian Message* (Cambridge: Cambridge University Press, 1980), 17–28.

8 *QS* 12 and cf. 13; *FOTL* 4:337–38; *FOTL* 13:172; Hans Walter Wolff, *Amos' geistige Heimat* (Neukirchen: Neukirchener Verlag, 1964), 30–36; *SKMS*^{2} 33*; s.v. Form and Structure of the Qur'ān, *EQ*.

9 Bell considers these to be stand-alone verses (*BCQ* 1:7).

This closes with an admonition.[10] Moreover, the *āyāt* in this pericope characterize sermons.[11]

Wa-waṣṣaynā l-insān bi-

The corpus preserves a highly stylized formula for exhortation, namely, *wa-waṣṣaynā l-insāna bi-* ("And We have enjoined upon man"). For example, Q. 31.14 (-*īC*) in Sūrat Luqmān reads,[12]

> *wa-waṣṣaynā l-insāna bi-wālidayhi ḥamalathu ummuhū wahnan ʿalā wahnin wa-fiṣāluhū fī ʿāmayni ani shkur lī wa-li-wālidayka ilayya l-maṣīru*
>
> And We have charged man concerning his parents
> – his mother bore him in weakness upon weakness,
> and his weaning was in two years
> – saying, 'Show thanks to Me and to your parents.
> The journeying is to Me.'

In fact, all three extant instances address appropriate behavior towards parents.[13] As far as exhortation is concerned, "what should be done right may consist either of a proper act or behavior."[14]

Dhālikum waṣṣākum bihī

The paraenetic formula (*dhālikum waṣṣākum bihī:* "that is what He has enjoined on you^{P}") occurs thrice in a series of verses in the corpus.[15] In all three cases it closes the respective verse in combination with the substitution formulation (*laʿallakum:* "so that you^{P} may…"). For example, Q. 6.151 ends,

> *dhālikum waṣṣākum bihī laʿallakum taʿqilūna*
>
> That is what He has enjoined on you,
> so that you may understand.

---

10 *BQA* 1:4–5.
11 *BCQ* 1:7.
12 Ostensibly part of "Luqmān's address to his son (vv. 12–19)" (*JQA* 376; *BCQ* 2:83–84).
13 *SKMS*^{2} 304 (vv. 14–15).
14 Cf. *FOTL* 2a:161.
15 S.v. Waṣṣā, *CQ*.

The subsequent verse (152) concludes,

> *dhālikum waṣṣākum bihī la'allakum tadhakkarūna*
>
> That is what He has enjoined on you,
> so that you may be reminded.

In the third instance, the last line of verse 153 reads,

> *dhālikum waṣṣākum bihī la'allakum tattaqūna*
>
> That is what He has enjoined on you,
> so that you may protect yourselves.

The triplicate possibly represents a substantial unit sharing the same end rhyme (*-ūC*). On the other hand, Bell notes, verses 152–53 are very likely incongruous.[16] Even so, Jonathan Draper states, serial disjunction, rather than seamless conjunction, typifies paraenesis in general.[17] In other words, "it may be composed of several genre elements and characteristic stylistic features, in a flexible arrangement."[18] In view of that, this paraenetic catalogue (Q. 6.151–53) includes, *inter alia*, divine prohibitions.[19]

Yā-ayyuhā n-nabī qul li-

Hirschfeld keenly observes that "domestic affairs form the substrata of a series...."[20] The corpus preserves a pair of codes that pertains to roles and relations within the household structure.[21] Significantly, Hirschfeld identifies one specific set of "household codes."[22] The highly stylized formula reads, *yā-ayyuhā n-nabiyyu qul li-* ("O prophet! Say to...").[23] For instance, consider Q. 33.28–29 (*-Can*)[24]:

---

16 *BCQ* 1:215.

17 Cf. Jonathan A. Draper, "Torah and Troublesome Apostles in the *Didache* Community," in *The Didache in Modern Research*, ed. idem (Leiden: E.J. Brill, 1996), 344.

18 *FOTL* 13:180.

19 *SKMS*[2] 291.

20 Hirschfeld, *New Researches*, 120.

21 James P. Hering, *The Colossian and Ephesian Haustafeln in Theological Context: An Analysis of Their Origins, Relationship, and Message* (New York: Peter Lang, 2007), 1; Dibelius, *A Fresh Approach to the New Testament and Early Christian Literature*, 220.

22 Ibid. Moreover, Hirschfeld notes that "with very few exceptions they refer to matrimonial matters" (idem, *New Researches*, 120). N.b. For "the form of instructions," *yā-ayyuhā n-nabiyyu:* "O prophet" (e.g., Q. 8.64–65), *yā-ayyuhā r-rasūlu:* "O messenger" (i.e., Q. 5.41 and Q. 5.67), *yā-*

yā-ayyuhā n-nabiyyu qul li-azwājika in kuntunna turidna l-ḥayāta d-dunyā wa-zīnatahā fa-ta'ālayna umatti'kunna wa-usarriḥkunna sarāḥan jamīlan

wa-in kuntunna turidna llāha wa-rasūlahū wa-d-dāra l-ākhirata fa-inna llāha a'adda li-l-muḥsināti minkunna ajran 'aẓīman

O prophet!
Say to your wives,
'If you want the life of this world and its ornament, come.
I shall make provision for you and release you fairly.

But if you want God and His messenger and the world to come,
God has prepared a great wage for those of you who do good.'

Bell comments, these verses lay down their marital rights and responsibilities.[25]

Yā nisā'a n-nabī

The vocative formula for the supplementary pair of household codes is "O wives of the prophet" (*yā nisā'a n-nabiyyi*). Take, for example, Q. 33.30 – 31 (-*Can*),

yā-nisā'a n-nabiyyi man ya'ti minkunna bi-fāḥishatin mubayyinatin yuḍā'af lahā l-'adhābu ḍi'fayni wa-kāna dhālika 'alā llāhi yasīran

wa-man yaqnut minkunna li-llāhi wa-rasūlihī wa-ta'mal ṣāliḥan nu'tihā ajrahā marratayni wa-a'tadnā lahā rizqan karīman

O wives of the prophet!
Whoever of you acts with clear impropriety,
the punishment for her will be doubled.
That is easy for God.

Whoever of you submits to God and His messenger and acts righteously
– We shall give her

ayyuhā r-rusulu: "O messengers" (i.e., Q. 23.51), *yā-ayyuhā l-muzzammilu:* "You[S] who are wrapped up in a robe!" (i.e., Q. 73.1), cf. Draper, "Torah and Troublesome Apostles in the *Didache* Community," 340 – 63, esp. 341 – 46; Dibelius, *A Fresh Approach to the New Testament and Early Christian Literature*, 234 – 37.

23 Hirschfeld, *New Researches*, 120. Cf. Q. 8.70 (*yā-ayyuhā n-nabiyyu qul li-man...*).

24 Bell notes that verses 28 – 29 are distinct and stand apart (*BCQ* 2:99).

25 Ibid.

her wage twice over.
We have prepared for her a generous provision.

In terms of structure, these lines are framed as "a personal exhortation."[26] As for content, Bell says, these call on the wives to shun evil and do good.[27]

Waylun li-

According to Tucker, "the prophets also utter admonitions or warnings of various kinds, as well as woe oracles."[28] Therefore, the woe formula (*waylun li-*) is also featured in the wisdom genre.[29] For instance, consider the woe cry (-*īC*) in the first verse (Q. 83.1) of Sūrat al-Muṭaffifīn ("The Skimpers")[30]:

waylun li-l-muṭaffifīna

Woe to the skimpers!

Similarly, the woe unto the worshippers in Q. 107.4 (-*īC*) reads,[31]

fa-waylun li-l-muṣallīna

So woe to the worshippers!

Bell notes that "*al-muṣallīn* are mentioned in Q. 74.43 and Q. 70.22 as a class to be commended, though in the latter passage 'who pray continually' is added, which brings it into relation with this, where it is implied that some were negligent."[32] Then naturally, the question of the reception of woe speech arises.[33] Consider the woe unto the repudiators in Q. 45.7–11 (-*īC*), which is accompanied by a catalogue of vices and a closing formula[34]:

26 Cf. Dibelius, *A Fresh Approach to the New Testament and Early Christian Literature*, 233.
27 *BCQ* 2:99.
28 Tucker, *Form Criticism of the Old Testament*, 66; *FOTL* 2a:166–67; Daniel J. Harrington, *Jesus Ben Sira of Jerusalem: A Biblical Guide to Living Wisely* (Collegeville, Minnesota: Liturgical Press, 2005), 71.
29 *SKMS*[2] 198.
30 Ibid., 222; Robinson, *Discovering the Qur'ān*, 129; *BCQ* 2:509.
31 *SKMS*[2] 234; Robinson, *Discovering the Qur'ān*, 127; *JQA* 591.
32 *BCQ* 2:589.
33 McLaughlin, *The Marzēaḥ in the Prophetic Literature*, 93.
34 *SKMS*[2] 312. Bell comments, the subsequent pair of verses (12–13) reverts to the *āyāt* (*BCQ* 2:258).

waylun li-kulli affākin athīmin

yasmaʿu āyāti llāhi tutlā ʿalayhi thumma yuṣirru mustakbiran ka-an lam yasmaʿhā fa-bashshirhu bi-ʿadhābin alīmin

wa-idhā ʿalima min āyātinā shay'an ittakhadhahā huzuwan ulā'ika lahum ʿadhābun muhīnun

min warā'ihim jahannamu wa-lā yughnī ʿanhum mā kasabū shay'an wa-lā mā ttakhadhū min dūni llāhi awliyā'a wa-lahum ʿadhābun ʿaẓīmun

hādhā hudan wa-lladhīna kafarū bi-āyāti rabbihim lahum ʿadhābun min rijzin alīmun

Woe to every sinful liar,

Who hears God's signs recited to Him,
and then persists in being haughty
as though he had not heard them.
Give[S] him the tidings of a painful torment.

When he knows anything of Our signs,
he takes them in mockery.
These people will have a humiliating torment.

Behind them is hell,
and that which they have amassed will avail them nothing,
nor will what they have taken as protectors
to the exclusion of God.
They will have a great torment.

This is a guidance
– and those who deny the truth of their Lord's signs
will have a painful torment of abomination.

In effect, woe speech openly grieves injustice.[35]

35 Klaus Koch, *Die Profeten I: Assyrische Zeit* (Stuttgart: Verlag W. Kohlhammer, 1978), 58; McLaughlin, *The Marzēaḥ in the Prophetic Literature*, 93.

Yā bunayya

Wansbrough notes, the text evidences "the wisdom formula *yā bunayya* (Q. 11.42; Q. 12.5; Q. 31.13, 16, 17; Q. 37.102)."[36] Take, for instance, Q. 11.42 (*-īC*) in the Noah saga, with the impending death of his son[37]:

> *wa-hiya tajrī bihim fī mawjin ka-l-jibāli wa-nādā nūḥun-i bnahū wa-kāna fī ma'zilin yā-bunayya rkab ma'anā wa-lā takun ma'a l-kāfirīna*
>
> It sailed with them among waves like mountains,
> and Noah called to his son,
> who was in an isolated place:
> 'O my son!
> Embark with us and do not be with the disbelievers.'

Here the direct address signals a contextualized order issued by the mnemohistorical Noah.[38] The conversation continues in verse 43 (*-īC*):

> *qāla sa-āwī ilā jabalin ya'ṣimunī mina l-mā'i qāla lā 'āṣima l-yawma min amri llāhi illā man raḥima wa-ḥāla baynahumā l-mawju fa-kāna mina l-mughraqīna*
>
> He [viz. son] said, 'I shall go and seek refuge on a mountain
> which will protect me from the water.'
> He [viz. Noah] said, 'Today there is no protector from God's command,
> except for the one on whom He has mercy.'
> And the waves came between the two of them,
> and he [viz. son] was among those drowned.

As a result, the conversation in verses Q. 11.42–43 (*-īC*) cements the "act-consequence connection" in qur'ānic wisdom literature.[39]

---

36 Wansbrough adds that this "third vocative found in the Qur'ān" is "attested also in the plural *yā baniyya* (Q. 12.67, 87 where Jacob addresses his sons; Q. 2.132 where Isaac and Jacob are addressed by Abraham)" (*QS* 15). Cf. s.v. Proverb, Genre of, *DOTWPW* (Prov 1–9; 22–24; e.g., Prov 1:8: "Listen, my son, to your father's instruction"; Prov 4:1: "Listen, my sons, to a father's instruction"); *The Didache*, trans. Aelred Cody, in *The Didache in Context: Essays on Its Text, History and Transmission*, ed. Clayton N. Jefford (Leiden: E.J. Brill, 1995), 6–8 ("My child"); Baumgartner, "Die literarischen Gattungen in der Weisheit des Jesus Sirach," 164–65.

37 *SKMS*^{2} 296; *JQA* 207 (vv. 25–49); *BCQ* 1:358.

38 *FOTL* 13:180.

39 S.v. Wisdom, *ER*^{2}.

Mā adrāka mā

The "expository" formulation (*mā adrāka mā:* "what can give you^{S} an idea of what"), according to Sinai, constitutes "the didactic question" proper.[40] This formula for one-on-one wisdom lessons occurs thirteen times in the corpus.[41] In Sūrat al-Qāriʿa ("The Smiter"), for example, verses Q. 101.1–3 (*-Cah*) model the quadripartite literary structure[42]:

> *al-qāriʿatu*
>
> *mā l-qāriʿatu*
>
> *wa-mā adrāka mā l-qāriʿatu*
>
> The smiter.
>
> What is the smiter?
>
> What can give you^{S} knowledge of what the smiter is?

The exposition, which constitutes the fourth element, ostensibly follows the question.[43] Worthy of note in the same sūra-unit, verse Q. 101.10 (*-Ciyah*) features a pronoun in the didactic formulation, which subsequently furnishes the new query[44]:

> *wa-mā adrāka mā hiyah*
>
> What can give you^{S} knowledge of what it is?

---

40 Sinai, "Qur'ān as Process," 426, fn. 30; Robinson, *Discovering the Qur'ān*, 119–20 ("Didactic Questions and Answers"); Douglas Estes, *The Questions of Jesus in John: Logic, Rhetoric and Persuasive Discourse* (Leiden: Brill, 2013), 107–9; *SPMC* xxv ("question-and-answer patterns of speech"); see Stewart, "The Mysterious Letters and Other Formal Features of the Qur'ān," 327–29; cf. Al-Azmeh, *The Emergence of Islam in Late Antiquity*, 439.

41 S.v. Adrá, *CQ*. Furthermore, Robinson notes, "Ten sūras have one or more didactic question of the form: 'And what will make thee comprehend what x is?'" (idem, *Discovering the Qur'ān*, 119–20).

42 *JQA* 585, fn. 1; *BCQ* 2:575; Robinson, *Discovering the Qur'ān*, 143.

43 *SKMS*^{2} 232.

44 Ibid. (vv. 10–11); *JQA* 585; cf. *BCQ* 2:577; Robinson, *Discovering the Qur'ān*, 128.

Furthermore, the text preserves abbreviated examples that commence with the didactic formula (*mā adrāka mā*).[45] For instance, Q. 74.27 (-*Cr*) begins with the question of *saqar*[46]:

wa-mā adrāka mā saqaru

What can give you^S knowledge of what *saqar* is?

Thereupon, verses Q. 74.28–30 (-*Cr*) follow up with a detailed description[47]:

lā tubqī wa-lā tadharu

lawwāḥatun li-l-bashari

ʿalayhā tisʿata ʿashara

It does not spare, nor does it leave alone,

Scorching the flesh.

Over it are nineteen.

Quite fittingly, the explanatory note glosses *saqar.*[48] Moreover, Robinson explains, the didactic formula in Q. 104 appears in nearly the same setting.[49] For that reason, Q. 104.5 (-*Cah*) opens with a question[50]:

wa-mā adrāka mā l-ḥuṭamatu

What can give you^S knowledge of what the insatiable is?

A qualified answer (vv. 6–7) to the question of *huṭama* comes afterwards[51]:

nāru llāhi l-mūqadatu

allatī taṭṭaliʿu ʿalā l-afʾidati

---

45 *JQA* 544 and 545, fn. 2; *SKMS*² 214.
46 *SKMS*² 214.
47 Ibid.
48 *BCQ* 2:452–53 (vv. 27–30); Robinson, *Discovering the Qurʾān*, 119–20.
49 Robinson, *Discovering the Qurʾān*, 119–20.
50 *SKMS*² 233.
51 Ibid.

– The fire of God, kindled,

Which rises over the hearts [of men].

These verses (-*Cah*) appropriately provide clarification.

Yas'alūnaka

The dialogic formula (*yas'alūnaka:* "they ask you^{S}") is ubiquitous in the corpus. Engaging a principal interlocutor, these questions are raised to elicit specific pieces of information.[52] For example, consider the stand-alone verse, Q. 2.189[53]:

yas'alūnaka 'ani l-ahillati qul hiya mawāqītu li-n-nāsi wa-l-ḥajji

They ask you^{S} about new moons.
Say^{S}: 'They are appointed times for the people and for the *Ḥajj*.'

According to Bell, "it answers a question as to the new moons, and condemns some pagan custom connected with them."[54] A related subject matter is touched upon in Q. 2.217, which addresses the place of conflict in sacred time[55]:

yas'alūnaka 'ani sh-shahri l-ḥarāmi qitālin fīhi qul qitālun fīhi kabīrun wa-ṣaddun 'an sabīli llāhi wa-kufrun bihī wa-l-masjidi l-ḥarāmi wa-ikhrāju ahlihī minhu akbaru 'inda llāhi wa-l-fitnatu akbaru mina l-qatli

They ask you^{S} about the sacred month and fighting in it.
Say^{S}: 'Fighting in it is grievous; but turning [people] from God's way and disbelief in Him and [turning people away from] the Sacred Mosque and expelling His people from it is more grievous with God. Persecution is more serious than killing.'

In addition, Sūrat al-Anfāl suitably turns to the vexed question of war booty.[56] Verse Q. 8.1 (-*īC*) is complete unto itself[57]:

yas'alūnaka 'ani l-anfāli quli l-anfālu li-llāhi wa-r-rasūli fa-ttaqū llāha wa-aṣliḥū dhāta baynikum wa-aṭī'ū llāha wa-rasūlahū in kuntum mu'minīna

---

52 *BCQ* 1:475.
53 Ibid., 1:39.
54 Ibid.
55 Ibid., 1:45; *JQA* 24 and 51, fn. 33.
56 *JQA* 169.
57 *BCQ* 1:269.

They ask you^{S} about the spoils of war.
Say^{S}: 'Spoils belong to God and to the messenger. Be^{P} God-fearing and put right what is between you, and obey God and His messenger, if you are believers.'

The response attempts to settle the matter of distribution equitably.[58]

Ḥamdala

According to Neuwirth, sermon-like sūras have come to be "stereotypically introduced by initial hymnal formulas."[59] Including variants, the sermon formula (*al-ḥamdu li-llāhi:* "Praise belongs to God") occurs twenty-four times in the corpus.[60] Regarding the *ḥamdala*, Hirschfeld notes that it is "used to invite the audience attending sermons to start praying, and is found both at the beginning and at the end of many discourses."[61] In terms of placement, the *ḥamdala* functions as a superscription, as well as a subscription.[62] For that reason it seems, the short formulaic doxology (Q. 1.2) marks the opening of the epilogue of the sermon, while doubling as the close of certain sūra-units.[63] Consider a mixed-type of peroration – doctrinal polemic in a doxology – concluding Sūrat al-Isrā᾽ (Q. 17.111):

wa-quli l-ḥamdu li-llāhi lladhī lam yattakhidh waladan wa-lam yakun lahū sharīkun fī l-mulki wa-lam yakun lahū waliyyun mina dh-dhuli wa-kabbirhu takbīran

And say:
Praise belongs to God,
who has not taken to himself a son
and who has no partner in sovereignty
nor any protector because He is humble.
Magnify^{S} him.

On a related matter, the last verse (Q. 27.93) of the sūra-unit closes with the *ḥamdala:*

wa-quli l-ḥamdu li-llāhi sa-yurīkum āyātihī fa-taʿrifūnahā wa-mā rabbuka bi-ghāfilin ʿammā taʿmalūna

---

58 Ibid.; *JQA* 170, fn. 1.
59 S.v. Form and Structure of the Qur᾽ān, *EQ*; *SKMS*^{2} 33*.
60 S.v. Ḥamada, *CQ.*
61 Hirschfeld, *New Researches*, 71; cf. Goitein, "Das Gebet im Qorān," 14–15.
62 Cf. Hirschfeld, *New Researches*, 71.
63 Baumstark, "Jüdischer und christlicher Gebetstypus im Koran," 237.

And say:
Praise belongs to God.
He will show you^P His signs
and you^P will recognize them.
Your^S Lord is not heedless of what you^P do.

Bell postulates that the reworked verse (93) is "spoken to the prophet."[64] Furthermore, Sūrat al-Jāthiya closes with an enlarged doxology (Q. 45.36 – 37) with both verses sharing the same end-rhyme (-*īC*):

fa-l-illāhi l-ḥamdu rabbi s-samāwāti wa-rabbi l-arḍi rabbi l-ʿālamīna

wa-lahu l-kibriyāʾu fī s-samāwāti wa-l-arḍi wa-huwa l-ʿazīzu l-ḥakīmu

Praise belongs to God,
Lord of the heavens and Lord of the earth,
Lord of all created beings.

To Him belongs the majesty in the heavens and the earth.
He is the Mighty and the Wise.

What is more, apart from their context, Q. 39.75 (*wa-qīla*) and Q. 37.182 (*wa-*) both share an identical closing doxology[65]:

al-ḥamdu li-llāhi rabbi l-ʿālamīna

Praise belongs to God, Lord of all beings.

The rhyme scheme for Q. 39.75 (-*īC*) largely conforms to that of the foregoing verses in the sūra-unit. In the case of Q. 37.182, it shares the same rhyme scheme (-*īC*) as that of the *benedictio* in the preceding verse (v. 181)[66]:

wa-salāmun ʿalā l-mursalīna

Peace be on those sent with the message.

In addition to this divine invocation, Jones argues that the concise doxology in verse 182 forms part of a longer epilogue (vv. 161 – 82).[67]

---

64 *BCQ* 2:36.
65 Regarding *al-ḥamdu li-llāhi*, see ibid., 1:1.
66 *QS* 310.
67 *JQA* 407.

Yā-ayyuhā lladhīna āmanū

The proclamation formula (*yā-ayyuhā lladhīna āmanū:* "O you who believe") also functions as a sermon formula. Take, for instance, the moral discourse promulgated in Q. 59.18–21 (-*ūC*)[68]:

yā-ayyuhā lladhīna āmanū ttaqū llāha wa-l-tanẓur nafsun mā qaddamat li-ghadin wa-ttaqū llāha inna llāha khabīrun bi-mā taʿmalūna

wa-lā takūnū ka-lladhīna nasū llāha fa-ansāhum anfusahum ulāʾika humu l-fāsiqūna

lā yastawī aṣḥābu n-nāri wa-aṣḥābu l-jannati aṣḥābu l-jannati humu l-fāʾizūna

law anzalnā hādhā l-qurʾāna ʿalā l-jabalin la-raʾaytahū khāshiʿan mutaṣaddiʿan min khashyati llāhi wa-tilka l-amthālu naḍribuhā li-n-nāsi laʿallahum yatafakkarūna

O you who believe!
Fear God;
and let every soul observe what it has sent on for the morrow;
and fear God.
God is informed of what you do.

Do not be like those who forgot God,
with the result that He caused them to forget themselves.
Those are the reprobates.

The companions of the Garden and the companions of the Fire are not equal.
The companions of the Garden are the winners.

Had We sent this Recitation down on a mountain,
you[S] would have seen it humbled and split asunder through fear of God.
These similitudes are coined by us for the people
so that they may reflect.

Also, consider the credal-type statements pronounced in Sūra 57.[69] The preaching fragment (vv. 28–29) that closes the chapter reads (-*īC*),

yā-ayyuhā lladhīna āmanū ttaqū llāha wa-āminū bi-rasūlihī yuʾtikum kiflayni min raḥmatihī wa-yajʿal lakum nūran tamshūna bihī wa-yaghfir lakum wa-llāhu ghafūrun raḥīmun

li-allā yaʿlama ahlu l-kitābi allā yaqdirūna ʿalā shayʾin min faḍli llāhi wa-anna l-faḍla bi-yadi

68 Ibid., 509.
69 Ibid., 501.

llāhi yu'tīhi man yashā'u wa-llāhu dhū l-faḍli l-'aẓīmi

O you who believe!
Fear God and believe in His messenger,
and He will give you a double portion of His mercy
and make for you a light,
by which you can walk;
and He will forgive you.
God is Forgiving and Merciful,

That the people of the scripture may know
that they have no power over any of God's bounty
but that the bounty is in the hand of God,
to give to those whom He wishes.
God is endowed with the great bounty.

Bell comments that "the point is the exclusiveness of the people of the Book; the Muslims are assured of the mercy of God, whose bounty the people of the Book have no power to limit."[70]

4.3 Wisdom Setting

Teaching Situation

John Bright (d. 1995) states that tribal, village, and townsfolk all pass down customs and mores.[71] In fact, von Rad concurs, "the existence of an older clan wisdom need not be contested in principle; its existence is, indeed, even highly probable."[72] In this case, tribal wisdom and ethics are also handed down

70 *BCQ* 2:355.

71 Bright, "Apodictic Prohibition," 185; Harrington, *Jesus Ben Sira of Jerusalem*, 67; Gerstenberger, *Wesen und Herkunft*, 110–17; Wolff, *Amos' geistige Heimat*, 60, fn. 5; cf. Hans-Jürgen Hermisson, *Studien zur israelitischen Spruchweisheit* (Neukirchen: Neukirchener Verlag des Erziehungsvereins, 1968), 81–92.

72 Von Rad, *Weisheit in Israel*, 24; idem, *Wisdom in Israel*, trans. James D. Martin (Nashville, Tennessee: Abingdon Press, 1972), 11; Gerstenberger, *Wesen und Herkunft*, 110–17; cf. Alt, *Die Ursprünge des israelitischen Rechts*, 1:278–332; Knut M. Heim, "The Phenomenon and Literature of Wisdom in Its Near Eastern Context and in the Biblical Wisdom Books," in *Hebrew Bible / Old Testament: The History of Its Interpretation*, vol. 3, pt. 2, ed. Magne Sæbø (Göttingen: Vandenhoeck & Ruprecht, 2015), 574–75.

through the ages.[73] This is patently evident in the vocative formula, "O my son" (*yā bunayya*). According to Jean-Paul Audet (d. 1993), "wisdom is *paideia*, an educational process that developed in the primitive body of the family."[74] Furthermore, the wisdom of the ages affects every sphere of society.[75] Thus, wisdom teaching is as extensive as it is varied.[76] Wisdom literature employs an adaptable set of delivery techniques intended for different audiences.[77] And so, "the *persona* of the authoritative sage" and terms of endearment come together to forge a powerful master-disciple bond.[78] The teaching situation ranges from private to small and large group instruction.[79] For example, the didactic question (*mā adrāka mā*) is ostensibly directed at a single person. On the other hand, the vocative address "O people" (*yā-ayyuhā n-nās*) is directed to a wider audience than the more exclusive address, "O you who believe" (*yā-ayyuhā lladhīna āmanū*). In the latter circumstance (e.g., Q. 3.118–19), the deictic formula (*hā-antum:* "here you are"), featured four times in the corpus, signposts real-time preaching.[80] In sum, the rich qur'ānic repertoire of wisdom includes sermons, lectures, lessons, etc.[81]

---

73 Bright, "Apodictic Prohibition," 185; von Rad, *Weisheit in Israel*, 24, fn. 9; Gerstenberger, *Wesen und Herkunft*, 110–17; cf. Alt, *Die Ursprünge des israelitischen Rechts*, 1:278–332; Margaret Mead, *Culture and Commitment: A Study of the Generation Gap* (Garden City, New York: Natural History Press, 1970), *passim*; Carole R. Fontaine, "The Sage in Family and Tribe," in *The Sage in Israel and the Ancient Near East*, ed. John G. Gammie and Leo G. Perdue (Winona Lake, Indiana: Eisenbrauns, 1990), 164.

74 Donn F. Morgan, *Wisdom in the Old Testament Traditions* (Atlanta, Georgia: John Knox Press, 1981), 40–41 ("Clan Wisdom"); Jean-Paul Audet, "Origines comparées de la double tradition de la loi et de la sagesse dans le Proche-Orient ancien," in *Proceedings of the International Congress of Orientalists* (Moscow: s.n., 1962), 1:352–57; Fontaine, "The Sage in Family and Tribe," 164.

75 *FOTL* 14:251 and cf. 14:257–58; *FOTL* 13:177.

76 Cf. Harrington, *Jesus Ben Sira of Jerusalem*, 78.

77 Huub van de Sandt and David Flusser, *The Didache: Its Jewish Sources and Its Place in Early Judaism and Christianity* (Minneapolis, Minnesota: Fortress Press, 2002), 67; cf. Dibelius, *A Fresh Approach to the New Testament and Early Christian Literature*, 234.

78 Ibid.; *FOTL* 14:251; *FOTL* 13:177; cf. Harrington, *Jesus Ben Sira of Jerusalem*, 78; s.vv. Initiation: Men's Initiation and Initiation: Women's Initiation, *ER*².

79 Cf. Wesselhoeft, "Making Muslim Minds," 793; s.vv. Initiation: Women's Initiation and Initiation: Men's Initiation, *ER*².

80 "Referring to the near, the deictic particle *hā-* is normally added, referring to the far, the suffixes *-ka* or more often *-lika* are attached" (Wolfdietrich Fischer, "Classical Arabic," in *The Semitic Languages*, ed. Robert Hetzron (London: Routledge, 1997), 200). "*Hā* affix occurring 904 times in the Qur'ān and functioning as: (i) attention-drawing particle, interjection 'look,' 'there!' 'this particular,' which is used to add emphasis or focus to one of the following: (1) (prefixally) independent pronouns (e.g., *antum* > *hā antum* 'here you are,' as in Q. 3.119: 'well here you are! – you love them, but they do not love you'..." (Elsaid M. Badawi and Muhammad Abdel Haleem, *Ara-*

4.4 Wisdom Forms

Admonition

According to Walter Baumgartner (d. 1970), admonition alternates between prohibition and command.[82] In terms of definition, admonition discourages the unethical, while encouraging the ethical, and as such imperatives abound.[83] For example, Q. 2.168 (-*īC*) admonishes listeners to steer clear of evil[84]:

> *yā-ayyuhā n-nāsu kulū mimmā fī l-arḍi ḥalālan ṭayyiban wa-lā tattabi'ū khuṭuwāti sh-shayṭāni innahū lakum 'aduwwun mubīnun*
>
> O people!
> Eat[P] what is allowable and good in the earth,
> and do not follow[P] the footsteps of Satan.
> He is a persuasive enemy for you[P].

Furthermore, consider Sūrat an-Nisā' wherein "the tone is set by the admonition made in the first verse and by lengthy injunctions about orphans" in Q. 4.1–2 (-*Can*)[85]:

> *yā-ayyuhā n-nāsu ttaqū rabbakumu lladhī khalaqakum min nafsin wāḥidatin wa-khalaqa minhā zawjahā wa-baththa minhumā rijālan kathīran wa-nisā'an wa-ttaqū llāha lladhī tasā'alūna bihī wa-l-arḥāma inna llāha kāna 'alaykum raqīban*
>
> *wa-ātū l-yatāmā amwālahum wa-lā tatabaddalū l-khabītha bi-ṭ-ṭayyibi wa-lā ta'kulū amwālahum ilā amwālikum innahū kāna ḥūban kabīran*
>
> O people!
> Fear your Lord,
> who created you from a single soul
> and who created from it its fellow
> and who spread many men and women from the two of them;

---

bic-English Dictionary of Qur'ānic Usage (Leiden: Brill, 2008), 976). Cf. *QS* 310; Qutbuddin, "*Khuṭba:* The Evolution of Early Arabic Oration," 212–13 and 216.

81 Cf. Wesselhoeft, "Making Muslim Minds," 793.

82 Baumgartner, "Die literarischen Gattungen in der Weisheit des Jesus Sirach," 165; Wolff, *Amos' geistige Heimat*, 30–36.

83 *FOTL* 4:337–38; *FOTL* 13:172.

84 *JQA* 24; *BCQ* 1:34.

85 Cf. *JQA* 87; *BCQ* 1:107. N.b. Robinson, *Discovering the Qur'ān*, 80 (vv. 1–14). "Towards the end of Q. 3, there is a reference to male and female (v. 195); the opening *āya* of Q. 4 refers to 'men and women' (v. 1)" (ibid., 266) ("The dovetailing of consecutive sūras").

and fear God,
through whom you seek rights from one another and from the ties of relationship.
God is a watcher over you.

Give^{P} orphans their property;
and do not substitute the bad for the good,
nor devour their property in addition to your own.
That is a great sin.

Bell surmises, it addresses the difficulties faced by those orphaned.[86] Likewise, verse 33 (*-ūC*) in Sūrat Luqmān (Q. 31) preserves an admonition to the general public[87]:

yā-ayyuhā n-nāsu ttaqū rabbakum wa-khshaw yawman lā yajzī wālidun ʿan waladihī wa-lā mawlūdun huwa jāzin ʿan wālidihī shayʾan inna waʿda llāhi ḥaqqun fa-lā taghurrannakumu l-ḥayātu d-dunyā wa-lā yaghurrannakum bi-llāhi l-gharūru

O people!
Fear your Lord,
and be afraid of a day when no father will give satisfaction for his child
and no child will give satisfaction for his father in anything.
God's promise is true.
So do not be deluded by the life of this world
and do not be deluded by the deluder concerning God.

In addition, Q. 4.170 (*-Can*) strikes a chord with listeners:

yā-ayyuhā n-nāsu qad jāʾakumu r-rasūlu bi-l-ḥaqqi min rabbikum fa-āminū khayran lakum wa-in takfurū fa-inna li-llāhi mā fī s-samāwāti wa-l-arḍi wa-kāna llāhu ʿalīman ḥakīman

O people!
The messenger has brought you the truth from your Lord.
So believe.
[That is] better for you.
If you disbelieve
– to God belongs what is in the heavens and the earth.
God is Knowing and Wise.

The admonition is to suspend disbelief.[88] In turn, Q. 4.174–5 (*-Can*) reads,

86 *BCQ* 1:107 (vv. 2–6).
87 *SKMS*^{2} 304 (vv. 33–34); *BCQ* 2:86.
88 Verse 170 likely stands apart (*BCQ* 1:142).

yā-ayyuhā n-nāsu qad jā'akum burhānun min rabbikum wa-anzalnā ilaykum nūran mubīnan

fa-ammā lladhīna āmanū bi-llāhi wa-'taṣamū bihī fa-sa-yudkhiluhum fī raḥmatin minhu wa-faḍlin wa-yahdīhim ilayhi ṣirāṭan mustaqīman

O people!
A proof has come to you from your Lord.
We have sent down to you a clear light.

As for those who believe in God and hold fast to Him,
He will admit them to mercy from Him and to bounty,
and He will guide them to Himself along a straight road.

According to Bell, these verses represent a stand-alone pericope.[89] Also, take into consideration verse Q. 10.57 (-*īC*), which addresses those assembled[90]:

yā-ayyuhā n-nāsu qad jā'atkum maw'iẓatun min rabbikum wa-shifā'un li-mā fī ṣ-ṣudūri wa-hudan wa-raḥmatun li-l-mu'minīna

O people!
There has come to you an admonition from your Lord
and a remedy for what is in [your] breasts
and a guidance and a mercy for the believers.

This verse "then calls the people's attention to what has been delivered."[91] Similarly, the admonition in verse Q. 22.1 (-*īC*) warns of a catastrophic end[92]:

yā-ayyuhā n-nāsu ttaqū rabbakum inna zalzalata s-sā'ati shay'un 'aẓīmun

O people!
Fear your Lord.
The earthquake of the Hour is a tremendous thing.

While this first verse concerns the eschaton, a subsequent one (Q. 22.5) dispels any doubt about the raising of the dead[93]:

yā-ayyuhā n-nāsu in kuntum fī raybin mina l-ba'thi fa-innā khalaqnākum min turābin thumma min nuṭfatin thumma min 'alaqatin thumma min muḍghatin mukhallaqatin wa-ghayri mukhallaqatin li-nubayyina lakum

---

89 Cf. ibid., 1:143.
90 *SKMS*² 294 (vv. 57–58); *BCQ* 1:339.
91 *BCQ* 1:339.
92 Ibid., 1:561 (vv. 1–4).
93 Ibid. (vv. 5–8).

O people!
If you^P are in doubt about the resurrection
– We have created you from dust,
then from a drop, then from a clot,
then from a lump, formed or unformed,
that We may make [things] clear to you^P.

Bell remarks, the integrity of this pericope is assured on the basis of the opening invocation.[94]

In terms of the wisdom genre, Q. 22.73 (-*ūC*) incorporates a *mathal* into the admonition, namely, the similitude of the fly[95]:

yā-ayyuhā n-nāsu ḍuriba mathalun fa-stamiʿū lahū inna lladhīna tadʿūna min dūni llāhi lan yakhluqū dhubāban wa-lawi jtamaʿū lahū wa-in yaslubhumu dh-dhubābu shayʾan lā yastanqidhūhu minhu ḍaʿufa ṭ-ṭālibu wa-l-maṭlūbu

O people!
A similitude has been coined.
Listen to it.
Those on whom you call,
to the exclusion of God,
will never create a fly,
though they combine to do it.
And if a fly robs them of anything,
they will not rescue that from it.
Weak are both the seeker and the sought.

On a similar note, Q. 35.3 (-*ūC*) warns,[96]

yā-ayyuhā n-nāsu dhkurū niʿmata llāhi ʿalaykum hal min khāliqin ghayru llāhi yarzuqukum mina s-samāʾi wa-l-arḍi lā ilāha illā huwa fa-annā tuʾfakūna

O people!
Remember God's blessing to you.
Is there any creator,
other than God,
who brings you sustenance from the sky and the earth?

94 Ibid.
95 Theodor Lohmann, "Die Gleichnisreden Muḥammeds im Koran (2. Teil)," *MIO* 12 (1966): 247; *BCQ* 1:575. For the formulation of simile, see Moses Sister, "Metaphern und Vergleiche im Koran," *MSOS* 34 (1931): 104–54, esp. 109–16; s.vv. Metaphor and Simile, *EQ*; Tucker, *Example Stories*, 103; William C. Scott, *The Oral Nature of the Homeric Simile* (Leiden: E.J. Brill, 1974), 56–95 and 126–65.
96 *JQA* 397 (vv. 3–8); *BCQ* 2:126.

There is no god but Him.
How are you caused to lie?

This verse admonishes listeners to remember past blessings by divine succour.[97] In the same vein, verse Q. 35.5 (-*ūC*) addresses the wider public[98]:

yā-ayyuhā n-nāsu inna wa'da llāhi ḥaqqun fa-lā taghurrannakumu l-ḥayātu d-dunyā wa-lā yaghurrannakum bi-llāhi l-gharūru

O people!
The promise of God is true.
So let not the life of this world deceive you.
Let not the deceiver deceive you about God.

According to Neuwirth, it constitutes an admonition to remember the divine promise.[99] Additionally, consider Q. 35.15–17 (-*īC*), which "renews the address to the people"[100]:

yā-ayyuhā n-nāsu antumu l-fuqarā'u ilā llāhi wa-llāhu huwa l-ghaniyyu l-ḥamīdu

in yasha' yudhhibkum wa-ya'ti bi-khalqin jadīdin

wa-mā dhālika 'alā llāhi bi-'azīzin

O people!
You^{P} are the ones who are in need of God.
God is the All-sufficient and the Laudable.

If He wishes, He can remove you^{P} and bring a new creation.

That is not a great matter for God.

Hanging by a thread, this admonition characterizes the human condition as one of absolute dependence.[101] Lastly, Q. 49.13 (-*īC*) reads,

97 *SKMS*^{2} 307.
98 Bell notes that "[t]he *ā*- assonance is found at *ad-dunyā*, and the rest of the verse is a repetition" (*BCQ* 2:126).
99 *SKMS*^{2} 307 (vv. 5–6).
100 Ibid.; *FOTL* 13:172; *BCQ* 2:129; *JQA* 397.
101 *SKMS*^{2} 307.

yā-ayyuhā n-nāsu innā khalaqnākum min dhakarin wa-unthā wa-ja'alnākum shu'ūban wa-qabā'ila li-ta'ārafū inna akramakum 'inda llāhi atqākum inna llāha 'alīmun khabīrun

O people!
We have created you male and female
and made you races and tribes
that you may know one another.
The noblest of you in the sight of God is the most God-fearing.
God is Knowing and Informed.

This verse "deals with *fakhr*, or self-glorification of the Arab tribes and recommends piety as the basis of nobility."[102]

Exhortation

As to definition, exhortation promotes pious living.[103] Here again, the *corpus coranicum* preserves due reverence to parents.[104] Accordingly, Q. 46.15 (-*īC*) reads,

wa-waṣṣaynā l-insāna bi-wālidayhi iḥsānan ḥamalathu ummuhū kurhan wa-waḍa'athu kurhan wa-ḥamluhū wa-fiṣāluhū thalāthūna shahran ḥattā idhā balagha ashuddahū wa-balagha arba'īna sanatan qāla rabbi awzi'nī an ashkura ni'mataka llatī an'amta 'alayya wa-'alā wālidayya wa-an a'mala ṣāliḥan tarḍāhu wa-aṣliḥ lī fī dhurriyyatī innī tubtu ilayka wa-innī mina l-muslimīna

And We have charged man to be kind to his parents
– his mother has carried him in travail
and given birth to him in travail,
and the carrying of him and the weaning of him are thirty months;
and then, when he attains maturity and reaches forty years,
he says, 'My Lord, press me to give thanks for Your blessing,
which You have bestowed on me and on my parents
and to act with righteousness that is pleasing to You;
and be good to me in my posterity.
I have turned towards You in repentance,
and I am one of those who have surrendered.'

Although Bell considers it a "legal prescription of kindness and respect to parents," it is well to bear in mind, however, that exhortation is not legislation.[105]

---

102 *BCQ* 2:289; s.v. Mufākhara, *EI*^{2}.
103 Cf. *FOTL* 2a:161.
104 *SKMS*^{2} 313 (vv. 15–16).
105 *BCQ* 2:265 (vv. 15–18); cf. *FOTL* 2a:161.

At the same time, Q. 29.8 (-*ūC*) adds a stipulation concerning recommended behavior towards pagan parents[106]:

> *wa-waṣṣaynā l-insāna bi-wālidayhi ḥusnan wa-in jāhadāka li-tushrika bī mā laysa laka bihī ʿilmun fa-lā tuṭiʿhumā ilayya marjiʿukum fa-unabbiʾukum bi-mā kuntum taʿmalūna*
>
> And We have enjoined man to treat his parents well;
> but if the two of them strive to make you^{S} associate with Me
> that of which you have no knowledge,
> do not obey them.
> To Me is your^{P} return,
> and I shall tell you^{P} what you used to do.

On filial piety, Bell comments that "the rule is further modified to permit disobedience to parents who strive to hold their children to polytheism."[107]

Paraenesis

With multiple wisdom forms at its disposal, paraenesis is "an address to an individual (or group) that seeks to persuade with reference to a goal."[108] In terms of literary structure, the paraenetic catalogue commences with the conveyance command formula (*qul*).[109] After the singular imperative comes the plural summons (*taʿālaw:* "Come^{P}!"), then follows a didactic formulation in the first person (*atlu mā:* "I shall recite what") and, in turn, the address proper. Lastly, the first segment closes with the standard phrase (*dhālikum waṣṣākum bihī laʿallakum*...). Thus Q. 6.151 (-*ūC*) reads,

> *qul taʿālaw atlu mā ḥarrama rabbukum ʿalaykum allā tushrikū bihī shayʾan wa-bi-l-wālidayni iḥsānan wa-lā taqtulū awlādakum min imlāqin naḥnu narzuqukum wa-iyyāhum wa-lā taqrabū l-fawāḥisha mā ẓahara minhā wa-mā baṭana wa-lā taqtulū n-nafsa llatī ḥarrama llāhu illā bi-l-ḥaqqi dhālikum waṣṣākum bihī laʿallakum taʿqilūna*
>
> Say: 'Come^{P} and I shall recite what your Lord has made sacred for you:
> that you associate nothing with him;
> that [you show] kindness to [your] parents;
> that you do not kill your children because of poverty

106 *SKMS*^{2} 302 (vv. 8–9).
107 *BCQ* 2:58 (vv. 8–9).
108 *FOTL* 13:180; cf. Dibelius, *Die Formgeschichte des Evangeliums*, 234–65; see Alan Kirk, *The Composition of the Sayings Source: Genre, Synchrony, and Wisdom Redaction in Q* (Leiden: Brill, 1998), 152–272.
109 *FOTL* 4:364; *QS* 16; Seybold, *Die Psalmen*, 52.

– We shall provide for you and them;
that you do not approach immoral acts,
whether open or concealed;
and do not kill the soul that God has made sacred,
except by right.
This is what He has enjoined on you,
so that you may understand.'

In addition, consider the subsequent verse (152) with the shared rhyme pattern (-*ūC*):

wa-lā taqrabū māla l-yatīmi illā bi-llatī hiya aḥsanu ḥattā yablugha ashuddahū wa-awfū l-kayla wa-l-mīzāna bi-l-qisṭi lā nukallifu nafsan illā wusʿahā wa-idhā qultum fa-ʿdilū wa-law kāna dhā qurbā wa-bi-ʿahdi llāhi awfū dhālikum waṣṣākum bihī laʿallakum tadhakkarū-na

'Do[P] not approach the wealth of the orphan,
save with what is better,
till he reaches maturity.
Fill up the measure and the balance, in justice.
(We do not impose burdens on any soul beyond its capacity.)
If you[P] speak, be just, even though it is a relative [who is involved].
Fulfill God's covenant.
This is what He has enjoined on you,
so that you may be reminded.'

The third and final verse (153) reads (-*ūC*),

wa-anna hādhā ṣirāṭī mustaqīman fa-ttabiʿūhu wa-lā tattabiʿū s-subula fa-tafarraqa bikum ʿan sabīlihī dhālikum waṣṣākum bihī laʿallakum tattaqūna

And 'This is My path, straight.
Follow[P] it and do not follow [other] ways
lest they take you away from His path.
That is what He has enjoined on you,
so that you may protect yourselves.'

As is evident from these verses, paraenesis incorporates multiple wisdom elements.[110]

110 *FOTL* 13:180.

Code

As for the prophetic household, one part contained in the corpus pertains directly to wives.[111] The household code in verses Q. 33.32–4 (-*Can*) reads,

> *yā-nisāʾa n-nabiyyi lastunna ka-aḥadin mina n-nisāʾi ini ttaqaytunna fa-lā takhḍaʿna bi-l-qawli fa-yaṭmaʿa lladhī fī qalbihī maraḍun wa-qulna qawlan maʿrūfan*
>
> *wa-qarna fī buyūtikunna wa-lā tabarrajna tabarruja l-jāhiliyyati l-ūlā wa-aqimna ṣ-ṣalāta wa-ātīna z-zakāta wa-aṭiʿna llāha wa-rasūlahū innamā yurīdu llāhu li-yudhhiba ʿankumu r-rijsa ahla l-bayti wa-yuṭahhirakum taṭhīran*
>
> *wa-dhkurna mā yutlā fī buyūtikunna min āyāti llāhi wa-l-ḥikmati inna llāha kāna laṭīfan khabīran*

O wives of the prophet!
You are not like any other women.
If you fear God,
do not be submissive in your speech,
lest someone in whose heart is sickness be filled with desire,
but speak in a way that is recognized as proper;

And stay in your apartments.
Do not adorn yourselves with the adornment of the age of ignorance of old.
Perform prayer and pay the *zakāt*
and obey God and His messenger.
God wants to remove abomination from you,
People of the household
and to cleanse you.

Remember those of the signs of God and of wisdom
that are recited to you in your apartments.
God is Gentle and Informed.

---

111 *BCQ* 2:99; see David L. Balch, *Let Wives Be Submissive: The Domestic Code in I Peter* (Atlanta, Georgia: Scholars Press, 1981), *passim*; Hering, *The Colossian and Ephesian Haustafeln in Theological Context*, 9 and cf. 17–20; Karl Weidinger, *Die Haustafeln: Ein Stück urchristlicher Paränese* (Leipzig: J.C. Hinrichs'sche Buchhandlung, 1928), *passim*; Klaus Berger, "Hellenistische Gattungen im Neuen Testament," in *Aufstieg und Niedergang der römischen Welt: Geschichte und Kultur Roms im Spiegel der neueren Forschung*, ed. Hildegard Temporini and Wolfgang Haase (Berlin: Walter de Gruyter, 1984), 2:1078–86.

Noteworthy, in this specific context, is the reference to the "people of the household" (*ahl al-bayt*).[112] According to Bell, these verses "warn them against conduct unbefitting their special position."[113] In addition, consider the second household code formulation featured in Q. 33.59 (-*Can*), which remains detached from its literary context[114]:

> *yā-ayyuhā n-nabiyyu qul li-azwājika wa-banātika wa-nisā'i l-mu'minīna yudnīna 'alayhinna min jalābībihinna dhālika adnā an yu'rafna fa-lā yu'dhayna wa-kāna llāhu ghafūran raḥīman*

> O prophet!
> Say to your wives and daughters and womenfolk of the believers
> to draw their robes close to them.
> That is more appropriate as a way for them to be recognized and not vexed.
> God is Forgiving and Compassionate.

Bell comments, this code "recommends the letting down of part of the mantle, as a means of recognition, so that they may not be subject to insult…."[115]

Oracle

"In all likelihood, the woes," states Gerstenberger, "were tools in the hands of the wise men as well."[116] Through the showcasing of shame, wisdom as critique bitterly bewails the ills of society for all to see.[117] In terms of structure, Tucker distinguishes three elements, namely, the woe formula, the subject of ridicule, and the damning.[118] As for "which motives govern the woe oracles," Gerstenberger cites "the injustice connected with the greedy accumulation of wealth…."[119] In

---

112 Bell comments that "*ahl al-bayt* is usually interpreted as meaning the prophet's family, as the context addressed to his wives would at first sight appear to imply. But the new address is peculiar…" (*BCQ* 2:99–100).

113 Ibid., 2:99.

114 Ibid., 2:106.

115 Ibid.

116 Gerstenberger, "The Woe-Oracles of the Prophets," 261–62; cf. McLaughlin, *The Marzēaḥ in the Prophetic Literature*, 91–92.

117 Ibid.; James L. Crenshaw, "Method in Determining Wisdom Influence upon 'Historical' Literature," *JBL* 88, no. 2 (1969): 129–42.

118 Tucker, *Form Criticism of the Old Testament*, 66, fn. 98; Westermann, *Grundformen prophetischer Rede*, 137–142; Wolff, *Amos' geistige Heimat*, 12–23; Gerstenberger, "The Woe-Oracles of the Prophets," 250, 256, fn. 27, 257–58, and 260–62; cf. McLaughlin, *The Marzēaḥ in the Prophetic Literature*, 91 and 93–94.

119 Gerstenberger, "The Woe-Oracles of the Prophets," 255.

the *corpus coranicum*, for instance, consider "the attack on rich disbelievers" in Sūrat al-Humaza ("The Backbiter").[120] Q. 104.1–4 (-*Cah*) reads,

> *waylun li-kulli humazatin lumazatin*
>
> *alladhī jamaʿa mālan wa-ʿaddadahū*
>
> *yaḥsabu anna mālahū akhladahū*
>
> *kallā la-yunbadhanna fī l-ḥuṭamati*
>
> Woe to every slandering backbiter,
>
> Who has gathered riches and counted them.
>
> He thinks his riches have made him immortal!
>
> No indeed! He will be flung to the insatiable.

Neuwirth considers the first two verses a woe cry with vices specified.[121] According to Gerstenberger, "woe cries or the wisdom texts do not try to preserve the old situation in a legal fashion with formulated laws; rather, they deal with this problem on a more private basis, with bitter puns, exhortations, and warnings."[122] Appropriate to the object, Neuwirth labels the third and fourth verses, dispelling a false sense of security.[123] As a result, Gerstenberger writes, "we observe in such records the unofficial struggle against economic corruption and exploitation...."[124] For that reason, the "lampoon" in this woe oracle "recalls the tone of early Arabic satirical poetry."[125]

---

120 *JQA* 588; *BCQ* 2:583.
121 *SKMS*² 233.
122 Gerstenberger, "The Woe-Oracles of the Prophets," 257–58; cf. McLaughlin, *The Marzēaḥ in the Prophetic Literature*, 91–92.
123 *SKMS*² 233.
124 Gerstenberger, "The Woe-Oracles of the Prophets," 257.
125 Robinson, *Discovering the Qur'ān*, 127; *JQA* 588.

Conversation

The corpus preserves several conversations between parent and child.[126] Take, for example, Q. 37.102, which begins (-*īC*),

> *fa-lammā balagha maʿahu s-saʿya qāla yā-bunayya innī arā fī l-manāmi annī adhbaḥuka fa-nẓur mādhā tarā*
>
> When [the boy] was old enough to run at his side, he said:
> 'O my son!
> I have seen in my dreams
> that I shall sacrifice you.
> Look, what do you think?'

The verse continues,

> *qāla yā-abati fʿal mā tuʾmaru sa-tajidunī in shāʾa llāhu mina ṣ-ṣābirīna*
>
> He said:
> 'O my father!
> Do what you are commanded.
> You will find me, if God wills,
> to be one of the steadfast.'

Therefore, Abraham's sacrifice preserves "a forthright expression of will."[127] To continue, orders either prescribe or proscribe behavior.[128] Q. 12.5 (-*īC*) advises against disclosing sensitive information.[129] In Q. 12.4 (-*īC*), the narrative formula (*idh*) introduces this father and son conversation that commences with a dream report[130]:

> *idh qāla yūsufu li-abīhi yā-abati innī raʾaytu aḥada ʿashara kawkaban wa-sh-shamsa wa-l-qamara raʾaytuhum lī sājidīna*
>
> When Joseph said to his father:
> 'O my father!
> I have seen eleven stars and the sun and the moon
> – I have seen them bowing down to me.'

---

126 Cf. Corvin, "Stylistic and Functional Study of the Prose Prayers," *passim*; s.v. Proverb, Genre of, *DOTWPW*; Michael V. Fox, *Proverbs 1–9* (New Haven, Connecticut: Yale University Press, 2000), 45–47; *FOTL* 2a:160.
127 *SKMS*² 281 (vv. 99–107); *FOTL* 13:180.
128 *FOTL* 13:180.
129 Ibid.
130 S.v. Narratives, *EQ*; *SKMS*² 297; *BCQ* 1:376.

The adjoining verse (5) in Sūrat Yūsuf reads,

> *qāla yā-bunayya lā taqṣuṣ ru'yāka 'alā ikhwatika fa-yakīdū laka kaydan inna sh-shayṭāna li-l-insāni 'aduwwun mubīnun*
>
> He said:
> 'O my son!
> Do not recount your dream to your brothers
> lest they devise some piece of guile against you.
> Satan is a very clear enemy to man.'

In the case of this conversation, the prohibition is deeply rooted in patriarchal authority.[131] Q. 12.6 (-*īC*) continues,

> *wa-ka-dhālika yajtabīka rabbuka wa-yu'allimuka min ta'wīli l-aḥādīthi wa-yutimmu ni'ma-tahū 'alayka wa-'alā āli ya'qūba ka-mā atammahā 'alā abawayka min qablu ibrāhīma wa-isḥāqa inna rabbaka 'alīmun ḥakīmun*
>
> 'In this way your Lord is choosing you;
> and He will teach you something of the interpretation of what you are told,
> and He will perfect His blessing on you
> and on the family of Jacob,
> just as he perfected it before, on your forefathers, Abraham and Isaac.
> Your Lord is Knowing and Wise.'

Murphy notes, the prohibition is effectual even without any grounds; however, on occasion, a reason is given.[132] In consequence, this conversation concludes by acknowledging Joseph's place among the elect.[133]

Lecture

Sūrat Luqmān frames a number of parental lectures.[134] For instance, Q. 31.13 (-*īC*) represents one such selection[135]:

---

131 *FOTL* 13:180.
132 Ibid.
133 *SKMS*[2] 297.
134 S.v. Proverb, Genre of, *DOTWPW*; Fox, *Proverbs 1–9*, 45–47; cf. Bultmann, *Geschichte der synoptischen Tradition*, 74 and 76; *KU* 132–36 (Luqmān).
135 Although verses 12–19 "go together as dealing with Luqmān," Bell questions the integrity of this sapiential cluster (*BCQ* 2:82; *JQA* 376). Bell further comments that verse 13 "would make a new beginning, though it is not certain that it is so, but the repetition of Luqmān is suspicious" (*BCQ* 2:82).

wa-idh qāla luqmānu li-bnihī wa-huwa ya'iẓuhū yā-bunayya lā tushrik bi-llāhi inna sh-shirka la-ẓulmun 'aẓīmun

And when Luqmān said to his son, admonishing him:
'O my son!
Do not associate any partner with God.
Associating partners with God is a grievous wrong.'

Murphy observes, there is in sapiential literature a preponderance of commands of the negative type.[136] It is clearly evident that the core principle consists of a theological prohibition.[137] What is more, it appears that the earnest appeal and the reasoning behind it both precede the lecture (*yā bunayya*) in this series.[138] Q. 31.12 (*-īC*) provides the narrative setting for this material[139]:

wa-la-qad ātaynā luqmāna l-ḥikmata ani shkur li-llāhi wa-man yashkur fa-innamā yashkuru li-nafsihī wa-man kafara fa-inna llāha ghaniyyun ḥamīdun

We gave Luqmān wisdom, saying:
'Give thanks to God.
Those who give thanks
do so only for the good of their own souls.'
Those who are ungrateful
– God is All-sufficient and Laudable.

The quintipartite literary structure of this father and son lecture concludes with a prescriptive injunction (v. 14) for full comprehension (*-īC*).[140]

The legacy of Luqmān also contains parental lectures exhibiting a dual literary structure.[141] As noted, the lecture form opens with a term of endearment: "O my son" (*yā bunayya*).[142] In these specific cases, the exhortation, motive clause, and conclusion are altogether dispensed with.[143] Secondly, the wisdom teaching follows the address.[144] For example, Q. 31.16 reads (*-īC*),

136 *FOTL* 13:180.
137 *SKMS*[2] 304; s.v. Proverb, Genre of, *DOTWPW*.
138 *FOTL* 2a:161; cf. Bultmann, *Geschichte der synoptischen Tradition*, 74 and 76; *FOTL* 13:177–78, 181, and 184; Phillip R. Callaway, "Deut 21:18–21: Proverbial Wisdom and Law," *JBL* 103, no. 3 (1984): 341. For instance, consider the doublet: *fa-inna ma'a l-'usri yusran, inna ma'a l-'usri yusran* (Q. 94.5–6). For aphorisms (sing. *mathal*) in the Qur'ān, see Hirschfeld, *New Researches*, 83–86; cf. Harrington, *Jesus Ben Sira of Jerusalem*, 68–70.
139 S.v. Proverb, Genre of, *DOTWPW*; s.v. Narratives, *EQ*; *KU* 132–36.
140 S.v. Proverb, Genre of, *DOTWPW*; Fox, *Proverbs 1–9*, 45.
141 *SKMS*[2] 304; s.v. Proverb, Genre of, *DOTWPW*.
142 S.v. Proverb, Genre of, *DOTWPW*.
143 Ibid.; *FOTL* 13:177.

yā-bunayya innahā in taku mithqāla ḥabbatin min khardalin fa-takun fī ṣakhratin aw fī s-samāwāti aw fī l-arḍi ya'ti bihā llāhu inna llāha laṭīfun khabīrun

O my son!
If it is the weight of a grain of mustard
and if it is in rock or in the heavens or on earth,
God will bring it forth.
God is Kind and Informed.

Neuwirth characterizes this as a lesson on God's omniscience.[145] In addition, the corpus preserves a lecture pair (Q. 31.17–18) that consists of a series of commands and prohibitions.[146] Verse 17 (-*ūC*) reads,[147]

yā-bunayya aqimi ṣ-ṣalāta wa-mur bi-l-ma'rūfi wa-nha 'ani l-munkari wa-ṣbir 'alā mā aṣābaka inna dhālika min 'azmi l-umūri

O my son!
Perform worship,
enjoin what is reputable
and forbid what is disreputable,
and endure patiently what befalls you.
That comes from determination in affairs.

The lecture focuses on performing worship and practicing patience.[148] The subsequent verse (18) immediately follows with serial prohibitions (-*ūC*)[149]:

wa-lā tuṣa''ir khaddaka li-n-nāsi wa-lā tamshi fī l-arḍi maraḥan inna llāha lā yuḥibbu kulla mukhtālin fakhūrin

Do not turn your cheek from men in disdain,
and do not walk in the land in exultation.
God does not love anyone who is conceited and boastful.

This is an appeal to exercise restraint and to tread lightly.[150]

144 S.v. Proverb, Genre of, *DOTWPW*.
145 *SKMS*² 304; *BCQ* 2:83.
146 *FOTL* 13:174 and 13:180.
147 Ibid., 13:174. Cf. Q. 3.104 and Q. 7.157 (*BCQ* 2:83).
148 *SKMS*² 304.
149 *FOTL* 13:180.
150 *SKMS*² 304 (vv. 18–19).

Lesson

Didactic and catechetic content assumes the lesson form with the frequent formula, *mā adrāka mā.*[151] Douglas Estes explains that "expository questions take this one step further by having the speaker answer the question in order to bring about a deeper reflection on the question at hand."[152] In other words, the header functions "as a rhetorical tool to preface an answer."[153] Sūrat al-Ḥāqqa ("The Reality") adopts an identical structure. Q. 69.1–3 (-*Cah*) reads,

> *al-ḥāqqatu*
>
> *mā l-ḥāqqatu*
>
> *wa-mā adrāka mā l-ḥāqqatu*
>
> The reality.
>
> What is the reality?
>
> What can give you[S] knowledge of what the reality is?

Neuwirth considers these didactic verses on *al-ḥāqqa.*[154] Additionally, Q. 82.17–19 introduces an exposition (with a doubled formulary) on the Last Judgment[155]:

> *wa-mā adrāka mā yawmu d-dīni*
>
> *thumma mā adrāka mā yawmu d-dīni*
>
> *yawma lā tamliku nafsun li-nafsin shay'an wa-l-amru yawma'idhin li-llāhi*
>
> What can give you[S] knowledge of what the Day of Judgment is?

---

151 Cf. Draper, "Torah and Troublesome Apostles in the *Didache* Community," 343; Soulen, *Handbook of Biblical Criticism*, 39 and 56; s.v. Catechesis, *EAC*; Bultmann, *Geschichte der synoptischen Tradition*, 76; Wolff, *Amos' geistige Heimat*, 5–12; *BCQ* 2:413.
152 N.b. "Quintilian treats expository questions as one type of question designed to emphasize a point rather than gather information – a category erroneously labeled 'rhetorical' in many modern discussions" (Estes, *The Questions of Jesus in John*, 71 and 108, fn. 105).
153 Ibid., 108.
154 *SKMS*[2] 212; cf. *JQA* 534.
155 *BCQ* 2:507; *JQA* 561.

Then what can give you^S knowledge of what the Day of Judgment is?

The day when no soul will have anything to help another soul,
The affair on that day will be God's.

Both elements in this wisdom lesson comprise a question and answer about *yawmu d-dīn.*[156] Although "the general purport of the term is clear enough," Robinson explains, "the didactic question allows for further elaboration."[157] This statement equally applies to Q. 77.14 (*-Cl*), whose query concerns "the day of decision" (*yawmu l-faṣl*).[158] It apparently applies less so to the terms *sijjīn* (Q. 83.8) and *ʿilliyyūn* (Q. 83.19).[159] Similarly, the second verse of Sūrat aṭ-Ṭāriq ("What Comes in the Night") preserves a question.[160] Q. 86.2 queries,

wa-mā adrāka mā ṭ-ṭāriqu

What can give you^S knowledge of what it is that comes in the night?

Commenting on *aṭ-ṭāriq*, Bell says, "that it needed explanation would seem to show that it was not a word commonly used in that sense."[161] In addition, Q. 90.12 (*-Cah*) enquires,

wa-mā adrāka mā l-ʿaqabatu

What can give you^S knowledge of what the ascent is?

The same fragmentary scenario applies to the didactic question here as well.[162]

At the same time, Sūrat al-Qadr (Q. 97) contains the answer (vv. 3–5) to the question (v. 2) on *al-qadr*. In consequence, the wisdom lesson in this sūra-unit (*-Cr*) begins with the second verse[163]:

wa-mā adrāka mā laylatu l-qadri

And what can give you^S knowledge of what the night of power is?

---

156 *SKMS*² 221.
157 Robinson, *Discovering the Qurʾān*, 120.
158 *SKMS*² 216.
159 Robinson, *Discovering the Qurʾān*, 120; *SKMS*² 222; *BCQ* 2:509–10; *JQA* 562.
160 *SKMS*² 224; Robinson, *Discovering the Qurʾān*, 120; *JQA* 567.
161 *BCQ* 2:523.
162 *SKMS*² 228; cf. Robinson, *Discovering the Qurʾān*, 120.
163 *SKMS*² 231; *JQA* 581, fn. 1; *BCQ* 2:563.

In an astute observation, Bell draws our attention to the fact that this term has undergone semantic reanalysis.[164] By means of a "better-than saying," verses 3 to 5 elaborate,[165]

laylatu l-qadri khayrun min alfi shahrin

tanazzalu l-malāʾikatu wa-r-rūḥu fīhā bi-idhni rabbihim min kulli amrin

salāmun hiya ḥattā maṭlaʿi l-fajri

The night of power is better than a thousand months;

The angels and the spirit descend during it,
by permission of their Lord in every matter.

Peace it is until the rising of the dawn.

Apparently, Neuwirth claims that this lesson corresponds to "a brief festal legend."[166]

Instruction

Murphy defines instruction as follows: "A teaching or doctrine that gives guidance to an individual or group, setting forth certain values, or prescribing rules of conduct, answering questions, etc."[167] Since these are issued by the man of God, the man of the cloth, and even the man of law, instructions are tailored accordingly.[168] In the *corpus coranicum*, moral teaching takes the form of

164 Ibid.; cf. Robinson, *Discovering the Qurʾān*, 120.
165 S.v. Proverb, Genre of, *DOTWPW*; Alexander A. Di Lella, introduction to *The Wisdom of Ben Sira*, trans. Patrick W. Skehan (New York: Doubleday & Company Inc., 1987), 24. According to Bell: "v. 3 introduces one of those time speculations which occur now and then in the Qurʾān, cf. Q. 22.47: One day = a thousand years; Q. 32.5 (*ditto*); Q. 70.4: one day = fifty thousand years. One would surmise that these belong to some one period, and the dating of this would then depend on the dating of these passages (in Q. 70, v. 4 is a later addition), most probably, early Medinan" (*BCQ* 2:563).
166 *SKMS*[2] 194; cf. Richter, *Der Sprachstil des Koran*, 24; Kees Wagtendonk, *Fasting in the Koran* (Leiden: E.J. Brill, 1968), 82–122; Robinson, *Discovering the Qurʾān*, 115 and 120; *JQA* 581.
167 *FOTL* 13:177; *FOTL* 14:251 and cf. 14:257–58.
168 *FOTL* 13:177.

dialogue.[169] As a matter of course, it assumes a threefold construction, which opens with the dialogic formula: "they ask you^{S}" (*yas'alūnaka*).[170] It then raises the issue at hand, followed by a solution of sorts.[171] In fact, Wansbrough observes, "*qul* may preface an apodosis after statements beginning *yas'alūnaka* (they ask you), often of halakhic content…."[172] He invites the reader to consider the first of "a series of answers formulated to questions which believers ask, or are likely to ask."[173] Accordingly, Q. 2.215 (-*īC*) reads,

> *yas'alūnaka mādhā yunfiqūna qul mā anfaqtum min khayrin fa-li-l-wālidayni wa-l-aqrabīna wa-l-yatāmā wa-l-masākīni wa-bni s-sabīli wa-mā taf'alū min khayrin fa-inna llāha bihī 'alīmun*
>
> They ask you^{S} what they are to spend.
> Say^{S}: 'Whatever good you^{P} spend should be for parents, close relatives, orphans, the destitute, and travellers. Whatever good you do, God is aware of it.'

Here again, Q. 2.219a-20 addresses expenditure[174]:

> *wa-yas'alūnaka mādhā yunfiqūna quli l-'afwa ka-dhālika yubayyinu llāhu lakumu l-āyāti la'allakum tatafakkarūna fī d-dunyā wa-l-ākhirati*
>
> And they ask you^{S} what they are to spend.
> Say^{S}: 'The surplus.'
> Thus God makes the signs clear for you^{P}, so that you may reflect
> on this world and the world to come.

At the same time, Q. 2.219 concerns practices of doubtful propriety[175]:

> *yas'alūnaka 'ani l-khamri wa-l-maysiri qul fīhimā ithmun kabīrun wa-manāfi'u li-n-nāsi wa-ithmuhumā akbaru min naf'ihimā*

---

169 Wesselhoeft, "Making Muslim Minds," 790; cf. *SPMC* xxv; Corvin, "Stylistic and Functional Study of the Prose Prayers," 67–68 and 70–78; Dibelius, *A Fresh Approach to the New Testament and Early Christian Literature*, 225 and 227; Harrington, *Jesus Ben Sira of Jerusalem*, 74; *FOTL* 13:175; *FOTL* 2a:160.
170 Wesselhoeft, "Making Muslim Minds," 792–93. "A slightly different pattern of question and response is reflected in the *ḥadīth* literature…" (Masud et al., "Muftis, Fatwas, and Islamic Legal Interpretation," 5–6).
171 Wesselhoeft, "Making Muslim Minds," 790 and 792.
172 *QS* 14.
173 Ibid. Bell comments, "The earliest of them, at least, were not intended to form part of the Book, and were not in rhyme" (*BCQ* 1:44).
174 *JQA* 24 and 51, fn. 35; *BCQ* 1:45.
175 *BCQ* 1:45; cf. Q. 5.90–91 (*JQA* 51, fn. 34).

They ask you^S about wine and *maysir.*
Say^S: 'In both these is great sin, but some benefits to the people; but the sin in them is greater than the benefit.'

On a related note, the fourth verse in Sūrat al-Māʾida fields a question about the permissibility of consuming wild game caught by tamed beasts of prey.[176] Q. 5.4 (-*āC*) reads,

yasʾalūnaka mādhā uḥilla lahum qul uḥilla lakumu ṭ-ṭayyibātu wa-mā ʿallamtum mina l-jawāriḥi mukallibīna tuʿallimūnahunna mimmā ʿallamakumu llāhu fa-kulū mimmā amsakna ʿalaykum wa-dhkurū sma llāhi ʿalayhi wa-ttaqū llāha inna llāha sarīʿu l-ḥisābi

They ask you^S what is permitted to them.
Say^S: 'Permitted to you^P are [all] good things; and those hunting beasts that you teach, training them, teaching them what God has taught you – eat what they catch for you, mentioning God's name over it and fearing God. God is swift to the reckoning.'

Q. 2.220a (-*īC*) turns to the care and treatment of orphans[177]:

wa-yasʾalūnaka ʿani l-yatāmā qul iṣlāḥun lahum khayrun wa-in tukhāliṭūhum fa-ikhwānukum wa-llāhu yaʿlamu l-mufsida mina l-muṣliḥi wa-law shāʾa llāhu la-aʿnatakum inna llāha ʿazīzun ḥakīmun

And they ask you^S about orphans.
Say^S: 'Setting their affairs right is good. If you^P mix with them, they are your brothers. God knows the one who causes mischief from the one who sets things right. Had He wished, He could have overburdened you. God is Mighty and Wise.'

As in this case, "wisdom instruction usually prescribes a rule of conduct or some value, whether positively or negatively. It may be very short and provided with a motive clause."[178] The latter element is also featured in Q. 2.222 (-*īC*):

wa-yasʾalūnaka ʿani l-maḥīḍi qul huwa adhan fa-ʿtazilū n-nisāʾa fī l-maḥīḍi wa-lā taqrabūhunna ḥattā yaṭhurna fa-idhā taṭahharna fa-tūhunna min ḥaythu amarakumu llāhu inna llāha yuḥibbu t-tawwābīna wa-yuḥibbu l-mutaṭahhirīna

They ask you^S about menstruation.
Say^S: 'It is a vexation. Withdraw^P from women during menstruation and do not approach them until they are clean. When they are clean, come to them as God has commanded you.' God loves those who repent, and He loves those who keep themselves clean.

---

176 *BCQ* 1:149.
177 Wesselhoeft, "Making Muslim Minds," 791. According to Bell, "The rhyme-phrase has again been added later" (*BCQ* 1:46).
178 *FOTL* 13:177.

This particular verse presents a question regarding the menstrual cycle, thus reflecting a wide array of questions put forth.[179]

What is more, Wansbrough notes that the dialogic formula (*yas'alūnaka*) even encompasses the Hour.[180] Take, for instance, the doublet in Q. 7.187[181]:

> *yas'alūnaka 'ani s-sā'ati ayyāna mursāhā qul innamā 'ilmuhā 'inda rabbī lā yujallīhā li-waqtihā illā huwa thaqulat fī s-samāwāti wa-l-arḍi lā ta'tīkum illā baghtatan*
>
> *yas'alūnaka ka-annaka ḥafiyyun 'anhā qul innamā 'ilmuhā 'inda llāhi wa-lākinna akthara n-nāsi lā ya'lamūna*
>
> They ask you^{S} about the Hour: 'When is the time of its anchoring?'
> Say^{S}: 'Knowledge of it is only with my Lord. Only He will reveal it at its proper time. It is heavy in the heavens and the earth – [but] it will only come to you^{P} suddenly.'
>
> They ask you^{S} as if you were well-informed about it.
> Say^{S}: 'Knowledge of it is only with God, but most of the people do not know.'

This verse represents a question and answer as to the time of reckoning.[182] Also, consider Q. 79.42–46 (-*Cā*) *sin* apodotic *qul*[183]:

> *yas'alūnaka 'ani s-sā'ati ayyāna mursāhā*
>
> *fī-ma anta min dhikrāhā*
>
> *ilā rabbika muntahāhā*
>
> *innamā anta mundhiru man yakhshāhā*
>
> *ka-annahum yawma yarawnahā lam yalbathū illā 'ashiyyatan aw ḍuḥāhā*
>
> They ask you^{S} about the Hour: 'When is the time of its anchoring?
>
> What mention can you^{S} make of it?'
>
> To your^{S} Lord is its goal.

---

179 *BCQ* 1:46; Wesselhoeft, "Making Muslim Minds," 791.
180 *QS* 14.
181 Cf. *BCQ* 1:263–64.
182 *SKMS*^{2} 293 (vv. 187–88).
183 Cf. ibid., 218–19 (vv. 42–43). Robinson considers the "messenger section" (vv. 42–46) "solace" (-*āhā*) (idem, *Discovering the Qur'ān*, 145–46, 177–88, esp. 186–88, and cf. 86–87).

You^{S} are merely the warner of those who fear it.

On the day they see it, it will be as if they had tarried only for an evening or its forenoon.

The sūra-unit ends by giving final notice.[184] According to Neuwirth, verses 44 and 45 offer clarification on the eschaton.[185] The subsequent verse (46) finishes with an oblique account of the sudden end.[186] Bell comments that it "is a reflex of the objection to the resurrection based on the length of time bodies had remained in the grave; souls will not be conscious of that."[187] In addition, with special reference to the issue of God's omniscience, Q. 17.85 (-*Can*) preserves a question with regard to the spirit (*rūḥ*)[188]:

wa-yas'alūnaka ani r-rūḥi quli r-rūḥu min amri rabbī wa-mā ūtītum mina l-ʿilmi illā qalīlan

And they ask you^{S} about the spirit.
Say^{S}: 'The spirit is part of the affair of my Lord; and you^{P} have been given only little knowledge.'

On the topic, "all that can be said is that it is connected with God's affair…."[189] Finally, Q. 20.105–7 (-*Can*) reads,[190]

wa-yas'alūnaka ʿani l-jibāli fa-qul yansifuhā rabbī nasfan

fa-yadharuhā qāʿan ṣafṣafan

lā tarā fīhā ʿiwajan wa-lā amtan

And they ask you^{S} about the mountains.
Say^{S}: 'My Lord will scatter them as ashes,

And leave them as an empty plain,

In which you^{S} will see no crookedness nor distortion.'

184 *JQA* 555.
185 *SKMS*^{2} 218.
186 Ibid.
187 *BCQ* 2:491.
188 *SKMS*^{2} 267.
189 *BCQ* 1:475.
190 *BCQ* 1:534 (vv. 105–108).

Bell writes, "Someone may have pointed to the mountains as a thing of permanence. The answer is that they will be reduced to a perfectly level plain."[191] Neuwirth considers these verses a threat of divine retribution for openly eschewing revelation.[192]

Sermon

Consider the "independent sermon" (Q. 27.59–64) preached to the whole.[193] It appropriately opens and closes with the conveyance command formula (*qul*), which "expresses the command to the recipient of a message to convey the message to a third party."[194] That is to say, the "relator," who is directed by prophetic authority to promulgate the announcement, "is simply a speaker in the name of a higher authority, whose orders must be obeyed."[195] According to the manner of delivery, this pericope constitutes a sermon proper: "A special kind of instruction and discourse develops which no longer announces a new truth, but which seeks instead to depict and spread the already announced truth."[196] Bell states that verse 59 "begins with what looks like the heading of a new passage, as this declaration preceded by *qul* probably once was."[197] The oration commences with the sermon formula (*ḥamdala*) and the *benedictio:*

> *quli l-ḥamdu li-llāhi wa-salāmun ʿalā ʿibādihi lladhīna ṣṭafā*
>
> Speak:
> Praise belongs to God,
> and peace be on His servants whom He has chosen.

Verse 59a immediately announces the theme with an expository question, which achieves, in some measure, the desired effect[198]:

> *āllāhu khayrun ammā yushrikūna*

---

191 Ibid., 1:534.
192 *SKMS*^{2} 270 (vv. 100–107).
193 *BCQ* 2:36; cf. Hirschfeld who considers Q. 27.59–93 to be the appropriate sermon unit (idem, *New Researches*, 77).
194 *FOTL* 4:364; *QS* 16; Seybold, *Die Psalmen*, 52.
195 S.v. Preaching, *EAC*.
196 Baeck, "Griechische und jüdische Predigt," 143; cf. Neuwirth, "Einige Bemerkungen," 1:736, note 1; *QSC* 253, fn. 1.
197 *BCQ* 2:36.
198 Estes, *The Questions of Jesus in John*, 107–110, esp. 108.

Is God better or that which they associate [with him]?

Bell notes that this *āyāt*-structured verse group (vv. 59–64) incorporates a reoccurring interrogative element.[199] In any case, the refrain-like *am-man* works in tandem with the "confirmation question" refrain (*a-ilāhun ma'a llāhi*) to ensure the structural integrity of this sermon-unit.[200] Verses 60 to 64 of Sūrat an-Naml involve question and answer[201]:

am-man khalaqa s-samāwāti wa-l-arḍa wa-anzala lakum mina s-samā'i mā'an fa-anbatnā bihī ḥadā'iqa dhāta bahjatin mā kāna lakum an tunbitū shajarahā a-ilāhun ma'a llāhi bal hum qawmun ya'dilūna

am-man ja'ala l-arḍa qarāran wa-ja'ala khilālahā anhāran wa-ja'ala lahā rawāsiya wa-ja'ala bayna l-baḥrayni ḥājizan a-ilāhun ma'a llāhi bal aktharuhum lā ya'lamūna

am-man yujību l-muḍṭarra idhā da'āhu wa-yakshifu s-sū'a wa-yaj'alukum khulafā'a l-arḍi a-ilāhun ma'a llāhi qalīlan mā tadhakkarūna

am-man yahdīkum fī ẓulumāti l-barri wa-l-baḥri wa-man yursilu r-riyāḥa bushran bayna yaday raḥmatihī a-ilāhun ma'a llāhi ta'ālā llāhu 'ammā yushrikūna

am-man yabda'u l-khalqa thumma yu'īduhū wa-man yarzuqukum mina s-samā'i wa-l-arḍi a-ilāhun ma'a llāhi

Is He not the one who has created the heavens and the earth
and sent down for you^{P} water from the sky,
through which We have caused to grow gardens full of beauty
whose trees you could not grow?
Is there a god in addition to God?
No, they are a people who deviate [from the truth].

Is He not the one who made the earth a firm place
and set rivers amid it
and placed on it firm mountains
and placed a partition between the two seas?
Is there a god in addition to God?
No, most of them have no knowledge.

Is He not the one who answers the harassed person

199 *BCQ* 2:36.
200 Estes, *The Questions of Jesus in John*, 37, fn. 18, and 113.
201 Cf. Bultmann, *Geschichte der synoptischen Tradition*, 76; Koch, *Die Profeten I*, 31; Westermann, *Der Psalter*, 22–24.

when he calls to Him
and removes evil and makes you viceroys of the earth?
Is there any god in addition to God?
Little are you^{P} reminded.

Is He not the one who guides you^{P} in the darkness of the land and the sea;
who looses the winds as harbingers of His mercy?
Is there any god in addition to God?
May God be exalted high above what they associate with Him.

Is He not the one who originates creation,
then causes it to happen again;
who gives you^{P} sustenance from the heaven and the earth?
Is there any god in addition to God?

Neuwirth considers verses 59–64 to be polemical questions regarding the Originator.[202] According to Jones, Q. 27.59–93 constitutes "a longish passage, partly polemic but mainly on God's attributes...."[203] Furthermore, the pronominal shift (vv. 60a and 60b) is not unprecedented.[204] Bell further adds that the theme of this sermon pericope (vv. 59–64) is His uniqueness.[205] Verse 64a concludes,

qul hātū burhānakum in kuntum ṣādiqīna

Speak:
Bring your^{P} proof, if you are truthful.

Speaking on behalf of prophetic authority, the *inclusio* of this directed sermon appropriately closes with the conveyance command formula (*qul*), followed by a rhetorical challenge addressed to the live audience.[206]

Beyond showing the way, sermons "were also intended to harness the persuasive power of the local pulpit to foster the populace's embrace of its new re-

202 *SKMS*^{2} 278.
203 *JQA* 345.
204 *BCQ* 2:36.
205 Ibid.
206 J. Clinton McCann, Jr., "The Shape and Shaping of the Psalter: Psalms in Their Literary Context," in *The Oxford Handbook of the Psalms*, ed. William P. Brown (Oxford: Oxford University Press, 2014), 356.

ligious beliefs and rhythms."[207] For instance, consider the "peroration urging belief and virtue" in Q. 47.33–38 (-*Cm*).[208] Verses 33 through 37 read,[209]

yā-ayyuhā lladhīna āmanū aṭīʿū llāha wa-aṭīʿū r-rasūla wa-lā tubṭilū aʿmālakum

inna lladhīna kafarū wa-ṣaddū ʿan sabīli llāhi thumma mātū wa-hum kuffārun fa-lan yaghfira llāhu lahum

fa-lā tahinū wa-tadʿū ilā s-salmi wa-antumu l-aʿlawna wa-llāhu maʿakum wa-lan yatirakum aʿmālakum

innamā l-ḥayātu d-dunyā laʿibun wa-lahwun wa-in tuʾminū wa-tattaqū yuʾtikum ujūrakum wa-lā yasʾalkum amwālakum

in yasʾalkumūhā fa-yuḥfikum tabkhalū wa-yukhrij aḍghānakum

O you who believe!
Obey God and obey the messenger,
and do not render your own works vain.

Those who do not believe and who turn [people] away from God's way
and then die when they are disbelievers,
God will not forgive them.

So do not weaken and call for peace,
when you have the upper hand;
for God is with you.
He will not grudge you your works.

The life of this world is only a sport and a diversion.
If you^{P} believe and protect yourselves,
He will give you your wages
and will not ask you for your possessions.

If He were to ask you for them and to press you,
you would be niggardly,
and He would bring to light your ill will.

---

207 Cf. Ashley Null, "Official Tudor Homilies," in *The Oxford Handbook of the Early Modern Sermon*, ed. Peter McCullough and Hugh Adlington (Oxford: Oxford University Press, 2011), 348; Greg Kneidel, "*Ars Prædicandi:* Theories and Practice," in op. cit., 6.
208 *JQA* 467.
209 Cf. Null, "Official Tudor Homilies," 358.

According to Bell, securing financial support proved to be more problematic than anticipated.[210] Noteworthy, therefore, is the deictic formula (*hā-antum*) that closes this sermon on charity (v. 38)[211]:

hā-antum hā'ulā'i tud'awna li-tunfiqū fī sabīli llāhi fa-minkum man yabkhalu wa-man yabkhal fa-innamā yabkhalu 'an nafsihī wa-llāhu l-ghaniyyu wa-antumu l-fuqarā'u wa-in tatawallaw yastabdil qawman ghayrakum thumma lā yakūnū amthālakum

Here you are.
You are called on to spend in God's way,
but there are some of you who are niggardly.
Those who are niggardly are only niggardly to themselves.
God is the All-sufficient, and you^{P} are the needy.
If you turn away, He will replace you by another people;
and then they will not be like you.

The same formulation is also present in the sermon on misplaced loyalty. Q. 3.118–19 (-*ūC*) reads,

yā-ayyuhā lladhīna āmanū lā tattakhidhū biṭānatan min dūnikum lā ya'lūnakum khabālan waddū mā 'anittum qad badati l-baghḍā'u min afwāhihim wa-mā tukhfī ṣudūruhum akbaru qad bayyannā lakumu l-āyāti in kuntum ta'qilūna

hā-antum ulā'i tuḥibbūnahum wa-lā yuḥibbūnakum wa-tu'minūna bi-l-kitābi kullihī wa-idhā laqūkum qālū āmannā wa-idhā khalaw 'aḍḍū 'alaykumu l-anāmila mina l-ghayẓi qul mūtū bi-ghayẓikum inna llāha 'alīmun bi-dhāti ṣ-ṣudūri

O you who believe!
Do not take intimates from outside yourselves,
who will spare no efforts to ruin you
and love what you are distressed at.
Their hatred has already appeared from their mouths,
and what their breasts conceal is greater.
We have made the signs clear for you,
if you understand.

Here you are.
You^{P} love them,
but they do not love you;
you believe in the whole of the scripture,
and when they meet you they say, 'We believe,'
but when they are alone, they bite their fingers in anger at you.

---

210 *BCQ* 2:279.
211 Cf. Null, "Official Tudor Homilies," 358; *BCQ* 2:280.

Say^S: 'Die^P through your anger.
God is aware of the thoughts in your breasts.'

Bell renders *khabāl* as "lack of morale."[212] Consider as well the sermon on "assurance of salvation" (Q. 33.41–44) that reads (*-Can*),[213]

yā-ayyuhā lladhīna āmanū dhkurū llāha dhikran kathīran

wa-sabbiḥūhu bukratan wa-aṣīlan

huwa lladhī yuṣallī ʿalaykum wa-malāʾikatuhū li-yukhrijakum mina ẓ-ẓulumāti ilā n-nūri wa-kāna bi-l-muʾminīna raḥīman

taḥiyyatuhum yawma yalqawnahū salāmun wa-aʿadda lahum ajran karīman

O you who believe!
remember God often,

And glorify Him morning and evening.

It is He who blesses you,
[as do] His angels,
to bring you out of the darkness into the light.
He is Merciful to the believers.

Their greeting on the day they meet Him will be, 'Peace.'
He has prepared for them a generous wage.

This sermon is intended to instill confidence and conviction.[214] In this context, the following point is worthy of note. The greeting on the day is indicative of "instructions for the hereafter."[215] In other words, *salām* constitutes a ritual pass for the dead.[216] Besides the foregoing sermon on salvation, the text contains an ex-

212 *BCQ* 1:88.
213 Cf. Null, "Official Tudor Homilies," 356. Regarding Q. 33, Jones states, "At two natural breaks more general passages have been added (35–36, then 41–44 plus 45–48 and a bridging verse 49)" (*JQA* 383).
214 *BCQ* 2:102.
215 *Gods, Heroes, and Monsters: A Sourcebook of Greek, Roman, and Near Eastern Myths*, ed. Carolina López-Ruiz (Oxford: Oxford University Press, 2014), 489.
216 Ibid., 489–91. These passes serve "the function of reminding the soul to declare something to an underworld authority in order to establish its identity as an initiate and therefore its right to pass into paradise" (Fritz Graf and Sarah Iles Johnston, *Ritual Texts for the Afterlife: Orpheus and the Bacchic Gold Tablets* (New York: Routledge, 2007), 133).

tensive one on mercy (Q. 33.9–27).[217] The long passage opens with the sermon formula in the ninth verse (-*Can*)[218]:

> *yā-ayyuhā lladhīna āmanū dhkurū niʿmata llāhi ʿalaykum idh jāʾatkum junūdun fa-arsalnā ʿalayhim rīḥan wa-junūdan lam tarawhā wa-kāna llāhu bi-mā taʿmalūna baṣīran*
>
> O you who believe!
> Remember God's blessing to you
> when hosts came [against] you,
> and We sent against them a wind
> and hosts that you^{P} did not see,
> though God is observer of what you do.

Following a narrow escape from disaster, this sermon stresses divine favor.[219]

4.5 Summary

The present chapter has examined the wisdom genre in the *corpus coranicum*. In particular, it has identified a broad range of sapiential formulae. For that reason, the speech-forms in wisdom literature comprise an equally expansive repertoire, spanning admonitions and exhortations to lectures and sermons. In addition to locating these pedagogical materials in household ethos and clan wisdom, it has also addressed the appropriation of these traditional forms to meet the growing demands present in multiple teaching situations. Significantly, Laurent Pernot considers sermon and story as aspects of pious performance.[220] Beyond this, the Qurʾān exhibits an interplay between wisdom and narrative writ large. Even in the biblical case, "the absence of wisdom forms does not disqualify a narrative text from having significant wisdom elements."[221] Accordingly, let us turn our attention to the narrative genre.

---

217 Cf. Null, "Official Tudor Homilies," 356. N.b. Q. 33.13: *yā-ahla yathriba* ("O people of Yathrib").

218 *JQA* 383.

219 *BCQ* 2:96; Robinson, *Discovering the Qurʾān*, 31.

220 Pernot, "The Rhetoric of Religion," 329.

221 Lindsay Wilson, *Joseph, Wise and Otherwise: The Intersection of Wisdom and Covenant in Genesis 37–50* (Eugene, Oregon: Wipf & Stock Publishers, 2004), 31, fn. 103; Roger N. Whybray, *The Intellectual Tradition in the Old Testament* (Berlin: Walter de Gruyter, 1974), 55, fn. 1, and 72–76.

Chapter 5: Narrative

5.1 Narrative Genre

Nearly a quarter of the *corpus coranicum* is composed of narrative material.[1] Hirschfeld explains, "the narrative element is so essential, that it must be carefully investigated...."[2] Accordingly, this chapter considers the narrative genre.[3] In terms of textual units, at least four gradient forms of the genre are immediately recognizable: saga, episode, legend, and report.[4] In the first place, Horovitz identifies those pericopae which, in their entirety, are composite constructions.[5] In other words, the saga form links a number of discrete episodes, then narrates these in a more or less coherent series.[6] Secondly, and for this reason, the original building blocks are not only discernable but also detachable.[7] Thirdly, these

---

1 Marshall, *God, Muḥammad and the Unbelievers*, 31–32; Faruq Sherif, *A Guide to the Contents of the Qurʾān* (London: Ithaca Press, 1985), 46; s.v. Narratives, *EQ*.

2 Hirschfeld, *New Researches*, 62. Claude Gilliot states, "It is well known that a wide variety of formulaic elements occur throughout the Qurʾān. This is in keeping with its basically oral nature, but perhaps is also a consequence of its reshaping" (s.v. Narratives, *EQ*; Sinai, *Fortschreibung und Auslegung*, 153–54; Angelika Neuwirth, "Erzählen als kanonischer Prozeß: Die Mose-Erzählung im Wandel der koranischen Geschichte," in *Islamstudien ohne Ende: Festschrift für Werner Ende zum 65. Geburtstag*, ed. Rainer Brunner, Monika Gronke, Jens Peter Laut, and Ulrich Rebstock (Würzburg: Ergon Verlag, 2002), 323–44).

3 S.v. Narratives, *EQ*; cf. *FOTL* 2a:166.

4 *FOTL* 2a:165–66; *FOTL* 10:312 and 10:313–14; *FOTL* 1:319; cf. Jolles, *Einfache Formen*, 62–90; Hirschfeld, *New Researches*, 62; Robert W. Neff, "Saga," in *Saga, Legend, Tale, Novella, Fable: Narrative Forms in Old Testament Literature*, ed. George W. Coats (Sheffield, England: JSOT Press, 1985), 22; Stephen H. Travis, "Form Criticism," in *New Testament Interpretation: Essays on Principles and Methods*, ed. I. Howard Marshall (Grand Rapids, Michigan: Wm. B. Eerdmans Publishing Company, 1977), 156–57; Ronald M. Hals, "Legend: A Case Study in Old Testament Form-Critical Terminology," *CBQ* 34, no. 2 (1972): 168. On the other hand, for legend in the restricted sense, cf. *FOTL* 1:318; *FOTL* 2a:164; *FOTL* 10:304; Jolles, *Einfache Formen*, 23–61; Sidersky, *Les origines des légendes musulmanes*, *passim*.

5 *KU* 2.

6 *FOTL* 2a:165–66.

7 *KU* 1–2. Wansbrough writes, Q. 12 is "often cited as a single instance of complete and sustained narrative in the Qurʾān. In fact, without benefit of exegesis the qurʾānic story of Joseph is anything but clear, a consequence in part of its elliptical presentation and in part of occasional allusion to extra-biblical tradition, e.g., vv. 24, 67, 77" (*QS* 1 and 229; *KU* 1; Speyer, *Die biblischen Erzählungen im Qoran*, 223; s.v. Narratives, *EQ*; *BCQ* 1:375–91; *JQA* 220; *SKMS*^{2} 297; Angelika Neuwirth, "Zur Struktur der Yūsuf-Sūre," in *Studien aus Arabistik und Semitistik: Anton Spitaler zum 70. Geburtstag von seinen Schülern überreicht*, ed. Werner Diem and Stefan Wild (Wiesbaden: Otto Harrassowitz, 1980), 123–52, esp. 127–38; Robinson, *Discovering the Qurʾān*,

https://doi.org/10.1515/9783110580884-005

episodes comprise further forms, that is, legends and reports.[8] Specifically, the "prophet legend," as defined by Burke Long, is "a type of legend which focuses chiefly on the prophet as main character and exemplar of virtue, goodness, piety, and divine favor."[9] In the Qur'ān, the prophet legends center upon those men of God and their role in the punishment stories.[10] Fourthly, the report is customarily just a jotted note.[11] While the narrative complex (e.g., saga, episode) evidences a change in rhyme pattern, the narrative simplex (e.g., report, legend) tends to be characterized by regular end rhyme. Furthermore, Claude Gilliot clarifies, *amthāl al-qur'ān* fall within "the semantic field of narratives in the Qur'ān."[12] In consideration of this, Mathias Zahniser notes, the sense of *mathal* in the corpus extends well beyond the limits of parable proper.[13] In the biblical case, Adolf Jülicher (d. 1938) distinguishes three forms of parable speeches: similitudes, parables, and example stories.[14] In addition, Dibelius has since introduced the form of

---

148–49; de Prémare, *Aux origines du Coran*, 40; idem, *Joseph et Muḥammad: Le chapitre 12 du Coran* (Aix-en-Provence: Publications de l'Université de Provence, 1989), 19–30; cf. Al-Azmeh, *Emergence of Islam in Late Antiquity*, 455, fn. 134; Yusuf Rahman, "Ellipsis in the Qur'ān: A Study of Ibn Qutayba's *Ta'wīl Mushkil al-Qur'ān*," in *Literary Structures of Religious Meaning in the Qur'ān*, ed. Issa J. Boullata (New York: Routledge, 2000), 278). In this connection, consider the following formula: *naḥnu naquṣṣu 'alayka...idh* ("We narrate to you^{S}...when"); minimal pair: Q. 12.3–4 and Q. 18.13–14 (*KU* 5; s.v. Narratives, *EQ*; H.T. Norris, "Qiṣaṣ Elements in the Qur'ān," in *Arabic Literature to the End of the Umayyad Period*, ed. A.F.L. Beeston, T.M. Johnstone, R.B. Serjeant, and G.R. Smith (Cambridge: Cambridge University Press, 1983), 246–59).

8 *FOTL* 2a:166.

9 *FOTL* 10:309–10.

10 *QS* 2; Ettinghausen, *Antiheidnische Polemik im Koran*, 45–53, esp. 45–46.

11 *FOTL* 1:10; *FOTL* 10:312.

12 S.v. Narratives, *EQ*.

13 "For Arabic literature in general, *mathal* can be translated by such terms as simile, similitude, example, parable, allegory, proverb, motto, apothegm, aphorism, fable, and maxim" (s.v. Parable, *EQ*; Frants Buhl, "Über Vergleichungen und Gleichnisse im Qur'ān," *AcOr* 2 (1924): 1–2; Lohmann, "Die Gleichnisreden Muḥammeds im Koran (2. Teil)," 269–71; cf. Di Lella, introduction, 21; Harrington, *Jesus Ben Sira of Jerusalem*, 67–68; Gwynne, "Patterns of Address," 73 and 77).

14 Jülicher, *Die Gleichnisreden Jesu*, 2:vii–viii; cf. Tucker, *Example Stories*, 16–17 and 109; Craig L. Blomberg, *Interpreting the Parables*, 2nd ed. (Downers Grove, Illinois: InterVarsity Press, 2012), 84 and 86–87; Charles H. Dodd (d. 1973), *The Parables of the Kingdom* (New York: Charles Scribner's Sons, 1961 [1935]), 7, fn. 1; Joachim Jeremias, *Die Gleichnisse Jesu*, 8th rev. ed. (Göttingen: Vandenhoeck & Ruprecht, 1970), 16–17; Bultmann, *Geschichte der synoptischen Tradition*, 179–222, esp. 188.

the paradigm.[15] With this in mind, then, let us proceed to discuss the narrative formulary.

5.2 Narrative Formulae

Yas'alūnaka

Wansbrough remarks that the dialogic formula (*yas'alūnaka*) also introduces narrative material.[16] In his foundational *Koranische Untersuchungen*, Horovitz elaborates: while this formula is found in general legislation and dogmatic formulation, it also begins one narration.[17] In this singular case, the first verse (Q. 18.83) about *bicornutus* opens with the anecdotal formula followed by *qul*[18]:

> *wa-yas'alūnaka 'an dhī l-qarnayni qul sa-atlū 'alaykum minhu dhikran*
>
> And they will ask you[S] about Dhū l-Qarnayn.
> Say[S]: 'I shall recite to you[P] a mention of him.'

Furthermore, Wansbrough claims that this formula is productive, meaning that it "may generate an etiological legend."[19]

Wa-ḍrib lahum mathal

Theodor Lohmann states, similitudes in the Qur'ān are clearly marked with the opening *mathal* formula.[20] In point of fact, it is a high frequency term in the text.[21] What is more, Frants Buhl (d. 1932) makes an important observation: in

---

15 Bultmann, *Geschichte der synoptischen Tradition*, 181–84; Ruben Zimmermann, *Puzzling the Parables of Jesus: Methods and Interpretation* (Minneapolis, Minnesota: Fortress Press, 2015), 107–9; Dibelius, *Die Formgeschichte des Evangeliums*, 34–66; Travis, "Form Criticism," 155–56; Repschinski, *Controversy Stories*, 236–38; Tucker, *Example Stories*, 16–17.

16 *QS* 14.

17 *KU* 6.

18 *JQA* 271; *BCQ* 1:495–97; Andrew Runni Anderson, "Alexander's Horns," *TAPA* 58 (1927): 111–22. Neuwirth considers verses 83–98 a report (*SKMS*[2] 238; *FOTL* 13:172 and 13:181).

19 *QS* 14, fn. 7, and 122–26; *KU* 6.

20 Lohmann, "Die Gleichnisreden Muḥammeds im Koran (2. Teil)," 274 and 276–77.

21 S.v. Parable, *EQ*.

many instances, *mathal* is accompanied by the verb *ḍaraba*.[22] The corpus preserves three instances (Q. 18.32, Q. 18.45, Q. 36.13) of the similitude formula: *wa-ḍrib lahum mathal* ("And coin^S for them a similitude").[23] For example, Q. 18.45–46 (-*Can*) reads,[24]

> *wa-ḍrib lahum mathala l-ḥayāti d-dunyā ka-māʾin anzalnāhu mina s-samāʾi fa-khtalaṭa bihī nabātu l-arḍi fa-aṣbaḥa hashīman tadhrūhu r-riyāḥu wa-kāna llāhu ʿalā kulli shayʾin muqtadiran*
>
> *al-mālu wa-l-banūna zīnatu l-ḥayāti d-dunyā wa-l-bāqiyātu ṣ-ṣāliḥātu khayrun ʿinda rabbika thawāban wa-khayrun amalan*
>
> And coin^S for them the similitude of the life of this world:
> [it is] like water that We send down from the sky,
> and the vegetation of the earth mingles with it,
> then [one] morning it becomes chaff that the winds scatter.
> God is omnipotent over everything.
>
> Wealth and children are the ornament of the life of this world;
> but the abiding things, the works of righteousness,
> are better with your^S Lord for reward and better for hope.

In this case, the formula functions in tandem with the simile marker (*ka*-).[25] Accordingly, Neuwirth considers this a similitude of this world.[26] Furthermore, Hirschfeld comments that this *mathal* places special emphasis on the transience of life.[27] For that reason, Lohmann appropriately labels this similitude, blowing in the wind.[28] In addition, he notes the repetition of the phrase *al-ḥayāti d-dunyā* in both verses, which reoccurs in a qurʾānic paradigm (Q. 3.117).[29] This similitude equates the mundane with the ephemeral.[30] Besides, this formula also introduces the controversy story.[31]

---

22 Buhl, "Über Vergleichungen und Gleichnisse im Qurʾān," 2; s.v. Parable, *EQ*; Andrew L. Rippin, "Studies in Qurʾānic Vocabulary: The Problem of the Dictionary," in *New Perspectives on the Qurʾān: The Qurʾān in Its Historical Context 2*, ed. Gabriel Said Reynolds (New York: Routledge, 2011), 40–41; Lohmann, "Die Gleichnisreden Muḥammeds im Koran (2. Teil)," 275.
23 Sister, "Metaphern und Vergleiche im Koran," 115–16; *KU* 5; cf. s.v. Narratives, *EQ* (Q. 36).
24 Lohmann, "Die Gleichnisreden Muḥammeds im Koran (2. Teil)," 275; *JQA* 271.
25 Sister, "Metaphern und Vergleiche im Koran," 112.
26 *SKMS*² 268.
27 Hirschfeld, *New Researches*, 87.
28 Theodor Lohmann, "Die Gleichnisreden Muḥammeds im Koran," *MIO* 12 (1966): 96 (v. 45).
29 Cf. ibid.
30 *BCQ* 1:489.

Ḍaraba llāhu mathal

The *corpus coranicum* contains a further similitude formula: *ḍaraba llāhu mathalan* ("God has coined a similitude").[32] For instance, Q. 16.75–6 preserves a pair.[33] Verse 75 (-*ūC*) recounts the similitude of two men, one enslaved, the other free[34]:

> *ḍaraba llāhu mathalan ʿabdan mamlūkan lā yaqdiru ʿalā shayʾin wa-man razaqnāhu minnā rizqan ḥasanan fa-huwa yunfiqu minhu sirran wa-jahran hal yastawūna l-ḥamdu li-llāhi bal aktharuhum lā yaʿlamūna*
>
> God has coined a similitude:
> a slave possessed by his master,
> who has control of nothing,
> [as compared with] the one for whom We have provided
> fair provision from Ourselves
> and who spends from it secretly and openly.
> Are they equal?
> Praise belongs to God.
> No, most of them do not know.

Bell comments, the meaning of this similitude is not readily evident.[35] In agreement, Buhl characterizes the construction of these two verses (75–76) as hard to discern.[36] To this, Lohmann adds, the exegetical problems are only compounded by the subsequent similitude, rendering interpretation especially difficult.[37] And so, Wansbrough reasons that "it may, indeed, be supposed that the public for whom Muslim scripture was intended could be expected to supply the missing detail."[38] In turn, the similitude on two men, one dumb, the other righteous, follows in Q. 16.76 (-*īC*)[39]:

---

31 Repschinski, *Controversy Stories*, *passim*.
32 Sister, "Metaphern und Vergleiche im Koran," 115–16; Lohmann, "Die Gleichnisreden Muḥammeds im Koran (2. Teil)," 275; *KU* 5; s.v. Narratives, *EQ*.
33 Cf. *SKMS*² 300; *JQA* 249.
34 Lohmann, "Die Gleichnisreden Muḥammeds im Koran," 76 and 101–4; idem, "Die Gleichnisreden Muḥammeds im Koran (2. Teil)," 275.
35 *BCQ* 1:447.
36 Buhl, "Über Vergleichungen und Gleichnisse im Qurʾān," 7–8; Lohmann, "Die Gleichnisreden Muḥammeds im Koran," 104.
37 Lohmann, "Die Gleichnisreden Muḥammeds im Koran," 101; *BCQ* 1:447.
38 *QS* 1.
39 Lohmann, "Die Gleichnisreden Muḥammeds im Koran," 104–6; *BCQ* 1:447.

wa-ḍaraba llāhu mathalan rajulayni aḥaduhumā abkamu lā yaqdiru ʿalā shayʾin wa-huwa kallun ʿalā mawlāhu aynamā yuwajjihhu lā yaʾti bi-khayrin hal yastawī huwa wa-man yaʾ-muru bi-l-ʿadli wa-huwa ʿalā ṣirāṭin mustaqīmin

And God has coined a similitude:
two men,
one of them dumb, who has control of nothing,
a burden on his owner
– wherever he sends him he brings back no good.
Is he equal to one who enjoins justice and is on a straight path?

In terms of the literary structure of similitudes, consider that of conflict and concord in Q. 39.29 (*-ūC*)[40]:

ḍaraba llāhu mathalan rajulan fīhi shurakāʾu mutashākisūna wa-rajulan salaman li-rajulin hal yastawiyāni mathalan al-ḥamdu li-llāhi bal aktharuhum lā yaʿlamūna

God has coined a similitude:
a man in whom disagreeing partners share
and a man belonging solely to one man.
Are the two equal in likeness?
Praise belongs to God.
No, most of them do not know.

This similitude is about the disparity between sole and joint proprietary interests.[41] Noteworthy is the formulation at its close, since it bears a close resemblance to that of Q. 16.75. The similitude formula doubles as the parable formula. Moreover, the same formula also introduces the example story.[42]

Mathalu lladhīna

First and foremost, paradigms are succinct.[43] Stephen Travis writes, these "culminate in an authoritative saying," in the biblical case.[44] It is pertinent, therefore, that paradigms frame and deliver aphorisms, so these narrative vehicles tend to stand apart.[45] Aside from slightly variant formulae, the pericopae gener-

40 *BCQ* 2:186; Lohmann, "Die Gleichnisreden Muḥammeds im Koran," 107–8; cf. idem, "Die Gleichnisreden Muḥammeds im Koran (2. Teil)," 276.
41 *SKMS*[2] 309; Buhl, "Über Vergleichungen und Gleichnisse im Qurʾān," 7.
42 *FOTL* 13:176; Tucker, *Example Stories*, 7, 17, and 19–41.
43 Travis, "Form Criticism," 155.
44 Ibid.
45 Hirschfeld, *New Researches*, 83; Travis, "Form Criticism," 155.

ally exhibit a concise tripartite structure, beginning with the double substitution formula: "the paradigm of those who...is like the paradigm of..." (*mathalu lladhī-na...ka-mathali...*).[46] Take, for instance, Q. 29.41 (-*ūC*):

> *mathalu lladhīna ttakhadhū min dūni llāhi awliyāʾa ka-mathali l-ʿankabūti ttakhadhat bay-tan wa-inna awhana l-buyūti la-baytu l-ʿankabūti law kānū yaʿlamūna*
>
> The paradigm of those who take for themselves patrons to the exclusion of God is like the paradigm of the spider that takes for itself a house:
> The frailest of houses is that of the spider.
> If they did but know.

In the second part of this paradigm, the proverbial spider marks the high point of the sūra-unit (*sūrat al-ʿankabūt*).[47] By design, special stress is laid upon the aphorism (*mathal*), which reads,[48] "The frailest of houses is that of the spider."[49] The third and last element finishes the laconic piece with an oral-formula.[50] By the same token, consider the following paradigm grounded in agriculture and associated natural phenomena.[51] Q. 2.261 (-*īC*) reads,[52]

> *mathalu lladhīna yunfiqūna amwālahum fī sabīli llāhi ka-mathali ḥabbatin anbatat sabʿa sanābila fī kulli sunbulatin miʾatu ḥabbatin wa-llāhu yuḍāʿifu li-man yashāʾu wa-llāhu wā-siʿun ʿalīmun*
>
> The paradigm of those who spend their possessions in the way of God
> is like the paradigm of a grain that produces seven ears, in each of which are a hundred grains:
> God multiplies for those whom He wills.
> God is Embracing and Knowing.

According to Bell, this stand-alone verse amounts to a call for collections.[53]

---

46 Travis, "Form Criticism," 155; Sister, "Metaphern und Vergleiche im Koran," 115; Lohmann, "Die Gleichnisreden Muḥammeds im Koran (2. Teil)," 276; Repschinski, *Controversy Stories*, 319–20.

47 Travis, "Form Criticism," 155; *SKMS*² 302 (vv. 41–43); *BCQ* 2:63 (vv. 41–43); cf. Lohmann, "Die Gleichnisreden Muḥammeds im Koran (2. Teil)," 276; *JQA* 363 (vv. 14–44).

48 Repschinski, *Controversy Stories*, 238; cf. Buhl, "Über Vergleichungen und Gleichnisse im Qurʾān," 8; Lohmann, "Die Gleichnisreden Muḥammeds im Koran (2. Teil)," 246 and 281; Sister, "Metaphern und Vergleiche im Koran," 125–28; Hirschfeld, *New Researches*, 93.

49 See Hirschfeld, *New Researches*, 85–86.

50 Repschinski, *Controversy Stories*, 238; Travis, "Form Criticism," 155.

51 Buhl, "Über Vergleichungen und Gleichnisse im Qurʾān," 4–5; Sister, "Metaphern und Vergleiche im Koran," 117–20 and 128–30.

52 Lohmann, "Die Gleichnisreden Muḥammeds im Koran (2. Teil)," 255–56.

53 *BCQ* 1:55; Hirschfeld, *New Researches*, 94.

Idh

Gilliot relates, narrative formulae "introduce something new in the development of the text...."[54] On this point, Horovitz observes, while *idh* happens to precede actual narrations, the perfect follows it.[55] To the point, Nöldeke justifiably suggests rendering the narrative formula as "days of yore."[56] Accordingly, *wa-idh* ("and when"), and *idh* ("when") on occasion, marks the opening of the legend form.[57] Amongst other things, these formulae indicate prophet legends and their constituent reports.[58] With special reference to "the serial employment of the presentative *wa-idh*," Wansbrough notes the fact that "the *exempla* achieve a kind of stylistic uniformity by resort to a scarcely varied stock of rhetorical convention."[59] For example, consider the first of two distinct episodes (Q. 26.10–68 and Q. 26.69–104) in Sūrat ash-Shuʿarāʾ, whose core (vv. 10–191) is predominantly narration.[60] The Moses legend opens with verse 10[61]:

> *wa-idh nādā rabbuka mūsā ani ʾti l-qawma ẓ-ẓālimīna*
>
> And when your[S] Lord called out to Moses,
> 'Go to the people who do wrong.'

Bell comments, the narrative progresses uninterrupted.[62] Furthermore, it closes with yet another device, that is, the refrain.[63]

---

54 S.v. Narratives, *EQ*; *KU* 4.
55 *KU* 4; Nöldeke, *Neue Beiträge*, 17.
56 Nöldeke, *Neue Beiträge*, 17.
57 S.v. Narratives, *EQ*; Nöldeke, *Neue Beiträge*, 17.
58 *FOTL* 10:309–10 and 10:312; s.v. Narratives, *EQ*.
59 *QS* 18–19. On these grounds, Gilliot concludes, "*wa-idh* is the most frequent sign of this type of transition" (s.v. Narratives, *EQ*).
60 *JQA* 335; Welch, "Formulaic Features of the Punishment-Stories," 79 and 81.
61 *SKMS*[2] 276; Welch, "Formulaic Features of the Punishment-Stories," 79.
62 *BCQ* 2:18.
63 *SKMS*[2] 276; Neuwirth, "Erzählen als kanonischer Prozeß," 336; *KU* 6; s.v. Narratives, *EQ*; *BIQ*[1] 71.

Wa...idh

In addition, the corpus preserves a substitution formula for introducing narrative pericopae: *wa...idh* ("and...when"). For instance, Sūrat al-Anbiyā᾽ (Q. 21.87–88) reads,[64]

> *wa-dhā n-nūni idh dhahaba mughāḍiban fa-ẓanna an lan naqdira ʿalayhi fa-nādā fī ẓ-ẓulu-māti an lā ilāha illā anta subḥānaka innī kuntu mina ẓ-ẓālimīna*
>
> *fa-stajabnā lahū wa-najjaynāhu mina l-ghammi wa-ka-dhālika nunjī l-mu᾽minīna*
>
> And Dhū l-Nūn
> – when he departed in anger
> and thought that We had no power over him;
> but he cried out in the darkness,
> 'There is no god but You.
> Glory be to You.
> I have been one of the wrong-doers.'
>
> So We responded to him and delivered him from his grief.
> Thus We deliver the believers.

Referencing Jonah as *Dhū l-Nūn* ("he of the fish"), this episode includes both his prayer and deliverance.[65] In other words, the dominant idea is rather "crime and forgiveness."[66] What is more, the same literary structure governs the subsequent Zachariah episode (Q. 21.89–90), as well as the preceding multi-episode saga (Q. 21.76–84).

Wa-fī...idh

Punishment stories in the Qur᾽ān incorporate the transitional *idh:* "And in... when" (*wa-fī...idh*).[67] Wansbrough says that this substitution phrase represents "the formula of commission."[68] For example, Q. 51.38 (-*īC*) reads,[69]

---

64 *SKMS*^{2} 271; *JQA* 298.
65 *SKMS*^{2} 271; *BCQ* 1:555–56.
66 Westermann, *Die Verheißungen an die Väter*, 47; idem, *The Promises to the Fathers: Studies on the Patriarchal Narratives*, trans. David E. Green (Philadelphia, Pennsylvania: Fortress Press, 1980), 44–45.
67 *QS* 2, 24, 28, and 314; Hirschfeld, *New Researches*, 62; Welch, "Formulaic Features of the Punishment-Stories," 78 and 100; Stewart, "Wansbrough, Bultmann, and the Theory of Variant Tra-

wa-fī mūsā idh arsalnāhu ilā fir'awna bi-sulṭānin mubīnin

And in Moses,
when We sent him to Pharaoh with a clear authority.

Along with terse introductory reports heading punishment episodes, the same formula also signals the "historical story" at large.[70]

Wa-ilā

According to Wansbrough, also found in the text "is a stereotype phrase employed exclusively for the non-biblical prophets."[71] The highly stylized formulation combines a personalized commission formula with a vocative address: *wa-ilā...akhāhum...qāla yā-qawmi 'budū llāha* ("And to...their brother...He said, 'O my tribe, serve God.'").[72] Furthermore, it introduces dialogic reports, as well as legends.[73] Q. 7.73 (-īC) narrates,[74]

wa-ilā thamūda akhāhum ṣāliḥan qāla yā-qawmi 'budū llāha mā lakum min ilāhin ghayruhū qad jā'atkum bayyinatun min rabbikum hādhihī nāqatu llāhi lakum āyatan fa-dharūhā ta'kul fī arḍi llāhi wa-lā tamassūhā bi-sū'in fa-ya'khudhakum 'adhābun alīmun

And to Thamūd their brother Ṣāliḥ.
He said, 'O my tribe, serve God.
You have no god other than Him.
A clear proof from your Lord has come to you.
This is the she-camel of God as a sign for you.
So let her eat in God's land,
and do not touch her with evil,
lest a painful torment seize you.

---

ditions," 35, 37, and 40; *KU* 1–10; s.v. Narratives, *EQ*; *FOTL* 1:5; *FOTL* 10:313. For a definition of "transition formula," see *FOTL* 2a:178.

68 *QS* 24 and 28; Stewart, "Wansbrough, Bultmann, and the Theory of Variant Traditions," 35, 37, and 40.

69 *SKMS*² 204 (vv. 38–40); *BCQ* 2:303 (vv. 38–40).

70 *QS* 24 and 28; Stewart, "Wansbrough, Bultmann, and the Theory of Variant Traditions," 35, 37, and 40; Welch, "Formulaic Features of the Punishment-Stories," 100; *FOTL* 10:301 and 10:312.

71 *QS* 24.

72 Welch, "Formulaic Features of the Punishment-Stories," 85–88; *QS* 24; *JQA* 156, fn. 6; *BCQ* 2:24.

73 *FOTL* 10:309–10 and 10:312. Wansbrough adds that this "might well be thought an editorial interpolation designed precisely to introduce reports of prophetical missions..." (*QS* 24).

74 *SKMS*² 292 (vv. 73–79); *BCQ* 1:239–40 (vv. 73–79).

In terms of its literary structure, this prophet legend on the she-camel opens with the substitution formulation and closes with a stylized warning.[75]

Wa-dhkur

As Horovitz rightly observes, the meaning of *dhikr* in the corpus is variable.[76] In the Qurʾān, legends and episodes constituting sagas feature a substitution formula, namely, "And remember..." (*wa-dhkur*).[77] For instance, there is a legend lodged in the longer David episode (Q. 38.17–29) which, in turn, is part of a more extensive piece (vv. 12–49).[78] The shorter David legend in Q. 38.17a-20 (-*āC*) reads,[79]

> *wa-dhkur ʿabdanā dāwūda dhā l-aydi innahū awwābun*
>
> *innā sakhkharnā l-jibāla maʿahū yusabbiḥna bi-l-ʿashiyyi wa-l-ishrāqi*
>
> *wa-ṭ-ṭayra maḥshūratan kullun lahū awwābun*
>
> *wa-shaddadnā mulkahū wa-ātaynāhu l-ḥikmata wa-faṣla l-khiṭābi*

> And remember Our servant David,
> the man of might.
> He was a penitent.
>
> With him We subdued the mountains
> to give glory at evening and sunrise;
>
> And the birds were rounded up,
> all turning to him.
>
> We strengthened his kingdom,
> and We gave him wisdom and decisive speech.

---

75 *BCQ* 1:239. Minimal pair: Q. 7.73 and Q. 11.64 (*fa-yaʾkhudhakum ʿadhābun...*).
76 *KU* 6–7; Goitein, "Das Gebet im Qorān," 3–13; *QS* 19.
77 *FOTL* 10:313–14.
78 *SKMS*[2] 282; *JQA* 415.
79 *SKMS*[2] 282 (vv. 17–20); *BCQ* 2:168 (vv. 16–20).

On a related note, take into account the further stylized formula, *wa-dhkur fī l-kitābi* ("And remember in the scripture..."), which provides the narrative framework for the core of Sūrat Maryam (Q. 19.16–58).[80]

Wa-tlu ʿalayhim nabaʾa...idh

An additional narrative formula appears in the text.[81] It reads, *wa-tlu ʿalayhim nabaʾa...idh* ("And recite^S to them the narrative of...when").[82] As an illustration, Q. 5.27 begins,[83]

> *wa-tlu ʿalayhim nabaʾa bnay ādama bi-l-ḥaqqi idh qarrabā qurbānan fa-tuqubbila min aḥadihimā wa-lam yutaqabbal mina l-ākhari qāla la-aqtulannaka qāla innamā yataqabbalu llāhu mina l-muttaqīna*
>
> And recite^S to them the narrative of
> the two sons of Adam,
> when they offered sacrifices,
> and it was accepted from one of them and not from the other.
> [The latter] said, 'I shall kill you.'
> [His brother] replied, 'God accepts
> only from those who are God-fearing.'

Jones comments, the identity of the children is undisclosed.[84] In addition, this stylized formula also signals the Noah episode in Q. 10.71–4.[85] The opening verse (71) reads,

> *wa-tlu ʿalayhim nabaʾa nūḥin idh qāla li-qawmihī yā-qawmi in kāna kabura ʿalaykum maqāmī wa-tadhkīrī bi-āyāti llāhi fa-ʿalā llāhi tawakkaltu fa-ajmiʿū amrakum wa-shurakāʾakum thumma lā yakun amrukum ʿalaykum ghummatan thumma qḍū ilayya wa-lā tunẓirūni*
>
> And recite^S to them the narrative of Noah,
> when he said to his people,
> 'O my people, if my staying here and my reminding you of God's signs weighs heavy on you,
> I put my trust in God.
> So resolve on your affair, with your associates.
> Let not your affair be a worry to you,

---

80 *SKMS*² 269.
81 Q. 5.27, Q. 10.71, Q. 26.69–70.
82 S.v. Narratives, *EQ*; *KU* 5; *QS* 19.
83 *BCQ* 1:154–55 (vv. 27–32).
84 *JQA* 115, fn. 9; *BCQ* 1:154.
85 *SKMS*² 295; *JQA* 195; *BCQ* 1:342–43 (vv. 71–73).

but make a decision about me.
Do not wait.'

Although in disagreement with alternate renditions in the corpus, it nonetheless shares certain points.[86]

Hal atāka ḥadīthu…idh

Wansbrough states, "these basic 'narrative' conventions are supplemented by others, which may be distinguished as interrogative, imperative, and simple declarative…."[87] In fact, the corpus evidences an interrogative formula, specifically, *hal atāka ḥadīthu…idh* ("Have you^S heard the narrative of…when…?").[88] To illustrate, take verses Q. 20.9–10, which open the Moses episode[89]:

wa-hal atāka ḥadīthu mūsā

idh ra'ā nāran fa-qāla li-ahlihi mkuthū innī ānastu nāran la'allī ātīkum minhā bi-qabasin aw ajidu 'alā n-nāri hudan

And have you^S heard the narrative of Moses?

When he saw a fire and said to his family,
'Wait. I have spotted a fire.
Perhaps I can bring you^P a brand from it
or find guidance at the fire.'

According to Wansbrough, "formally interrogative locutions function almost exclusively as rhetorical questions, e.g., *hal atāka ḥadīthu/naba'u*, preceding mention of Abraham, Moses, Pharaoh, Thamūd, and other representatives of the *umam khāliya*."[90]

86 *BCQ* 1:342.
87 *QS* 19.
88 Ibid.; s.v. Narratives, *EQ*; *KU* 5 and 7.
89 *SKMS*^{2} 270 (vv. 9–99); *BCQ* 1:522–33 (vv. 9–98).
90 *QS* 19; *KU* 7.

Wa-la-qad ataynā

Wansbrough observes that "the messenger formula, also designated formula of legitimation (*corroboratio*), may be merely understood, and constructions including only the term of commission, e.g., *la-qad ataynā, la-qad arsalnā*, are common in Muslim scripture."[91] For example, the report in Q. 21.48 (-*īC*) reads,[92]

> *wa-la-qad ātaynā mūsā wa-hārūna l-furqāna wa-ḍiyā'an wa-dhikran li-l-muttaqīna*
>
> And in the past We gave to Moses and Aaron the salvation (*al-furqān*)
> and illumination and a reminder for those who protect themselves.

In addition, consider Q. 23.49 (-*ūC*):

> *wa-la-qad ātaynā mūsā l-kitāba la'allahum yahtadūna*
>
> And in the past We gave Moses the scripture,
> so that they might be guided aright.

This report ends the Moses episode (vv. 45–49).[93] Furthermore, in Sūrat al-Furqān (Q. 25), verses 35 to 36 narrate,[94]

> *wa-la-qad ātaynā mūsā l-kitāba wa-ja'alnā ma'ahū akhāhu hārūna wazīran*
>
> *fa-qulnā dhhabā ilā l-qawmi lladhīna kadhdhabū bi-āyātinā fa-dammarnāhum tadmīran*
>
> And in the past We gave Moses the scripture
> and made his brother Aaron as minister with him.
>
> So We said, 'Go to the people who do not believe the truth of Our signs.'
> Then We destroyed them completely.

Aaron is introduced as nothing less than *wazīr* in this terse episode.[95]

---

91 *QS* 13; *KU* 5.
92 *SKMS*² 271; *JQA* 298.
93 *JQA* 314; *SKMS*² 272; *BCQ* 1:583.
94 *JQA* 329; *SKMS*² 273; *BCQ* 2:7.
95 *BCQ* 2:7.

Arsalnā...ilā

As one in a series in the sūra-unit, Q. 11.25–49 preserves an episode on Noah.[96] Its opening formula reads (v. 25),

wa-la-qad arsalnā nūḥan ilā qawmihī innī lakum nadhīrun mubīnun

And We sent Noah to his people,
'I am a clear warner for you.'

According to Neuwirth, the final verse (49) constitutes commentary.[97] Additionally, the corpus features a signature Noah formulation: *la-qad arsalnā nūḥan ilā qawmihī fa-qāla yā-qawmi ʿbudū llāha mā lakum min ilāhin ghayruhū.*[98] To continue, the Moses episode (Q. 23.45–49), in which Aaron features again, opens (vv. 45–46),[99]

thumma arsalnā mūsā wa-akhāhu hārūna bi-āyātinā wa-sulṭānin mubīnin

ilā firʿawna wa-malaʾihī fa-stakbarū wa-kānū qawman ʿālīna

Then We sent Moses and his brother Aaron with Our signs and a clear authority

to Pharaoh and his nobles,
but they were proud and were exalted people.

Bell comments, "it may be noted that they are not sent to their own people but to Pharaoh, to whom their people are subject."[100]

---

96 *JQA* 207; *BCQ* 1:355–60.
97 *SKMS*[2] 296; cf. Carlos A. Segovia, *The Quranic Noah and the Making of the Islamic Prophet: A Study of Intertextuality and Religious Identity Formation in Late Antiquity* (Berlin: Walter de Gruyter, 2015), 28–30; Geza Vermes, "Bible and Midrash: Early Old Testament Exegesis," in *The Cambridge History of the Bible*, ed. Peter R. Ackroyd (Cambridge: Cambridge University Press, 1970), 1:203–23.
98 Minimal pair: Q. 7.59 and Q. 23.23.
99 *JQA* 314; *SKMS*[2] 272; *BCQ* 1:583.
100 *BCQ* 1:583.

Kadhdhabat

The *kadhdhabat* formula is peculiar to punishment stories.[101] In the first instance, the simple formula (*kadhdhabat*) introduces the "summary report."[102] In the second place, the text preserves a fine specimen of the long saga (Q. 54.9–40).[103] Comprised of no less than four episodes, this punishment saga features the opening formula (*kadhdhabat*), a reoccurring oral-formulaic phrase (*ʿadhābī wa-nudhur:* "My punishment and warnings"), a refrain-like (vv. 19, 31, 34) substitution phrase (*innā arsalnā ʿalayhim…:* "We sent against them…"), and a refrain proper (*wa-la-qad yassarnā l-qurʾāna li-dh-dhikri fa-hal min muddakirin:* "And We have made the recitation easy to remember – but are there any that are reminded?") that also brings the saga to an end.[104] With reference to Sūrat al-Qamar (Q. 54), Bell observes how it avails itself of refrain clusters.[105] Moreover, a "schematic" formulation introduces episodes embedded in the saga form.[106] Accordingly, the substitution formula begins, *kadhdhabat…l-mursalīna* ("…denied the truth of those who were sent").[107] Featuring the transitional formula (*idh*), the commission follows, *idh qāla lahum akhūhum…a-lā tattaqūna* ("when their brother…said to them, 'will you not protect yourselves?'"). It continues, *innī lakum rasūlun amīnun* ("I am a faithful messenger for you"). The fourth verse of the saga formulation reads, "So fear God and obey me" (*fa-ttaqū llāha wa-aṭīʿūni*). The opening piece concludes, "I am not asking you for any wage for this. My reward is only with the Lord of all beings."[108] For example, consider the Hūd episode in Q. 26.123–40[109]:

kadhdhabat ʿādun al-mursalīna

idh qāla lahum akhūhum hūdun a-lā tattaqūna

innī lakum rasūlun amīnun

fa-ttaqū llāha wa-aṭīʿūni

---

101 *KU* 5.
102 *FOTL* 2a:172f.
103 *SKMS*² 286; *BCQ* 2:324–27; Hirschfeld, *New Researches*, 62–63; *JQA* 491.
104 *SKMS*² 286; Hirschfeld, *New Researches*, 62; Al-Azmeh, *Emergence of Islam in Late Antiquity*, 440; *BIQ*¹ 71.
105 *BIQ*¹ 71.
106 *FOTL* 10:313–14; Welch, "Formulaic Features of the Punishment-Stories," 78–79.
107 Welch, "Formulaic Features of the Punishment-Stories," 78.
108 Ibid., 80.
109 *BCQ* 2:22; *SKMS*² 276–77; *JQA* 335.

wa-mā as'alukum 'alayhi min ajrin in ajriya illā 'alā rabbi l-'ālamīna

'Ād denied the truth of those who were sent,

When their brother Hūd said to them,
'Will you not protect yourselves?

I am a faithful messenger for you.

Fear God and obey me.

I am not asking you for any wage for this.
My reward is only with the Lord of all beings.'

Apart from core narrative content, this pericope closes with an oral-formulaic phrase (*-īC*), which represents the saga episode "divider" (Q. 26.139a-40)[110]:

inna fī dhālika la-āyatan wa-mā kāna aktharuhum mu'minīna

wa-inna rabbaka la-huwa l-'azīzu r-raḥīmu

In that there is a sign,
but most of them have not become believers.

Your Lord is the Mighty and the Compassionate.

As a matter of fact, this Hūd episode is part of a narrative saga.[111]

5.3 Narrative Setting

Life Contexts

To begin with, Neuwirth observes that parables (*amthāl*) in the Qur'ān are "taken largely from the agricultural and commercial worlds of seventh-century Arabia...."[112] Since some are grounded in nature, with hints of rustic coloring,

110 *SKMS*^{2} 277; *JQA* 340; Welch, "Formulaic Features of the Punishment-Stories," 78 and 81.
111 Welch, "Formulaic Features of the Punishment-Stories," 80; Hirschfeld, *New Researches*, 62.
112 S.v. Parable, *EQ*; Robinson, *Discovering the Qur'ān*, 150.

these constitute "established village wisdom."[113] On the other hand, since the narrative genre draws from a wide repertoire of literary forms, ranging from parables to prophet legends, these consequently mirror multiple settings.[114] Let us consider for a moment the proposition that these forms trace back to not one, but several originating circumstances.[115] Take, for instance, the narrative form of the controversy story.[116] According to Boris Repschinski, "the stories can no longer be understood as tools of the earliest catechetical or kerygmatic activities," *contra* Wansbrough.[117] Neither "can they be easily associated with the historical," *contra* Hirschfeld.[118] The performative contexts of narrative forms therefore vary to a great extent; parables appear in traditional tellings, while paradigms feature prominently in religious sermons.[119] Travis notes the special function paradigms play in the delivery of a sermon.[120] In point of fact, the prophetic speech-form in the proclamation genre (i.e., Q. 2.264–65) incorporates multiple illustrative paradigms (*amthāl*).[121] Thus, in terms of the paradigm, "this use was decisive for the development of the form."[122] Similar to the parable,

---

113 S.v. Parable, *EQ*; Bright, "Apodictic Prohibition," 185; Wolff, *Amos' geistige Heimat*, 60–61; cf. McLaughlin, *The Marzēaḥ in the Prophetic Literature*, 91; Blomberg, *Interpreting the Parables*, 84–85.

114 Robinson, *Discovering the Qur'ān*, 150; *FOTL* 10:309–10; Repschinski, *Controversy Stories*, 241; Arland J. Hultgren, *Jesus and His Adversaries: The Form and Function of the Conflict Stories in the Synoptic Tradition* (Minneapolis, Minnesota: Augsburg Publishing House, 1979), 197–98.

115 Cf. Repschinski, *Controversy Stories*, 241; Hultgren, *Jesus and His Adversaries*, 197–98.

116 Repschinski, *Controversy Stories*, 240; Hultgren, *Jesus and His Adversaries*, 52–59.

117 Repschinski, *Controversy Stories*, 241; cf. Hultgren, *Jesus and His Adversaries*, 50–52 and 197–99; *QS* 14 and 20; Hirschfeld, *New Researches*, 59–71, esp. 63. For example, Stewart advances the reasonable claim: "Sūras of the type that include the punishment stories resemble the form of a sermon. They adopt a tripartite structure, with an introduction, a series of *exempla* from salvation history, and a conclusion" (idem, "Wansbrough, Bultmann, and the Theory of Variant Traditions," 45).

118 Cf. Repschinski, *Controversy Stories*, 241; Hultgren, *Jesus and His Adversaries*, 198; Marshall, *God, Muḥammad and the Unbelievers*, 29–30. Wansbrough comments on Hirschfeld: "This kind of argument was a corollary of that scholar's acceptance of the Nöldeke-Schwally chronology of revelation, a feasible but hardly the only method of interpreting the qur'ānic data" (*QS* 2).

119 Blomberg, *Interpreting the Parables*, 84–85 and 92; Bultmann, *Geschichte der synoptischen Tradition*, 179; Hirschfeld, *New Researches*, 59; Edgar V. McKnight, *What is Form Criticism?* (Philadelphia, Pennsylvania: Fortress Press, 1969), 52–53; Dodd, *Parables of the Kingdom*, 85; Blomberg, *Interpreting the Parables*, 84–85 and 91.

120 Dibelius, *Die Formgeschichte des Evangeliums*, 66; Travis, "Form Criticism," 155–56; Repschinski, *Controversy Stories*, 238.

121 Westermann, *Grundformen prophetischer Rede*, *passim*; Hirschfeld, *New Researches*, 83 and 93.

122 Repschinski, *Controversy Stories*, 238.

"legend belongs to the world of oral folklore and storytellers."[123] Legends were recounted "at religious shrines, in family and tribal settings, and on pilgrimages to holy sites."[124] What is more, in the hands of the saga-teller, sagas are retold at equally numerous venues.[125] Furthermore, narrative criticism is particularly focused on form and its relevance to the work.[126] In view of that, Marvin Sweeney has an eye on both the life setting as well as the literary one.[127]

5.4 Narrative Forms

Anecdote

Q. 18.83–98 (*-Can*) preserves an entertaining piece terse in expression.[128] In this anecdote about Dhū l-Qarnayn, familiar words reoccur twice in verses 89 and 92[129]:

> *thumma atbaʿa sababan*
>
> Then he followed a way.

In a teaching situation, repetition as technique improves memory and concentration.[130] The final verse (98) drives home the point:

> *qāla hādhā raḥmatun min rabbī fa-idhā jā'a waʿdu rabbī jaʿalahū dakkā'a wa-kāna waʿdu rabbī ḥaqqan*
>
> He said: 'This is a mercy from my Lord.
> But when the promise of my Lord comes to pass,

---

123 *FOTL* 10:304; *KU* 7.
124 *FOTL* 10:304.
125 *Genesis*, xxxv; *FOTL* 1:6–7; Burke O. Long, *1 Kings with an Introduction to Historical Literature, FOTL* (Grand Rapids, Michigan: Wm. B. Eerdmans Publishing Company, 1984), 9:260; *FOTL* 10:313–14; Welch, "Formulaic Features of the Punishment-Stories," 110; Stewart, "Wansbrough, Bultmann, and the Theory of Variant Traditions," 42.
126 Repschinski, *Controversy Stories*, 292; cf. Marshall, *God, Muḥammad and the Unbelievers*, 32–36.
127 Marvin A. Sweeney, *Isaiah 1–39 with an Introduction to Prophetic Literature, FOTL* (Grand Rapids, Michigan: Wm. B. Eerdmans Publishing Company, 1996), 16:12.
128 *FOTL* 13:173.
129 Harrington, *Jesus Ben Sira of Jerusalem*, 74–75.
130 Ibid., 75; André Lemaire, "The Sage in School and Temple," in *The Sage in Israel and the Ancient Near East*, ed. John G. Gammie and Leo G. Perdue (Winona Lake, Indiana: Eisenbrauns, 1990), 181.

He will make it a flattened surface.
The promise of my Lord is true.'

Murphy concludes, the sole objective of this form is to marshall anecdotal evidence in order to make a point.[131]

Similitude

For instance, consider the similitude of the cultivator and pauper in Q. 18.32–44 (-*Can*).[132] Verse 32 opens with the formula[133]:

wa-ḍrib lahum mathalan rajulayni ja'alnā li-aḥadihimā jannatayni min a'nābin wa-ḥafafnāhumā bi-nakhlin wa-ja'alnā baynahumā zar'an

Coin^{S} for them a similitude:
two men,
to one of whom We assigned two vineyards
and surrounded them with palm trees
and set cultivated land between them.

In this similitude, God affords a man two vineyards and his counterpart none.[134] Hirschfeld comments, the narrative juxtaposes wealth with poverty.[135] In this lengthy piece, the final pair of verses (vv. 43–44) paints a poignant picture[136]:

wa-lam takun lahū fi'atun yanṣurūnahū min dūni llāhi wa-mā kāna muntaṣiran

hunālika l-walāyatu li-llāhi l-ḥaqqi huwa khayrun thawāban wa-khayrun 'uqban

He had no group to help him apart from God,
and he was helpless.

Protection there belongs only to God, the True.
He is better for reward and better for consequence.

131 *FOTL* 13:173.
132 Buhl, "Über Vergleichungen und Gleichnisse im Qur'ān," 5–7.
133 Lohmann, "Die Gleichnisreden Muḥammeds im Koran," 76 and 88–96.
134 *SKMS*^{2} 268; *BCQ* 1:487; *BIQ*^{1} 78.
135 Hirschfeld, *New Researches*, 87.
136 *JQA* 271; Lohmann, "Die Gleichnisreden Muḥammeds im Koran," 91.

"In narratives, too," Bell states, "the homiletic element is apt to intrude."[137] That being the case, this similitude ends on a sobering note.[138]

Parable

According to Harrington, "a parable is an example of comparative speech…."[139] Following Jülicher, "the narrative form" of parables sets them apart from similitudes at large.[140] What is more, Wansbrough states that "a distinctly referential, as contrasted with expository, style characterizes qurʾānic treatment of most of what I have alluded to as schemata of revelation…."[141] For instance, Sūrat an-Naḥl ("The Bees") preserves one such parable.[142] The *mathal* in Q. 16.112–13 (-*ūC*) opens with the formula[143]:

> *wa-ḍaraba llāhu mathalan qaryatan kānat āminatan muṭmaʾinnatan yaʾtīhā rizquhā raghadan min kulli makānin fa-kafarat bi-anʿumi llāhi fa-adhāqahā llāhu libāsa l-jūʿi wa-l-khawfi bi-mā kānū yaṣnaʿūna*
>
> *wa-la-qad jāʾahum rasūlun minhum fa-kadhdhabūhu fa-akhadhahumu l-ʿadhābu wa-hum ẓālimūna*

> And God has coined a parable:
> a settlement that was secure, at rest,
> with its provision coming to it in plenty from every place;
> yet it was ungrateful for the blessings of God,
> and so God let it taste the garb of hunger and fear
> because of what they were doing.

137 *BIQ*[1] 78.
138 Lohmann, "Die Gleichnisreden Muḥammeds im Koran," 91.
139 Harrington, *Jesus Ben Sira of Jerusalem*, 68.
140 Adolf Jülicher, *Die Gleichnisreden Jesu* (Tübingen: Verlag von J.C.B. Mohr (Paul Siebeck), 1888), 1:97; Tucker, *Example Stories*, 109; *BIQ*[1] 78; Neuwirth, *Der Koran als Text der Spätantike*, 504–9; s.v. Parable, *EQ*; McKnight, *What is Form Criticism?* 55; cf. s.v. Narratives, *EQ*. Rosalind Ward Gwynne writes, "Muslim scholars did not confine a passage to a single category, however; they were acutely aware that a historical precedent or a parable, for example, though in the form of a third-person narrative, is a form of address, and its surrounding apparatus places it in one or more of the first three categories," namely, "vocative," "imperative," or "effect on the audience" (eadem, "Patterns of Address," 73 and 77).
141 *QS* 1; Stewart, "Wansbrough, Bultmann, and the Theory of Variant Traditions," 22.
142 Cf. Buhl, "Über Vergleichungen und Gleichnisse im Qurʾān," 10.
143 *SKMS*[2] 301; *BCQ* 1:455.

A messenger had come to them from among their own number,
but they accused him of falsehood,
and they were smitten by punishment
while they were wrong-doers.

Bell states that these verses set a precedent.[144]

Paradigm

As determined by Dibelius, "the paradigm reveals itself in fact as the narrative form…."[145] In this case, the narrative element is short, and lacks description or elaboration.[146] For example, Q. 2.171 (-*ūC*) reads,[147]

wa-mathalu lladhīna kafarū ka-mathali lladhī yanʿiqu bi-mā lā yasmaʿu illā duʿāʾan wa-nidāʾan ṣummun bukmun ʿumyun fa-hum lā yaʿqilūna

And the paradigm of those who do not believe
is like the paradigm of one who shouts out to what can hear nothing but a shout and a cry:
Deaf, dumb, and blind.
They have no understanding.

Buhl remarks that such bold imagery is inspired by the polemic against idolatry.[148] Q. 2.17–18 (-*ūC*) also has a different version of the paradigm:

mathaluhum ka-mathali lladhī stawqada nāran fa-lammā aḍāʾat mā ḥawlahū dhahaba llāhu bi-nūrihim wa-tarakahum fī ẓulumātin lā yubṣirūna

ṣummun bukmun ʿumyun fa-hum lā yarjiʿūna

Their paradigm is like the paradigm of that of those who light a fire,
and when it lights up all around them
God takes away their light and leaves them in darkness, unable to see:

Deaf, dumb, and blind.
They do not return.

---

144 *BCQ* 1:455.
145 Dibelius, *Die Formgeschichte des Evangeliums*, 66; idem, *From Tradition to Gospel*, 69.
146 Repschinski, *Controversy Stories*, 238.
147 Lohmann, "Die Gleichnisreden Muḥammeds im Koran," 77; idem, "Die Gleichnisreden Muḥammeds im Koran (2. Teil)," 248–49.
148 Buhl, "Über Vergleichungen und Gleichnisse im Qurʾān," 8–9.

Furthermore, the corpus contains a variant formulation: "the paradigm of those who...is like" (*mathalu lladhīna...ka-*).[149] Q. 14.18 (*-īC*) seals the fate of the faithless[150]:

> *mathalu lladhīna kafarū bi-rabbihim aʿmāluhum ka-ramādin ishtaddat bihi r-rīḥu fī yawmin ʿāṣifin lā yaqdirūna mimmā kasabū ʿalā shayʾin dhālika huwa ḍ-ḍalālu l-baʿīdu*
>
> The paradigm of those who do not believe in their Lord
> is their works are like ashes which the wind scatters on a stormy day:
> They have no power over any of what they have earned.
> That is distant error.

Bell comments, this stand-alone paradigm likens the disbelievers to dust.[151] Moreover, Q. 62.5 (*-īC*) reads,[152]

> *mathalu lladhīna ḥummilū t-tawrāta thumma lam yaḥmilūhā ka-mathali l-ḥimāri yaḥmilu asfāran biʾsa mathalu l-qawmi lladhīna kadhdhabū bi-āyāti llāhi wa-llāhu lā yahdī l-qawma ẓ-ẓālimīna*
>
> The paradigm of those who have been loaded with the Torah and then have not carried it
> is like the paradigm of the donkey who carries books:
> Bad is the paradigm of the people who deny the truth of God's signs.
> God does not guide people who do wrong.

On a related matter, consider the final verse of Sūrat al-Fatḥ (Q. 48.29), headlining the sanctioned statement (*-Can*)[153]:

> *muḥammadun rasūlu llāhi wa-lladhīna maʿahū ashiddāʾu ʿalā l-kuffāri ruḥamāʾu baynahum tarāhum rukkaʿan sujjadan yabtaghūna faḍlan mina llāhi wa-riḍwānan sīmāhum fī wujūhihim min athari s-sujūdi dhālika mathaluhum fī t-tawrāti wa-mathaluhum fī l-injīli ka-zarʿin akhraja shaṭʾahū fa-āzarahū fa-staghlaẓa fa-stawā ʿalā sūqihī yuʿjibu z-zurrāʿa li-yaghīẓa bihimu l-kuffāra waʿada llāhu lladhīna āmanū wa-ʿamilū ṣ-ṣāliḥāti minhum maghfiratan wa-ajran ʿaẓīman*
>
> Muḥammad is the messenger of God.
> Those who are with him are hard on the disbelievers,
> merciful among themselves.

---

149 Cf. Sister, "Metaphern und Vergleiche im Koran," 114–15.

150 Buhl, "Über Vergleichungen und Gleichnisse im Qurʾān," 8; Lohmann, "Die Gleichnisreden Muḥammeds im Koran," 76 and 116; Hirschfeld, *New Researches*, 88.

151 *BCQ* 1:410; *SKMS*² 299; cf. *JQA* 239 (vv. 18–23).

152 *JQA* 518 (vv. 5–6); Lohmann, "Die Gleichnisreden Muḥammeds im Koran," 77; idem, "Die Gleichnisreden Muḥammeds im Koran (2. Teil)," 264–65.

153 Travis, "Form Criticism," 155; Hirschfeld, *New Researches*, 96 and 140.

You see them bowing and prostrating themselves,
seeking bounty and approval from God.
Their mark is on their faces from the effect of prostration.
That is their paradigm in the Torah;
And their paradigm in the Gospel
is like a seed that puts forth its shoot and strengthens it,
so that it grows stout and rises firm on its stalk,
delighting the sowers
– that He may enrage the disbelievers through them.
God has promised those of them who believe and do righteous deeds forgiveness and a great wage.

The paradigm employs a simplified substitution formula: "the paradigm of...is like" (*mathalu...ka-*).[154] By way of closing, this sūra-unit extends a promise to people of faith.[155]

A further paradigm ends on a similar note to that of Q. 62.5. Beyond that, Q. 3.117 (*-ūC*) features an additional variant: "the paradigm of what...is like the paradigm of..." (*mathalu mā...ka-mathali...*)[156]:

mathalu mā yunfiqūna fī hādhihi l-ḥayāti d-dunyā ka-mathali rīḥin fīhā ṣirrun aṣābat ḥartha qawmin ẓalamū anfusahum fa-ahlakathu wa-mā ẓalamahumu llāhu wa-lākin anfusahum yaẓlimūna

The paradigm of what they spend in the life of the world
is like the paradigm of an icy wind which smites the tillage of a people
who have wronged themselves and destroys it:
God does not wrong them.
But they wrong themselves.

According to Lohmann, the image panel depicts death and direful destruction from heaven, while the object panel speaks to the sins of men.[157] And again,

154 Sister, "Metaphern und Vergleiche im Koran," 114–15; Lohmann, "Die Gleichnisreden Muḥammeds im Koran," 77; idem, "Die Gleichnisreden Muḥammeds im Koran (2. Teil)," 267–69; Buhl, "Über Vergleichungen und Gleichnisse im Qur'ān," 5 (Matt 13:8); Hirschfeld, *New Researches*, 96 (Mark 4:8); *JQA* 474, fn. 4 (Mark 4:26–28); *BCQ* 2:286 (Mark 4:26–28, 30–32); cf. Jülicher, *Die Gleichnisreden Jesu*, 2:514–46 and 2:569–81; Dibelius, *Die Formgeschichte des Evangeliums*, 229.

155 Robinson, *Discovering the Qur'ān*, 268.

156 *BCQ* 1:87; Buhl, "Über Vergleichungen und Gleichnisse im Qur'ān," 5; Lohmann, "Die Gleichnisreden Muḥammeds im Koran," 77; idem, "Die Gleichnisreden Muḥammeds im Koran (2. Teil)," 244–46.

157 Lohmann, "Die Gleichnisreden Muḥammeds im Koran (2. Teil)," 244; Tucker, *Example Stories*, 18; Neuwirth, *Der Koran als Text der Spätantike*, 501–4.

Sūrat an-Nūr features the simple formula (*mathalu…ka-*).[158] On the other hand, verse Q. 24.35 eloquently opens with an oral-formulaic construction framing the paradigm (*mathal*)[159]:

> *allāhu nūru s-samāwāti wa-l-arḍi mathalu nūrihī ka-mishkātin fīhā miṣbāḥun al-miṣbāḥu fī zujājatin az-zujājatu ka-annahā kawkabun durriyyun yūqadu min shajaratin mubārakatin zaytūnatin lā sharqiyyatin wa-lā gharbiyyatin yakādu zaytuhā yuḍī'u wa-law-lam tamsashu nārun*
>
> God is the light of the heavens and the earth.
> The paradigm of His light
> is like a niche in which there is a lamp
> – the lamp in a glass, and the glass like a brilliant star
> – lit from a blessed tree, an olive-tree
> neither from the East nor from the West,
> whose oil almost glows, even though no fire has touched it:

Verse 35a contains the eponymous saying[160]:

> *nūrun ʿalā nūrin yahdī llāhu li-nūrihī man yashā'u wa-yaḍribu llāhu l-amthāla li-n-nāsi wa-llāhu bi-kulli shay'in ʿalīmun*
>
> Light upon light,
> God guides to His light those whom He wishes;
> and God coins parables for the people.
> God is aware of everything.

As Buhl notes in passing, this is the well-known verse of light.[161]

---

158 Sister, "Metaphern und Vergleiche im Koran," 114–15.
159 *BCQ* 1:601–3; Lohmann, "Die Gleichnisreden Muḥammeds im Koran," 77; idem, "Die Gleichnisreden Muḥammeds im Koran (2. Teil)," 262–64; Sister, "Metaphern und Vergleiche im Koran," 118–19. For the oral-formulaic base phrase (*as-samāwāt wa-l-arḍ*), see s.v. Samā', *CQ.*
160 *JQA* 321.
161 Buhl, "Über Vergleichungen und Gleichnisse im Qur'ān," 9. The latter half of the verse is of equal interest, given the oral-formulaic use of the parabolic (*mathal*) phrase: "God coins parables" (*yaḍribu llāhu l-amthāla*) (Q. 13.17, Q. 14.25, and Q. 24.35a); ibid., 2. Elsewhere in the corpus, analogous phrases with a similar function occur with variants. For example: "And We have coined for the people in this *qur'ān* every kind of parable" (*wa-la-qad ḍarabnā li-n-nāsi fī hādhā l-qur'āni min kulli mathalin*); minimal pair: Q. 30.58 and Q. 39.27; alternate formulation: *wa-la-qad ṣarrafnā li-n-nāsi fī hādhā l-qur'āni min kulli mathalin* (Q. 17.89); variant order: Q. 18.54; cf. Q. 17.41, Q. 20.113, and Q. 46.27; additional formulation: *wa-tilka l-amthālu naḍribuhā li-n-nāsi* (Q. 29.43 and Q. 59.21).

Controversy Story

Repschinski writes, "At the heart of the controversy stories is the controversy."[162] Their tripartite order is literally (i) setting, (ii) objection, and (iii) riposte.[163] Take, for example, the narrative of rejection (Q. 36.13–16) in the *mathal aṣḥāb al-qarya* (-*ūC*).[164] The pericope opens with the scene.[165] The introductory formula (v. 13) reads,[166]

> *wa-ḍrib lahum mathalan aṣḥāba l-qaryati idh jā'ahā l-mursalūna*
>
> Coin^{S} for them a controversy story (*mathal*):
> the inhabitants of the village,
> when those who were sent came to them;

The latter portion of this verse incorporates the transitional formula (*idh*).[167] At the same time, *idh* in the subsequent verse (14) also doubles as a narrative formula proper.[168] A further distinctive feature is the presence of dialogue.[169] Accordingly, the controversy story turns to the objection and the riposte (vv. 14–16):

> *idh arsalnā ilayhimu thnayni fa-kadhdhabūhumā fa-ʿazzaznā bi-thālithin fa-qālū innā ilaykum mursalūna*
>
> *qālū mā antum illā basharun mithlunā wa-mā anzala r-raḥmānu min shay'in in antum illā takdhibūna*
>
> *qālū rabbunā yaʿlamu innā ilaykum la-mursalūna*
>
> When We sent two men to them, but they called them liars;
> so We reinforced them with a third.
> The [three] said: 'We are sent to you^{P}.'
>
> They said: 'You^{P} are only mortals like us. The Merciful has not sent down anything. You^{P} are

162 Repschinski, *Controversy Stories*, 273. Paradigms and controversy stories share "a literary affinity" (ibid., 277–83).
163 Ibid., 264–70 and 273.
164 *SKMS*^{2} 279 (vv. 13–19); *BCQ* 2:138–41 (vv. 13–29); *JQA* 402 (vv. 13–29); Robinson, *Discovering the Qur'ān*, 150–51 (vv. 14–30).
165 Repschinski, *Controversy Stories*, 266–67 and 273.
166 Robinson, *Discovering the Qur'ān*, 150–51.
167 S.v. Narratives, *EQ*.
168 Nöldeke, *Neue Beiträge*, 17; *KU* 4; *QS* 18–19; s.v. Narratives, *EQ*. The presence of the dual *idh* formulae leads Bell to doubt the integrity of the piece (*BCQ* 2:139).
169 Repschinski, *Controversy Stories*, 280.

simply telling lies.'

The [three] said: 'Our Lord knows we are sent to you^{P}.'

This "motif of hostility" dominates the controversy story, and for that reason, it employs the debate formula (*qālū:* "they said").[170] Furthermore, "the decisive elements of the controversy story do not lie in a dialogue but in the dominical saying or activity concluding the story," in this case, twice repeated: "We are sent to you^{P}."[171]

Example Story

According to Zahniser, *mathal* as "an illustrative story teaching a lesson" represents an important form in the corpus.[172] The example story, specifically, "provides a concrete example to illustrate a point."[173] For instance, consider the set of three example stories (vv. 10–12) in Sūrat at-Taḥrīm ("Prohibition").[174] Q. 66.10 (*-īC*) begins with the formula for introducing the example story:

ḍaraba llāhu mathalan li-lladhīna kafarū mra'ata nūḥin wa-mra'ata lūṭin kānatā taḥta 'abdayni min 'ibādinā ṣāliḥayni fa-khānatāhumā fa-lam yughniyā 'anhumā mina llāhi shay'an wa-qīla dkhulā n-nāra ma'a d-dākhilīna

God has coined an example story for those who disbelieve:
the wife of Noah and the wife of Lot.
They were married to two righteous servants of Ours,
but they betrayed them;
so [their husbands] were of no avail to them against God.
They were told, 'Enter the Fire with those who are entering.'

On this and the subsequent verse, Buhl comments that in connection with *ḍaraba*, *mathal* has the semantically narrow sense of "example."[175] More often than not, these examples deliver warnings and bear bad tidings (e.g., Q.

170 Ibid., 292; cf. Azaiez, *Le contre-discours coranique*, 8; Neuwirth, "Structural, Linguistic, and Literary Features," 108.
171 Repschinski, *Controversy Stories*, 238; *BCQ* 2:382; Buhl, "Über Vergleichungen und Gleichnisse im Qur'ān," 4 and 11.
172 S.v. Parable, *EQ*; Hirschfeld, *New Researches*, 84; Neuwirth, *Der Koran als Text der Spätantike*, 502 and 509.
173 *FOTL* 1:318; *FOTL* 13:176; Tucker, *Example Stories*, 7.
174 *JQA* 526.
175 Buhl, "Über Vergleichungen und Gleichnisse im Qur'ān," 10.

14.45–46, Q. 25.39; Q. 43.56; Q. 16.112, Q. 36.13; Q. 66.10).[176] But at the same time, Buhl states, there can also be good examples to emulate (e.g., Q. 43, vv. 57 and 59; Q. 66.11).[177] And so, the second verse (11) relates (-*īC*),

> *wa-ḍaraba llāhu mathalan li-lladhīna āmanū mraʾata firʿawna idh qālat rabbi bni lī ʿindaka baytan fī l-jannati wa-najjinī min firʿawna wa-ʿamalihī wa-najjinī mina l-qawmi ẓ-ẓālimīna*
>
> And God has coined an example story for those who believe:
> the wife of Pharaoh when she said,
> 'My Lord, build for me a house with You in the Garden
> and deliver me from Pharaoh and his work,
> and deliver me from the people who do wrong.'

Quite appropriately, the cultic formula (*rabbi*) stands at the head of this prayer. The third verse of this series (12) concludes the sūra-unit (-*īC*):

> *wa-maryama bnata ʿimrāna llatī aḥṣanat farjahā fa-nafakhnā fīhi min rūḥinā wa-ṣaddaqat bi-kalimāti rabbihā wa-kutubihī wa-kānat mina l-qānitīna*
>
> And Mary, the daughter of ʿImrān,
> who guarded her private parts;
> and We breathed into it some of Our Spirit,
> and she counted true the words of her Lord and His scriptures
> and was one of the obedient.

As is evident from the final verse in this series of example stories, the introductory formula is omitted in favor of the coordinating conjunction (*wa-*). To close with, Wansbrough observes the following: "Analysis of the qur'ānic application of these shows that they have been adapted to the essentially paraenetic character of that document, and that, for example, originally narrative material was reduced almost invariably to a series of discrete and parabolic utterances."[178] Therefore, these example stories constitute narratives writ small.

Report

The report form narrates a shorthand version of an historical happening.[179] Put otherwise, a report consists of a simple scenario, a single drama.[180] Although the

---

176 Ibid.
177 Ibid.; Sister, "Metaphern und Vergleiche im Koran," 115–16; cf. *BCQ* 2:399.
178 *QS* 1.
179 *FOTL* 10:312; *FOTL* 1:10; *FOTL* 13:181.

topic of a report varies considerably, the calling down of divine retribution is notable.[181] Q. 7.65 (-*ūC*) contains a report on Hūd[182]:

> *wa-ilā ʿādin akhāhum hūdan qāla yā-qawmi ʿbudū llāha mā lakum min ilāhin ghayruhū a-fa-lā tattaqūna*
>
> And to ʿĀd their brother Hūd.
> He said, 'O my tribe, serve God.
> You have no god other than Him.
> Will you not protect yourselves?'

Additionally, consider Q. 51.43 (-*īC*)[183]:

> *wa-fī thamūda idh qīla lahum tamattaʿū ḥattā ḥīnin*
>
> And in Thamūd,
> when they were told, 'Take your enjoyment for a time.'

Interestingly enough, there is an affinity here between the report and the paradigm.[184]

Summary Report

In addition to the report proper, there is also the summary report.[185] According to George Coats (d. 2006), summaries occur at turning points and act as bridge narratives.[186] In other words, "the purpose of its transitional function is to move the larger narrative effectively forward."[187] Pertinent in this regard is Q. 29.36–9 (-*īC*), which commences with the commission formulation. However, it is highly

180 *FOTL* 10:312.
181 Ibid.
182 *SKMS*² 292 (vv. 65–72); *BCQ* 1:239–40 (vv. 65–72).
183 *SKMS*² 204 (vv. 43–45); *BCQ* 2:303 (vv. 43–45); Welch, "Formulaic Features of the Punishment-Stories," 100.
184 *FOTL* 10:312.
185 *FOTL* 2a:172–73.
186 Ibid., 2a:173.
187 Ibid.

significant in that it seamlessly transitions from the prophet legend to the summary report (*wa-*). Evoking the *ubi sunt* motif, verses 38 to 39 read,[188]

> *wa-ʿādan wa-thamūda wa-qad tabayyana lakum min masākinihim wa-zayyana lahumu sh-shayṭānu aʿmālahum fa-ṣaddahum ʿani s-sabīli wa-kānū mustabṣirīna*
>
> *wa-qārūna wa-firʿawna wa-hāmāna wa-la-qad jāʾahum mūsā bi-l-bayyināti fa-stakbarū fī l-arḍi wa-mā kānū sābiqīna*
>
> And ʿĀd and Thamūd,
> for it is clear to you from their dwelling-places.
> Satan made their deeds seem fair to them,
> and turned them from the way,
> though they thought they saw clearly.
>
> And Qārūn and Pharaoh and Hāmān.
> Moses brought them clear proofs,
> but they were haughty in the land.
> Yet they did not outstrip [Us].

What is more, the subsequent verse Q. 29.40 recapitulates,[189]

> *fa-kullan akhadhnā bi-dhanbihī fa-minhum man arsalnā ʿalayhi ḥāṣiban wa-minhum man akhadhathu ṣ-ṣayḥatu wa-minhum man khasafnā bihi l-arḍa wa-minhum man aghraqnā wa-mā kāna llāhu li-yaẓlimahum wa-lākin kānū anfusahum yaẓlimūna*
>
> We took each one for his sin.
> Among them were those on whom We sent a sandstorm,
> and among them were those who were taken by the shout,
> and among them were those whom We caused the earth to swallow
> and among them were those whom We drowned.
> God would not wrong them,
> but they wronged themselves.

Alford Welch observes that "this concluding verse is unique in providing a summary of the methods used by God in destroying earlier peoples who rejected his messengers."[190] Therefore, it is quite appropriate when Neuwirth says, summary

---

188 *SKMS*^{2} 302 (vv. 38–40); *QS* 7; Stewart, "Wansbrough, Bultmann, and the Theory of Variant Traditions," 29–30; Becker, "Ubi sunt qui ante nos in mundo fuere," 87–105; Lidzbarski, "Ubi sunt qui ante nos in mundo fuere," 300; *BCQ* 2:63.
189 *JQA* 363.
190 Welch, "Formulaic Features of the Punishment-Stories," 98.

reports (vv. 38–40) evoke other narratives.[191] Similarly, Welch notes that Q. 53.50–54 (-*Cā*) is full of brief allusions to a series of punishment stories.[192] Using the same assonance, the list begins with the coordinating conjunction (*wa-*) combined with a variant (*ahlaka:* "He destroyed") of a narrative formula[193]:

wa-annahū ahlaka ʿādan al-ūlā

wa-thamūda fa-mā abqā

wa-qawma nūḥin min qablu innahum kānū hum aẓlama wa-aṭghā

wa-l-muʾtafikata ahwā

fa-ghashshāhā mā ghashshā

And that He destroyed ʿĀd, the first,

And Thamūd, and He did not spare them,

And the people of Noah before
– for they did grievous wrong and were vile transgressors –

And He also overthrew the overturned settlements,

So that they were covered by that which covered [them].

On *ʿĀd al-ūlā*, Bell comments that it "apparently can only mean ʿĀd, the first of the peoples to be destroyed."[194] Also, consider the self-contained summary report, which features a "narrative frame" and stands at the head of a subsequent prophet episode.[195] Q. 38.12–14 (-*āC*) reads,[196]

kadhdhabat qablahum qawmu nūḥin wa-ʿādun wa-firʿawnu dhū l-awtādi

wa-thamūdu wa-qawmu lūṭin wa-aṣḥābu l-aykati ulāʾika l-aḥzābu

191 *SKMS*² 302; *BCQ* 2:63.
192 *SKMS*² 207; Welch, "Formulaic Features of the Punishment-Stories," 101–2 (vv. 50–56).
193 *JQA* 488; *SKMS*² 207; *KU* 8 (*ahlaknā*); *FOTL* 1:318.
194 *BCQ* 2:321; s.v. Iram, *EI*¹.
195 *SKMS*² 282; *FOTL* 2a:166.
196 *SKMS*² 282 (vv. 12–16).

in kullun illā kadhdhaba r-rusula fa-ḥaqqa ʿiqābi

Before them the people of Noah denied,
and ʿĀd, and Pharaoh,
the man with the pegs,

And Thamūd and the people of Lot
and the men of the thicket
– they were the parties.

Every one of them denied the truth of the messengers,
and My punishment was justified.

The simple formula (*kadhdhabat*) and its variant (*kadhdhaba*) bracket the list of punishment stories.[197] On a note related to verse Q. 38.12 (*kadhdhabat qabla-hum*), Ettinghausen states, the summary reports on the fallen nations sound formulaic and contrived at best.[198]

Historical Story

Compared to the report form, the historical story narrates single occurrences in a slightly more elaborate fashion.[199] For example, Q. 51.41–42 (*-īC*) reads,[200]

wa-fī ʿādin idh arsalnā ʿalayhimu r-rīḥa l-ʿaqīma

mā tadharu min shayʾin atat ʿalayhi illā jaʿalathu ka-r-ramīmi

And in ʿĀd,
when We sent loose on them the withering wind,

Which spared nothing on which it came, but turned it into decayed matter.

Although Neuwirth places these verses under the rubric of the lessons of history, the historical story is primarily concerned with recording what happened, plain

197 Ibid.; *BCQ* 2:167.
198 Ettinghausen, *Antiheidnische Polemik im Koran*, 51.
199 Cf. *FOTL* 10:301; *QS* 311 (*historia*).
200 *SKMS*² 204.

and simple.[201] In brief, Bell comments, "Story of ʿĀd, only shortly indicated; destruction due to withering wind."[202]

Legend

To continue, Sūrat Hūd also furnishes a fine example of the legend form. For instance, verse 84 of the Shuʿayb legend in Q. 11.84–9 (-*īC*) commences with the commission formulation:

> *wa-ilā madyana akhāhum shuʿayban qāla yā-qawmi ʿbudū llāha mā lakum min ilāhin ghayruhū wa-lā tanquṣū l-mikyāla wa-l-mīzāna innī arākum bi-khayrin wa-innī akhāfu ʿalaykum ʿadhāba yawmin muḥīṭin*

> And to Madyan their brother Shuʿayb.
> He said, 'My people, serve God.
> You have no god other than Him.
> Do not give short measure or short weight.
> I see that you are faring well,
> but I fear for you the punishment of an all-encompassing day.

Bell remarks that the scales-topos persists in the Madyan narratives.[203] Verse 89 ends the legend:

> *wa-yā-qawmi lā yajrimannakum shiqāqī an yuṣībakum mithlu mā aṣāba qawma nūḥin aw qawma hūdin aw qawma ṣāliḥin wa-mā qawmu lūṭin minkum bi-baʿīdin*

> O my people, let not the split with me incite you
> lest you are smitten by the like of what smote the people of Noah
> or the people of Hūd or the people of Ṣāliḥ;
> and the people of Lot are not far from you.

Plainly, this embedded summary report marks off the unit. However, Bell recognizes, "the beginning shows that it formed part of the series, Noah, ʿĀd, Thamūd."[204] The frame indicates that the Shuʿayb legend (Q. 11.84–9) belongs to a larger narrative, namely, the Shuʿayb episode (Q. 11.84–95).[205] To clarify,

---

201 Ibid.; *FOTL* 10:301.
202 *BCQ* 2:303.
203 Ibid., 1:365.
204 Ibid.
205 *FOTL* 2a:166; *JQA* 207; *BCQ* 1:365–67; *SKMS*² 296; Stewart, "Wansbrough, Bultmann, and the Theory of Variant Traditions," 26–27 and 37–38.

it is a type of *inclusio*, whose brackets serve a resumptive function.[206] In the case of the Shuʿayb episode, the short commission formula (*wa-ilā madyana:* "And to Madyan") in the first verse (84) echoes the abbreviated formula for condemnation (*buʿdan li-madyana:* "Away with Madyan") in the final verse (95).[207] In addition to the legend, the Shuʿayb episode also features counter-discourse and employs multiple vocative formulations.[208]

On a related note, the Shuʿayb legend in Q. 7.85–9 (-*īC*) begins with the exact same formula. Moreover, Jones indicates that the prophetic narratives in this sūra-unit are by far the most extensive in the corpus.[209] The commission opens the first part of verse 85:

> *wa-ilā madyana akhāhum shuʿayban qāla yā-qawmi ʿbudū llāha mā lakum min ilāhin ghayruhu*
>
> And to Madyan their brother Shuʿayb.
> He said, 'O my people, serve God.
> You have no god other than Him.'

The remainder and subsequent verses (Q. 7.85a-87) constitute an extensive paraenetic catalogue, in which the scales-topos resurfaces.[210] This vocative address sets the scene for the objection and riposte (vv. 88–89), akin to the controversy story. Here again, the Shuʿayb legend (Q. 7.85–9) is one element within the larger Shuʿayb episode (Q. 7.85–93).[211] Furthermore, Q. 26 preserves yet one more Shuʿayb episode (vv. 176–91).[212] Verses 176–80 introduce the episode by means of the localized (*kadhdhaba*) schematic formulation[213]:

> *kadhdhaba aṣḥābu l-aykati l-mursalīna*
>
> *idh qāla lahum shuʿaybun a-lā tattaqūna*
>
> *innī lakum rasūlun amīnun*

---

206 *FOTL* 2a:166.
207 *BQA* 1:204; Welch, "Formulaic Features of the Punishment-Stories," 90–91 and 113, fn. 23.
208 *SKMS*² 296; *BCQ* 1:365–67; *JQA* 207.
209 *JQA* 147.
210 *BCQ* 1:241.
211 *SKMS*² 292; *BCQ* 1:241–42; Stewart, "Wansbrough, Bultmann, and the Theory of Variant Traditions," 25–26 and 35–37.
212 *SKMS*² 276–77; *BCQ* 2:24; *JQA* 335; Stewart, "Wansbrough, Bultmann, and the Theory of Variant Traditions," 27 and 39–40.
213 Welch, "Formulaic Features of the Punishment-Stories," 78–79.

fa-ttaqū llāha wa-aṭīʿūni

wa-mā asʾalukum ʿalayhi min ajrin in ajriya illā ʿalā rabbi l-ʿālamīna

The men of the thicket denied the truth of those who were sent:

When their brother Shuʿayb said to them,
'Will you not protect yourselves?

I am a faithful messenger for you.

Fear God and obey me.

I am not asking you for any wage for this.
My reward is only with the Lord of all beings.'

Attuned to detail, Bell observes that "Shuʿayb is not called their brother, but it is uncertain whether any significance should be attached to this."[214] The remaining verses include a partial paraenetic catalogue, a debate formulation, and a punishment.[215] Stewart writes, "Wansbrough is probably correct in referring to the punishment stories as *exempla* in the Qurʾān...."[216]

Episode

At the outset, episodes assume the form of shortened sagas.[217] The saga-teller splices together different genres, such as prayer, liturgy, wisdom, etc.[218] For instance, Q. 26.69–104 preserves an episode on Abraham.[219] Specifically, verses 69 to 70 narrate,

214 *BCQ* 2:24.
215 *SKMS*² 277. With regard to Wansbrough, Stewart comments on "his generally correct understanding that the stories have been adapted to a paraenetic framework" (idem, "Wansbrough, Bultmann, and the Theory of Variant Traditions," 28).
216 Stewart, "Wansbrough, Bultmann, and the Theory of Variant Traditions," 29 and 41; *QS* 2, 18, 310, and 314; s.v. Narratives, *EQ*.
217 Gunkel, *Die Sagen der Genesis*, 19–21; *FOTL* 2a:172; Hirschfeld, *New Researches*, 62; cf. Roger N. Whybray, *The Making of the Pentateuch: A Methodological Study* (Sheffield, England: JSOT Press, 1987), 133–34.
218 *FOTL* 1:5; *FOTL* 9:260.
219 *SKMS*² 276; *JQA* 335; *BCQ* 2:20–21.

wa-tlu ʿalayhim nabaʾa ibrāhīma

idh qāla li-abīhi wa-qawmihī mā taʿbudūna

And recite[S] to them the narrative of Abraham,

When he said to his father and his people,
'What do you worship?'

This episode contains pericopae drawn from other genres (e. g., hymn, prayer).[220] According to Bell, the prayer of Abraham, *inter alia*, fills out the narrative nicely.[221] Finally, it ends with a refrain (vv. 103–4).[222] Related to this, Sūrat al-Anbiyāʾ (Q. 21) also recounts an episode on Abraham (vv. 51–72).[223] Immediately followed by *idh*, the narrative begins (vv. 51–52),

wa-la-qad ātaynā ibrāhīma rushdahū min qablu wa-kunnā bihī ʿālimīna

idh qāla li-abīhi wa-qawmihī mā hādhihi t-tamāthīlu llatī antum lahā ʿākifūna

And in the past We gave Abraham his right course
– for We knew him –

When he said to his father and to his people,
'What are these images to which you cleave?'

This episode apparently closes (v. 72) with the formulaic phrase, *wa-wahabnā li-* ("And We bestowed upon…")[224]:

wa-wahabnā lahū isḥāqa wa-yaʿqūba nāfilatan wa-kullan jaʿalnā ṣāliḥīna

And We bestowed upon him Isaac and Jacob as a special gift.
Each one [of them] We made righteous.

The corpus contains yet another Abraham episode (Q. 51.24–37) that starts (vv. 24–25),[225]

---

220 *FOTL* 9:260; *FOTL* 1:5; *SKMS*² 276.
221 *BCQ* 2:20.
222 *SKMS*² 276.
223 Ibid., 271; *JQA* 298; *BCQ* 1:551–53.
224 For the refrain-like phrase, see Q. 6.84, Q. 19.50, Q. 19.53, Q. 29.27, Q. 38.30, and Q. 38.43.
225 *SKMS*² 204; *BCQ* 2:301–2; *JQA* 481.

hal atāka ḥadīthu ḍayfi ibrāhīma l-mukramīna

idh dakhalū ʿalayhi fa-qālū salāman qāla salāmun qawmun munkarūna

Have you[S] heard the narrative of the honored guests of Abraham?

When they came to see him and said, 'Peace.'
He said, 'Peace, people unknown.'

In addition, consider the Noah episode in Q. 26.105–22.[226] Verses 105–9 open this short saga:

kadhdhabat qawmu nūḥin-i l-mursalīna

idh qāla lahum akhūhum nūḥun a-lā tattaqūna

innī lakum rasūlun amīnun

fa-ttaqū llāha wa-aṭīʿūni

wa-mā asʾalukum ʿalayhi min ajrin in ajriya illā ʿalā rabbi l-ʿālamīna

The people of Noah denied the truth of those who were sent,

When their brother Noah said to them,
'Will you not protect yourselves?

I am a faithful messenger for you.

Fear God and obey me.

I am not asking you for any wage for this.
My reward is only with the Lord of all beings.'

The body consists of a number of distinct genres.[227] Q. 26.111–16 features the debate formula, thus representing a "controversy dialogue."[228] Because of the cultic formula, verses 117–20 constitute a petitionary prayer.[229] The short Noah saga

226 *BCQ* 2:21; *SKMS*^{2} 276; *JQA* 335.
227 Welch, "Formulaic Features of the Punishment-Stories," 80–81.
228 *SKMS*^{2} 276; Neuwirth, "Structural, Linguistic, and Literary Features," 108; cf. Azaiez, *Le contre-discours coranique*, 8; Repschinski, *Controversy Stories*, 236–38.
229 *SKMS*^{2} 276 (vv. 117–18).

terminates with a twofold closing refrain.[230] What is more, Horovitz holds, several sūra-units are filled with narrative content.[231] To illustrate, he cites Sūrat Nūḥ (Q. 71), which combines a number of pieces.[232] Verse Q. 71.1 opens,

> *innā arsalnā nūḥan ilā qawmihī an andhir qawmaka min qabli an ya'tiyahum ʿadhābun alīmun*
>
> We sent Noah to his people, saying,
> 'Warn your[S] people before a painful punishment comes upon them.'

When considered collectively, the intricate structure involves, (i) "commission," (ii) "admonition," (iii) "prediction of disaster," (iv) "contestation," (v) "justification," (vi) "monologue/dialogue," (vii) "apocalyptic" motif, and (viii) so-called "eschatological coda."[233]

Saga

The long saga is arranged either serially or concurrently.[234] As is often the case with short sagas, the Noah episode (Q. 26.105–22) is part of a progression cast in one mold, otherwise known as the "saga cycle."[235] For example, consider the literary structure of the central episode (Q. 26.141–59) in this long saga. The familiar schematic formulation (Q. 26.141–5) leads off the Ṣāliḥ episode[236]:

> *kadhdhabat thamūdu l-mursalīna*
>
> *idh qāla lahum akhūhum ṣāliḥun a-lā tattaqūna*
>
> *innī lakum rasūlun amīnun*
>
> *fa-ttaqū llāha wa-aṭīʿūni*

---

230 Ibid., 276–77; Welch, "Formulaic Features of the Punishment-Stories," 80–81 and cf. 82.
231 *KU* 1–2.
232 Ibid., 1; *JQA* 538.
233 Segovia, *The Quranic Noah*, 28–30.
234 *FOTL* 2a:166.
235 Welch, "Formulaic Features of the Punishment-Stories," 80; Hirschfeld, *New Researches*, 62; *BCQ* 2:22; Gunkel, *Die Sagen der Genesis*, 19–21; cf. *FOTL* 1:5.
236 *SKMS*^{2} 277; Welch, "Formulaic Features of the Punishment-Stories," 78–79; Stewart, "Wansbrough, Bultmann, and the Theory of Variant Traditions," 39.

wa-mā as'alukum 'alayhi min ajrin in ajriya illā 'alā rabbi l-'ālamīna

Thamūd denied the truth of those who were sent,

When their brother Ṣāliḥ said to them,
'Will you not protect yourselves?

I am a faithful messenger for you.

Fear God and obey me.

I am not asking you for any wage for this.
My reward is only with the Lord of all beings.'

In turn, this episode finishes off with the characteristic refrain (vv. 158a-59) for this saga[237]:

inna fī dhālika la-āyatan wa-mā kāna aktharuhum mu'minīna

wa-inna rabbaka la-huwa l-'azīzu r-raḥīmu

In that there is a sign,
but most of them have not become believers.

Your Lord is the Mighty and the Compassionate.

This long saga consists of five episodes (i.e., Noah, Hūd, Ṣāliḥ, Lot, and Shu'ayb), conforming to a "parallel schematic form."[238] Therefore, Jones remarks that these episodes coalesce into a single narrative that holds together.[239]

In addition, Sūrat Hūd also preserves the long saga form (Q. 11.50–68). Given its title, verse 50 opens the episode (Q. 11.50–60) with the stylized formulation[240]:

wa-ilā 'ādin akhāhum hūdan qāla yā-qawmi 'budū llāha mā lakum min ilāhin ghayruhū in antum illā muftarūna

237 *SKMS*² 277; *JQA* 341.

238 Welch, "Formulaic Features of the Punishment-Stories," 80; cf. s.v. Narratives, *EQ*. N.b. Q. 26.176 (*kadhdhaba*).

239 *JQA* 335.

240 Ibid., 207; *BCQ* 1:360–61; *SKMS*² 296.

And to ʿĀd their brother Hūd.
He said, 'O my tribe, serve God.
You have no god other than Him.
You are merely inventing.'

Significantly, the substitution formula (*buʿd*) concludes both episodes in this long saga: "...disbelieved in their Lord. Away with..." (*a-lā inna...kafarū rabba-hum a-lā buʿdan li-*).[241] For instance, Q. 11.60 reads,

wa-utbiʿū fī hādhihi d-dunyā laʿnatan wa-yawma l-qiyāmati a-lā inna ʿādan kafarū rabba-hum a-lā buʿdan li-ʿādin qawmi hūdin

A curse was made to follow them in this world
and on the Day of Resurrection.
ʿĀd disbelieved in their Lord.
Away with ʿĀd, the people of Hūd.

The saga continues with the Ṣāliḥ episode (Q. 11.61–8).[242] Verse 61 begins,

wa-ilā thamūda akhāhum ṣāliḥan qāla yā-qawmi ʿbudū llāha mā lakum min ilāhin ghayruhū huwa anshaʾakum mina l-arḍi wa-staʿmarakum fīhā fa-staghfirūhu thumma tūbū ilayhi inna rabbī qarībun mujībun

And to Thamūd their brother Ṣāliḥ.
He said, 'O my tribe, serve God.
You have no god other than Him.
It is He who has raised you from the earth
and settled you in it.
Seek His forgiveness,
then turn to Him in repentance.
My Lord is Near and Responsive.'

This episode features counter-discourse, as indicated by the debate formula (*qālū:* "they said").[243] Q. 11.62–4 relates,

qālū yā-ṣāliḥu qad kunta fīnā marjuwwan qabla hādhā a-tanhānā an naʿbuda mā yaʿbudu ābāʾunā wa-innanā la-fī shakkin mimmā tadʿūnā ilayhi murībin

qāla yā-qawmi a-raʾaytum in kuntu ʿalā bayyinatin min rabbī wa-ātānī minhu raḥmatan fa-

241 Cf. *BQA* 1:204; Welch, "Formulaic Features of the Punishment-Stories," 90–91 and 113, fn. 23.
242 *JQA* 207; *BCQ* 1:362–63; *SKMS*² 296.
243 *SKMS*² 296; cf. Azaiez, *Le contre-discours coranique*, 8; Neuwirth, "Structural, Linguistic, and Literary Features," 108.

man yanṣurunī mina llāhi in ʿaṣaytuhū fa-mā tazīdūnanī ghayra takhsīrin

wa-yā-qawmi hādhihī nāqatu llāhi lakum āyatan fa-dharūhā taʾkul fī arḍi llāhi wa-lā tamassūhā bi-sūʾin fa-yaʾkhudhakum ʿadhābun qarībun

They said, 'O Ṣāliḥ, up to now you were the one among us
about whom there were hopes.
Do you forbid us to serve what our fathers served?
We are in doubt about what you are calling us to.'

He said, 'O my tribe, have you considered:
if I stand on a clear proof from my Lord
and He has given me mercy from Him
Who will save me from God if I disobey Him?
You would increase me only in loss.

O my tribe, this is the she-camel of God, a sign to you.
Let her eat in God's land
and do not touch her with evil,
lest you are seized by a punishment that is near.'

The communal crime follows (v. 65),[244]

fa-ʿaqarūhā fa-qāla tamattaʿū fī dārikum thalāthata ayyāmin dhālika waʿdun ghayru makdhūbin

But they hamstrung her, and he said,
'Enjoy yourselves in your dwellings for three days.
That is a promise that will not be found false.'

Interestingly, both episodes narrate the deliverance in formulaic fashion: "When our command came, We saved...and those who believed with him through mercy from Us" (*lammā jāʾa amrunā najjaynā...wa-lladhīna āmanū maʿahū bi-raḥmatin minnā*).[245] Accordingly, Q. 11.66 reads,

fa-lammā jāʾa amrunā najjaynā ṣāliḥan wa-lladhīna āmanū maʿahū bi-raḥmatin minnā wa-min khizyi yawmiʾidhin inna rabbaka huwa l-qawiyyu l-ʿazīzu

When our command came,
We saved Ṣāliḥ and those who believed with him
through mercy from Us

244 *SKMS*² 296.
245 Ibid.; cf. Stewart, "Wansbrough, Bultmann, and the Theory of Variant Traditions," 37.

from the shame of that day.
Your Lord is the Strong and Mighty.

The subsequent punishment (Q. 11.67–68) brings closure to the two-episode saga[246]:

wa-akhadha lladhīna ẓalamū ṣ-ṣayḥatu fa-aṣbaḥū fī diyārihim jāthimīna

ka-an lam yaghnaw fīhā a-lā inna thamūda kafarū rabbahum a-lā buʿdan li-thamūda

And the Cry seized the wrong-doers,
and in the morning they were prostrate in their abodes,

As if they had never flourished there.
Thamūd disbelieved in their Lord.
Away with Thamūd.

Notably, Bell submits, the *buʿd* formula will be issued at the time of reckoning.[247]

In light of these considerations, it is clear that the saga is "a long, traditional narrative, composed of episodic units," gravitating towards a central motif, otherwise building upon layered motifs.[248] Take, for example, the punishment stories in the *corpus coranicum*, "where all the narratives share the basic motif of crime and punishment."[249] Welch writes,[250]

> Their basic plot is that God sends or selects a messenger from among the people of a tribe or town, who urges his people to serve only the true God, warns them that they will be destroyed if they reject his message, which the majority do, and then God rescues the messenger and those who believe him, and destroys those who do not.

In terms of literary structure, these aligned punishment episodes begin with the schematic saga formulation and close with the dual refrain functioning as an episode divider.[251] The core content varies, otherwise.[252] What is more, Long notes,

---

246 *SKMS*² 296; cf. Welch, "Formulaic Features of the Punishment-Stories," 91.
247 *BQA* 1:204; Welch, "Formulaic Features of the Punishment-Stories," 113, fn. 23.
248 *FOTL* 10:313; *FOTL* 1:5; cf. *FOTL* 13:178 and 13:183–84.
249 Cf. Westermann, *Die Verheißungen an die Väter*, 89; idem, *Promises to the Fathers*, 92; Welch, "Formulaic Features of the Punishment-Stories," 78.
250 Welch, "Formulaic Features of the Punishment-Stories," 78; Stewart, "Wansbrough, Bultmann, and the Theory of Variant Traditions," 29.
251 Hirschfeld, *New Researches*, 62; *SKMS*² 276–77; Welch, "Formulaic Features of the Punishment-Stories," 78–79 and 81.

the saga incorporates pericopae taken from other abbreviated narrative forms.[253] For instance, the body of the Noah episode in Q. 26.111–16 opens with the debate formula[254]:

qālū a-nu'minu laka wa-ttaba'aka l-ardhalūna

qāla wa-mā 'ilmī bi-mā kānū ya'malūna

in ḥisābuhum illā 'alā rabbī law tash'urūna

wa-mā ana bi-ṭāridi l-mu'minīna

in ana illā nadhīrun mubīnun

qālū la-in lam tantahi yā-nūḥu la-takūnanna mina l-marjūmīna

They said, 'Shall we believe you,
when the vilest are your followers?'

He said, 'What knowledge have I about what they have been doing?

Their reckoning rests only with my Lord, if you^{P} did but know it.

I am not going to drive away the believers.

I am only a clear warner.'

They said, 'If you do not desist, O Noah, you will be amongst those who are stoned.'

In addition to the controversy dialogue, Q. 26.117–20 also features the aforementioned prayer genre[255]:

qāla rabbi inna qawmī kadhdhabūni

fa-ftaḥ baynī wa-baynahum fatḥan wa-najjinī wa-man ma'iya mina l-mu'minīna

fa-anjaynāhu wa-man ma'ahū fī l-fulki l-mashḥūni

---

252 Welch, "Formulaic Features of the Punishment-Stories," 80.
253 *FOTL* 10:313–14; *FOTL* 1:319; cf. Welch, "Formulaic Features of the Punishment-Stories," 111, fn. 6.
254 *SKMS*^{2} 276; cf. Neuwirth, "Structural, Linguistic, and Literary Features," 108; Azaiez, *Le contre-discours coranique*, 8.
255 *SKMS*^{2} 276 (vv. 117–18).

thumma aghraqnā baʿdu l-bāqīna

He said, 'My Lord, my people have disbelieved me.

Make an opening between me and them;
and save me and those of the believers who are with me.'

So We saved him and those who were with him in the laden ship.

Then, afterwards, We drowned the rest.

In fact, Coats observes, as a favorite topic of the "primeval saga," it involves inundation.[256] Accordingly, Westermann concludes with regard to retribution: "We are therefore justified in speaking of a basic motif fundamental to the primal history."[257] On a related matter, Sūrat al-Anbiyā' includes a three-episode saga (Q. 21.76–84), whose motifs include paying the penalty and delivery from danger.[258] To illustrate, the remarkably brief Noah episode (vv. 76–77) reads,[259]

wa-nūḥan idh nādā min qablu fa-stajabnā lahū fa-najjaynāhu wa-ahlahū mina l-karbi l-ʿaẓīmi

wa-naṣarnāhu mina l-qawmi lladhīna kadhdhabū bi-āyātinā innahum kānū qawma saw'in fa-aghraqnāhum ajmaʿīna

And Noah,
when he called out before that,
and We responded to him,
and saved him and his family from the great disaster,

And We helped him against the people who denied the truth of Our signs.
They were an evil people, and so We drowned them all.

Two subsequent episodes feature David and Solomon (vv. 78–82), as well as Job (vv. 83–84).[260]

---

256 *FOTL* 1:5.
257 Westermann, *Die Verheißungen an die Väter*, 47; idem, *Promises to the Fathers*, 44–45.
258 Segovia, *The Quranic Noah*, 29.
259 *BCQ* 1:554; *SKMS*^{2} 271; *JQA* 298.
260 *BCQ* 1:554–55; *SKMS*^{2} 271; *JQA* 298.

The saga form is also centered upon the principle of promise.[261] Particularly pronounced is that for progeny.[262] Suitably, Sūrat Āl ʿImrān (Q. 3.33–34) has a familial frame (-*īC*)[263]:

inna llāha ṣṭafā ādama wa-nūḥan wa-āla ibrāhīma wa-āla ʿimrāna ʿalā l-ʿālamīna

dhurriyyatan baʿḍuhā min baʿḍin wa-llāhu samīʿun ʿalīmun

God chose Adam and Noah and the family of Abraham
and the family of ʿImrān above all created beings,

The seed of one another.
God is the Hearer and the Knower.

This promise saga contains two episodes: the first episode (Q. 3.35–41) follows with the narrative formula *idh* ("when"), while the second opens (v. 42) with *wa-idh* ("and when"). Additionally, Sūrat Maryam (Q. 19) preserves a pair of annunciation episodes on Zachariah and John the Baptist (vv. 2–15), as well as Mary and Jesus (vv. 16–33).[264] Notably, the complete saga (vv. 2–33) shares the same assonance (-*iyyā*).[265] In terms of the "annunciation scene," Long discerns three patterned elements: (i) "appearance of a divine emissary," (ii) "announcement of birth," and (iii) "reactions to the announcement."[266] As in the biblical case, Westermann says, "a different form of the promise of a child is addressed to the father."[267] And so, the promise to Zachariah begins with a variant formulation (*dhikr:* "remembrance") in combination with *idh* ("when"), followed by divine-human dialogue.[268] Q. 19.2–3 reads,

dhikru raḥmati rabbika ʿabdahū zakariyyā

---

261 Westermann, *Die Verheißungen an die Väter*, 11, 59–60, and cf. 92.
262 Ibid., 123–27.
263 Ibid., 61.
264 *JQA* 282; *BCQ* 1:501–5. On the other hand, Robinson considers verse 2 separately (idem, *Discovering the Qurʾān*, 146–48). Bell similarly treats verses 1–2 (*BCQ* 1:501).
265 *JQA* 282; *BCQ* 1:503.
266 *FOTL* 10:293.
267 Westermann, *Die Verheißungen an die Väter*, 125; idem, *Promises to the Fathers*, 135.
268 Balentine, *Prayer in the Hebrew Bible*, 30; Corvin, "Stylistic and Functional Study of the Prose Prayers," 239. Robinson comments, "The last word of the sūra is *rikz* ('slightest sound'). It is a pun on *dhikr* ('mention'), the word with which the sūra begins, and on *Zakariyyā* ('Zachariah'), who is first mentioned in v. 2" (idem, *Discovering the Qurʾān*, 147–48).

idh nādā rabbahū nidā'an khafiyyan

Remembrance of the mercy of your[S] Lord to His servant Zachariah,

When he called out to his Lord in secret.

In Q. 19.7–9, the promise is made[269]:

yā-zakariyyā innā nubashshiruka bi-ghulāmin ismuhū yaḥyā lam naj'al lahū min qablu samiyyan

qāla rabbi annā yakūnu lī ghulāmun wa-kānati mra'atī 'āqiran wa-qad balaghtu mina l-kibari 'itiyyan

qāla ka-dhālika qāla rabbuka huwa 'alayya hayyinun wa-qad khalaqtuka min qablu wa-lam taku shay'an

'O Zachariah, We give you very good tidings of a son
whose name will be John,
a name We have never given to anyone before.'

He said, 'My Lord, how can I have a son
when my wife is barren,
and I have become infirm through old age?'

He said, "[It will be] so. Your Lord says,
'It is easy for Me, for I created you before
when you were nothing.'"

Importantly, the John the Baptist episode ends on a note similar to that of the Jesus episode. Q. 19.14–15 concludes with the "blessing formula" (*salām 'alā*)[270]:

wa-barran bi-wālidayhi wa-lam yakun jabbāran 'aṣiyyan

wa-salāmun 'alayhi yawma wulida wa-yawma yamūtu wa-yawma yub'athu ḥayyan

And dutiful to his parents,
and he was not overweening or rebellious.

Blessings be upon him the day he was born,

---

269 *SKMS*[2] 269.
270 Ibid.; *FOTL* 10:294; *FOTL* 4:363; *FOTL* 14:258–59.

the day he dies,
and the day he is raised up alive.

In the second episode, "the announcement of the birth of a child comes through a messenger of God."[271] In combination with *idh*, the annunciation in Q. 19.16–19 employs the stylized formulation: *wa-dhkur fī l-kitābi* ("And remember in the scripture...")[272]:

wa-dhkur fī l-kitābi maryama idhi ntabadhat min ahlihā makānan sharqiyyan

fa-ttakhadhat min dūnihim ḥijāban fa-arsalnā ilayhā rūḥanā fa-tamaththala lahā basharan sawiyyan

qālat innī aʿūdhu bi-r-raḥmāni minka in kunta taqiyyan

qāla innamā ana rasūlu rabbiki li-ahaba laki ghulāman zakiyyan

Remember Mary in the scripture,
when she withdrew from her folk to a place in the east.

And she put between them and herself a barrier.
And We sent to her Our Spirit [who] appeared to her as a perfect man.

She said, 'I seek refuge from you with the Merciful,
if you are God-fearing.'

He said, 'I am only the messenger of your Lord,
that I may give you a pure son.'

Apparently, the messenger scene in verse 19 includes a cameo role for "an angel who appeared in visible form."[273] In turn, the Jesus episode closes the intervening hagiography with familiar verses (Q. 19.32–33), including the blessing formula[274]:

wa-barran bi-wālidatī wa-lam yajʿalnī jabbāran shaqiyyan

wa-s-salāmu ʿalayya yawma wulidtu wa-yawma amūtu wa-yawma ubʿathu ḥayyan

---

271 Westermann, *Die Verheißungen an die Väter*, 125; idem, *Promises to the Fathers*, 134.
272 *SKMS*² 269; *BCQ* 1:503.
273 *SKMS*² 269; Robinson, *Discovering the Qurʾān*, 96.
274 *SKMS*² 269; *FOTL* 4:363; *FOTL* 10:294; *FOTL* 14:258–59.

'And dutiful to my mother,
and He has not made me overweening and wretched.

Blessings be upon me the day I was born,
the day I die,
and the day I shall be raised alive.'

Related to this promise saga is an abbreviated version rendered in Sūrat al-Anbiyā' (Q. 21.89–91).

Equally relevant is the saga that stresses the prophet.[275] In a clear and concise manner, Q. 38.41–8 exhibits the key features.[276] The narrative formula, "And remember..." (*wa-dhkur*), delimits the relatively short episodes in this middling saga. Notice the fact that the Job episode (vv. 41–44: *-āC*) employs *idh* ("when") in conjunction with the complaint prayer. Q. 38.41 reads,[277]

wa-dhkur 'abdanā ayyūba idh nādā rabbahū annī massaniya sh-shayṭānu bi-nuṣbin wa-'adhābin

And remember Our servant Job,
when he called out to his Lord, saying,
'Satan has touched me with fatigue and torment.'

Upon completion of the Job episode with his recompense, the subsequent pair of episodes features prophets in triplicate.[278] Take, for instance, Q. 38.45–47 (*-āC*) and the *udhkur* opening[279]:

wa-dhkur 'ibādanā ibrāhīma wa-isḥāqa wa-ya'qūba ulī l-aydī wa-l-abṣāri

innā akhlaṣnāhum bi-khāliṣatin dhikrā d-dāri

wa-innahum 'indanā la-mina l-muṣṭafayna l-akhyāri

And remember Our servants Abraham and Isaac and Jacob,
men of might and vision.

We distinguished them with a pure quality,
remembrance of the Abode.

275 John Lierman, *The New Testament Moses* (Tübingen: Mohr Siebeck, 2004), 62–63.
276 *SKMS²* 282.
277 *BCQ* 2:173.
278 *SKMS²* 282; *BCQ* 2:174 (vv. 45–48).
279 *SKMS²* 282.

With Us they are of the chosen, the good.

Then comes the third and final episode, Q. 38.48 (-*āC*)[280]:

wa-dhkur ismāʿīla wa-l-yasaʿa wa-dhā l-kifli wa-kullun mina l-akhyāri

And remember Ishmael and al-Yasaʿ and Dhū l-Kifl.
Each is one of the chosen.

Bell notes, these episodes are brief by design.[281] To this, Gunkel insightfully adds, "Now, of course, the brief compass of the old sagas is at the same time an index of their character. They deal with very simple occurrences, which can be adequately described in a few words."[282]

Furthermore, Q. 19.41–58 preserves a multipart saga on Abraham and other envoys.[283] On this Jones remarks, these prophetic narrations feature a singular -*iyyā* assonance.[284] Concerning Abraham (vv. 41–50), the opening two verses (vv. 41–42) exhibit the double substitution formula: *wa-dhkur fī l-kitābi... innahū kāna...* ("And remember in the scripture...He was...").[285] Q. 19.41 recollects,

wa-dhkur fī l-kitābi ibrāhīma innahū kāna ṣiddīqan nabiyyan

And remember Abraham in the scripture.
He was a true friend of God, a prophet.

Facilitated by *idh*, the narrative then transitions into Abraham's confrontation with his parent and his people (vv. 42–46).[286] Both the first and second episodes (vv. 51–53) close with a stylized refrain-like phrase: *wa-wahabnā li-...min raḥmatinā* ("And We bestowed upon...from Our Mercy").[287] For instance, Q. 19.50 reads,

280 Ibid.; *BCQ* 2:174–75.

281 *BCQ* 2:173. Furthermore, Bell adds, "That al-Yasaʿ is Elisha seems practically certain, but Dhū l-Kifl remains an enigma...The most feasible identification is with Elijah" (ibid., 2:175).

282 Gunkel, *Die Sagen der Genesis*, 21; idem, *The Legends of Genesis*, trans. W.H. Carruth (Chicago: The Open Court Publishing Co., 1901), 46–47.

283 *SKMS*[2] 269 (vv. 41–65).

284 *JQA* 282.

285 *SKMS*[2] 269; *BCQ* 1:507–9.

286 *SKMS*[2] 269.

287 Cf. *BCQ* 1:510. For the formulaic phrase, *wa-wahabnā li-* ("And We bestowed upon..."), see Q. 6.84, Q. 21.72, Q. 29.27, Q. 38.30, and Q. 38.43.

wa-wahabnā lahum min raḥmatinā wa-jaʿalnā lahum lisāna ṣidqin ʿaliyyan

And We bestowed upon them some of Our Mercy
and gave them a tongue of truth, high [in renown].

Recounted thereafter is the Moses episode (vv. 51–53), which shares a similar literary structure[288]:

wa-dhkur fī l-kitābi mūsā innahū kāna mukhlaṣan wa-kāna rasūlan nabiyyan

wa-nādaynāhu min jānibi ṭ-ṭūri l-aymani wa-qarrabnāhu najiyyan

wa-wahabnā lahū min raḥmatinā akhāhu hārūna nabiyyan

And remember Moses in the scripture.
He was devoted [to God] and a messenger and a prophet.

We called to him from the right side of the mountain
and brought him near in communion.

And We bestowed upon him, from Our Mercy, his brother Aaron as a prophet.

In addition to Moses and his calling, it also includes Aaron's joint vocation.[289] Subsequent to this is the Ishmael episode (Q. 19.54–55)[290]:

wa-dhkur fī l-kitābi ismāʿīla innahū kāna ṣādiqa l-waʿdi wa-kāna rasūlan nabiyyan

wa-kāna yaʾmuru ahlahū bi-ṣ-ṣalāti wa-z-zakāti wa-kāna ʿinda rabbihī marḍiyyan

And remember Ishmael in the scripture.
He was true to his promise and was a messenger and prophet.

He used to tell his people to pray and give alms,
and he was pleasing to his Lord.

The fourth and final prophet episode (vv. 56–57) concerns Idrīs[291]:

wa-dhkur fī l-kitābi idrīsa innahū kāna ṣiddīqan nabiyyan

---

288 *SKMS*² 269; *BCQ* 1:509–11.
289 *SKMS*² 269.
290 Ibid.; *BCQ* 1:510.
291 *SKMS*² 269; *BCQ* 1:510–11.

wa-rafa'nāhu makānan 'aliyyan

And remember Idrīs in the scripture.
He was a true friend of God, a prophet.

We raised him to a high position.

Jones notes, the designation eludes commentators.[292] Ostensibly, Q. 19.58 completes the prophet series:

ulā'ika lladhīna an'ama llāhu 'alayhim mina n-nabiyyīna min dhurriyyati ādama wa-mimman ḥamalnā ma'a nūḥin wa-min dhurriyyati ibrāhīma wa-isrā'īla wa-mimman hadaynā wa-jtabaynā idhā tutlā 'alayhim āyātu r-raḥmāni kharrū sujjadan wa-bukiyyan

These are those whom God has favored
among the prophets of the seed of Adam
and of those whom we carried with Noah
and of the seed of Abraham and Israel
and of those whom We guided and chose.
When the signs of the Merciful are recited to them,
they fall down, prostrating themselves and weeping.

At first glance, this saga closes with a summary report.[293] However, Bell rightly concludes, there is evidently a discrepancy between the episodes narrated and the final condensed report.[294]

5.5 Summary

As Coats explains, "at least form-critically, narrative includes all texts that are determined by narrative style...."[295] Although *mathal* begins with simple comparison, Hirschfeld holds that it extends to parables, paradigms, and example stories alike.[296] Given its breadth, Horovitz even seems to consider *amthāl* as *exempla*.[297] In addition, the *corpus coranicum* also preserves prophetic narratives that

292 *JQA* 286, fn. 3. Bell comments, "There has been considerable discussion as to the identity of Idrīs...It is impossible to say whether there is any significance in the fact that in both places his name follows that of Ishmael. Muslims usually identify him with Enoch" (*BCQ* 1:510–11).
293 According to Bell, this verse (58) "rouses suspicion by its length" (*BCQ* 1:511–12).
294 Ibid., 1:512.
295 *FOTL* 2a:165.
296 Hirschfeld, *New Researches*, 83.
297 *KU* 7.

contain allusions to mnemohistorical figures and events.[298] On the other hand, the narrative genre is "distinguished from those kinds of texts that either describe permanent conditions or define attitudes or express commands, prohibitions, admonitions, exhortations, and even laws and prophetic announcements, in which narrative style is also used."[299] Presently, let us turn our attention to the prophetic speech-forms in the proclamation genre.

---

298 *QS* 239; *KU* 32–44.
299 *FOTL* 2a:165.

Chapter 6: Proclamation

6.1 Proclamation Genre

Regarding prophetic speech, Koch makes an astute observation: "Although the saying is based on divine inspiration, its construction is none the less subject to the rules of art."[1] What is more, Greßmann writes, "Since the prophetical genres have not been handed on in tradition, they must first be recovered and reconstructed."[2] Following Gunkel, concision tends to characterize early messages.[3] Thus making an equally strong claim, Westermann concludes, these are sentential in nature.[4] According to Gwynne, "analysis of qur'ānic address is the first step to understanding audience response to the Qur'ān, as it is the first step to understanding the context of any passage."[5] In the corpus, the vocative typically introduces prophetic speech, and proclamation formulae begin with the corresponding particle (*yā-ayyuhā*).[6] Wansbrough notes that "the addressees may be either 'you believers, disbelievers, Jews, scriptuaries' (*alladhīna āmanū, kafarū, hādū, ūtū l-kitāb*), or finally, one of several epithets referring to God's messengers, e.g., *rasūl, rusul, mursalūn, nabī, muzzammil, muddaththir*, etc."[7] He concludes, "it would thus not be impossible to see in that phrase the primary form of prophetical announcement in Muslim scripture."[8] The proclama-

---

1 Koch, *Die Profeten I*, 29–31; idem, *The Prophets*, trans. Margaret Kohl (Philadelphia, Pennsylvania: Fortress Press, 1988), 1:21; Neuwirth, "Einige Bemerkungen," 1:736; Oden, "Historical Understanding and Understanding the Religion of Israel," 20.

2 Greßmann, "Die literarische Analyse Deuterojesajas," 259; Hayes, *Interpreting Ancient Israelite History, Prophecy, and Law*, 190.

3 Hermann Gunkel, "Propheten: II. Seit Amos," *RGG*[1], vol. 4, ed. Friedrich Michael Schiele and Leopold Zscharnack (Tübingen: Verlag von J.C.B. Mohr (Paul Siebeck), 1913), cols. 1866–86, esp. cols. 1877–78; Westermann, *Grundformen prophetischer Rede*, 15 and 39; Smith, *Isaiah Chapters XL-LV*, 8; Hayes, *Interpreting Ancient Israelite History, Prophecy, and Law*, 190, fn. 123; *FOTL* 16:14.

4 Westermann, *Grundformen prophetischer Rede*, 16 and cf. 75.

5 Gwynne, "Patterns of Address," 86.

6 Cf. Rolf Rendtorff (d. 2014), "Botenformel und Botenspruch," *ZAW* 74, no. 2 (1962): 165; s.v. Form and Structure of the Qur'ān, *EQ*; Thackston, *Introduction to Koranic and Classical Arabic*, 114–15; Jones, *Arabic through the Qur'ān*, 180–81; *QS* 15; Aune, *Prophecy*, 90; Westermann, *Grundformen prophetischer Rede*, 19, 25, and 79; Johannes Lindblom, *Die literarische Gattung der prophetischen Literatur: Eine literargeschichtliche Untersuchung zum Alten Testament* (Uppsala: A.-B. Lundequistska Bokhandeln, 1924), 100–1. For example, "Hear, O my people" (Ps 50:7).

7 Wansbrough further adds, "Most often the formula introduces an imperative (e.g., Q. 35.3) or a prohibitive (e.g., Q. 24.27), but also a conditional construction (e.g., Q. 8.29), and occasionally a nominal (e.g., Q. 33.50) or interrogative sentence (e.g., Q. 61.10)" (*QS* 15).

8 Ibid.

https://doi.org/10.1515/9783110580884-006

tion genre in the *corpus coranicum* preserves a number of vocative formulae, along with a range of regulatory prophetic speech-forms.[9] Together these proclamations constitute communal rules and regulations.[10] For the moment, let us consider this one question: "Who is the audience for the Qur'ān?"[11]

6.2 Proclamation Formulae

Yā-ayyuhā lladhīna āmanū

Fred Donner identifies the *mu'minūn* ("believers") as the intended audience.[12] In fact, the formula, "O you who believe" (*yā-ayyuhā lladhīna āmanū*), permeates throughout.[13] In addition, Bell also shows familiarity with this pattern of address.[14] Consider the proclamation (Q. 2.153) sans *qul* that represents messenger speech enjoining worship (*ṣalāt*)[15]:

> *yā-ayyuhā lladhīna āmanū sta'īnū bi-ṣ-ṣabri wa-ṣ-ṣalāti inna llāha ma'a ṣ-ṣābirīna*
>
> O you who believe!
> Seek help in patience and in worship.
> God is with the steadfast.

On a similar subject, consider Q. 2.104:

> *yā-ayyuhā lladhīna āmanū lā taqūlū rā'inā wa-qūlū nẓurnā wa-sma'ū wa-li-l-kāfirīna 'adhābun alīmun*

---

9 Westermann, *Grundformen prophetischer Rede, passim.*
10 Cf. Eric F. Bishop, "The Qumrān Scrolls and the Qur'ān," *MW* 48, no. 3 (1958): 223–36; *The Dead Sea Scrolls*, vol. 1: Rule of the Community and Related Documents, ed. James H. Charlesworth (Tübingen: Verlag von J.C.B. Mohr (Paul Siebeck), 1994), *passim*; Draper, "Torah and Troublesome Apostles in the *Didache* Community," 342.
11 Gwynne, "Patterns of Address," 74.
12 Ibid.; Fred M. Donner, *Muhammad and the Believers: At the Origins of Islam* (Cambridge, Massachusetts: The Belknap Press of Harvard University Press, 2010), 57; cf. Stefan Heidemann, "The Evolving Representation of the Early Islamic Empire and Its Religion on Coin Imagery," in *The Qur'ān in Context: Historical and Literary Investigations into the Qur'ānic Milieu*, ed. Angelika Neuwirth, Nicolai Sinai, and Michael Marx (Leiden: Brill, 2011), 165, fn. 52.
13 According to al-Zarkashī, this form of address is directed at "the people of Medina" (*ahl al-madīna*) (idem, *al-Burhān fī 'ulūm al-Qur'ān*, 2:247; Gwynne, "Patterns of Address," 78).
14 *BCQ* 1:43.
15 *QS* 13 and 15; cf. Westermann, *Grundformen prophetischer Rede*, 64; Soulen, *Handbook of Biblical Criticism*, 69. Q. 2.153–242 "is the section that lays down regulations for the Islāmic community" (Robinson, *Discovering the Qur'ān*, 201).

O you who believe!
Do not say, 'Regard us,'
but say, 'Observe us,' and listen.
The disbelievers will have a painful torment.

In passing, Jones notes this verse poses a philological problem.[16] It is semantically related to Q. 4.46, which incorporates the debate formula (*yaqūlūna:* "they say").[17] He further remarks, Sūrat an-Nisāʾ is embroiled in controversy, with a high concentration of authoritative proclamations.[18]

Qul yā-ayyuhā n-nās

Consider the literary structure of Q. 7.158 (-*ūC*) which, according to Wansbrough, represents qurʾānic messenger speech.[19] In particular, note that the introduction of first-person discourse is not equivalent to divine self-predication[20]:

qul yā-ayyuhā n-nāsu innī rasūlu llāhi ilaykum jamīʿan alladhī lahū mulku s-samāwāti wa-l-arḍi lā ilāha illā huwa yuḥyī wa-yumītu fa-āminū bi-llāhi wa-rasūlihi n-nabiyyi l-ummiyyi lladhī yuʾminu bi-llāhi wa-kalimātihī wa-ttabiʿūhu laʿallakum tahtadūna

Say:
'O people!
I am the messenger of God to you all
– of Him to whom belongs the sovereignty of heaven and earth.
There is no God but Him.

16 *JQA* 37, fn. 21; *BCQ* 1:19.
17 *JQA* 94, fn. 7 (Q. 5, vv. 13 and 41); cf. Azaiez, *Le contre-discours coranique*, 8; Neuwirth, "Structural, Linguistic, and Literary Features," 108.
18 *JQA* 87.
19 *QS* 12 and cf. 13; *BCQ* 1:254. Q. 82.6 and Q. 84.6 both exhibit a variant formulation of the prophetic speech-form: "O man" (*yā-ayyuhā l-insānu*). Upon closer inspection, this particular vocative category is eschatological (cf. Westermann, *Grundformen prophetischer Rede*, 17, 21, and 61; Greßmann, *Der Messias* (Göttingen: Vandenhoeck & Ruprecht, 1929), 69). This is exemplified by the titles of the respective sūra-units: "The Rending" (*al-infiṭār*) and "The Splitting" (*al-inshiqāq*).
20 Cf. Westermann, *Grundformen prophetischer Rede*, 89. On this point, Wansbrough states, "Finally, but most significantly, *qul* may introduce statements not predicable of the deity and usually containing finite verb-forms like 'I fear' (Q. 6.15), 'I have been ordered' (Q. 13.36), 'If I err' (Q. 34.50), but also descriptions of the type 'I am only a warner' (Q. 38.65 etc.), as well as stereotype formulae like 'God suffices as witness between us' (Q. 29.52)" (*QS* 14–15).

> He gives life and causes death.
> Believe in God and His messenger,
> the prophet of his community,
> who believes in God and His words,
> and follow him so that you may be guided aright.'

The quadripartite structure opens with the "divine imperative."[21] Evidently, when it combines with a vocative formula, such as "O people" (*yā-ayyuhā n-nās*) or "O disbelievers" (*yā-ayyuhā l-kāfirūn*), it yields a sentential phrase, which authenticates the message as divinely dispensed.[22] The presentation that follows the vocative address features the qur'ānic "emissarial self-introduction formula," whereby the envoy discloses the identity of the sender.[23] Then, lastly, comes the content which, in this case, appears without the formulaic phrase.[24] As a matter of course, this is the proclamation proper.[25] The commission constitutes a glaring omission, however.[26]

Yā-ayyuhā l-muddaththir

Accordingly, Q. 74 bears the prophetic commission.[27] What is more, "messenger speech expresses the self-conceptualization of the prophets as messengers or

---

21 Cf. *QS* 8, 14–15, and 35; *SKMS*² 33*; Gwynne, "Patterns of Address," 74; see Nicholas Wolterstorff, *Divine Discourse* (Cambridge: Cambridge University Press, 1995), *passim*.
22 Cf. Westermann, *Grundformen prophetischer Rede*, 66; Matthias Radscheit, "Word of God or Prophetic Speech? Reflections on the Qur'ānic *Qul*-statements," in *Encounters of Words and Texts: Intercultural Studies in Honor of Stefan Wild*, ed. Lutz Edzard and Christian Szyska (Hildesheim: Georg Olms Verlag, 1997), 38 and 42; *QS* 15; Gwynne, "Patterns of Address," 81.
23 *QS* 12; *FOTL* 10:321. Localized formulary: Q. 7.104 (*innī rasūlun min rabbi l-ʿālamīna*); Q. 19.19 (*qāla innamā ana rasūlu rabbiki*); Q. 43.46 (*qāla innī rasūlu rabbi l-ʿālamīna*); Q. 61.6 (*innī rasūlu llāhi ilaykum*).
24 *QS* 12–13. According to Wansbrough, the "messenger formula proper (*Botenformel*) may be isolated as *kadhālika qāla rabbuki(ka)*..." (*QS* 13; Westermann, *Grundformen prophetischer Rede*, 107–9). N.b. "In Isa 6:9 the commission formula is present, but the messenger formula itself is lacking: 'Go, and say to this people...'" (Aune, *Prophecy*, 90). Furthermore, Wansbrough states, "Though it is possible to argue that the use of the vocative dispenses with a specific phrase of legitimation (*corroboratio*), such as the messenger formula, the elements are by no means mutually exclusive" (*QS* 15).
25 Westermann, *Grundformen prophetischer Rede*, 67.
26 *QS* 12.
27 Robinson, *Discovering the Qur'ān*, 121.

ambassadors of God to human recipients."[28] In view of that, verses Q. 74.1–7 exhibiting assonance (-*Cr*) read,[29]

yā-ayyuhā l-muddaththiru
qum fa-andhir
wa-rabbaka fa-kabbir
wa-thiyābaka fa-ṭahhir
wa-r-rujza fa-hjur
wa-lā tamnun tastakthiru
wa-li-rabbika fa-ṣbir

You[S] who are wrapped up in a cloak,
Arise and warn,
And magnify your Lord.
Purify your clothes
And shun abomination.
Do not show favors, seeking gain.
Be patient for the sake of your Lord.

Neuwirth considers these verses to be an invocation with an imperative series subjoined.[30] In fact, an imperative formula is traditionally used to designate prophets and to present their message formally.[31]

Yā-ayyuhā r-rasūl

"Utterances addressed to members" (i.e., *rasūl, rusul, mursalūn, nabī, muzzammil, muddaththir*), Wansbrough states, "might of course be interpreted as containing implicitly the divine imperative, and hence the equivalent to expressions prefaced by *qul*."[32] Q. 5.67 (-*īC*) reads,[33]

yā-ayyuhā r-rasūlu balligh mā unzila ilayka min rabbika wa-in lam taf'al fa-mā ballaghta risālatahū wa-llāhu ya'ṣimuka mina n-nāsi inna llāha lā yahdī l-qawma l-kāfirīna

---

28 Cf. Marvin A. Sweeney, "The Prophets and the Prophetic Books, Prophetic Circles and Traditions – New Trends, Including Religio-psychological Aspects," in *Hebrew Bible / Old Testament: The History of Its Interpretation*, vol. 3, pt. 2, ed. Magne Sæbø (Göttingen: Vandenhoeck & Ruprecht, 2015), 514.

29 Cf. *JQA* 544; *BCQ* 2:449–50; Hirschfeld, *New Researches*, 34 and 38.

30 *SKMS*[2] 214.

31 *FOTL* 10:296 and 10:320; Westermann, *Grundformen prophetischer Rede*, 93; *SKMS*[2] 214; Aune, *Prophecy*, 90; *BCQ* 2:449. For example, 1Kgs 21:18.

32 *QS* 15; *SKMS*[2] 33*.

33 Gwynne, "Patterns of Address," 74; cf. al-Zarkashī, *al-Burhān fī 'ulūm al-Qur'ān*, 2:247.

O messenger!
Proclaim what has been sent down to you from your Lord!
If you do not do that,
you are not delivering His message.
God will protect you from the people.
God does not guide the people who do not believe.

According to Bell, this is apparently intended for a single recipient.[34]

6.3 Proclamation Setting

Messenger Situation

In the biblical case, the delivery of divine communiqués is deeply rooted in profane practice.[35] That is to say, "the proclamation formula introduces royal decrees, ordinances, and commands inasmuch as these convey irrevocable authoritative words of the king."[36] Accordingly, "it follows from the requirements of the oral transmission that the message that the messenger has to deliver must be short."[37] What is more, Westermann stresses, "the speech itself which is to be transmitted assumes, as a message, definite, fixed forms which first make it into a message."[38] At the end of the day, these are shaped by the original setting.[39] In point of fact, the vocative formula signaling qurʾānic messenger speech occurs four times in the corpus (Q. 7.158, Q. 10.104, Q. 10.108, Q. 22.49). Each time it features first-person discourse. Moreover, the predominant form represented in the proclamation genre is regulatory. Heralded by the messenger, communal rules and regulations are thereby put into effect.[40] In consequence, the text preserves the "community rule."[41] This merits further consideration.

34 *BCQ* 1:163; Gwynne, "Patterns of Address," 75.
35 Sweeney, "The Prophets and the Prophetic Books, Prophetic Circles and Traditions," 3:514.
36 Westermann, *Grundformen prophetischer Rede*, 79; idem, *Basic Forms of Prophetic Speech*, trans. Hugh Clayton White (Philadelphia, Pennsylvania: The Westminster Press, 1967), 111.
37 Westermann, *Grundformen prophetischer Rede*, 75; idem, *Basic Forms*, 105.
38 Westermann, *Grundformen prophetischer Rede*, 79; idem, *Basic Forms*, 111; Rendtorff, "Botenformel und Botenspruch," 177.
39 Ludwig Köhler, *Deuterojesaja (Jesaja 40–55) stilkritisch untersucht* (Giessen: Verlag von Alfred Töpelmann, 1923), 102–9; idem, *Kleine Lichter: Fünfzig Bibelstellen erklärt* (Zürich: Zwingli-Verlag, 1945), 11–17; Westermann, *Grundformen prophetischer Rede*, 25–28 and 64; cf. Rendtorff, "Botenformel und Botenspruch," 165–77, esp. 169; Koch, *Was ist Formgeschichte?* 265.
40 Sarianna Metso, "In Search of the *Sitz im Leben* of the *Community Rule*," in *The Provo International Conference on the Dead Sea Scrolls: Technological Innovations, New Texts, and Reformu-*

6.4 Regulatory Forms

Rules of Inclusion

The Qur'ān contains prescriptive guidelines for "the admissions procedure of the community."[42] Consider, for example, Q. 2.208–9 (-*īC*):

yā-ayyuhā lladhīna āmanū dkhulū fī s-silmi kāffatan wa-lā tattabiʿū khuṭuwāti sh-shayṭāni innahū lakum ʿaduwwun mubīnun

fa-in zalaltum min baʿdi mā jāʾatkumu l-bayyinātu fa-ʿlamū anna llāha ʿazīzun ḥakīmun

O you who believe!
Enter the peace, all of you.
Do not follow the footsteps of Satan.
He is a clear enemy to you.

But if you slip after the clear proofs have come to you,
know that God is Mighty and Wise.

As a matter of fact, "*silm* occurs only here," which connotes "peace," or "living in accord with each other."[43] At this point, Bell even notes that the phrase (*lā tattabiʿū khuṭuwāti sh-shayṭāni*) also appears in Q. 2.168, Q. 6.142, and Q. 24.21.[44] He further states that "the phrase seems to be used in reference to conduct which causes division."[45] Q. 24.21 opens with a prohibition:

yā-ayyuhā lladhīna āmanū lā tattabiʿū khuṭuwāti sh-shayṭāni wa-man yattabiʿ khuṭuwāti sh-shayṭāni fa-innahū yaʾmuru bi-l-faḥshāʾi wa-l-munkari

O you who believe!
Do not follow Satan's footsteps!
Those who follow Satan's footsteps
– he enjoins immoral behavior and wrong-doing.

---

lated Issues, ed. Donald W. Parry and Eugene Ulrich (Leiden: Brill, 1999), 312–14; cf. *QS* 170–202.

41 *The Dead Sea Scrolls*, 1:1 and 1:145–75; *FOTL* 2a:167; s.v. Form and Structure of the Qur'ān, *EQ*; Sherif, *Guide to the Contents of the Qur'ān*, 108–47.

42 Cf. Metso, "In Search of the *Sitz im Leben* of the *Community Rule*," 308; *The Dead Sea Scrolls*, 1:1 and 1:8–11.

43 *BCQ* 1:43.

44 Ibid., 1:596.

45 Ibid.

In addition, Q. 9.119 (-*īC*) implores,[46]

yā-ayyuhā lladhīna āmanū ttaqū llāha wa-kūnū maʿa ṣ-ṣādiqīna

O you who believe!
Protect yourselves against God and be with the truthful!

At the same time, these communal rules reflect the process of othering. Take, for instance, verses Q. 3.100 – 1, which speak to the dangers of relapsing into error (-*īC*)[47]:

yā-ayyuhā lladhīna āmanū in tuṭīʿū farīqan mina lladhīna ūtū l-kitāba yaruddūkum baʿda īmānikum kāfirīna

wa-kayfa takfurūna wa-antum tutlā ʿalaykum āyātu llāhi wa-fīkum rasūluhū wa-man yaʿtaṣim bi-llāhi fa-qad hudiya ilā ṣirāṭin mustaqīmin

O you who believe!
If you obey a party of those who have been given the scripture,
they will turn you back into disbelievers
after you have believed.

How can you^P be disbelievers
when the signs of God are recited to you,
and His messenger is among you?
Those who hold fast to God are guided to a straight path.

An analogous passage in Q. 3.149 (-*īC*), which also bears the same announcement formula, voices similar concerns. What is more, Q. 5.54 (-*īC*) cautions against falling back into error[48]:

yā-ayyuhā lladhīna āmanū man yartadda minkum ʿan dīnihī fa-sawfa yaʾtī llāhu bi-qawmin yuḥibbuhum wa-yuḥibbūnahū adhillatin ʿalā l-muʾminīna aʿizzatin ʿalā l-kāfirīna yujāhidūna fī sabīli llāhi wa-lā yakhāfūna lawmata lāʾimin dhālika faḍlu llāhi yuʾtīhi man yashāʾu wa-llāhu wāsiʿun ʿalīmun

O you who believe!
[In the case of] those of you who turn away from their religion,
God will bring [in their stead] a people who love Him and whom He loves,
humble towards the believers,
mighty towards the disbelievers,

46 Ibid., 1:321; *JQA* 179.
47 *BCQ* 1:84; *The Dead Sea Scrolls*, 1:10 – 11.
48 *BCQ* 1:161 (vv. 54 – 56).

striving in the way of God,
not fearing the blame of any blamer.
That is the bounty of God which He gives to those whom He wishes.
God is Embracing and Knowing.

Moreover, prohibitory injunctions are issued to stave off dissension amongst the ranks.[49] For example, Q. 3.102 (-*ūC*) reads,[50]

yā-ayyuhā lladhīna āmanū ttaqū llāha ḥaqqa tuqātihī wa-lā tamūtunna illā wa-antum muslimūna

O you who believe!
Fear God with the fear that is due to him
and die only as people who have submitted [to Him].

According to Bell, in the face of disagreement and conflict, verse 103 (-*ūC*) urges otherwise[51]:

wa-ʿtaṣimū bi-ḥabli llāhi jamīʿan wa-lā tafarraqū wa-dhkurū niʿmata llāhi ʿalaykum idh kuntum aʿdāʾan fa-allafa bayna qulūbikum fa-aṣbaḥtum bi-niʿmatihī ikhwānan wa-kuntum ʿalā shafā ḥufratin mina n-nāri fa-anqadhakum minhā ka-dhālika yubayyinu llāhu lakum āyātihī laʿallakum tahtadūna

Hold fast to God's rope, all together,
and do not split up;
and recall God's blessing to you:
when you were enemies
and He brought reconciliation to your hearts,
and by His blessing you became brothers;
and you were on the lip of a pit of fire
and He saved you from it.
Thus God makes His signs plain for you, so that you may be guided.

Then, verse 104 (-*ūC*) earnestly pleads with them[52]:

wa-l-takun minkum ummatun yadʿūna ilā l-khayri wa-yaʾmurūna bi-l-maʿrūfi wa-yanhawna ʿani l-munkari wa-ulāʾika humu l-mufliḥūna

Let there be [one] community from you,
summoning [people] to good and enjoining what is reputable

---

49 Cf. *The Didache*, 7 and 13.
50 *BCQ* 1:84.
51 Ibid.
52 Ibid., 1:84–85.

and forbidding what is disreputable.
Those will be the ones who prosper.

It issues a call for unity and an end to intercommunal strife.[53] Lastly, Q. 3.200 (-*ūC*) closes the sūra-unit with a moral injunction:

yā-ayyuhā lladhīna āmanū ṣbirū wa-ṣābirū wa-rābiṭū wa-ttaqū llāha laʿallakum tufliḥūna

O you who believe!
Be patient and vie in patience,
make ready and fear God,
so that you may prosper.

Questioning the integrity of the passage, Bell states that this verse (200) remains isolated.[54]

Rules of Exclusion

The corpus contains a series of denunciations.[55] To start with, verse Q. 9.23 (-*ūC*) reads,

yā-ayyuhā lladhīna āmanū lā tattakhidhū ābāʾakum wa-ikhwānakum awliyāʾa ini staḥabbū l-kufra ʿalā l-īmāni wa-man yatawallahum minkum fa-ulāʾika humu ẓ-ẓālimūna

O you who believe!
Do not take your fathers and your brothers as allies
if they prefer disbelief to belief.
Those of you who take them as allies
– those are the wrong-doers.

In like manner, Q. 63.9 (-*ūC*) in Sūrat al-Munāfiqūn ("The Hypocrites") is addressed to the faithful[56]:

yā-ayyuhā lladhīna āmanū lā tulhikum amwālukum wa-lā awlādukum ʿan dhikri llāhi wa-man yafʿal dhālika fa-ulāʾika humu l-khāsirūna

O you who believe!
Let neither your possessions nor your children

53 Ibid., 1:84.
54 Ibid., 1:105.
55 Cf. *The Dead Sea Scrolls*, 1:1 and 1:12–13.
56 *JQA* 520 (vv. 9–11); *BCQ* 2:386–87.

divert you from remembrance of God.
Those who do that – those are the losers.

Bell says, with regard to Sūrat at-Taghābun ("Mutual Fraud"), it appears that the believers "were finding opposition among their wives and children…."[57] At the same time, the text contains a statute for "agreeable atonement."[58] Accordingly, verses Q. 64.14–15 (-*īC*) read,[59]

yā-ayyuhā lladhīna āmanū inna min azwājikum wa-awlādikum ʿaduwwan lakum fa-ḥdharū-hum wa-in taʿfū wa-taṣfaḥū wa-taghfirū fa-inna llāha ghafūrun raḥīmun

innamā amwālukum wa-awlādukum fitnatun wa-llāhu ʿindahū ajrun ʿaẓīmun

O you who believe!
Among your wives and your children there are enemies for you.
So beware of them.
If you^{p} pardon and overlook and forgive
– God is Forgiving and Compassionate.

Your^{p} possessions and your children are a temptation,
and God – with Him is a mighty reward.

Therefore, Q. 66, verse 6 (-*ūC*) implores,[60]

yā-ayyuhā lladhīna āmanū qū anfusakum wa-ahlīkum nāran waqūduhā n-nāsu wa-l-ḥijāratu ʿalayhā malāʾikatun ghilāẓun shidādun lā yaʿṣūna llāha mā amarahum wa-yafʿalūna mā yuʾ-marūna

O you who believe!
Protect yourselves and your families against a fire
whose fuel is the people and stones,
over which are harsh, severe angels,
who do not disobey God in what He commands them
but do what they are commanded.

---

57 Regarding Q. 64.14, Bell further states, "The sense is not quite clear. Is *ʿadūw* to be taken in a concrete sense, i.e., are there definite enemies among the Muslims' wives and children, or is it to be taken abstractly as al-Bayḍāwī suggests, i.e., is preoccupation with them inimical to the Muslims' wholehearted obedience? The word would naturally be concrete and the end of the verse seems also to imply that sense. If it were taken abstractly, v. 15 would be little more than a repetition" (*BCQ* 2:390–91).
58 Cf. *The Dead Sea Scrolls*, 1:1 and 1:14–15.
59 Cf. *JQA* 522.
60 *BCQ* 2:398.

For that reason, Q. 66.8 (-*īC*) sternly admonishes,

> *yā-ayyuhā lladhīna āmanū tūbū ilā llāhi tawbatan naṣūḥan 'asā rabbukum an yukaffira 'ankum sayyi'ātikum wa-yudkhilakum jannātin tajrī min taḥtihā l-anhāru yawma lā yukhzī llāhu n-nabiyya wa-lladhīna āmanū ma'ahū nūruhum yas'ā bayna aydīhim wa-bi-aymānihim yaqūlūna rabbanā atmim lanā nūranā wa-ghfir lanā innaka 'alā kulli shay'in qadīrun*
>
> O you who believe!
> Turn to God in sincere repentance.
> It may be that your Lord will redeem your evil deeds for you
> and admit you to gardens,
> through which rivers flow,
> on the day when God will not shame the prophet and those who believe with him.
> Their light will run in front of them and on their right hands,
> and they will say, 'Our Lord, perfect our light for us and forgive us. You have power over everything.'

Evidently, this composite verse incorporates a proclamation (*yā-ayyuhā lladhīna āmanū*), conjoined (*wa-*) with a collective prayer (*rabbanā*), and prefaced by the debate formula (*yaqūlūna*).[61]

In continuation of Sūrat at-Tawba ("Repentance"), "verses 17–28 form a further passage of polemic, somewhat different in thrust and tone to what has preceded, but still aimed at the polytheists (*mushrikūn*)."[62] For example, Q. 9.28 (-*īC*) parts with the pagans[63]:

> *yā-ayyuhā lladhīna āmanū innamā l-mushrikūna najasun fa-lā yaqrabū l-masjida l-ḥarāma ba'da 'āmihim hādhā wa-in khiftum 'aylatan fa-sawfa yughnīkumu llāhu min faḍlihī in shā'a inna llāha 'alīmun ḥakīmun*
>
> O you who believe!
> The polytheists are unclean.
> Let them not approach the sacred shrine after this year of theirs.
> If you fear poverty,
> God will give you sufficiency from His bounty, if He wishes.
> God is Knowing and Wise.

However, according to Bell, it does not prevent them from performing the sacred rite.[64] Furthermore, Q. 4.144 (-*Can*) bars the faithful from fraternizing with the enemy[65]:

---

61 Ibid.
62 *JQA* 178.
63 *BCQ* 1:298.
64 Ibid.

> *yā-ayyuhā lladhīna āmanū lā tattakhidhū l-kāfirīna awliyāʾa min dūni l-muʾminīna a-turīdū-na an tajʿalū li-llāhi ʿalaykum sulṭānan mubīnan*
>
> O you who believe!
> Do not choose the disbelievers as allies
> to the exclusion of the believers.
> Do you want to give God a clear authority against you?

Additionally, Q. 5.57 (-*īC*) prohibits them from associating with the scoffers[66]:

> *yā-ayyuhā lladhīna āmanū lā tattakhidhū lladhīna ttakhadhū dīnakum huzuwan wa-laʿiban mina lladhīna ūtū l-kitāba min qablikum wa-l-kuffāra awliyāʾa wa-ttaqū llāha in kuntum muʾ-minīna*
>
> O you who believe!
> Do not take as allies
> those who take your religion in mockery and as a sport,
> whether they are from the ones who were given the scripture before you
> or from the disbelievers.
> Fear God if you are believers.

In turn, denunciations reflect the "theological atmosphere."[67] For instance, Q. 4.136 (-*Can*) reads,[68]

> *yā-ayyuhā lladhīna āmanū āminū bi-llāhi wa-rasūlihī wa-l-kitābi lladhī nazzala ʿalā rasūlihī wa-l-kitābi lladhī anzala min qablu wa-man yakfur bi-llāhi wa-malāʾikatihī wa-kutubihī wa-rusulihī wa-l-yawmi l-ākhiri fa-qad ḍalla ḍalālan baʿīdan*
>
> O you who believe!
> Believe in God and His messenger
> and in the scripture which He has sent down to His messenger
> and in the scripture which He has sent down previously.
> Those who do not believe in God and His angels and His scriptures and His Messengers and the Last Day
> have wandered far astray.

Regarding Sūrat al-Māʾida, Jones states that "the polemic is for the most part directed at the Jews and the Christians."[69] According to Bell, Q. 5.51 (-*īC*) "commands the breaking off of relations with Jews and Christians"[70]:

65 Ibid., 1:137.
66 Ibid., 1:161.
67 Cf. *The Dead Sea Scrolls*, 1:4.
68 *BCQ* 1:135.
69 *JQA* 110.

yā-ayyuhā lladhīna āmanū lā tattakhidhū l-yahūda wa-n-naṣārā awliyāʾa baʿḍuhum awliyāʾu baʿḍin wa-man yatawallahum minkum fa-innahū minhum inna llāha lā yahdī l-qawma ẓ-ẓālimīna

O you who believe!
Do not take the Jews and Christians as allies.
They are allies of each other.
Whoever of you makes them his allies is one of them.
God does not guide the people who do wrong.

Q. 5.11 (-*ūC*) issues a call to remembrance:

yā-ayyuhā lladhīna āmanū dhkurū niʿmata llāhi ʿalaykum idh hamma qawmun an yabsuṭū ilaykum aydiyahum fa-kaffa aydiyahum ʿankum wa-ttaqū llāha wa-ʿalā llāhi fa-l-yatawakkali l-muʾminūna

O you who believe!
Remember God's blessing to you
when a people intended to stretch their hands towards you.
He restrained their hands from you.
So fear God.
Let the believers put their trust in God.

Also, consider Q. 5.35 (-*ūC*), which beseeches[71]:

yā-ayyuhā lladhīna āmanū ttaqū llāha wa-btaghū ilayhi l-wasīlata wa-jāhidū fī sabīlihī laʿallakum tufliḥūna

O you who believe!
Fear God and seek the means to approach Him
and strive in His way so that you may prosper.

Finally, Q. 5.105 (-*ūC*) recommends, it is better to tend to one's own soul[72]:

yā-ayyuhā lladhīna āmanū ʿalaykum anfusakum lā yaḍurrukum man ḍalla idhā htadaytum ilā llāhi marjiʿukum jamīʿan fa-yunabbiʾukum bi-mā kuntum taʿmalūna

O you who believe!
Take care of your souls.
Those who have gone astray cannot harm you
if you are guided aright.

---

70 *BCQ* 1:160 (vv. 51–53).
71 Ibid., 1:156.
72 Ibid., 1:171.

You will all return to God,
and He will tell you what you were doing.

"Whether this indicates a time when defections were taking place," Bell concludes, "it is impossible to say with certainty."[73]

Rules of Authority

In terms of authority, Q. 4.59 (*-Can*) establishes the ground rules:

yā-ayyuhā lladhīna āmanū aṭīʿū llāha wa-aṭīʿū r-rasūla wa-ulī l-amri minkum fa-in tanāzaʿ-tum fī shayʾin fa-ruddūhu ilā llāhi wa-r-rasūli in kuntum tuʾminūna bi-llāhi wa-l-yawmi l-ākhiri dhālika khayrun wa-aḥsanu taʾwīlan

O you who believe!
Obey God and obey the messenger and those of you who have authority.
If you quarrel with one another about anything,
refer it to God and the messenger,
if you believe in God and the Last Day.
That is better and fairer as a course.

In case of dispute, it is to be resolved through those who wield the power of adjudication.[74] In practice, decision-making falls to "the representative of God" who, by virtue of position, is vested with authority (Q. 4.59; Q. 8.20).[75] Take, for instance, Q. 58.12 (*-īC*), which concerns audiences held with God's herald[76]:

yā-ayyuhā lladhīna āmanū idhā nājaytumu r-rasūla fa-qaddimū bayna yaday najwākum ṣa-daqatan dhālika khayrun lakum wa-aṭharu fa-in lam tajidū fa-inna llāha ghafūrun raḥīmun

O you who believe!
When you have private audience with the messenger,
offer alms before your meeting.
That is better and purer for you.
But if you do not find [the means]
God is Forgiving and Compassionate.

---

73 Ibid.

74 Ibid., 1:122.

75 Ibid., 1:122 and 1:274.

76 *JQA* 505.

Bell comments, this "evidently treats of conduct in the *majlis* of the prophet...."[77] Therefore, the proscription in Q. 49.1 (-*īC*) establishes the boundaries of acceptable behavior[78]:

> *yā-ayyuhā lladhīna āmanū lā tuqaddimū bayna yadayi llāhi wa-rasūlihī wa-ttaqū llāha inna llāha samī'un 'alīmun*
>
> O you who believe!
> Do not be forward before God and His messenger.
> Fear God; God is Hearing and Knowing.

Elaborating on the special rules of etiquette, Q. 49.2 (-*ūC*) dictates,

> *yā-ayyuhā lladhīna āmanū lā tarfa'ū aṣwātakum fawqa ṣawti n-nabiyyi wa-lā tajharū lahū bi-l-qawli ka-jahri ba'ḍikum li-ba'ḍin an taḥbaṭa a'mālukum wa-antum lā tash'urūna*
>
> O you who believe!
> Do not raise your voices above that of the prophet,
> and do not speak loudly to him,
> as you do to one another,
> lest your works fail whilst you are not aware.

Simply put, it touches on the principles of polite conversation.[79] Likewise, verses Q. 5.101–2 (-*īC*) broach the matter of impolite speech[80]:

> *yā-ayyuhā lladhīna āmanū lā tas'alū 'an ashyā'a in tubda lakum tasu'kum wa-in tas'alū 'anhā ḥīna yunazzalu l-qur'ānu tubda lakum 'afā llāhu 'anhā wa-llāhu ghafūrun ḥalīmun*
>
> *qad sa'alahā qawmun min qablikum thumma aṣbaḥū bihā kāfirīna*
>
> O you who believe!
> Do not ask about things which,
> if they are revealed to you,
> will trouble you.
> Yet if you do ask about them
> when the recitation is being sent down
> they will be revealed to you.
> God forgives that.
> God is Forgiving and Prudent.

---

77 *BCQ* 2:359.
78 Ibid., 2:287.
79 Ibid.
80 Ibid., 1:170.

A people before you asked about them,
but then did not believe in them.

Bell reasons that "the answer might not please the questioner, and the matter may be one better left undefined."[81] What is more, Q. 33.69 offers a word of caution to "deprecate insults to the prophet, alleging the example of Moses who was cleared of the insult leveled at him"[82]:

yā-ayyuhā lladhīna āmanū lā takūnū ka-lladhīna ādhaw mūsā fa-barra'ahu llāhu mimmā qālū wa-kāna ʿinda llāhi wajīhan

O you who believe!
Do not be like those who vexed Moses,
and then God declared him innocent of what they said,
and he was eminent with God.

Moreover, Q. 33.70 – 71 shores up the authority of the messenger:

yā-ayyuhā lladhīna āmanū ttaqū llāha wa-qūlū qawlan sadīdan

yuṣliḥ lakum aʿmālakum wa-yaghfir lakum dhunūbakum wa-man yuṭiʿi llāha wa-rasūlahū fa-qad fāza fawzan ʿaẓīman

O you who believe!
Fear God and speak straight speech,

And He will set right your deeds for you
and forgive you your sins.
Those who obey God and His messenger gain a great triumph.

Additionally, Q. 8.24 (*-ūC*) reads,

yā-ayyuhā lladhīna āmanū stajībū li-llāhi wa-li-r-rasūli idhā daʿākum li-mā yuḥyīkum wa-ʿlamū anna llāha yaḥūlu bayna l-mar'i wa-qalbihī wa-annahū ilayhi tuḥsharūna

O you who believe!
Respond to God and to the messenger
when He calls you to that which will give you life;
and know that God can come between a man and his own heart
and that you will be rounded up to Him.

81 Ibid.
82 Ibid., 2:108; Hirschfeld, *New Researches*, 122.

Bell writes, this "seems to appeal for a response to something from which the hearts of the prophet's followers revolted...."[83] He further addresses Q. 8.27 (-*ūC*):

> *yā-ayyuhā lladhīna āmanū lā takhūnū llāha wa-r-rasūla wa-takhūnū amānātikum wa-antum ta'lamūna*
>
> O you who believe!
> Do not betray God and the messenger.
> Do not betray your trusts knowingly.

This seems to be an extension of the earlier entreaty.[84]

Rules of Purity

Extant in the Qur'ān are regulations pertaining to the optimal state of ritual purity.[85] In point of fact, food-related customs (e.g., Q. 2.168–69, 172–73) involve issues relevant to the group as a whole.[86] Take, for instance, Q. 2.172 (-*ūC*) that lightly touches on the subject[87]:

> *yā-ayyuhā lladhīna āmanū kulū min ṭayyibāti mā razaqnākum wa-shkurū li-llāhi in kuntum iyyāhu ta'budūna*
>
> O you who believe!
> Eat the good things that we have provided for your sustenance,
> and be grateful to God, if you worship Him.

According to Robinson, this verse calls upon them to consume what is best.[88] And so, the text proceeds to list specific dietary taboos (Q. 2.173; Q. 5.3; Q. 16.115).[89] In addition to parallel construction, noteworthy is the fact that all three verses conclude with the identical oral formula (*inna llāha ghafūrun raḥīmun*).[90] For example, Q. 2.173 reads (-*īC*),

---

83 *BCQ* 1:275.
84 Ibid., 1:276 (vv. 27–28).
85 Cf. *The Dead Sea Scrolls*, 1:178–79.
86 *JQA* 24; Robinson, *Discovering the Qur'ān*, 212–13; *BCQ* 1:34.
87 Regarding Sūra 2, Jones observes, "From verse 142 onwards there is a radical change of subject matter. Narratives disappear, and they are replaced by injunctions, ordinances, and some prohibitions for the faithful" (*JQA* 24).
88 Robinson, *Discovering the Qur'ān*, 212.
89 *JQA* 44, fn. 29; Robinson, *Discovering the Qur'ān*, 212–13.
90 Welch, "Formulaic Features of the Punishment-Stories," 77–78; see Milman Parry, "The Epithet and the Formula I: The Usage of the Fixed Epithet," in *The Making of Homeric Verse: The*

innamā ḥarrama ʿalaykumu l-maytata wa-d-dama wa-laḥma l-khinzīri wa-mā uhilla bihī li-ghayri llāhi fa-mani ḍṭurra ghayra bāghin wa-lā ʿādin fa-lā ithma ʿalayhi inna llāha ghafūrun raḥīmun

He has forbidden for you carrion,
blood, the flesh of the pig,
and anything that has been dedicated to any other than God;
but if anyone is compelled,
without wishing [to do so] or [without] transgressing
– it is no sin for him.
God is Forgiving and Compassionate.

Verse Q. 5.87 (-*īC*) also concerns comestibles[91]:

yā-ayyuhā lladhīna āmanū lā tuḥarrimū ṭ-ṭayyibāti mā aḥalla llāhu lakum wa-lā taʿtadū inna llāha lā yuḥibbu l-muʿtadīna

O you who believe!
Do not forbid the good things
which God has made lawful for you,
and do not transgress,
God does not love transgressors.

Furthermore, Q. 5.1 (-*ūC*) enjoins,[92]

yā-ayyuhā lladhīna āmanū awfū bi-l-ʿuqūdi

O you who believe!
Fulfill your undertakings.

Sūrat al-Māʾida boasts a wide repertoire of customary rules.[93]

In terms of ritual pollution and ablution, Q. 5.6 addresses worship (*ṣalāt*)[94]:

Collected Papers of Milman Parry, ed. Adam Parry (Oxford: Clarendon Press, 1971), 37–117; Albert B. Lord, "The Formula," in *The Singer of Tales* (New York: Atheneum, 1978), 30–67; Paolo Vivante, *The Epithets in Homer: A Study in Poetic Values* (New Haven, Connecticut: Yale University Press, 1982), *passim*; Robert C. Culley, "Formulas and Formulaic Systems," in *Oral Formulaic Language in the Biblical Psalms* (Toronto: University of Toronto Press, 1967), 32–101; Andrew G. Bannister, *An Oral-Formulaic Study of the Qur'ān* (Lanham, Maryland: Lexington Books, 2014), 25–31.

91 *BCQ* 1:166 (vv. 87–88).

92 *BCQ* 1:145; *JQA* 110.

93 *JQA* 110.

94 *BCQ* 1:150.

yā-ayyuhā lladhīna āmanū idhā qumtum ilā ṣ-ṣalāti fa-ghsilū wujūhakum wa-aydiyakum ilā l-marāfiqi wa-msaḥū bi-ru'ūsikum wa-arjulakum ilā l-ka'bayni

O you who believe!
When you rise to worship,
wash your faces and your hands up to the elbows,
and wipe your heads and your feet up to the ankles.

Also, consider the isolated verse, Q. 4.43 (-*Can*)[95]:

yā-ayyuhā lladhīna āmanū lā taqrabū ṣ-ṣalāta wa-antum sukārā ḥattā ta'lamū mā taqūlūna wa-lā junuban illā 'ābirī sabīlin ḥattā taghtasilū wa-in kuntum marḍā aw 'alā safarin aw jā'a aḥadun minkum mina l-ghā'iṭi aw lāmastumu n-nisā'a fa-lam tajidū mā'an fa-tayammamū ṣa'īdan ṭayyiban fa-msaḥū bi-wujūhikum wa-aydīkum inna llāha kāna 'afuwwan ghafūran

O you who believe!
Do not draw near to worship when you are intoxicated,
until you know what you say;
nor when you are polluted,
save when you are traversing a way,
until you have washed yourselves.
If you are sick or on a journey
or one of you comes from the closet
or if you have had contact with women
and you do not find water, have recourse to clean soil
and wipe your faces and your hands with it.
God is Pardoning and Forgiving.

Here, inebriation is a clear breach of session protocol.[96] Additionally, Bell draws the inference that "the exception in favor of those on a journey would imply that the permission to use sand instead of water was not in the original form of the verse."[97] Moreover, verses Q. 5.90–91 (-*ūC*) prohibit wine and wagering[98]:

yā-ayyuhā lladhīna āmanū innamā l-khamru wa-l-maysiru wa-l-anṣābu wa-l-azlāmu rijsun min 'amali sh-shayṭāni fa-jtanibūhu la'allakum tufliḥūna

innamā yurīdu sh-shayṭānu an yūqi'a baynakumu l-'adāwata wa-l-baghḍā'a fī l-khamri wa-l-

---

95 Ibid., 1:118.

96 "The offender is said to have been 'Abd al-Raḥmān b. 'Awf (d. 31/652)," who "tried to recite Sūra 109 but became muddled and intoned, 'Say! O disbelievers, I worship what you worship...' instead of the correct version which runs, 'Say! O disbelievers, I do *not* worship what you worship...'" (ibid.; Robinson, *Discovering the Qur'ān*, 61).

97 *BCQ* 1:119.

98 Ibid., 1:167–68; cf. Q. 2.219.

maysiri wa-yaṣuddakum ʿan dhikri llāhi wa-ʿani ṣ-ṣalāti fa-hal antum muntahūna

O you who believe!
Wine, *maysir*, idols, and divining arrows
are an abomination that is of the work of Satan.
Avoid it, so that you may prosper.

Satan only desires to cause enmity and hatred among you
through wine and *maysir*
and to turn you from remembrance of God and from worship.
Are you going to desist?

Altruistic intent aside, in its basest form, *maysir* had a poor reputation.[99]

Rules of Ritual

In addition to rules for ritual purity, the corpus also includes prescriptions regulating fasting. Q. 2.183 reads (-*ūC*)[100]:

yā-ayyuhā lladhīna āmanū kutiba ʿalaykumu ṣ-ṣiyāmu ka-mā kutiba ʿalā lladhīna min qabli-kum laʿallakum tattaqūna

O you who believe!
Fasting is prescribed for you,
as it was prescribed for those who were before you,
so that you may protect yourselves –

Following the same end rhyme pattern (-*ūC*), the subsequent verse (184) proceeds to stipulate a series of exemption clauses relating to the fast:

ayyāman maʿdūdātin fa-man kāna minkum marīḍan aw ʿalā safarin fa-ʿiddatun min ayyāmin ukhara wa-ʿalā lladhīna yuṭīqūnahū fidyatun ṭaʿāmu miskīnin fa-man taṭawwaʿa khayran fa-huwa khayrun lahū wa-an taṣūmū khayrun lakum in kuntum taʿlamūna

For a fixed number of days.
Those of you who are sick or on a journey,
a number of other days;
and, for those who are able to do it,
there may be a redemption:
the feeding of a destitute person.

99 *JQA* 123, fn. 15.
100 Robinson, *Discovering the Qur'ān*, 213; *BCQ* 1:36; s.v. Form and Structure of the Qur'ān, *EQ*.

And those who do better voluntarily,
it is better for them.
For you to fast is better for you,
if you but know.

In the same vein, verse 185 (-*ūC*) specifies the designated period for the observance of the fast[101]:

shahru ramaḍāna lladhī unzila fīhi l-qur'ānu hudan li-n-nāsi wa-bayyinātin mina l-hudā wa-l-furqāni fa-man shahida minkumu sh-shahra fa-l-yaṣumhu wa-man kāna marīḍan aw-'alā safarin fa-'iddatun min ayyāmin ukhara yurīdu llāhu bikumu l-yusra wa-lā yurīdu bikumu l-'usra wa-li-tukmilū l-'iddata wa-li-tukabbirū llāha 'alā mā hadākum wa-la'allakum tashkurūna

[It is] the month of Ramaḍān,
in which the Qur'ān was sent down
as a guidance to the people
and as clear proofs of the guidance and of the salvation.
Let those of you who witness the month
fast during it.
Those of you who are sick or on a journey,
a number of other days.
God desires ease for you, not hardship,
and [He desires] you to complete the period
and to magnify God for having guided you and to be thankful.

"In old Semitic practice," writes William Robertson Smith (d. 1894), "religious fasting meant abstinence from all food, not merely from flesh."[102] Bell notes the fact that verse 186 switches its focus from fasting to prayer (*du'ā'*).[103] The question of ritual purity is resumed in the subsequent verse (187).[104]

On a related topic, Q. 5.2 (-*Cū*) demarcates sacred space and time[105]:

yā-ayyuhā lladhīna āmanū lā tuḥillū sha'ā'ira llāhi wa-lā sh-shahra l-ḥarāma wa-lā l-hadya wa-lā l-qalā'ida wa-lā āmmīna l-bayta l-ḥarāma yabtaghūna faḍlan min rabbihim wa-riḍwānan wa-idhā ḥalaltum fa-ṣṭādū

---

101 Bell notes, "There has been considerable discussion as to why Ramaḍān was thus distinguished, but no satisfactory reason has been suggested..." (*BCQ* 1:37).
102 William Robertson Smith, *Lectures on the Religion of the Semites: The Fundamental Institutions*, 3rd ed. (New York: The Macmillan Company, 1927), 303, fn. 1.
103 *BCQ* 1:38.
104 Ibid.; *JQA* 24.
105 *BCQ* 1:145.

O you who believe!
Do not profane God's waymarks
nor the sacred month nor offerings nor garlands
nor those repairing to the sacred house,
seeking bounty and approval from their Lord.
When you leave the pilgrim state, you may hunt.

Jones says, "this is traditionally understood to mean any of the four sacred months."[106] In this connection, Q. 5.94 (*-īC*) addresses a breach of ethics[107]:

yā-ayyuhā lladhīna āmanū la-yabluwannakumu llāhu bi-shay'in mina ṣ-ṣaydi tanāluhū aydīkum wa-rimāḥukum li-ya'lama llāhu man yakhāfuhū bi-l-ghaybi fa-mani 'tadā ba'da dhālika fa-lahū 'adhābun alīmun

O you who believe!
God will indeed test you
in [the matter of] some of the game taken by your hands and your spears,
that God may know who fears Him in the Invisible.
Those who transgress after this will have a painful punishment.

Similarly, Q. 5.95 (*-āC*) pertains to slaying animals on hallowed ground[108]:

yā-ayyuhā lladhīna āmanū lā taqtulū ṣ-ṣayda wa-antum ḥurumun wa-man qatalahū minkum muta'ammidan fa-jazā'un mithlu mā qatala mina n-na'ami yaḥkumu bihī dhawā 'adlin minkum hadyan bāligha l-ka'bati aw kaffāratun ṭa'āmu masākīna aw 'adlu dhālika ṣiyāman li-yadhūqa wabāla amrihī 'afā llāhu 'ammā salafa wa-man 'āda fa-yantaqimu llāhu minhu wa-llāhu 'azīzun dhū ntiqāmin

O you who believe!
Do not kill game while you are in the sacred state.
If any of you kill [such game] intentionally,
[there must be] recompense
– the like of what he has killed from [his] livestock,
as two men of justice from you decide,
an offering to reach the Ka'ba or expiation:
food for the destitute or the equivalent of that in fasting,
that he may taste the mischief of his action.
God forgives what has happened in the past;
but God will take vengeance on those who repeat [the offense].
God is Mighty and a Wielder of vengeance.

---

106 Jones further remarks, "another interpretation is that it means the season of the *Ḥajj*" (*JQA* 110, fn. 1).
107 *BCQ* 1:168.
108 Ibid., 1:168–69.

This verse suitably addresses making amends for the wrong.[109] Finally, Q. 8.29 (-*īC*) "holds out the hope of the coming of the enigmatical *furqān*"[110]:

yā-ayyuhā lladhīna āmanū in tattaqū llāha yaj'al lakum furqānan wa-yukaffir 'ankum sayyi'ātikum wa-yaghfir lakum wa-llāhu dhū l-faḍli l-'aẓīmi

O you who believe!
If you fear God,
He will assign a salvation to you
and will absolve you of your evil deeds
and will forgive you.
God is Possessed of great bounty.

Bell infers that *furqān*, in this context, connotes "salvation."[111]

Rules of Order

The Qur'ān preserves "rules for the congregation" (*jumu'a*).[112] For example, Sūrat al-Jumu'a advocates proper behavior befitting worship.[113] The proclamation contained in verses Q. 62.9 – 10 (-*ūC*) makes direct reference to "the day of the assembly"[114]:

yā-ayyuhā lladhīna āmanū idhā nūdiya li-ṣ-ṣalāti min yawmi l-jumu'ati fa-s'aw ilā dhikri llāhi wa-dharū l-bay'a dhālikum khayrun lakum in kuntum ta'lamūna

fa-idhā quḍiyati ṣ-ṣalātu fa-ntashirū fī l-arḍi wa-btaghū min faḍli llāhi wa-dhkurū llāha kathīran la'allakum tufliḥūna

O you who believe!
When call is made for worship on the day of assembly,
hasten to remembrance of God and leave [your] trading.
That is better for you, did you but know.

And when worship is ended,
disperse in the land and seek some of God's bounty,

---

109 Cf. *The Dead Sea Scrolls*, 1:1 and 1:12 – 15.
110 *BCQ* 1:276 – 77.
111 Ibid., 1:277.
112 Cf. *The Dead Sea Scrolls*, 1:1 and 1:34 – 45.
113 *JQA* 518 (vv. 9 – 11).
114 *BCQ* 2:382 – 83.

and remember God much,
so that you may prosper.

In addition, the *corpus coranicum* includes "rules for the session" (*majlis*).[115] In its minimal expression, the vocative particle of the proclamation is omitted in favor of the formula *qul.*[116] Significantly, Pernot notes that "another rhetorical device is naming and designation."[117] Take, for instance, Q. 17.110 (*-Can*) that reads,[118]

quli dʿū llāha awi dʿū r-raḥmāna ayyan mā tadʿū fa-lahu l-asmāʾu l-ḥusnā wa-lā tajhar bi-ṣalātika wa-lā tukhāfit bihā wa-btaghi bayna dhālika sabīlan

Say^{S}:
'Pray^{P} to God or pray to the Merciful.
Whichever you pray to is possessed of the fairest names.
Do not be loud in your worship, nor hushed in it.
Seek a way between that.'

In this particular case, the content of the twofold announcement addresses a collective audience, which is instructed in the cultic invocation and the subject of prayer etiquette. In connection with rules of the session, also consider Q. 58.11 (*-īC*)[119]:

yā-ayyuhā lladhīna āmanū idhā qīla lakum tafassaḥū fī l-majālisi fa-fsaḥū yafsaḥi llāhu lakum wa-idhā qīla nshuzū fa-nshuzū yarfaʿi llāhu lladhīna āmanū minkum wa-lladhīna ūtū l-ʿilma darajātin wa-llāhu bi-mā taʿmalūna khabīrun

O you who believe!
When you are asked to make room in assemblies, make room,
God will make room for you;
and when you are asked to move up, move up
– and God will raise in rank those of you who have believed and have been given knowl-

---

115 Cf. *The Dead Sea Scrolls*, 1:26–27.
116 *QS* 16; Seybold, *Die Psalmen*, 52.
117 Pernot, "The Rhetoric of Religion," 329.
118 *The Dead Sea Scrolls*, 1:1. According to Bell, verse 110 "has no necessary connection with the preceding. It belongs to the period when al-Raḥmān is being introduced as a name of the deity and question has arisen regarding it. This was probably in Mecca. The verse identifies al-Raḥmān and Allāh, either name may be used; there is no indication that al-Raḥmān was to be dropped" (*BCQ* 1:479–80).
119 Bell writes, verse 11 "evidently treats of conduct in the *majlis* of the prophet, and therefore belongs probably to a comparatively late date in the Medinan period" (*BCQ* 2:359–60; *JQA* 505).

edge.
God is informed of what you do.

The verse opens with the proclamation formula. Although it proceeds to address a day-to-day matter, these graduated spatial arrangements in fact indicate the relative stations of initiates upon "entering the covenant community."[120] In turn, as intimated in the second portion of the verse, these correspond to the "disclosure of sacred knowledge, particularly mythical paradigms."[121] In addition, Q. 7.204 (-*ūC*) treats the rules of conduct during the ritual recitation[122]:

wa-idhā quriʾa l-qurʾānu fa-stamiʿū lahū wa-anṣitū laʿallakum turḥamūna

And when the recitation is recited,
Listen^{P} to it and be^{P} silent,
so that you^{P} may receive mercy.

Lastly, on a related note, Q. 46.29 narrates (-*īC*),[123]

wa-idh ṣarafnā ilayka nafaran mina l-jinni yastamiʿūna l-qurʾāna fa-lammā ḥaḍarūhu qālū anṣitū fa-lammā quḍiya wallaw ilā qawmihim mundhirīna

And [recall] when We turned to you^{S}
a number of the Jinn,
who listened to the recitation.
When they attended it, they said, 'Be^{P} silent,'
and when it was finished, they went back to their people as warners.

Evidently embedded in this composite mythopoeic narrative is a plural imperative relating a specific session rule, which instructs the audience to remain quiet and listen attentively.[124] In line with this, Q. 22.77 (-*ūC*) reads,

yā-ayyuhā lladhīna āmanū rkaʿū wa-sjudū wa-ʿbudū rabbakum wa-fʿalū l-khayra laʿallakkum tufliḥūna

O you who believe!
Bow down and prostrate yourselves and serve your Lord and do good, so that you may prosper.

---

120 *JQA* 505; cf. *The Dead Sea Scrolls*, 1:1; s.v. Catechesis, *EAC*.
121 Cf. s.vv. Initiation: Men's Initiation and Initiation: Women's Initiation, *ER*^{2}. This reflects "oral religious instruction, especially as it was imparted during initiation into a worshipping community" (s.v. Catechesis, *EAC*).
122 *BCQ* 1:267.
123 *JQA* 462.
124 S.v. Anṣata, *CQ*.

This equally concerns session prayer protocol.

Rules of Propriety

To open with, the Qur'ān contains "domestic legislation."[125] For example, Q. 24.27 (-*ūC*) addresses how to properly call on or visit someone[126]:

> *yā-ayyuhā lladhīna āmanū lā tadkhulū buyūtan ghayra buyūtikum ḥattā tasta'nisū wa-tusallimū ʿalā ahlihā dhālikum khayrun lakum laʿallakum tadhakkarūna*
>
> O you who believe!
> Do not enter houses other than your own until you have sought permission
> and greeted the people of the house.
> That is better for you,
> so that you may be reminded.

By the same token, Q. 24.58 (-*īC*) also insists on common decency[127]:

> *yā-ayyuhā lladhīna āmanū li-yastaʾdhinkumu lladhīna malakat aymānukum wa-lladhīna lam yablughū l-ḥuluma minkum thalātha marrātin min qabli ṣalāti l-fajri wa-ḥīna taḍaʿūna thiyābakum mina ẓ-ẓahīrati wa-min baʿdi ṣalāti l-ʿishāʾi thalāthu ʿawrātin lakum laysa ʿalaykum wa-lā ʿalayhim junāḥun baʿdahunna ṭawwāfūna ʿalaykum baʿḍukum ʿalā baʿḍin ka-dhālika yubayyinu llāhu lakumu l-āyāti wa-llāhu ʿalīmun ḥakīmun*
>
> O you who believe!
> Let those whom your right hands possess
> and those of you who have not reached puberty
> ask permission of you three times:
> before dawn worship;
> when you lay aside your garments in the noon heat;
> and after evening worship
> – three times of nakedness for you.
> It is no sin for you or them to go round to one another
> beyond [these three times].
> – Thus God makes the signs clear for you.
> God is Knowing and Wise.

125 *BCQ* 1:606.
126 Ibid., 1:598; *JQA* 321.
127 *BCQ* 1:606; *JQA* 321.

Speaking to the "unguarded intervals in the day," this verse specifies the persons and times when "they must announce themselves and ask permission before entering."[128] To continue, a special stricture is imposed in Q. 33.53[129]:

> *yā-ayyuhā lladhīna āmanū lā tadkhulū buyūta n-nabiyyi illā an yu'dhana lakum ilā ṭa'āmin ghayra nāẓirīna ināhu wa-lākin idhā du'ītum fa-dkhulū fa-idhā ṭa'imtum fa-ntashirū wa-lā musta'nisīna li-ḥadīthin inna dhālikum kāna yu'dhī n-nabiyya fa-yastaḥyī minkum wa-llāhu lā yastaḥyī mina l-ḥaqqi*
>
> O you who believe!
> Do not enter the apartments of the prophet
> unless invited for a meal
> without waiting for the proper time.
> When you are invited, enter;
> and when you have fed, disperse,
> without lingering for conversation.
> That would vex the prophet,
> but he is ashamed to [ask] you [to leave];
> but God is not ashamed of the truth.

Following Bell, this pertains to protocol during audiences with the prophet at his private residence.[130]

Jones states, Sūrat al-Ḥujurāt provides some additional guidelines.[131] As far as *correptio fraterna* is concerned, Q. 49.11 (-ūC) reminds them to be on guard against envy[132]:

> *yā-ayyuhā lladhīna āmanū lā yaskhar qawmun min qawmin 'asā an yakūnū khayran minhum wa-lā nisā'un min nisā'in 'asā an yakunna khayran minhunna wa-lā talmizū anfusakum wa-lā tanābazū bi-l-alqābi bi'sa l-ismu l-fusūqu ba'da l-īmāni wa-man lam yatub fa-ulā'ika humu ẓ-ẓālimūna*
>
> O you who believe!
> Let not a people scorn another people who may be better than them;
> nor let women scorn women who may be better than them.

---

128 Then again, "at other times of the day when people are accustomed to go about calling on each other, there is no need for these persons to announce themselves" (*BCQ* 1:606).
129 *JQA* 383.
130 *BCQ* 2:104–5.
131 *JQA* 475.
132 *BCQ* 2:289; Claudio Gianotto, "The Lucan Parable of the Good Samaritan and Its Interpretations in Christian Antiquity," in *The Quest for a Common Humanity: Human Dignity and Otherness in the Religious Traditions of the Mediterranean*, ed. Katell Berthelot and Matthias Morgenstern (Leiden: Brill, 2011), 126; s.v. Correction, *Augustine through the Ages*, ed. Allan D. Fitzgerald (Grand Rapids, Michigan: Wm. B. Eerdmans Publishing Company, 1999).

Do not find fault with one another,
nor insult each other with nicknames.
Evil is the term 'vicious conduct,' after belief.
Those who do not turn in repentance
– those are the wrong-doers.

It flatly rejects the practice of name-calling.[133] Yet again, Q. 49.12 (*-īC*) expresses disapproval of malicious gossip[134]:

yā-ayyuhā lladhīna āmanū jtanibū kathīran mina ẓ-ẓanni inna baʿḍa ẓ-ẓanni ithmun wa-lā tajassasū wa-lā yaghtab baʿḍukum baʿḍan a-yuḥibbu aḥadukum an yaʾkula laḥma akhīhi maytan fa-karihtumūhu wa-ttaqū llāha inna llāha tawwābun raḥīmun

O you who believe!
Avoid much suspicion:
some suspicion is a sin.
Do not spy; nor be backbiters of one another.
Would one of you like to eat the flesh of his brother
when he is dead?
You would hate it.
Fear God. God is Relenting and Compassionate.

Bell notes that "to slander a person behind his back" is here reprimanded, and then "compared, in a striking question," to anthropophagy.[135] On a closely related matter, verses Q. 58.9–10 (*-ūC*) address "secret colloguing" and "the venting of discontent"[136]:

yā-ayyuhā lladhīna āmanū idhā tanājaytum fa-lā tatanājaw bi-l-ithmi wa-l-ʿudwāni wa-maʿṣiyati r-rasūli wa-tanājaw bi-l-birri wa-t-taqwā wa-ttaqū llāha lladhī ilayhi tuḥsharūna

innamā n-najwā mina sh-shayṭāni li-yaḥzuna lladhīna āmanū wa-laysa bi-ḍārrihim shayʾan illā bi-idhni llāhi wa-ʿalā llāhi fa-l-yatawakkali l-muʾminūna

O you who believe!
When you meet together privately,
do not do so in sin and enmity
and disobedience to the messenger
but in piety and fear of God.
Fear God to whom you will be rounded up.

---

133 *BCQ* 2:289.
134 Ibid.
135 Ibid.
136 *JQA* 505; *BCQ* 2:358.

Private meetings are from Satan,
that he may sadden those who believe;
but he cannot harm them at all,
save with God's permission.
Let the believers put their trust in God.

The initial verse "does not forbid private conversations, but rather certain subjects of them."[137] Nonetheless, the subsequent verse deplores these clandestine activities altogether.[138]

Rules of Property

Certain pericopae in the *corpus coranicum* provide a mechanism for equitable distribution in the community.[139] For instance, Q. 2.254 (-*ūC*) reads,

yā-ayyuhā lladhīna āmanū anfiqū mimmā razaqnākum min qabli an ya'tiya yawmun lā bay'un fīhi wa-lā khullatun wa-lā shafā'atun wa-l-kāfirūna humu ẓ-ẓālimūna

O you who believe!
Spend some of that which We have given you as provision
before a day comes
on which there will be neither bargain nor friendship nor intercession.
The disbelievers are the wrong-doers.

Bell states that this verse likely stands alone.[140] On the subject of *ṣadaqāt* ("alms"), and sharing the same opening formula, Q. 2.264 (-*īC*) reads,[141]

yā-ayyuhā lladhīna āmanū lā tubṭilū ṣadaqātikum bi-l-manni wa-l-adhā ka-lladhī yunfiqu mālahū ri'ā'a n-nāsi wa-lā yu'minu bi-llāhi wa-l-yawmi l-ākhiri fa-mathaluhū ka-mathali ṣafwānin 'alayhi turābun fa-aṣābahū wābilun fa-tarakahū ṣaldan lā yaqdirūna 'alā shay'in mimmā kasabū wa-llāhu lā yahdī l-qawma l-kāfirīna

O you who believe!
Do not render your alms void by reproach or vexation,
like the one who spends his possessions to make a show to the people

137 *BCQ* 2:359.
138 Ibid.
139 Catherine M. Murphy, *Wealth in the Dead Sea Scrolls and in the Qumran Community* (Leiden: Brill, 2002), 115; cf. *The Dead Sea Scrolls*, 1:6–7 and cf. 1:12–13; *Didache*, 7.
140 *BCQ* 1:53.
141 *JQA* 24; cf. *Didache*, 5 and 13.

and does not believe in God and the Last Day.
His paradigm is like the paradigm of a rock on which is soil,
which is struck by heavy rain, leaving it bare.
They have no power over any of that which they have acquired.
God does not guide people who do not believe.

In terms of the "circulation of wealth," following Michael Bonner, "alms move down the social scale and persons gain wealth and move up and give alms once again in a repeated cycle of exchange."[142] The next verse (265), joined by the coordinating conjunction (*wa-*), immediately follows (*-īC*) with a second illustrative paradigm (*mathal*):

wa-mathalu lladhīna yunfiqūna amwālahumu btighā'a marḍāti llāhi wa-tathbītan min anfusihim ka-mathali jannatin bi-rabwatin aṣābahā wābilun fa-ātat ukulahā ḍi'fayni fa-in lam yuṣibhā wābilun fa-ṭallun wa-llāhu bi-mā ta'malūna baṣīrun

And the paradigm of those who spend their possessions in seeking God's approval and in strengthening their souls
is like the paradigm of a garden on a hill,
which is struck by heavy rain,
and which then yields its produce in double quantity.
If no rain strikes it, there is dew.
God is observer of what you^{P} do.

Therefore, it is evident that both the proclamation and narrative genres comingle here (vv. 264–65).[143] Bell adds that these verses combined are actually a single unit.[144] Jones notes that Q. 2.267–68 (*-īC*) similarly regulates the flow of material goods[145]:

yā-ayyuhā lladhīna āmanū anfiqū min ṭayyibāti mā kasabtum wa-mimmā akhrajnā lakum mina l-arḍi wa-lā tayammamū l-khabītha minhu tunfiqūna wa-lastum bi-ākhidhīhi illā an tughmiḍū fīhi wa-'lamū anna llāha ghaniyyun ḥamīdun

ash-shayṭānu ya'idukumu l-faqra wa-ya'murukum bi-l-faḥshā'i wa-llāhu ya'idukum maghfiratan minhu wa-faḍlan wa-llāhu wāsi'un 'alīmun

---

142 Natalie Zemon Davis, conclusion to *Poverty and Charity in Middle Eastern Contexts*, ed. Michael Bonner, Mine Ener, and Amy Singer (Albany: State University of New York Press, 2003), 316; Michael Bonner, "Poverty and Charity in the Rise of Islam," in op. cit., 13–30.
143 *BCQ* 1:55.
144 Ibid.
145 *JQA* 24.

O you who believe!
Spend some of the good things you have acquired
and of the things We have brought forth from the earth for you;
and do not have recourse to the bad things to spend
when you would not take them [for yourselves]
without shutting your eyes over them.
Know that God is All-sufficient and Laudable.

Satan promises you poverty
and urges you to immorality;
but God promises you forgiveness and bounty from Himself.
God is Embracing and Knowing.

Moreover, according to Bonner, "wealth, at least surplus wealth, must keep moving."[146] In this connection, Q. 9.34 (-*īC*) reads,

yā-ayyuhā lladhīna āmanū inna kathīran mina l-aḥbāri wa-r-ruhbāni la-ya'kulūna amwāla n-nāsi bi-l-bāṭili wa-yaṣuddūna 'an sabīli llāhi wa-lladhīna yaknizūna dh-dhahaba wa-l-fiḍḍata wa-lā yunfiqūnahā fī sabīli llāhi fa-bashshirhum bi-'adhābin alīmin

O you who believe!
Many of the rabbis and monks consume people's possessions in vanity and bar [people] from God's way.
Those who hoard gold and silver
and do not spend it in God's way
– give them the tidings of a painful torment.

Bell reasons that *alladhīna yaknizūna* "might designate a section of the Muslims who were niggardly in their contributions to the cause of God."[147] In addition, Q. 2.278 (-*īC*) contains an injunction against *ribā* ("usury") directed at the believers[148]:

yā-ayyuhā lladhīna āmanū ttaqū llāha wa-dharū mā baqiya mina r-ribā in kuntum mu'minīna

O you who believe!
Fear God and give up the usury that is outstanding,
if you are believers.

Furthermore, consider Q. 3.130 (-*ūC*)[149]:

146 Davis, conclusion, 316; Bonner, "Poverty and Charity," 14 (*ribā*).
147 *BCQ* 1:300.
148 *JQA* 24; *BCQ* 1:58.
149 *JQA* 64.

yā-ayyuhā lladhīna āmanū lā ta'kulū r-ribā aḍʿāfan muḍāʿafatan wa-ttaqū llāha laʿallakum tufliḥūna

O you who believe!
Do not live on usury,
[receiving the sum lent] multiplied many times.
Fear God so that you may prosper.

This pericope is set apart from its surroundings.[150] Bonner notes, "it is difficult to say what *ribā* actually means in the Qur'ān."[151] At the same time, "one passage where it occurs (Q. 30.39) clearly contrasts some kind of bad circulation (*ribā*) with good circulation (*zakāt* or almsgiving)."[152]

On a related matter, Q. 2.282–83a discusses contract law at considerable length, particularly concerning monetary obligations.[153] The injunction to record financial transactions begins (v. 282),

yā-ayyuhā lladhīna āmanū idhā tadāyantum bi-daynin ilā ajalin musamman fa-ktubūhu wa-l-yaktub baynakum kātibun bi-l-ʿadli wa-lā ya'ba kātibun an yaktuba ka-mā ʿallamahu llāhu fa-l-yaktub wa-l-yumlili lladhī ʿalayhi l-ḥaqqu wa-l-yattaqi llāha rabbahū wa-lā yabkhas minhu shay'an

O you who believe!
When you contract debts with one another for a fixed term,
record it in writing.
Let a scribe record it justly in writing between you.
Let no scribe refuse to write in the way that God has taught him.
Let him write and let the one who has incurred the debt dictate,
and let him fear his Lord, God,
and let him not diminish any of it.

Thereafter follow stipulations on verifying agreements.[154] Additionally, verses Q. 4.29–30, according to Bell, constitute "early legislation."[155] Verse 29 (-*Can*) begins,

yā-ayyuhā lladhīna āmanū lā ta'kulū amwālakum baynakum bi-l-bāṭili illā an takūna tijāratan ʿan tarāḍin minkum wa-lā taqtulū anfusakum inna llāha kāna bikum raḥīman

150 *BCQ* 1:90 (vv. 130–36).
151 Bonner, "Poverty and Charity," 14.
152 Ibid. Q. 30.39 reads, *wa-mā ātaytum min riban li-yarbuwa fī amwāli n-nāsi fa-lā yarbū ʿinda llāhi wa-mā ātaytum min zakātin turīdūna wajha llāhi fa-ulā'ika humu l-muḍʿifūna.*
153 *JQA* 24.
154 Ibid.
155 *BCQ* 1:115.

O you who believe!
Do not consume your property among you in vanity,
but let there be trading by mutual consent among you.
Do not kill yourselves.
God is merciful to you.

Bell states that verse 30 (*-Can*) naturally comes next[156]:

wa-man yafʿal dhālika ʿudwānan wa-ẓulman fa-sawfa nuṣlīhi nāran wa-kāna dhālika ʿalā llāhi yasīran

Those who do that through wrong-doing and aggression,
We shall roast them in a fire
– that is easy for God.

In this connection, consider Q. 5.106–8 (*-īC*) on securing the inheritance of property. The pericope begins,

yā-ayyuhā lladhīna āmanū shahādatu baynikum idhā ḥaḍara aḥadakumu l-mawtu ḥīna l-waṣiyyati thnāni dhawā ʿadlin minkum aw ākharāni min ghayrikum in antum ḍarabtum fī l-arḍi fa-aṣābatkum muṣībatu l-mawti

O you who believe!
[Let there be] witnessing between you
when death comes to one of you
at the time when bequests are made:
two witnesses, just men from among you,
or two persons from another people
if you are travelling in the land and the misfortune of death befalls you.

The subsequent portion addresses the resolution of inheritance disputes. All in all, these verses are specifically directed at leaving a last will and testament.[157]

Rules of Matrimony

Sūrat an-Nisāʾ attends to marriage.[158] For example, Q. 4.19 (*-Can*) opens with the "suitability for marriage"[159]:

156 Ibid.
157 Ibid., 1:171.
158 Ibid., 1:112; Moshe J. Bernstein, *Reading and Re-reading Scripture at Qumran* (Leiden: Brill, 2013), 2:621.
159 Bernstein, *Reading and Re-reading Scripture at Qumran*, 2:621.

yā-ayyuhā lladhīna āmanū lā yaḥillu lakum an tarithū n-nisāʾa karhan wa-lā taʿḍulūhunna li-tadhhabū bi-baʿḍi mā ātaytumūhunna illā an yaʾtīna bi-fāḥishatin mubayyinatin wa-ʿāshirū-hunna bi-l-maʿrūfi fa-in karihtumūhunna fa-ʿasā an takrahū shayʾan wa-yajʿala llāhu fīhi khayran kathīran

O you who believe!
It is not lawful for you to inherit women against their will
or to coerce them that you may take away part of what you have given them
unless they commit a flagrant indecency.
Consort with them properly.
If you dislike them,
perhaps you dislike something when God has put much good into it.

Bell writes that "the usual interpretation is that it refers to a pagan Arab custom, according to which the wife of a man who had died might be claimed by the heir."[160] The subsequent two verses (20 – 21) address the dissolution of marriage (-*Can*)[161]:

wa-in aradtumu stibdāla zawjin makāna zawjin wa-ātaytum iḥdāhunna qinṭāran fa-lā taʾ-khudhū minhu shayʾan a-taʾkhudhūnahū buhtānan wa-ithman mubīnan

wa-kayfa taʾkhudhūnahū wa-qad afḍā baʿḍukum ilā baʿḍin wa-akhadhna minkum mīthāqan ghalīẓan

If you wish to replace a wife by another
and you have given one of them a large sum,
take nothing from it.
Would you take it by calumny and manifest sin?

How can you take it after you have come together with one another,
and they have taken a binding pledge from you?

Also, consider a related verse (Q. 33.49) that reads,[162]

yā-ayyuhā lladhīna āmanū idhā nakaḥtumu l-muʾmināti thumma ṭallaqtumūhunna min qabli an tamassūhunna fa-mā lakum ʿalayhinna min ʿiddatin taʿtaddūnahā fa-mattiʿūhunna wa-sarriḥūhunna sarāḥan jamīlan

O you who believe!
If you marry believing women
and divorce them before you touch them

160 *BCQ* 1:112.
161 *JQA* 87; *BCQ* 1:112 – 13.
162 *BCQ* 2:103; *JQA* 383.

you have no period to count against them.
Make provision for them and release them fairly.

This regulation clarifies that *ʿidda* ("prescribed period of waiting") is rendered inapplicable in the case of an unconsummated marriage.[163] In addition, Sūrat al-Mumtaḥana ("She who is to be Examined") (Q. 60.10) regulates "mixed marriages" (-*īC*)[164]:

yā-ayyuhā lladhīna āmanū idhā jāʾakumu l-muʾminātu muhājirātin fa-mtaḥinūhunna llāhu aʿlamu bi-īmānihinna fa-in ʿalimtumūhunna muʾminātin fa-lā tarjiʿūhunna ilā l-kuffāri lā hunna ḥillun lahum wa-lā hum yaḥillūna lahunna wa-ātūhum mā anfaqū wa-lā junāḥa ʿalaykum an tankiḥūhunna idhā ātaytumūhunna ujūrahunna wa-lā tumsikū bi-ʿiṣami l-kawāfiri wa-sʾalū mā anfaqtum wa-l-yasʾalū mā anfaqū dhālikum ḥukmu llāhi yaḥkumu baynakum wa-llāhu ʿalīmun ḥakīmun

O you who believe!
When believing women come to you as emigrants, examine them.
God is well aware of their faith.
If you know them to be believers
do not return them to the disbelievers.
[Such women] are not lawful for them,
nor are they lawful for those women.
So give them [back] what they have spent.
It is no sin for you to marry them
when you have given them their wages.
Do not hold on to the ties with disbelieving women,
but ask for what you spent
– and let [the disbelievers] ask for what they have spent.
That is the judgment of God.
He judges between you.
God is Knowing and Wise.

The sum in question refers to *mahr* ("dowry").[165] Significantly, "it is obvious that laws which pertain directly to marriage (and several kinds of laws fall under this broad rubric) furnish the most critical evidence regarding the presence or absence of women in the society presupposed by the text which contains those regulations."[166]

---

163 *BCQ* 2:103; s.v. ʿIdda, *EI*[1].
164 Cf. Dibelius, *A Fresh Approach to the New Testament and Early Christian Literature*, 224.
165 *BCQ* 2:373.
166 Bernstein, *Reading and Re-reading Scripture at Qumran*, 2:621.

Rules of Punishment

On equality in the eyes of the law, Q. 4.135 (-*Can*) stipulates,[167]

> *yā-ayyuhā lladhīna āmanū kūnū qawwāmīna bi-l-qisṭi shuhadā'a li-llāhi wa-law ʿalā anfusi-kum awi l-wālidayni wa-l-aqrabīna in yakun ghaniyyan aw faqīran fa-llāhu awlā bihimā fa-lā tattabiʿū l-hawā an taʿdilū wa-in talwū aw tuʿriḍū fa-inna llāha kāna bi-mā taʿmalūna khabī-ran*
>
> O you who believe!
> Be steadfast in justice, witnesses for God,
> even if it is against your selves or your parents or your close relatives.
> Whether the person be rich or poor,
> God is closer to both.
> Do not follow whim lest you turn [away from justice].
> If you twist or turn away,
> you will find that God is informed of what you do.

The subject of retribution (e.g., Q. 2.178–79) likewise affects communal relations.[168] In terms of the penalty for homicide, consider Q. 2.178 (-*īC*),[169]

> *yā-ayyuhā lladhīna āmanū kutiba ʿalaykumu l-qiṣāṣu fī l-qatlā l-ḥurru bi-l-ḥurri wa-l-ʿabdu bi-l-ʿabdi wa-l-unthā bi-l-unthā fa-man ʿufiya lahū min akhīhi shay'un fa-ttibāʿun bi-l-maʿrūfi wa-adā'un ilayhi bi-iḥsānin dhālika takhfīfun min rabbikum wa-raḥmatun fa-mani ʿtadā baʿda dhālika fa-lahū ʿadhābun alīmun*
>
> O you who believe!
> Retaliation is prescribed for you concerning the slain:
> the free man for the free man;
> the slave for the slave;
> the female for the female.
> For the [killer] who receives some forgiveness
> from the brother of [the slain],
> prosecution according to what is recognized as proper
> and payment to [the brother] in kindness.
> That is an alleviation and a mercy from your Lord.
> Those who transgress after this will have a painful torment.

In fact, Robinson considers Q. 2.153 to 242 "legislation" proper.[170]

---

167 *JQA* 104, fn. 13.
168 Ibid., 24; *BCQ* 1:35–36.
169 *The Dead Sea Scrolls*, 1:1 and 1:28–35; Robinson, *Discovering the Qur'ān*, 213.
170 Robinson, *Discovering the Qur'ān*, 211.

Rules of War

On the subject of war, Q. 9.38 (*-īC*) is concerned "with warlike expeditions, to which the believers, or some of them, are averse"[171]:

> *yā-ayyuhā lladhīna āmanū mā lakum idhā qīla lakumu nfirū fī sabīli llāhi ththāqaltum ilā l-arḍi a-raḍītum bi-l-ḥayāti d-dunyā mina l-ākhirati fa-mā matāʿu l-ḥayāti d-dunyā fī l-ākhirati illā qalīlun*
>
> O you who believe!
> What is the matter with you[P]?
> When you are told, 'Go out in God's way,'
> you sink heavily to the ground.
> Are you content with the life of this world
> rather than the world to come?
> The enjoyment of the life of this world is a little thing,
> compared with the world to come.

Bell notes that this verse remains isolated.[172] Furthermore, Q. 47.7 is "a promise of God's help in overthrowing the disbelievers"[173]:

> *yā-ayyuhā lladhīna āmanū in tanṣurū llāha yanṣurkum wa-yuthabbit aqdāmakum*
>
> O you who believe!
> If you help God, He will help you and make your feet firm.

In Q. 9.123 (*-īC*), "the believers are urged to make raids upon them," namely, the disbelievers[174]:

> *yā-ayyuhā lladhīna āmanū qātilū lladhīna yalūnakum mina l-kuffāri wa-l-yajidū fīkum ghilẓa-tan wa-ʿlamū anna llāha maʿa l-muttaqīna*

---

171 Bell writes, "This is usually supposed to refer to the northern expedition, upon which many were reluctant to embark" (*BCQ* 1:302). Cf. *The Dead Sea Scrolls*, vol. 2: Damascus Document, War Scroll, and Related Documents, ed. James H. Charlesworth (Tübingen: Verlag von J.C.B. Mohr (Paul Siebeck), 1995), 80–203. N.b. "Inheriting the rules for warfare, the sect lived in preparation for the eschatological war" (*The Dead Sea Scrolls*, 1:3; Bishop, "The Qumrān Scrolls and the Qur'ān," 230–32 ("Fighting in God's Way")).
172 *BCQ* 1:302.
173 Ibid., 2:273; cf. Q. 2.250a, Q. 3.147, and Q. 8.11.
174 In addition, Bell tentatively suggests that "the injunction might of course be more general" (*BCQ* 1:323).

O you who believe!
Fight those of the disbelievers who are near you, and let them find harshness in you and know that God is with those who protect themselves.

Turning to the rules of engagement, Q. 4.94 (*-Can*) reads,

yā-ayyuhā lladhīna āmanū idhā ḍarabtum fī sabīli llāhi fa-tabayyanū wa-lā taqūlū li-man alqā ilaykumu s-salāma lasta mu'minan tabtaghūna 'araḍa l-ḥayāti d-dunyā fa-'inda llāhi maghānimu kathīratun ka-dhālika kuntum min qablu fa-manna llāhu 'alaykum fa-tabayyanū inna llāha kāna bi-mā ta'malūna khabīran

O you who believe!
When you journey in the way of God,
act with discrimination and do not say to someone who offers peace to you,
'You are not a believer,'
seeking chance gain in the life of this world.
There is abundant booty with God.
You were like that previously,
but God has been gracious to you.
So act with discrimination.
God is informed of what you do.

This proclamation "deals with the high-handedness of Muslim raiders, who refuse to receive a greeting of assurance that a man is a Muslim and therefore free from attack."[175]

On a related problem, Q. 49.6 (*-īC*) clarifies the handling and use of military disinformation:

yā-ayyuhā lladhīna āmanū in jā'akum fāsiqun bi-naba'in fa-tabayyanū an tuṣībū qawman bi-jahālatin fa-tuṣbiḥū 'alā mā fa'altum nādimīna

O you who believe!
If some reprobate brings you tidings,
be clear about it,
lest you smite a people in ignorance
and next morning regret what you have done.

Bell comments, it was "occasioned by some false report...."[176] In terms of drawing up in battle array, verses 2 to 4 (*-ūC*) in Sūrat aṣ-Ṣaff ("The Ranks") read,[177]

---

175 Ibid., 1:129; cf. Ibn Isḥāq, *Das Leben Muhammed's nach Muhammed Ibn Ishâk*, ed. Ferdinand Wüstenfeld, vol. 1, pt. 2 (Göttingen: Dieterichsche Universitäts-Buchhandlung, 1859), 987.
176 *BCQ* 2:287–88.
177 Ibid., 2:377.

yā-ayyuhā lladhīna āmanū li-ma taqūlūna mā lā tafʿalūna

kabura maqtan ʿinda llāhi an taqūlū mā lā tafʿalūna

inna llāha yuḥibbu lladhīna yuqātilūna fī sabīlihī ṣaffan ka-annahum bunyānun marṣūṣun

O you who believe!
Why do you say what you do not do?

It is most hateful to God that you say what you do not do.

God loves those who fight in His way in ranks,
as though they are a solid building.

These verses, Bell writes, "refer to some incident in fighting...."[178] Additionally, Q. 4.71 issues the following orders:

yā-ayyuhā lladhīna āmanū khudhū ḥidhrakum fa-nfirū thubātin awi-nfirū jamīʿan

O you who believe!
Take precautions.
Advance in companies or advance all together.

In a similar fashion, Sūrat al-Anfāl follows suit. Take, for instance, the "military instruction" in Q. 8.15–16[179]:

yā-ayyuhā lladhīna āmanū idhā laqītumu lladhīna kafarū zaḥfan fa-lā tuwallūhumu l-adbāra

wa-man yuwallihim yawmaʾidhin duburahū illā mutaḥarrifan li-qitālin aw mutaḥayyizan ilā fiʾatin fa-qad bāʾa bi-ghaḍabin mina llāhi wa-maʾwāhu jahannamu wa-biʾsa l-maṣīru

O you who believe!
When you meet those who disbelieve marching into battle,
do not turn your backs to them.

Those who turn their backs to them on that day
– unless turning away to fight
or withdrawing to [join another] company –
are burdened with anger from God.
Their abode will be hell
– an evil journey's end.

178 Ibid.; *JQA* 516.
179 *BCQ* 1:273.

According to Bell, "*zaḥfan* only occurs here; the root means to creep or go slowly and is used of an army going into battle perhaps because the men are then dismounted."[180] Furthermore, Q. 8.45 (-*ūC*) gives the order to stand and fight:

yā-ayyuhā lladhīna āmanū idhā laqītum fi'atan fa-thbutū wa-dhkurū llāha kathīran la'allakum tufliḥūna

O you who believe!
When you meet a party [of the enemy],
stand firm, and call God frequently to mind,
so that you may prosper.

Bell states that it "is an exhortation to the believers to be steady in battle."[181] In this context, *fi'a* ("detachment") refers to "a small company."[182] On the raids (sing. *ghazwa*) and the casualties of war, Q. 3.156 (-*īC*) reads,[183]

yā-ayyuhā lladhīna āmanū lā takūnū ka-lladhīna kafarū wa-qālū li-ikhwānihim idhā ḍarabū fī l-arḍi aw kānū ghuzzan law kānū 'indanā mā mātū wa-mā qutilū li-yaj'ala llāhu dhālika ḥasratan fī qulūbihim wa-llāhu yuḥyī wa-yumītu wa-llāhu bi-mā ta'malūna baṣīrun

O you who believe!
Do not be like those who do not believe
and who say about their brothers
who travel in the land or go on raids,
'Had they been with us,
they would not have died or been slain.'
[This is] so that God may make that a cause of anguish in their hearts.
God gives life and brings death.
God is observer of what you do.

This is conveyed "in very much softened form, so as to be a comfort to the believers, rather than a reproach."[184]

In the making of alliances, Q. 60.1 (-*īC*) lays out the following[185]:

yā-ayyuhā lladhīna āmanū lā tattakhidhū 'aduwwī wa-'aduwwakum awliyyā'a tulqūna ilayhim bi-l-mawaddati wa-qad kafarū bi-mā jā'akum mina l-ḥaqqi yukhrijūna r-rasūla wa-iyyākum an tu'minū bi-llāhi rabbikum in kuntum kharajtum jihādan fī sabīlī wa-btighā'a marḍātī

180 Ibid.
181 Ibid., 1:281 (vv. 45–47).
182 Cf. ibid.
183 S.v. Ghazw, *EI*².
184 *BCQ* 1:95 (vv. 156–57).
185 Hirschfeld, *New Researches*, 127; *BCQ* 2:375.

tusirrūna ilayhim bi-l-mawaddati wa-ana aʿlamu bi-mā akhfaytum wa-mā aʿlantum wa-man yafʿalhu minkum fa-qad ḍalla sawāʾa s-sabīli

O you who believe!
Do not take my enemy and your enemy as allies,
offering them friendship
when they have disbelieved in the truth that has come to you,
driving out you and the messenger
because you believe in God, your Lord.
If you go forth to strive in my way and to seek my approval
[and yet] secretly show them friendship
– when I am well aware of what you hide and what you proclaim
– those of you who do that stray from the straight way.

Q. 60.13 (-*ūC*) makes this point in no uncertain terms:

yā-ayyuhā lladhīna āmanū lā tatawallaw qawman ghaḍiba llāhu ʿalayhim qad yaʾisū mina l-ākhirati ka-mā yaʾisa l-kuffāru min aṣḥābi l-qubūri

O you who believe!
Do not take as allies
a people with whom God is angry
and who have despaired of the world to come,
as the disbelievers have despaired of those who are in the graves.

This verse draws the sūra-unit to a close. Lastly, in a telling proclamation, Q. 61.10 (-*īC*) reads,[186]

yā-ayyuhā lladhīna āmanū hal adullukum ʿalā tijāratin tunjīkum min ʿadhābin alīmin

O you who believe!
Shall I show you a trade
that will deliver you from a painful torment?

Prima facie, this is "a rather curious passage."[187] Bell further comments, "its main sense evidently is to recommend fighting, but it is couched in rather vague language...."[188] In effect, this invokes the principal *casus fœderis* for all al-

186 With reference to Q. 61.10 and Q. 43.61, Robinson states, "These could conceivably have been spoken by God, but an examination of them in the light of Qurʾānic usage suggests that we should probably infer that Muḥammad is the speaker" (idem, *Discovering the Qurʾān*, 236).
187 *BCQ* 2:379 (vv. 10–13).
188 Ibid.

lies. Furthermore, Q. 61.14 (-*īC*) closes the sūra-unit by "invoking divine assistance"[189]:

> *yā-ayyuhā lladhīna āmanū kūnū anṣāra llāhi ka-mā qāla ʿīsā bnu maryama li-l-ḥawāriyyīna man anṣārī ilā llāhi qāla l-ḥawāriyyūna naḥnu anṣāru llāhi fa-āmanat ṭāʾifatun min banī isrāʾīla wa-kafarat ṭāʾifatun fa-ayyadnā lladhīna āmanū ʿalā ʿaduwwihim fa-aṣbaḥū ẓāhirīna*
>
> O you who believe!
> Be God's helpers,
> just as Jesus, son of Mary, said to the disciples,
> 'Who are my helpers towards God?'
> The disciples said, 'We are God's helpers.'
> And a party of the Children of Israel believed
> and another party did not believe.
> So We strengthened those who believed,
> and they prevailed.

This verse "also hints at the assistance of his followers to be rendered to God, presumably in the punishment" of those who "suffer divine retribution."[190]

6.5 Summary

As determined by Greßmann, "the prophetical sayings are usually very simply constructed."[191] Accordingly, the proclamation genre evidences a cluster of formulae relating to the messenger situation. Particularly noteworthy is the preponderance of communal announcements that commence with "O you who believe" (*yā-ayyuhā lladhīna āmanū*). Further analysis confirms the presence of multiple regulatory forms covering a comprehensive set of community rules. As copiously illustrated in the present chapter, these proclamations address not only identity, alterity, and structure, but also even questions pertaining directly to prophetic authority. What is more, these rules equally dictate matters martial and marital, ritual and retributive. That is to say, these prescriptive proclamations in the public sphere shed critical light on "the formation of community."[192]

---

189 Cf. Monica White, *Military Saints in Byzantium and Rus, 900–1200* (Cambridge: Cambridge University Press, 2013), 39.

190 Cf. *BCQ* 2:380; White, *Military Saints*, 39.

191 Greßmann, "Die literarische Analyse Deuterojesajas," 260; cf. idem, *Der Messias*, 69; Hayes, *Interpreting Ancient Israelite History, Prophecy, and Law*, 190; Westermann, *Grundformen prophetischer Rede*, 21.

192 Stewart, "Wansbrough, Bultmann, and the Theory of Variant Traditions," 24; *QS* 148.

Chapter 7: Conclusion

7.1 Genre Classification

In all literary pursuits, discerning genre is not only necessary, but inevitable.[1] As a case in point, in his monumental *Jāmiʿ al-bayān ʿan taʾwīl al-Qurʾān*, al-Ṭabarī transmits an oft-debated tradition (*ḥadīth*), wherein "the Qurʾān was sent down according to seven *aḥruf* (*ʿalā sabʿati aḥruf*): regulation (glossing *amr*), prohibition (*zajr*), exhortation (*targhīb*), admonition (*tarhīb*), debate (*jadal*), narrative (*qaṣaṣ*), and parable (*mathal*)."[2] In examining the tradition, Gilliot concludes, "this seems to be a primitive attempt to classify the essential genres contained in the Qurʾān."[3] Consider, in addition, Hirschfeld who offers yet another reading of scripture, according to the following types: confirmatory, declamatory, narrative, descriptive, and legislative revelations, as well as parable.[4] Aziz Al-Azmeh clarifies, "Not unnaturally, this implied, as is well attested by the character of the received qurʾānic text, the preservation of what may appear as random and diffuse materials...."[5] Put otherwise, the canon fuses together "a set of literary bones," which vastly restricts the movement of materials.[6] Naturally, the question arises, "What kind of literature lay at the living point?"[7] Regarded as first, in the order of development, Mikhail Bakhtin (d. 1975) accords "simple" genres pride of place.[8] And so, at the time of closing the canon, "these primary

---

1 George W. Coats, "Genres: Why Should They Be Important for Exegesis," in *Saga, Legend, Tale, Novella, Fable: Narrative Forms in Old Testament Literature*, ed. idem (Sheffield, England: JSOT Press, 1985), 9; Han Young Lee, *From History to Narrative Hermeneutics* (Frankfurt am Main: Peter Lang, 2004), 90.

2 al-Ṭabarī, *Tafsīr*, 1:69 (given on the authority of Abū Qilāba); s.v. Narratives, *EQ*; Claude Gilliot, "Les sept 'lectures': Corps social et écriture révélée (Première partie)," *SI* 61 (1985): 5–25; idem, "Les sept 'lectures': Corps social et écriture révélée (Seconde partie)," *SI* 63 (1986): 49–62.

3 S.v. Narratives, *EQ*.

4 Hirschfeld, *New Researches*, 34 and 36; s.v. Post-Enlightenment Academic Study of the Qurʾān, *EQ*.

5 Al-Azmeh, *Emergence of Islam in Late Antiquity*, 454–55.

6 Coats, "Genres," 8.

7 Ibid.

8 Mikhail M. Bakhtin, "The Problem of Speech Genres," in *Speech Genres and Other Late Essays* [*Éstetika slovesnogo tvorchestva*], ed. Caryl Emerson and Michael Holquist, trans. Vern W. McGee (Austin, Texas: University of Texas Press, 1986), 61–62; Clive Thomson, "Bakhtin's 'Theory' of Genre," *STCL* 9, no. 1 (1984): 36; Buss, *Biblical Form Criticism*, 165–66; Roland Boer, "Introduction: Bakhtin, Genre and Biblical Studies," in *Bakhtin and Genre Theory in Biblical Studies*, ed. idem (Atlanta, Georgia: Society of Biblical Literature, 2007), 3.

https://doi.org/10.1515/9783110580884-007

genres are altered and assume a special character when they enter into complex ones."[9] Once severed from their principal source, simple genres become, in effect, empty shells of their former selves.[10] By the same token, Guillaume Dye draws a fine distinction between their place in life and their placement in the canon.[11] However, shorn of their original context, these constitute decontextualized fragments.[12] Thus, once more, the task at hand is to breathe new life into these texts.[13]

This dovetails nicely with the root question: "What precisely constitutes a genre?"[14] Coats isolates a set of criteria to determine the proper boundaries.[15] To start with, a distinguishing characteristic of a given genre is its formulary.[16] Next comes literary structure and, as such, formulary and form are closely related.[17] Directly follows social context, which locates a genre's setting in life before it entered literature.[18] Lastly, there is function, literally whereby a given genre achieves its intended ends.[19] To this John Collins appends the caveat that "while a complete study of a genre must consider function and social setting, neither of these factors can determine the definition."[20] For all that, the latter remains an exacting task and a serious matter, not taken lightly.[21] Stewart states, "Genres, whether written or spoken, follow conventional rules, and an under-

---

9 Bakhtin, "The Problem of Speech Genres," 62; Thomson, "Bakhtin's 'Theory' of Genre," 36.
10 Bakhtin, "The Problem of Speech Genres," 62.
11 *The Qur'ān Seminar Commentary / Le Qur'ān Seminar: A Collaborative Study of 50 Qur'ānic Passages / Commentaire collaboratif de 50 passages coraniques*, ed. Mehdi Azaiez, Gabriel Said Reynolds, Tommaso Tesei, and Hamza M. Zafer (Berlin: Walter de Gruyter, 2016), 16; Guillaume Dye, "Pourquoi et comment se fait un texte canonique? Quelques réflexions sur l'histoire du Coran," in *Hérésies: une construction d'identités religieuses*, ed. idem, Christian Brouwer, and Anja van Rompaey (Bruxelles: Editions de l'Université de Bruxelles, 2015), 95; Bakhtin, "The Problem of Speech Genres," 61–62.
12 Dye, "Pourquoi et comment se fait un texte canonique?" 104.
13 Angelika Neuwirth and Michael A. Sells, introduction to *Qur'ānic Studies Today*, ed. eadem (New York: Routledge, 2016), 3.
14 Coats, "Genres," 11.
15 Ibid., 11 and 15; cf. Buss, *Changing Shape of Form Criticism*, 29–30.
16 Coats, "Genres," 12.
17 Ibid., 11–13.
18 Ibid., 13.
19 Ibid.
20 John J. Collins, "Introduction: Towards the Morphology of a Genre," *Semeia* 14 (1979): 1–2.
21 Coats, "Genres," 8, 10–11, and 15; cf. Smith, *Isaiah Chapters XL-LV*, 10. In line with Goethe, "to name a thing is not necessarily to explain it" (Carey A. Moore, introduction to *Esther*, trans. idem (New York: Doubleday & Company Inc., 1971), lv; Werner Dommershausen, *Die Estherrolle: Stil und Ziel einer alttestamentlichen Schrift* (Stuttgart: Verlag Katholisches Bibelwerk, 1968), 154–56).

standing of those rules helps one to understand better texts that draw on those genres."[22] In the end, by identifying formulae, examining forms, and determining settings, genre criticism establishes the crucial link between life and literature in the past.[23]

7.2 Genre History

In his "Der Koran als Geschichtsquelle," Rudi Paret (d. 1983) claims, the distinction is readily apparent between the history of religion and salvation history.[24] Yet, this is not as self-evident as it seems at first. For instance, the historical-critical examination of the corpus is built on, and therefore, ultimately dependent upon, the extra-qur'ānic tradition (in particular, *sīra-maghāzī*).[25] Otherwise, and even on this point, scholarship is far from a consensus. Reflecting this state of affairs, the assumptions of sacred history are foundational, if not axiomatic.[26] In point of fact, Michael Pregill specifies, "Form criticism of the Qur'ān almost always proceeds through the hermeneutic lens of the *sīra* tradition; that is, our understanding of the evolution of qur'ānic discourse is typically anchored in the biography of a particular individual, which then seems to limit the possibilities for formal analysis considerably."[27] That was clearly the case at least

22 *Qur'ān Seminar Commentary*, 37–38; Coats, "Genres," 9–10. Significantly, Collins notes, "While the study of genre inevitably involves a diachronic, historical dimension, its identification and definition are independent of historical considerations" (idem, "Introduction: Towards the Morphology of a Genre," 1).

23 Coats, "Genres," 10; Hayes, *Interpreting Ancient Israelite History, Prophecy, and Law*, 165.

24 Rudi Paret, "Der Koran als Geschichtsquelle," *Isl.* 37, nos. 1–3 (1961): 26; Buss, *Changing Shape of Form Criticism*, 18–21; Oden, "Historical Understanding and Understanding the Religion of Israel," 15–18.

25 Neuwirth and Sells, introduction, 4. Fred M. Donner states, "Clearly, the *sīra*'s vision, as a historical reconstruction of Islām's origins, has grave weaknesses...But at this point, it seems likely that some aspects of the traditional *sīra* framework may, in the end, emerge as historically sound" (idem, "The Historian, the Believers, and the Qur'ān," in *New Perspectives on the Qur'ān: The Qur'ān in Its Historical Context 2*, ed. Gabriel Said Reynolds (New York: Routledge, 2011), 30). In conjunction with this particular article, see Heikki Räisänen, "Word of God, Word of Muḥammad: Could Historical Criticism of the Qur'ān be Pursued by Muslims?" in *Marcion, Muḥammad and the Mahatma: Exegetical Perspectives on the Encounter of Cultures and Faiths* (London: SCM Press Ltd., 1997), 118–36, esp. 123–25; s.v. Narratives, *EQ*.

26 Neuwirth and Sells, introduction, 1–2; Lee, *From History to Narrative Hermeneutics*, 104 and 183–85.

27 *Qur'ān Seminar Commentary*, 340.

until Wansbrough.[28] Accordingly, from a purely historical standpoint, Dye finds it necessary to sever the link between text and tradition.[29]

And yet, the question remains, whether the *seriatim* Weil–Nöldeke chronology involves a serious case of circular reasoning.[30] Writing in response, Gabriel Said Reynolds argues that reading scripture in light of hagiography is deeply flawed and locked in a "vicious circle."[31] Nonetheless, the fact of the matter remains, chronology is the logic of history.[32] For this reason, Sinai points to the pressing need for a diachronic reading of the Qur'ān.[33] In fact, Paret considers the corpus a primary source *par excellence.*[34] In other words, one could say without reservation that the Qur'ān – and the Qur'ān alone – is the key document.[35] In the light of this reality, Pregill poses a critical question: "What would be the requisite methodological commitments for the field to advance to a serious and disciplined form criticism of the Qur'ān that was not primarily grounded in the *sīra* tradition?"[36]

To begin with, Hawting holds, the objective is to restore scripture to history.[37] Patricia Crone (d. 2015) says, this more or less amounts to reclaiming the literary

---

28 Ibid.; Donner, "The Historian, the Believers, and the Qur'ān," 27; Neuwirth, "Qur'ānic Studies and Philology," 181–82; Lee, *From History to Narrative Hermeneutics*, 104 and 183–85. Wansbrough writes, "Now, the Muslim concept of *Heilsgeschichte* depended, not unexpectedly, upon the didactic value of *exempla*, and those constitute in turn a major portion of scripture. Whether such reflect Muḥammad's idea(s) of history is irrelevant. That they represent the organizing principle of Ibn Isḥāq's composition is relevant...Indeed, an important problem in the analysis of the *Sīra*, and one only alluded to by Sellheim, is Ibn Isḥāq's treatment of material preserved also as the canonical text of revelation" (*QS* 58).

29 *Qur'ān Seminar Commentary*, 16.

30 Sinai, *Fortschreibung und Auslegung*, 60–73, esp. 60–61; Madigan, *The Qur'ān's Self-Image*, 86; cf. Neuwirth, "Meccan Texts – Medinan Additions? Politics and the Re-reading of Liturgical Communications," in *Words, Texts and Concepts Cruising the Mediterranean Sea*, ed. Rüdiger Arnzen and Jörn Thielmann (Leuven: Peeters, 2004), 93.

31 Gabriel Said Reynolds, "Le problème de la chronologie du Coran," *Arabica* 58 (2011): 501; cf. Sinai, *Fortschreibung und Auslegung*, 61.

32 Cf. Gabriel Said Reynolds, *The Emergence of Islam: Classical Traditions in Contemporary Perspective* (Minneapolis, Minnesota: Fortress Press, 2012), 138–39.

33 Sinai, *Fortschreibung und Auslegung*, 60.

34 Paret, "Der Koran als Geschichtsquelle," 26.

35 Neuwirth and Sells, introduction, 5; *Qur'ān Seminar Commentary*, 21.

36 *Qur'ān Seminar Commentary*, 340–41.

37 Ibid., 21; Gabriel Said Reynolds, introduction to op. cit., 2; Francis E. Peters, "The Quest of the Historical Muḥammad," *IJMES* 23, no. 3 (1991): 300; Madigan, *The Qur'ān's Self-Image*, 86, fn. 24; Izutsu, *God and Man in the Koran*, 29 and 37; see Steck, *Exegese des Alten Testaments*, 148–55.

heritage of the text.[38] Similarly, by casting a wider net, Dye's proposal moves beyond Weil and Nöldeke, beyond Meccan and Medinan.[39] Al-Azmeh, on the other hand, posits "an older form of continuity with antiquity."[40] And yet it is equally evident, Reynolds writes, that ascertaining this has proven difficult, and so continues to elude historians.[41] Be that as it may, the *corpus coranicum* is twice removed from history.[42] For that reason, Donner sensibly suggests,[43]

> Given this grave uncertainty over the Qur'ān's context, scholars must reverse the usual procedure when studying a text: rather than using the context to illuminate the meaning of the text, we must start with the Qur'ān text itself, and try to deduce from hints inside it what a plausible historical context (or several contexts, in the case it is not a unitary text) might be.

In this regard, it is certainly pertinent, that of all research, Neuwirth's is the least susceptible to chronological problems, since she pays particular attention to structural features.[44] As it happens, Gunkel resolves, with reference to psalm criticism,[45]

---

38 *Qur'ān Seminar Commentary*, 14; Segre, *Avviamento all'analisi del testo letterario*, 131–59; Neuwirth, "Qur'ānic Studies and Philology," 186; *SPMC* xxi.

39 *Qur'ān Seminar Commentary*, 17; Dye, "Pourquoi et comment se fait un texte canonique?" 96.

40 Al-Azmeh, *Emergence of Islam in Late Antiquity*, 1. Marco Schöller relates, "Indeed, it might be supposed, and there is some rumor to that effect among contemporary scholars of early Islām, that Wansbrough's hypothesis of a cumulative creation of the Qur'ān and its gradual evolution into scripture in a sectarian setting of broadly Near Eastern monotheistic stamp might still be safeguarded if the period of the Qur'ān's origin is no longer placed in the first Islāmic centuries but ante-dated to the time prior to the prophet's mission" (s.v. Post-Enlightenment Academic Study of the Qur'ān, *EQ*; cf. Patricia Crone, "Historiographical Introduction," in *Slaves on Horses: The Evolution of the Islamic Polity* (Cambridge: Cambridge University Press, 1980), 13–14).

41 Gabriel Said Reynolds, "Introduction: The Golden Age of Qur'ānic Studies?" in *New Perspectives on the Qur'ān: The Qur'ān in Its Historical Context 2*, ed. idem (New York: Routledge, 2011), 21; Donner, "The Historian, the Believers, and the Qur'ān," 25–26 and 37; Reynolds, *Emergence of Islam*, 136 and cf. 168; *SPMC* xxiii and xxvi–xxviii.

42 *Qur'ān Seminar Commentary*, 21; Donner, "The Historian, the Believers, and the Qur'ān," 25.

43 Donner, "The Historian, the Believers, and the Qur'ān," 25; Reynolds, *Emergence of Islam*, 145.

44 Sinai, *Fortschreibung und Auslegung*, 66. According to Rippin, "Neuwirth's *Studien* marks a significant re-orientation of interests for the historical-critical school of analysis of the Qur'ān in the sense that, despite the expectations perhaps raised by the title, actual chronological considerations barely play a role within the book..." (idem, review of *Studien zur Komposition der mekkanischen Suren*, by Angelika Neuwirth, *BSOAS* 45, no. 1 (1982): 149).

45 *EinlPs*[4] 31; Gunkel and Begrich, *Introduction to Psalms*, 21; s.v. Narratives, *EQ*; Neuwirth, "Qur'ānic Studies and Philology," 184–86.

> Using genres creates new relationships between the individual psalms and often provides a new understanding. All of this affects the assignation of time. In particular, genre research provides new standards for differentiating the new from the old within the psalms, and finally a vast internal history of the entire poetry can be recognized.

John Hayes (d. 2013) recapitulates, genre criticism is a means to determine the historical development of these literary materials.[46]

Neuwirth stresses time and again the centrality of the text to any reconstruction.[47] Then again, Madigan clearly notes, there is the vexing question of identifying an objective criterion on which to base a sound chronology.[48] "Assuming, then, that we are desirous of adopting as thoroughly historical a method," Edward Sapir (d. 1939) writes, "the question immediately suggests itself: how [to] inject a chronology into this confusing mass of purely descriptive fact?"[49] Whereas slow sanding produces smooth surfaces read along the grain, fissures in fact facilitate internal criticism against it.[50] Therefore, multiplicity and variance take precedence in genre criticism, so as to derive a chronology from the corpus.[51] To this end, scholars are committed to furthering higher criticism.[52] Paret affirms that historical criticism has proved its worth many times over.[53] Maurice Gaudefroy-Demombynes (d. 1957) remarks, no account of the Qurʾān is complete without accounting for chronology.[54] Notwithstanding the foregoing, in her critical assessment of the field, Crone states, "After Wellhausen the most striking feature of Islāmic *Quellenkritik* was its absence."[55]

Most notably, then, Henning Bernhard Witter (wr. 1711) and Jean Astruc (wr. 1753) laid the foundations of the Graf-Wellhausen hypothesis for historical

46 Hayes, *Interpreting Ancient Israelite History, Prophecy, and Law*, 165; Lee, *From History to Narrative Hermeneutics*, 89.

47 Neuwirth and Sells, introduction, 5.

48 Madigan, *The Qur'ān's Self-Image*, 86; see W. Montgomery Watt, "The Dating of the Qurʾān: A Review of Richard Bell's Theories," in *Early Islam: Collected Articles* (Edinburgh: Edinburgh University Press, 1990), 24–33.

49 Edward Sapir, *Time Perspective in Aboriginal American Culture: A Study in Method* (Ottawa: Government Printing Bureau, 1916), 2.

50 Cf. Crone, "Historiographical Introduction," 12.

51 Weren, *Windows on Jesus*, 113; Sinai, *Fortschreibung und Auslegung*, 72; Bakhtin, "The Problem of Speech Genres," 60.

52 Neuwirth and Sells, introduction, 3–4.

53 Paret, "Der Koran als Geschichtsquelle," 24.

54 Maurice Gaudefroy-Demombynes, "Sur quelques noms d'Allāh dans le Coran," *Annuaire* (1929): 21.

55 Cf. Crone, "Historiographical Introduction," 13–14.

reconstruction.[56] This, in turn, provides a powerful means of analyzing scripture with reference to the past.[57] Highly significant, therefore, is the statement of Toshihiko Izutsu (d. 1993) that "the qur'ānic worldview is essentially theocentric."[58] Reminiscent of Graf-Wellhausen, and with special reference to the second Meccan period, Nöldeke advances the perceptive claim[59]:

> In this period, Muḥammad started to introduce the specific name, *al-Raḥmān*, 'the Merciful,' for his God, concurrently with *Allāh*, which was familiar also to the pagans. This name, which was previously used only once, now becomes in places even more frequent than the usual *Allāh*. *al-Raḥmān*, on the other hand, disappears in the sūras of the third period, apart from a few exceptions, and is completely lacking in the Medinan period.

With an eye to Nöldeke, Madigan first of all objects that his argument is specious at best.[60] At once, Sinai dismisses this objection as untenable.[61] In addition to *al-Raḥmān*, Joseph Chelhod (d. 1994) insightfully states, a close examination of the theonyms *Allāh* and *Rabb* in the text would go a long way toward restoring its chronology.[62] In the second place, *pace* Nöldeke, Bell cautions against depend-

---

56 Rylaarsdam, foreword, iii; Bray, *Biblical Interpretation*, 240–41; Jean Astruc, *Conjectures sur les mémoires originaux dont il paroit que Moyse s'est servi pour composer le Livre de la Genese* (Bruxelles: Chez Fricx, 1753), *passim*; s.v. Documentary Hypothesis, *NIDB*; s.v. Diachronic Interpretation, *OEBI*; Sinai, *Fortschreibung und Auslegung*, 61. For a sustained critique of the Graf-Wellhausen hypothesis, form criticism, and tradition criticism, see Whybray, *The Making of the Pentateuch*, 9; Lee, *From History to Narrative Hermeneutics*, 93–94. See Lawrence Boadt, *Reading the Old Testament: An Introduction* (New York: Paulist Press, 1984), 96.

57 Lee, *From History to Narrative Hermeneutics*, 87.

58 Toshihiko Izutsu, *Ethico-Religious Concepts in the Qur'ān* (Montreal: McGill-Queen's University Press, 2002), 18; idem, *God and Man in the Koran*, 41; Madigan, *The Qur'ān's Self-Image*, 84.

59 *GdQ*[2] 1:117 and 1:121; Theodor Nöldeke, Friedrich Schwally, Gotthelf Bergsträßer, and Otto Pretzl, *The History of the Qur'ān*, trans. Wolfgang H. Behn (Leiden: Brill, 2013), 99; *BIQ*[1] 101.

60 Madigan, *The Qur'ān's Self-Image*, 86.

61 Sinai, *Fortschreibung und Auslegung*, 61.

62 Joseph Chelhod, "Note sur l'emploi du mot *Rabb* dans le Coran," *Arabica* 5, no. 2 (1958): 167; s.vv. *Allāh*, *Basmala*, and *Rabb*, *EI*[2]; Jeffery, *Foreign Vocabulary*, 66–67 (*Allāh*), 136–37 (*Rabb*), and 140–41 (*al-Raḥmān*); Izutsu, *God and Man in the Koran*, 40–41 (*Allāh*), 47–52 (*Allāh:* "Post-Koranic System"), 95–119 (*Allāh*), 103 (*Rabb*), 109 (*Rabb*), 121 (*Rabb*), and 198–219 (*Rabb*); Alford T. Welch, "Allāh and Other Supernatural Beings: The Emergence of the Qur'ānic Doctrine of Tawḥīd," in *Studies in Qur'ān and Tafsīr*, ed. idem (Chico, California: American Academy of Religion, 1979), 733–58; Jacques Jomier, "Le nom divin 'al-Raḥmān' dans le Coran," in *Mélanges Louis Massignon* (Damascus: Institut Français de Damas, 1957), 2:361–81, esp. 379–80; Patricia Crone, "The Religion of the Qur'ānic Pagans: God and the Lesser Deities," *Arabica* 57, nos. 2–3 (2010): 151–200, esp. 166–69; Peters, "The Quest of the Historical Muḥammad," 300–301; Tilman Seidensticker, "Sources for the History of Pre-Islamic Religion," in *The Qur'ān in Context: Historical and Literary Investigations into the Qur'ānic Milieu*, ed. Angelika

ence on elements of style.[63] Conversely, Chelhod notes, it is well known that Nöldeke based his work on content and style alike.[64]

Evidently, the problem rests less with style than with Nöldeke's conjecture, wherein "historical intuition, as it was sometimes called, began to take the place of sound criticism."[65] Nevertheless, Bell concedes the indisputable fact that elements of style indeed evolve over time.[66] Along similar lines, Madigan concludes, there is no question that the corpus preserves traces of this stylistic drift; rather, the problem is one of recognizing limits.[67] However, Bakhtin counters, "All this is a result of an inadequate understanding of the generic nature of linguistic styles, and the absence of a well-thought-out classification of speech genres in terms of spheres of human activity."[68] He unequivocally declares, "Where there is style there is genre."[69] Moreover, Greßmann positively asserts, judgments of style are bound to those of form.[70] Bakhtin also sounds a sensible note of caution: "It is especially harmful to separate style from genre when elaborating historical problems."[71] For all that, Madigan reasonably holds, a single measure is insufficient for control.[72]

Neuwirth, Nicolai Sinai, and Michael Marx (Leiden: Brill, 2011), 301–15, esp. 301; Robinson, *Discovering the Qur'ān*, 78–79, 89–91, and cf. 95.

63 *BIQ*[1] 102.

64 Chelhod, "Note sur l'emploi du mot *Rabb* dans le Coran," 167.

65 Cf. Joseph Schacht, "A Reevaluation of Islamic Traditions," *JRAS* 2 (1949): 143; *BIQ*[1] 103; *GdQ*[2] 1:121; Robinson, *Discovering the Qur'ān*, 93.

66 *BIQ*[1] 103.

67 Madigan, *The Qur'ān's Self-Image*, 86; Calder, "History and Nostalgia," 58, fn. 7; Andrew L. Rippin, "The Qur'ānic *asbāb al-nuzūl* Material: An Analysis of Its Use and Development in Exegesis" (PhD diss., McGill University, 1981), 439, fn. 1.

68 Bakhtin, "The Problem of Speech Genres," 65. Consequently, "to fail to consider the peculiarities of generic subcategories of speech in any area of linguistic study leads to perfunctoriness and excessive abstractness, distorts the historicity of the research, and weakens the link between language and life" (ibid., 63; Boer, "Introduction: Bakhtin, Genre and Biblical Studies," 3).

69 Bakhtin, "The Problem of Speech Genres," 64 and 66; idem, *The Dialogic Imagination: Four Essays* [*Voprosy literatury i ėstetiki*], trans. Caryl Emerson and Michael Holquist (Austin, Texas: University of Texas Press, 1981), 428. Bakhtin defines "linguistic style" to mean "the selection of the lexical, phraseological, and grammatical resources of the language" (idem, "The Problem of Speech Genres," 60 and 64, fn. 4).

70 Greßmann, "Die literarische Analyse Deuterojesajas," 259; cf. Smith, *Isaiah Chapters XL-LV*, 7.

71 Bakhtin, "The Problem of Speech Genres," 64.

72 Madigan, *The Qur'ān's Self-Image*, 87.

Genre comprises various forms, the intersection of which once stirred debate.[73] And so, it is no small matter when Klaus Berger extrapolates its historical character.[74] Although constrained by Gunkel's conception of the history of literature, Berger nonetheless establishes the deceptively simple and elusive fact: "Genres have history."[75] In turn, genre history is founded on comparison.[76] Stemming from this observation, Robinson calls for a twofold analysis.[77] Foremost is gathering a substantial body of evidence, independent of seriation. Then, at the diachronic level, relative dating is used to arrange this material. This affords a temporal clue to the corpus; among other things, mapping the distribution of divine epithets according to the genres and forms surveyed.[78] Chelhod's comment

---

73 Klaus Berger, *Einführung in die Formgeschichte* (Tübingen: Francke Verlag, 1987), 36. "Formal analysis is a comprehensive category that includes attention to structure and function. It deals not only with synchronic but also with diachronic processes insofar as these are 'organic,' that is, involved in an organization of the material" (Buss, *Changing Shape of Form Criticism*, 17–18 and 27–28; Gunkel, "Fundamental Problems of Hebrew Literary History," 62).

74 Berger, *Einführung in die Formgeschichte*, 36 and 43; Buss, *Changing Shape of Form Criticism*, 26.

75 Berger, *Einführung in die Formgeschichte*, 38; idem, *Formen und Gattungen im Neuen Testament* (Tübingen: Francke Verlag, 2005), 10–15. "Genre history pertains to the reception of a particular text-type through the course of world history...Self-consciously retrieving Gunkel and Norden's unfinished project of genre-research (a project that, it is to be recalled, Dibelius repudiated), Berger insists on the paramount importance of genre (as opposed to oral form), insofar as this literary property, more than any other factor, provides the communicative meeting ground and decisive point of contact between the author and the author's readers...Berger recognizes that some genres will fall in and out of fashion in different times and in different places; accordingly, theories of genealogical development are ruled out, and any attempts to plot biblical texts against a reconstructed 'genre timeline' must be deemed futile" (s.v. Form Criticism: New Form Criticism, *DJG*).

76 Berger, *Einführung in die Formgeschichte*, 38 and 43; Buss, *Changing Shape of Form Criticism*, 23–24.

77 Robinson, *Discovering the Qur'ān*, 95.

78 Sapir, *Time Perspective in Aboriginal American Culture*, 2; Madigan, *The Qur'ān's Self-Image*, 87; Robinson, *Discovering the Qur'ān*, 78–79, 89–91, and cf. 95. Lexical criteria: for "pre-redactional" subcorpora "titles" (e.g., *kitāb, furqān, qur'ān*), see Madigan, *The Qur'ān's Self-Image*, 125–32 ("The Names of Particular Revelations"); Robinson, *Discovering the Qur'ān*, 83–84 and 94; Neuwirth, "Meccan Texts – Medinan Additions?" 93; Arthur Jeffery, *The Qur'ān as Scripture* (New York: Books for Libraries, 1980 [1952]), 3–17, esp. 7 and 9–17; for "semantic fields" (e.g., *īmān, islām*), see Madigan, *The Qur'ān's Self-Image*, 84; Toshihiko Izutsu, *The Concept of Belief in Islamic Theology: A Semantic Analysis of Īmān and Islām* (Tokyo: The Keio Institute of Cultural and Linguistic Studies, 1965), *passim*; Donner, *Muhammad and the Believers*, 57; cf. *QS* 73–84, esp. 75, fn. 2; Whybray, *The Intellectual Tradition in the Old Testament*, 74–76. Neuwirth notes, "There is, then, not one ancient Bible but two Late Antique Bibles" (eadem, "Qur'ānic Studies and Philology," 190).

is appropriate here: though the foregoing is merely a clue, in the absence of any other, it would be intellectually irresponsible to ignore.[79]

The repository is a fitting image as a point of departure from formal classification to historical reconstruction.[80] Accordingly, the investigation begins with a representative selection of different genres, with the purpose of identifying a diachronic sequence in the *corpus coranicum*.[81] What is more, Dye recognizes that the history and trajectory of a particular pericope is contingent upon its genre.[82] Therefore, "the validity of abstract generic typologies that hypostasize a group of texts synchronically is denied in favor of a diachronic perspective where the operative factor is transformation."[83] Resonating with Coats' classification, qurʾānic genres encapsulate the form-critical elements of formulae, forms, themes, settings, and functions, as well as a genre-historical dimension.[84] On this firm basis, Bakhtin determines, "one must develop a special history of speech genres that reflects more directly, clearly, and flexibly all the changes taking place in social life."[85]

---

79 Chelhod, "Note sur l'emploi du mot *Rabb* dans le Coran," 167.

80 Neuwirth, "Vom Rezitationstext über die Liturgie zum Kanon," 98; Madigan, *The Qurʾān's Self-Image*, 88–89; Neal Robinson, "Hands Outstretched: Towards a Re-reading of Sūrat al-Māʾida," *JQS* 3, no. 1 (2001): 1, fn. 2; Sinai, *Fortschreibung und Auslegung*, 65; Dye, "Pourquoi et comment se fait un texte canonique?" 96, fn. 157.

81 Cf. Madigan, *The Qurʾān's Self-Image*, 86; Martin J. Buss, "Dialogue in and among Genres," in *Bakhtin and Genre Theory in Biblical Studies*, ed. Roland Boer (Atlanta, Georgia: Society of Biblical Literature, 2007), 16; Boer, "Introduction: Bakhtin, Genre and Biblical Studies," 4. Izutsu states, "vocabulary, far from being a single homogeneous plain, consists of a great number – or rather we should say, an indefinite number – of strata of associative connections or spheres of conceptual association, each one of which corresponds to a predominant interest of a community in a given period of history…" (idem, *God and Man in the Koran*, 29).

82 Dye, "Pourquoi et comment se fait un texte canonique?" 97.

83 Thomson, "Bakhtin's 'Theory' of Genre," 32. Similarly, Buss contends, "Negatively (*contra* Gunkel), I reject the notion that genres have 'essences,' that is, the idea that there are right or wrong ways to categorize genres. Instead, together with other relational theorists, I accept the view that genres are more or less useful ways of treating similar literary phenomena together" (idem, "Dialogue in and among Genres," 9).

84 Bakhtin, "The Problem of Speech Genres," 60, 64, and 76–78; Coats, "Genres," 11–13; Buss, *Changing Shape of Form Criticism*, 17. For themes, see Lee, *From History to Narrative Hermeneutics*, 137; Martin Noth, *Überlieferungsgeschichte des Pentateuch* (Stuttgart: Verlag W. Kohlhammer, 1948), *passim*; Noth, *Quellenkritische Studien*, 30. For tendencies, see Barthold Georg Niebuhr's (d. 1831) *Römische Geschichte*, 3 vols. (Berlin: Realschulbuchhandlung, 1811–32), and Ferdinand Christian Baur's (d. 1860) *Paulus, der Apostel Jesu Christi* (Stuttgart: Verlag von Becher & Müller, 1845).

85 "Speech genres," for Bakhtin, "are the drive belts from the history of society to the history of language" (idem, "The Problem of Speech Genres," 65).

7.3 Summary

Cesare Segre (d. 2014) states, "It is not just possible, but absolutely necessary, to orient literary texts historically."[86] That is to say, "formal analysis alone cannot possibly be sufficient in form-critical research."[87] This is but a prelude to history; and if not that, "then our most important witness for sounding out the gradual crystallization of the pre-conquest Islāmic *Urgemeinde* is left unexplored."[88] The present volume on genre criticism investigated the application of form criticism in the identification of genres within the *corpus coranicum.* "Let us ask once more: can this synchronic taxonomy be interpreted diachronically?"[89] By way of closing, genre history is the key.[90]

86 Segre, *Avviamento all'analisi del testo letterario*, 133; idem, *Introduction to the Analysis of the Literary Text*, trans. John Meddemmen (Bloomington: Indiana University Press, 1988), 117.
87 Gerstenberger, "Psalms," 223.
88 Sinai and Neuwirth, introduction, 6. Neuwirth states, "A new attempt to trace the qur'ānic development is overdue...The still powerful shibboleth that lurks behind this deficiency is chronology – but not in the simple sense of accepting or rejecting a particular sequence of sūras such as that established by Theodor Nöldeke in the beginning of critical scholarship. What is at stake is a deeper understanding of chronology – that Nöldeke only vaguely conceived of..." (eadem, "Qur'ānic Studies and Philology," 182).
89 Cf. Sinai, "Qur'ān as Process," 426; Buss, *Changing Shape of Form Criticism*, 24.
90 Gunkel, foreword, vi.

Bibliography

Abdel Haleem, Muhammad. "Context and Internal Relationships: Keys to Qur'ānic Exegesis: A Study of Sūrat al-Raḥmān." In *Approaches to the Qur'ān*, edited by Gerald R. Hawting and Abdul-Kader A. Shareef, 71–98. London: Routledge, 1993.

Abdul-Raof, Hussein. "Textual Progression and Presentation Technique in Qur'ānic Discourse: An Investigation of Richard Bell's Claims of 'Disjointedness' with Especial Reference to Q. 17–20." *JQS* 7, no. 2 (2005): 36–60.

Abrahamov, Binyamin. "Theology." In *The Blackwell Companion to the Qur'ān*, edited by Andrew Rippin, 420–33. Oxford: Blackwell Publishing, 2006.

Adams, Charles J. "Reflections on the Work of John Wansbrough." *MTSR* 9, no. 1 (1997): 75–90.

Aejmelaeus, Anneli. *The Traditional Prayer in the Psalms.* Berlin: Walter de Gruyter, 1986.

Al-Azmeh, Aziz. *The Emergence of Islam in Late Antiquity: Allāh and His People.* Cambridge: Cambridge University Press, 2014.

Albertz, Rainer. *Persönliche Frömmigkeit und offizielle Religion: Religionsinterner Pluralismus in Israel und Babylon.* Stuttgart: Calwer Verlag, 1978.

Ali, Kecia. *The Lives of Muhammad.* Cambridge, Massachusetts: Harvard University Press, 2014.

Alt, Albrecht. *Die Ursprünge des israelitischen Rechts.* In *Kleine Schriften zur Geschichte des Volkes Israel*, 278–332. Vol. 1. 2nd rev. ed. München: C.H. Beck'sche Verlagsbuchhandlung, 1959 [1934].

Anderson, Andrew Runni. "Alexander's Horns." *TAPA* 58 (1927): 100–122.

Anderson, Bernhard W. "Introduction: Martin Noth's Traditio-Historical Approach in the Context of Twentieth-Century Biblical Research." In *A History of Pentateuchal Traditions*, by Martin Noth, xiii–xxxii. Atlanta, Georgia: Scholars Press, 1981.

Anderson, Bernhard W. *Understanding the Old Testament.* 4th ed. Englewood Cliffs, New Jersey: Prentice-Hall, 1986.

Anderson, George W. *A Critical Introduction to the Old Testament.* London: Gerald Duckworth & Co. Ltd., 1979.

Annet, Peter. *The Free Enquirer.* London: R. Carlile, 1826 [1761].

Annet, Peter. *The Resurrection of Jesus Considered.* 3rd ed. London: M. Cooper, 1744.

Annet, Peter. *The Resurrection Defenders.* London: s.n., 1745.

Aristotle. *The Complete Works of Aristotle.* Vol. 2. Edited by Jonathan Barnes. Princeton, New Jersey: Princeton University Press, 1984.

Assmann, Aleida, and Jan Assmann. "Kanon und Zensur als kultursoziologische Kategorien." In *Kanon und Zensur: Beiträge zur Archäologie der literarischen Kommunikation II*, edited by eadem, 7–27. München: Wilhelm Fink Verlag, 1987.

Assmann, Jan. *Moses the Egyptian: The Memory of Egypt in Western Monotheism.* Cambridge, Massachusetts: Harvard University Press, 1997.

Astruc, Jean. *Conjectures sur les mémoires originaux dont il paroit que Moyse s'est servi pour composer le Livre de la Genese.* Bruxelles: Chez Fricx, 1753.

Audet, Jean-Paul. "Origines comparées de la double tradition de la loi et de la sagesse dans le Proche-Orient ancien." In *Proceedings of the International Congress of Orientalists*, 352–57. Vol. 1. Moscow: s.n., 1962.

https://doi.org/10.1515/9783110580884-008

Augustine through the Ages. Edited by Allan D. Fitzgerald. Grand Rapids, Michigan: Wm. B. Eerdmans Publishing Company, 1999.

Aune, David E. *Prophecy in Early Christianity and the Ancient Mediterranean World*. Grand Rapids, Michigan: Wm. B. Eerdmans Publishing Company, 1983.

Ayoub, Mahmoud. *The Qur'ān and Its Interpreters*. Vol. 1. Albany: State University of New York Press, 1984.

Azaiez, Mehdi. *Le contre-discours coranique*. Berlin: Walter de Gruyter, 2015.

Badawi, Elsaid M., and Muhammad Abdel Haleem. *Arabic-English Dictionary of Qur'ānic Usage*. Leiden: Brill, 2008.

Baeck, Leo. "Griechische und jüdische Predigt." In *Aus Drei Jahrtausenden: Wissenschaftliche Untersuchungen und Abhandlungen zur Geschichte des jüdischen Glaubens*, 142–56. Tübingen: Verlag von J.C.B. Mohr (Paul Siebeck), 1958.

Bakhtin, Mikhail M. *The Dialogic Imagination: Four Essays* [*Voprosy literatury i ėstetiki*]. Translated by Caryl Emerson and Michael Holquist. Austin, Texas: University of Texas Press, 1981.

Bakhtin, Mikhail M. "The Problem of Speech Genres." In *Speech Genres and Other Late Essays* [*Ėstetika slovesnogo tvorchestva*], edited by Caryl Emerson and Michael Holquist, 60–102. Translated by Vern W. McGee. Austin, Texas: University of Texas Press, 1986.

Balch, David L. *Let Wives Be Submissive: The Domestic Code in I Peter*. Atlanta, Georgia: Scholars Press, 1981.

Balentine, Samuel E. *Prayer in the Hebrew Bible: The Drama of Divine-Human Dialogue*. Minneapolis, Minnesota: Fortress Press, 1993.

Bannister, Andrew G. *An Oral-Formulaic Study of the Qur'ān*. Lanham, Maryland: Lexington Books, 2014.

Barth, Jakob. *Studien zur Kritik und Exegese des Qorans*. Strassburg: Verlag von Karl J. Trübner, 1915.

Barth, Karl. *Die protestantische Theologie im 19. Jahrhundert: Ihre Vorgeschichte und ihre Geschichte*. 2nd rev. ed. Zollikon-Zürich: Evangelischer Verlag AG, 1952.

Barton, John. *Reading the Old Testament: Method in Biblical Study*. 2nd rev. ed. Louisville, Kentucky: Westminster John Knox Press, 1996.

Baumgartner, Walter. "Die literarischen Gattungen in der Weisheit des Jesus Sirach." *ZAW* 34, no. 3 (1914): 161–98.

Baumstark, Anton. *Comparative Liturgy*. Translated by F.L. Cross. Westminster, Maryland: The Newman Press, 1958.

Baumstark, Anton. "Jüdischer und christlicher Gebetstypus im Koran." *Isl.* 16, no. 1 (1927): 229–48.

Baumstark, Anton. *Liturgie comparée. Principes et Méthodes pour l'étude historique des liturgies chrétiennes*. 3rd ed. Chevetogne, Belgique: Éditions de Chevetogne, 1953.

Baur, Ferdinand Christian. *Paulus, der Apostel Jesu Christi*. Stuttgart: Verlag von Becher & Müller, 1845.

Bautch, Richard J. *Developments in Genre between Post-Exilic Penitential Prayers and the Psalms of Communal Lament*. Atlanta, Georgia: Society of Biblical Literature, 2003.

Becker, Carl H. "Ubi sunt qui ante nos in mundo fuere." In *Aufsätze zur Kultur- und Sprachgeschichte vornehmlich des Orients: Ernst Kuhn zum 70. Geburtstage am 7. Februar 1916 gewidmet von Freunden und Schülern*, 87–105. Breslau: Verlag von M. & H. Marcus, 1916.

Bell, Richard. *A Commentary on the Qur'ān*. 2 vols. Edited by C. Edmund Bosworth and M. E.J. Richardson. Manchester, England: University of Manchester, 1991.

Bell, Richard. *Introduction to the Qur'ān*. Edinburgh: Edinburgh University Press, 1953.

Bell, Richard, and W. Montgomery Watt. *Bell's Introduction to the Qur'ān*. Rev. ed. Edinburgh: Edinburgh University Press, 1970.

Berger, Klaus. *Einführung in die Formgeschichte*. Tübingen: Francke Verlag, 1987.

Berger, Klaus. *Formen und Gattungen im Neuen Testament*. Tübingen: Francke Verlag, 2005.

Berger, Klaus. "Hellenistische Gattungen im Neuen Testament." In *Aufstieg und Niedergang der römischen Welt: Geschichte und Kultur Roms im Spiegel der neueren Forschung*, edited by Hildegard Temporini and Wolfgang Haase, 1031–432. Vol. 2. Berlin: Walter de Gruyter, 1984.

Bernstein, Moshe J. *Reading and Re-reading Scripture at Qumran*. Vol. 2. Leiden: Brill, 2013.

Bierl, Anton. "Maenadism as Self-referential Chorality in Euripides' *Bacchae*." In *Choral Mediations in Greek Tragedy*, edited by Renaud Gagné and Marianne Govers Hopman, 211–26. Cambridge: Cambridge University Press, 2013.

Bishop, Eric F. "The Qumrān Scrolls and the Qur'ān." *MW* 48, no. 3 (1958): 223–36.

Blomberg, Craig L. *Interpreting the Parables*. 2nd ed. Downers Grove, Illinois: InterVarsity Press, 2012.

Blum, Erhard. "Formgeschichte – A Misleading Category? Some Critical Remarks." In *The Changing Face of Form Criticism for the Twenty-first Century*, edited by Marvin A. Sweeney and Ehud Ben Zvi, 32–45. Grand Rapids, Michigan: Wm. B. Eerdmans Publishing Company, 2003.

Boadt, Lawrence. *Reading the Old Testament: An Introduction*. New York: Paulist Press, 1984.

Bobzin, Hartmut. *Der Koran: Eine Einführung*. 7th ed. München: Verlag C.H. Beck, 2007.

Boeckh, August. *Encyklopädie und Methodologie der philologischen Wissenschaften*. Leipzig: Teubner, 1877.

Boer, Roland. "Introduction: Bakhtin, Genre and Biblical Studies." In *Bakhtin and Genre Theory in Biblical Studies*, edited by idem, 1–7. Atlanta, Georgia: Society of Biblical Literature, 2007.

Bonner, Michael. "Poverty and Charity in the Rise of Islam." In *Poverty and Charity in Middle Eastern Contexts*, edited by idem, Mine Ener, and Amy Singer, 13–30. Albany: State University of New York Press, 2003.

Boullata, Issa J. Introduction to *Literary Structures of Religious Meaning in the Qur'ān*, edited by idem, ix–xii. New York: Routledge, 2000.

Braaten, Carl E. *History and Hermeneutics*. Philadelphia, Pennsylvania: The Westminster Press, 1966.

Bray, Gerald. *Biblical Interpretation: Past & Present*. Downers Grove, Illinois: InterVarsity Press, 1996.

Briggs, Charles Augustus. *Biblical Study: Its Principles, Methods, and History*. New York: Charles Scribner's Sons, 1883.

Bright, John. "The Apodictic Prohibition: Some Observations." *JBL* 92, no. 2 (1973): 185–204.

Brueggemann, Dale A. "Brevard Childs' Canon Criticism: An Example of Post-Critical Naiveté." *JETS* 32, no. 3 (1989): 311–26.

Buhl, Frants. "Über Vergleichungen und Gleichnisse im Qur'ān." *AcOr* 2 (1924): 1–11.

al-Bukhārī. *Ṣaḥīḥ al-Bukhārī*. Damascus: Dār Ibn Kathīr, 2002.

al-Bukhārī. *Ṣaḥīḥ al-Bukhārī*. Vol. 8. Translated by Muhammad Muhsin Khan. Riyadh: Maktabat Dār al-Salām, 1997.

Bullinger, E.W. *Figures of Speech in the Bible, Explained and Illustrated.* London: Eyre & Spottiswoode, 1898.

Bullock, C. Hassell. *Encountering the Book of Psalms: A Literary and Theological Introduction.* Grand Rapids, Michigan: Baker Academic, 2001.

Bultmann, Rudolf. *Die Geschichte der synoptischen Tradition.* 3rd rev. ed. Göttingen: Vandenhoeck & Ruprecht, 1957 [1921].

Bultmann, Rudolf. *The History of the Synoptic Tradition.* Translated by John Marsh. Oxford: Basil Blackwell, 1963.

Buss, Martiṇ J. *Biblical Form Criticism in Its Context.* Sheffield, England: Sheffield Academic Press, 1999.

Buss, Martin J. *The Changing Shape of Form Criticism: A Relational Approach.* Edited by Nickie M. Stipe. Sheffield, England: Sheffield Phoenix Press, 2010.

Buss, Martin J. "Dialogue in and among Genres." In *Bakhtin and Genre Theory in Biblical Studies*, edited by Roland Boer, 9–18. Atlanta, Georgia: Society of Biblical Literature, 2007.

Buss, Martin J. "The Idea of *Sitz im Leben:* History and Critique." *ZAW* 90, no. 2 (1978): 157–70.

Butler, Trent. "Narrative Form Criticism: Dead or Alive?" In *A Biblical Itinerary: In Search of Method, Form and Content: Essays in Honor of George W. Coats*, edited by Eugene E. Carpenter, 39–59. Sheffield, England: Sheffield Academic Press, 1997.

Calder, Norman. "History and Nostalgia: Reflections on John Wansbrough's *The Sectarian Milieu.*" *MTSR* 9, no. 1 (1997): 47–73.

Calder, Norman. "Tafsīr from Ṭabarī to Ibn Kathīr: Problems in the Description of a Genre, Illustrated with Reference to the Story of Abraham." In *Approaches to the Qur'ān*, edited by Gerald R. Hawting and Abdul-Kader A. Shareef, 101–40. New York: Routledge, 1993.

Callaway, Phillip R. "Deut 21:18–21: Proverbial Wisdom and Law." *JBL* 103, no. 3 (1984): 341–52.

Campbell, Antony F. "The Emergence of the Form-Critical and Traditio-Historical Approaches." In *Hebrew Bible / Old Testament: The History of Its Interpretation*, vol. 3, pt. 2, edited by Magne Sæbø, 125–47. Göttingen: Vandenhoeck & Ruprecht, 2015.

Caspari, Carl P. *A Grammar of the Arabic Language.* 2 vols. 3rd rev. ed. Edited and translated by William Wright. Cambridge: Cambridge University Press, 1896–98.

Chaniotis, Angelos. "Ritual Performances of Divine Justice: The Epigraphy of Confession, Atonement, and Exaltation in Roman Asia Minor." In *From Hellenism to Islam: Cultural and Linguistic Change in the Roman Near East*, edited by Hannah M. Cotton, Robert G. Hoyland, Jonathan J. Price, and David J. Wasserstein, 115–53. Cambridge: Cambridge University Press, 2009.

Chapman, Mark D. *Ernst Troeltsch and Liberal Theology: Religion and Cultural Synthesis in Wilhelmine Germany.* Oxford: Oxford University Press, 2001.

Chelhod, Joseph. "Note sur l'emploi du mot *Rabb* dans le Coran." *Arabica* 5, no. 2 (1958): 159–67.

Childs, Brevard S. *Biblical Theology in Crisis.* Philadelphia, Pennsylvania: The Westminster Press, 1970.

Childs, Brevard S. *Biblical Theology of the Old and New Testaments: Theological Reflection on the Christian Bible.* Minneapolis, Minnesota: Fortress Press, 1993.

Childs, Brevard S. *Introduction to the Old Testament as Scripture.* Philadelphia, Pennsylvania: Fortress Press, 1979.

Childs, Brevard S. *The Struggle to Understand Isaiah as Christian Scripture.* Grand Rapids, Michigan: Wm. B. Eerdmans Publishing Company, 2004.

Clines, David J.A. "Contemporary Methods in Hebrew Bible Criticism." In *Hebrew Bible / Old Testament: The History of Its Interpretation*, vol. 3, pt. 2, edited by Magne Sæbø, 148–69. Göttingen: Vandenhoeck & Ruprecht, 2015.

Clines, David J.A. *On the Way to the Postmodern: Old Testament Essays, 1967–1998.* Vol. 2. Sheffield, England: Sheffield Academic Press, 1998.

Coats, George W. *Exodus 1–18. FOTL* 2a. Grand Rapids, Michigan: Wm. B. Eerdmans Publishing Company, 1999.

Coats, George W. *Genesis with an Introduction to Narrative Literature. FOTL* 1. Grand Rapids, Michigan: Wm. B. Eerdmans Publishing Company, 1983.

Coats, George W. "Genres: Why Should They Be Important for Exegesis." In *Saga, Legend, Tale, Novella, Fable: Narrative Forms in Old Testament Literature.* Edited by idem. Sheffield, England: JSOT Press, 1985.

Collins, John J. "Introduction: Towards the Morphology of a Genre." *Semeia* 14 (1979): 1–19.

Conrad, Lawrence I. "Qur'ānic Studies: A Historian's Perspective." In *Results of Contemporary Research on the Qur'ān: The Question of a Historio-Critical Text of the Qur'ān*, edited by Manfred S. Kropp, 9–15. Beirut: Orient-Institut, 2007.

Corvin, Jack W. "A Stylistic and Functional Study of the Prose Prayers in the Historical Narratives of the Old Testament." PhD diss., Emory University, 1972.

Crenshaw, James L. *Gerhard von Rad.* Waco, Texas: Word Books, 1978.

Crenshaw, James L. "Method in Determining Wisdom Influence upon 'Historical' Literature." *JBL* 88, no. 2 (1969): 129–42.

Crollius, Ary A. Roest. "The Prayer in the Qur'ān." *SM* 24 (1975): 223–52.

Crone, Patricia. "The Religion of the Qur'ānic Pagans: God and the Lesser Deities." *Arabica* 57, nos. 2–3 (2010): 151–200.

Crone, Patricia. *Slaves on Horses: The Evolution of the Islamic Polity.* Cambridge: Cambridge University Press, 1980.

Crüsemann, Frank. *Studien zur Formgeschichte von Hymnus und Danklied in Israel.* Neukirchen-Vluyn: Neukirchener Verlag, 1969.

Crutchfield, John Charles. "Circles of Context: An Interpretation of Psalms 107–118." PhD diss., Hebrew Union College, 2000.

Culley, Robert C. *Oral Formulaic Language in the Biblical Psalms.* Toronto: University of Toronto Press, 1967.

Cullmann, Oscar. *Prayer in the New Testament.* Translated by John Bowden. Minneapolis, Minnesota: Fortress Press, 1995.

Davids, Peter H. *The Epistle of James: A Commentary on the Greek Text.* Grand Rapids, Michigan: Wm. B. Eerdmans Publishing Company, 1982.

Davis, Natalie Zemon. Conclusion to *Poverty and Charity in Middle Eastern Contexts*, edited by Michael Bonner, Mine Ener, and Amy Singer, 315–24. Albany: State University of New York Press, 2003.

The Dead Sea Scrolls. Edited by James H. Charlesworth. Vols. 1 and 2. Tübingen: Verlag von J.C.B. Mohr (Paul Siebeck), 1994–95.
Deißmann, Gustav Adolf. "Der Beter Jesus: Ein vergessenes Kapitel der Neutestamentlichen Theologie." *ChrW* 13 (1899): cols. 701–7.
Di Lella, Alexander A. Introduction to *The Wisdom of Ben Sira*, 3–92. Translated by Patrick W. Skehan. New York: Doubleday & Company Inc., 1987.
Dibelius, Martin. "Die alttestamentlichen Motive in der Leidensgeschichte des Petrus- und des Johannes-Evangeliums." In *Abhandlungen zur semitischen Religionskunde und Sprachwissenschaft*, edited by Wilhelm Frankenberg and Friedrich Küchler, 125–50. Giessen: Verlag von Alfred Töpelmann, 1918.
Dibelius, Martin. *Die Formgeschichte des Evangeliums*. 2nd rev. ed. Tübingen: J.C.B. Mohr (Paul Siebeck), 1933 [1919].
Dibelius, Martin. *A Fresh Approach to the New Testament and Early Christian Literature*. New York: Charles Scribner's Sons, 1936.
Dibelius, Martin. *From Tradition to Gospel*. Translated by Bertram Lee Woolf. New York: Charles Scribner's Sons, 1965.
Dibelius, Martin. "Zur Formgeschichte der Evangelien." *ThR*, N.F., 1 (1929): 185–216.
The Didache. Translated by Aelred Cody. In *The Didache in Context: Essays on Its Text, History and Transmission*, edited by Clayton N. Jefford, 3–14. Leiden: E.J. Brill, 1995.
Dietrich, Walter. "Historiography in the Old Testament." In *Hebrew Bible / Old Testament: The History of Its Interpretation*, vol. 3, pt. 2, edited by Magne Sæbø, 467–99. Göttingen: Vandenhoeck & Ruprecht, 2015.
The Divine Liturgy of St. John Chrysostom. Translated by Milan G. Popovich. McKeesport and Duquesne, Pennsylvania: Sava, 1968.
Dodd, Charles H. *The Parables of the Kingdom*. New York: Charles Scribner's Sons, 1961 [1935].
Dommershausen, Werner. *Die Estherrolle: Stil und Ziel einer alttestamentlichen Schrift*. Stuttgart: Verlag Katholisches Bibelwerk, 1968.
Donner, Fred M. "The Historian, the Believers, and the Qurʾān." In *New Perspectives on the Qurʾān: The Qurʾān in Its Historical Context 2*, edited by Gabriel Said Reynolds, 25–37. New York: Routledge, 2011.
Donner, Fred M. *Muhammad and the Believers: At the Origins of Islam*. Cambridge, Massachusetts: The Belknap Press of Harvard University Press, 2010.
Donner, Fred M. *Narratives of Islamic Origins: The Beginnings of Islamic Historical Writing*. Princeton, New Jersey: The Darwin Press, Inc., 1998.
Donner, Fred M. "The Qurʾān in Recent Scholarship: Challenges and Desiderata." In *The Qurʾān in Its Historical Context*, edited by Gabriel Said Reynolds, 29–50. New York: Routledge, 2008.
Draper, Jonathan A. "Torah and Troublesome Apostles in the *Didache* Community." In *The Didache in Modern Research*, edited by idem, 340–63. Leiden: E.J. Brill, 1996.
Driver, S.R. *An Introduction to the Literature of the Old Testament*. New York: Meridian Books, 1957.
Dye, Guillaume. "Pourquoi et comment se fait un texte canonique? Quelques réflexions sur l'histoire du Coran." In *Hérésies: une construction d'identités religieuses*, edited by idem, Christian Brouwer, and Anja van Rompaey, 55–104. Bruxelles: Editions de l'Université de Bruxelles, 2015.

Ernst, Carl W. *How to Read the Qur'ān*. Chapel Hill: University of North Carolina Press, 2011.
Estes, Douglas. *The Questions of Jesus in John: Logic, Rhetoric and Persuasive Discourse*. Leiden: Brill, 2013.
Ettinghausen, Richard. *Antiheidnische Polemik im Koran*. Gelnhausen: F.W. Kalbfleisch, 1934.
Farrin, Raymond. *Structure and Qur'ānic Interpretation*. Ashland, Oregon: White Cloud Press, 2014.
Farris, Stephen. *The Hymns of Luke's Infancy Narratives*. Sheffield, England: JSOT Press, 1985.
Finlay, Timothy D. *The Birth Report Genre in the Hebrew Bible*. Tübingen: Mohr Siebeck, 2005.
Fischer, Wolfdietrich. "Classical Arabic." In *The Semitic Languages*, edited by Robert Hetzron, 187–219. London: Routledge, 1997.
Fischer, Wolfdietrich. *Grammatik des klassischen Arabisch*. Wiesbaden: Otto Harrassowitz, 1972.
Fontaine, Carole R. "The Sage in Family and Tribe." In *The Sage in Israel and the Ancient Near East*, edited by John G. Gammie and Leo G. Perdue, 155–64. Winona Lake, Indiana: Eisenbrauns, 1990.
Forster, Michael N. Introduction to *Philosophical Writings*, by Johann Gottfried von Herder, vii–xxxv. Cambridge: Cambridge University Press, 2002.
Fox, Michael V. *Character and Ideology in the Book of Esther*. 2nd ed. Grand Rapids, Michigan: Wm. B. Eerdmans Publishing Company, 2001.
Fox, Michael V. *Proverbs 1–9*. New Haven, Connecticut: Yale University Press, 2000.
Fugate, Joe K. *The Psychological Basis of Herder's Aesthetics*. Paris: Mouton & Co., 1966.
Futato, Mark D. *The Book of Psalms*. Wheaton, Illinois: Tyndale House Publishers, 2009.
Gager, John G. *Curse Tablets and Binding Spells from the Ancient World*. Oxford: Oxford University Press, 1992.
Gaudefroy-Demombynes, Maurice. "Sur quelques noms d'Allāh dans le Coran." *Annuaire* (1929): 3–21.
Gelin, Albert. "La question des 'relectures' bibliques à l'intérieur d'une tradition vivante." In *Sacra Pagina*, edited by Joseph Coppens, Albert Descamps, and Édouard Massaux, 303–15. Vol. 1. Gembloux, Belgium: J. Duculot, 1959.
Genesis. Translated by Hermann Gunkel. 3rd ed. Göttingen: Vandenhoeck & Ruprecht, 1910.
Gerstenberger, Erhard S. *Der bittende Mensch: Bittritual und Klagelied des Einzelnen im Alten Testament*. Neukirchen: Neukirchener Verlag, 1980.
Gerstenberger, Erhard S. "Psalms." In *Old Testament Form Criticism*, edited by John H. Hayes, 179–223. San Antonio, Texas: Trinity University Press, 1977.
Gerstenberger, Erhard S. *Psalms: Part I with an Introduction to Cultic Poetry*. *FOTL* 14. Grand Rapids, Michigan: Wm. B. Eerdmans Publishing Company, 1988.
Gerstenberger, Erhard S. *Wesen und Herkunft des "apodiktischen Rechts."* Neukirchen: Neukirchener Verlag des Erziehungsvereins, 1965.
Gerstenberger, Erhard S. "The Woe-Oracles of the Prophets." *JBL* 81, no. 3 (1962): 249–63.
Geyer, Rudolf. "Zur Strophik des Qurāns." *WZKM* 22 (1908): 265–86.
Gianotto, Claudio. "The Lucan Parable of the Good Samaritan and Its Interpretations in Christian Antiquity." In *The Quest for a Common Humanity: Human Dignity and Otherness in the Religious Traditions of the Mediterranean*, edited by Katell Berthelot and Matthias Morgenstern, 125–38. Leiden: Brill, 2011.

Gilliot, Claude. "Les sept 'lectures': Corps social et écriture révélée (Première partie)." *SI* 61 (1985): 5–25.
Gilliot, Claude. "Les sept 'lectures': Corps social et écriture révélée (Seconde partie)." *SI* 63 (1986): 49–62.
Gjesdal, Kristin. "Hegel and Herder on Art, History, and Reason." *P&L* 30 (2006): 17–32.
Gods, Heroes, and Monsters: A Sourcebook of Greek, Roman, and Near Eastern Myths. Edited by Carolina López-Ruiz. Oxford: Oxford University Press, 2014.
Goethe, Johann Wolfgang von. *Goethes Werke: Schriften zur Kunst, Schriften zur Literatur, Maximen und Reflexionen*. 12th rev. ed. München: Verlag C.H. Beck, 1994.
Goitein, Fritz. "Das Gebet im Qorān." Diss., Universität Frankfurt am Main, 1923.
Goitein, Fritz. "Das Gebet im Qorān." Published Abstract. Diss., Frankfurt am Main, 1923.
Goitein, Fritz. *Studies in Islamic History and Institutions*. Leiden: Brill, 2010.
Goldziher, Ignaz. *Die Richtungen der islamischen Koranauslegung*. Leiden: E.J. Brill, 1920.
Goldziher, Ignaz. *Schools of Koranic Commentators*. Edited and translated by Wolfgang H. Behn. Wiesbaden: Harrassowitz Verlag, 2006.
Gracyk, Theodore A. "Sublimity, Ugliness, and Formlessness in Kant's Aesthetic Theory." *JAAC* 45, no. 1 (1986): 49–56.
Graf, Fritz. "Fluch und Segen: Ein Grabepigramm und seine Welt." In *Zona archeologica: Festschrift für Hans Peter Isler zum 60. Geburtstag*, edited by Sabrina Buzzi, Daniel Käch, Erich Kistler, Elena Mango, Marek Palaczyk, and Olympia Stefani, 183–91. Bonn: Habelt, 2001.
Graf, Fritz, and Sarah Iles Johnston. *Ritual Texts for the Afterlife: Orpheus and the Bacchic Gold Tablets*. New York: Routledge, 2007.
Greenberg, Moshe. *Biblical Prose Prayer as a Window to the Popular Religion of Ancient Israel*. Berkeley: University of California Press, 1983.
Greenwood, David. "Rhetorical Criticism and Formgeschichte: Some Methodological Considerations." *JBL* 89, no. 4 (1970): 418–26.
Greßmann, Hugo. *Albert Eichhorn und Die Religionsgeschichtliche Schule*. Göttingen: Vandenhoeck & Ruprecht, 1914.
Greßmann, Hugo. "Die literarische Analyse Deuterojesajas." *ZAW* 34, no. 4 (1914): 254–97.
Greßmann, Hugo. *Der Messias*. Göttingen: Vandenhoeck & Ruprecht, 1929.
Gunkel, Hermann. "Formen der Hymnen." *ThR* 20, nos. 10–11 (1917): 265–304.
Gunkel, Hermann. "The 'Historical Movement' in the Study of Religion." *ExpTim* 38, no. 12 (1927): 532–36.
Gunkel, Hermann. "Die israelitische Literatur." In *Die orientalischen Literaturen*, edited by Paul Hinneberg, 51–102. Leipzig: Verlag B.G. Teubner, 1906.
Gunkel, Hermann. *The Legends of Genesis*. Translated by W.H. Carruth. Chicago: The Open Court Publishing Co., 1901.
Gunkel, Hermann. "The Literature of Ancient Israel." Translated by Armin Siedlecki. In *Relating to the Text: Interdisciplinary and Form-Critical Insights on the Bible*, edited by Timothy J. Sandoval and Carleen Mandolfo, 26–83. London: T&T Clark International, 2003.
Gunkel, Hermann. *Reden und Aufsätze*. Göttingen: Vandenhoeck & Ruprecht, 1913.
Gunkel, Hermann. *Die Sagen der Genesis*. Göttingen: Vandenhoeck & Ruprecht, 1901.
Gunkel, Hermann. *What Remains of the Old Testament and Other Essays*. New York: The Macmillan Company, 1928.

Gunkel, Hermann, and Joachim Begrich. *Einleitung in die Psalmen: Die Gattungen der religiösen Lyrik Israels.* 4th ed. Göttingen: Vandenhoeck & Ruprecht, 1985 [1933].

Gunkel, Hermann, and Joachim Begrich. *Introduction to Psalms: The Genres of the Religious Lyric of Israel.* Translated by James D. Nogalski. Macon, Georgia: Mercer University Press, 1998.

Gunneweg, Antonius H.J. *Vom Verstehen des Alten Testaments: Eine Hermeneutik.* Göttingen: Vandenhoeck & Ruprecht, 1977.

Güttgemanns, Erhardt. *Offene Fragen zur Formgeschichte des Evangeliums: Eine methodologische Skizze der Grundlagenproblematik der Form- und Redaktionsgeschichte.* 2nd rev. ed. München: Chr. Kaiser Verlag, 1971.

Gwynne, Rosalind Ward. "Patterns of Address." In *The Blackwell Companion to the Qur'ān*, edited by Andrew Rippin, 73–87. Oxford: Blackwell Publishing, 2006.

Habel, Norman. *Literary Criticism of the Old Testament.* Philadelphia: Fortress Press, 1986 [1971].

Hainsworth, Bryan. *The Iliad: A Commentary.* Vol. 3. Cambridge: Cambridge University Press, 1993.

Hals, Ronald M. "Legend: A Case Study in Old Testament Form-Critical Terminology." *CBQ* 34, no. 2 (1972): 166–76.

Hammann, Konrad. *Hermann Gunkel: Eine Biographie.* Tübingen: Mohr Siebeck, 2014.

Harnack, Adolf von. *Reden und Aufsätze.* Vol. 2. Gieszen: J. Ricker'sche Verlagsbuchhandlung, 1904.

Harrington, Daniel J. *Interpreting the New Testament.* Wilmington, Delaware: Michael Glazier, Inc., 1979.

Harrington, Daniel J. *Jesus Ben Sira of Jerusalem: A Biblical Guide to Living Wisely.* Collegeville, Minnesota: Liturgical Press, 2005.

Hartog, Paul. *Polycarp and the New Testament: The Occasion, Rhetoric, Theme, and Unity of the Epistle to the Philippians and Its Allusions to New Testament Literature.* Tübingen: Mohr Siebeck, 2002.

Hayes, John H. *Interpreting Ancient Israelite History, Prophecy, and Law.* Eugene, Oregon: Cascade Books, 2013.

Hayes, John H., and Frederick C. Prussner. *Old Testament Theology: Its History and Development.* Atlanta, Georgia: John Knox Press, 1985.

Hegel, Georg Wilhelm Friedrich. *Vorlesungen über die Ästhetik I.* Frankfurt am Main: Suhrkamp, 1970.

Hegel, Georg Wilhelm Friedrich. *Vorlesungen über die Ästhetik II.* Frankfurt am Main: Suhrkamp, 1970.

Heidemann, Stefan. "The Evolving Representation of the Early Islamic Empire and Its Religion on Coin Imagery." In *The Qur'ān in Context: Historical and Literary Investigations into the Qur'ānic Milieu*, edited by Angelika Neuwirth, Nicolai Sinai, and Michael Marx, 149–95. Leiden: Brill, 2011.

Heiler, Friedrich. *Das Gebet: Eine religionsgeschichtliche und religionspsychologische Untersuchung.* 5th ed. München: Verlag von Ernst Reinhardt, 1923.

Heiler, Friedrich. *Prayer: A Study in the History and Psychology of Religion.* Translated by Samuel McComb. Oxford: Oxford University Press, 1932.

Heim, Knut M. "The Phenomenon and Literature of Wisdom in Its Near Eastern Context and in the Biblical Wisdom Books." In *Hebrew Bible / Old Testament: The History of Its*

Interpretation, vol. 3, pt. 2, edited by Magne Sæbø, 559–93. Göttingen: Vandenhoeck & Ruprecht, 2015.
Hempel, Johannes. *Die althebräische Literatur und ihr hellenistisch-jüdisches Nachleben.* Wildpark-Potsdam: Akademische Verlagsgesellschaft Athenaion, 1930.
Hengel, Martin. *Studies in the Gospel of Mark.* Eugene, Oregon: Wipf & Stock Publishers, 2003.
Herder, Johann Gottfried von. *Abhandlung über den Ursprung der Sprache.* Berlin: Bey Christian Friedrich Voß, 1772.
Herder, Johann Gottfried von. *Auch eine Philosophie der Geschichte zur Bildung der Menschheit.* S.l.: s.n., 1774.
Herder, Johann Gottfried von. *Briefe, das Studium der Theologie betreffend.* Vol. 1. 2nd rev. ed. Weimar: Carl Ludolf Hoffman, 1785.
Herder, Johann Gottfried von. *Kleinere Aufsätze I.* Cambridge: Cambridge University Press, 1952.
Herder, Johann Gottfried von. *Kritische Wälder.* Edited by Heinrich Dünker. Berlin: Gustav Hempel, 1879.
Herder, Johann Gottfried von. *Vom Geist der ebräischen Poesie.* 2 vols. Deßau: Verlag-Kasse, 1782–83.
Hering, James P. *The Colossian and Ephesian Haustafeln in Theological Context: An Analysis of Their Origins, Relationship, and Message.* New York: Peter Lang, 2007.
Hermisson, Hans-Jürgen. *Studien zur israelitischen Spruchweisheit.* Neukirchen: Neukirchener Verlag des Erziehungsvereins, 1968.
Hinds, Martin. "Sayf ibn ʿUmar's Sources on Arabia." In *Studies in Early Islamic History*, edited by Jere Bacharach, Lawrence I. Conrad, and Patricia Crone, 143–59. Princeton, New Jersey: The Darwin Press, Inc., 1996.
Hirschfeld, Hartwig. *New Researches into the Composition and Exegesis of the Qorān.* London: Royal Asiatic Society, 1902.
Hjelde, Sigurd. *Sigmund Mowinckel und seine Zeit: Leben und Werk eines norwegischen Alttestamentlers.* Tübingen: Mohr Siebeck, 2006.
Hornig, Barbara. "Das Prosagebet der nachexilischen Literatur." Published Abstract. Diss., Universität Leipzig, 1957. *ThLZ* 83, no. 9 (1958): cols. 644–46.
Horovitz, Josef. *Koranische Untersuchungen.* Berlin: Walter de Gruyter, 1926.
Hultgren, Arland J. *Jesus and His Adversaries: The Form and Function of the Conflict Stories in the Synoptic Tradition.* Minneapolis, Minnesota: Augsburg Publishing House, 1979.
Human, Dirk J. "Psalm 136: A Liturgy with Reference to Creation and History." In *Psalms and Liturgy*, edited by idem and Cas J.A. Vos, 73–88. London: T&T Clark International, 2004.
Ibn Isḥāq. *Das Leben Muhammed's nach Muhammed Ibn Ishâk.* Edited by Ferdinand Wüstenfeld. Vol. 1, pt. 2. Göttingen: Dieterichsche Universitäts-Buchhandlung, 1859.
Ibn al-Kalbī, Abū l-Mundhir Hishām b. Muḥammad. *Le livre des idoles* (*Kitāb al-aṣnām*). 2nd ed. Edited by Ahmed Zeki Pacha. Cairo: Imprimerie bibliothèque egyptienne, 1924.
Izutsu, Toshihiko. *The Concept of Belief in Islamic Theology: A Semantic Analysis of Īmān and Islām.* Tokyo: The Keio Institute of Cultural and Linguistic Studies, 1965.
Izutsu, Toshihiko. *Ethico-Religious Concepts in the Qurʾān.* Montreal: McGill-Queen's University Press, 2002.
Izutsu, Toshihiko. *God and Man in the Koran: Semantics of the Koranic Weltanschauung.* Tokyo: The Keio Institute of Cultural and Linguistic Studies, 1964.

Izutsu, Toshihiko. *Language and Magic: Studies in the Magical Function of Speech*. Tokyo: The Keio Institute of Philological Studies, 1956.
Jeffery, Arthur. *The Foreign Vocabulary of the Qur'ān*. Leiden: Brill, 2007 [1938].
Jeffery, Arthur. *The Qur'ān as Scripture*. New York: Books for Libraries, 1980 [1952].
Jeremias, Joachim. *Die Gleichnisse Jesu*. 8th rev. ed. Göttingen: Vandenhoeck & Ruprecht, 1970.
Jolles, André. *Einfache Formen: Legende, Sage, Mythe, Rätsel, Spruch, Kasus, Memorabile, Märchen, Witz*. Halle: Max Niemeyer Verlag, 1930.
Jomier, Jacques. "Le nom divin 'al-Raḥmān' dans le Coran." In *Mélanges Louis Massignon*, 361–81. Vol. 2. Damascus: Institut Français de Damas, 1957.
Jones, Alan. *Arabic through the Qur'ān*. Cambridge: The Islamic Texts Society, 2005.
Jülicher, Adolf. *Die Gleichnisreden Jesu*. 2 vols. Tübingen: Verlag von J.C.B. Mohr (Paul Siebeck), 1888–99.
Kandil, Lamya. "Die Schwüre in den mekkanischen Suren." In *The Qur'ān as Text*, edited by Stefan Wild, 41–57. Leiden: E.J. Brill, 1996.
Kapelrud, A.S. Review of *The Divine Warrior in Early Israel*, by P.D. Miller, Jr. *JSS* 20, no. 1 (1975): 116–17.
Kassis, Hanna E. *A Concordance of the Qur'ān*. Berkeley: University of California Press, 1983.
Kirk, Alan. *The Composition of the Sayings Source: Genre, Synchrony, and Wisdom Redaction in Q*. Leiden: Brill, 1998.
Klatt, Werner. *Hermann Gunkel: Zu seiner Theologie der Religionsgeschichte und zur Entstehung der formgeschichtlichen Methode*. Göttingen: Vandenhoeck & Ruprecht, 1969.
Klingbeil, Martin G. "Off the Beaten Track: An Evangelical Reading of the Psalms without Gunkel." *BBR* 16, no. 1 (2006): 25–39.
Kloppenborg, John S. *The Formation of Q: Trajectories in Ancient Wisdom Collections*. Philadelphia, Pennsylvania: Fortress Press, 1987.
Kneidel, Greg. "*Ars Prædicandi:* Theories and Practice." In *The Oxford Handbook of the Early Modern Sermon*, edited by Peter McCullough and Hugh Adlington, 3–20. Oxford: Oxford University Press, 2011.
Knierim, Rolf P., and George W. Coats. *Numbers*. *FOTL* 4. Grand Rapids, Michigan: Wm. B. Eerdmans Publishing Company, 2005.
Koch, Klaus. *The Growth of the Biblical Tradition: The Form-Critical Method*. Translated by S.M. Cupitt. New York: Charles Scribner's Sons, 1969.
Koch, Klaus. *Die Profeten I: Assyrische Zeit*. Stuttgart: Verlag W. Kohlhammer, 1978.
Koch, Klaus. *The Prophets*. Vol. 1. Translated by Margaret Kohl. Philadelphia, Pennsylvania: Fortress Press, 1988.
Koch, Klaus. *Was ist Formgeschichte? Neue Wege der Bibelexegese*. 2nd rev. ed. Neukirchen: Neukirchener Verlag des Erziehungsvereins, 1967.
Köhler, Ludwig. *Deuterojesaja (Jesaja 40–55) stilkritisch untersucht*. Giessen: Verlag von Alfred Töpelmann, 1923.
Köhler, Ludwig. *Kleine Lichter: Fünfzig Bibelstellen erklärt*. Zürich: Zwingli-Verlag, 1945.
Law, David R. *The Historical-Critical Method*. London: T&T Clark International, 2012.
Lee, Han Young. *From History to Narrative Hermeneutics*. Frankfurt am Main: Peter Lang, 2004.

Lemaire, André. "The Sage in School and Temple." In *The Sage in Israel and the Ancient Near East*, edited by John G. Gammie and Leo G. Perdue, 165–81. Winona Lake, Indiana: Eisenbrauns, 1990.
Lidzbarski, Mark. "Ubi sunt qui ante nos in mundo fuere." *Isl.* 8, nos. 3–4 (1918): 300.
Lierman, John. *The New Testament Moses.* Tübingen: Mohr Siebeck, 2004.
Lightfoot, J.L. *The Sibylline Oracles.* Oxford: Oxford University Press, 2007.
Lindblom, Johannes. *Die literarische Gattung der prophetischen Literatur: Eine literargeschichtliche Untersuchung zum Alten Testament.* Uppsala: A.-B. Lundequistska Bokhandeln, 1924.
Lohmann, Theodor. "Die Gleichnisreden Muḥammeds im Koran." *MIO* 12 (1966): 75–118.
Lohmann, Theodor. "Die Gleichnisreden Muḥammeds im Koran (2. Teil)." *MIO* 12 (1966): 241–87.
Long, Burke O. *1 Kings with an Introduction to Historical Literature. FOTL* 9. Grand Rapids, Michigan: Wm. B. Eerdmans Publishing Company, 1984.
Long, Burke O. *2 Kings. FOTL* 10. Grand Rapids, Michigan: Wm. B. Eerdmans Publishing Company, 1991.
Lord, Albert B. *The Singer of Tales.* New York: Atheneum, 1978.
Lowth, Robert. *De sacra poesi Hebræorum.* Oxford: Clarendon Press, 1753.
Lüdemann, Gerd. "Die 'Religionsgeschichtliche Schule' und die Neutestamentliche Wissenschaft." In *Die "Religionsgeschichtliche Schule": Facetten eines theologischen Umbruchs*, edited by idem, 9–22. Frankfurt am Main: Peter Lang, 1996.
Lüdemann, Gerd, and Martin Schröder. *Die religionsgeschichtliche Schule in Göttingen: Eine Dokumentation.* Göttingen: Vandenhoeck & Ruprecht, 1987.
Lüling, Günter. *Über den Urkoran: Ansätze zur Rekonstruktion der vorislamisch-christlichen Strophenlieder im Koran.* 2nd ed. Erlangen: Verlagsbuchhandlung H. Lüling, 1993.
Luxenberg, Christoph. *Die syro-aramäische Lesart des Koran: Ein Beitrag zur Entschlüsselung der Koransprache.* Berlin: Das Arabische Buch, 2000.
Madigan, Daniel A. *The Qur'ān's Self-Image: Writing and Authority in Islam's Scripture.* Princeton, New Jersey: Princeton University Press, 2001.
Madigan, Daniel A. "Reflections on Some Current Directions in Qur'ānic Studies." *MW* 85, nos. 3–4 (1995): 345–62.
Magonet, Jonathan. "On Reading Psalms as Liturgy: Psalms 96–99." In *The Shape and Shaping of the Book of Psalms: The Current State of Scholarship*, edited by Nancy L. deClaissé-Walford, 161–77. Atlanta, Georgia: SBL Press, 2014.
The Making of Homeric Verse: The Collected Papers of Milman Parry. Edited by Adam Parry. Oxford: Clarendon Press, 1971.
Marshall, David. *God, Muḥammad and the Unbelievers: A Qur'ānic Study.* Richmond, Surrey: Curzon Press, 1999.
Martyn, James Louis. *History and Theology in the Fourth Gospel.* 3rd rev. ed. Louisville, Kentucky: Westminster John Knox Press, 2003.
Masud, Muhammad Khalid, Brinkley Messick, and David S. Powers. "Muftis, Fatwas, and Islamic Legal Interpretation." In *Islamic Legal Interpretation: Muftis and Their Fatwas*, edited by idem, 3–32. Cambridge, Massachusetts: Harvard University Press, 1996.
Mathews, Thomas F. *The Early Churches of Constantinople: Architecture and Liturgy.* University Park: The Pennsylvania State University Press, 1971.

McAuliffe, Jane Dammen. Introduction to *The Cambridge Companion to the Qur'ān*, edited by eadem, 1–20. Cambridge: Cambridge University Press, 2006.
McCann, J. Clinton, Jr. *The Book of Psalms: Introduction, Commentary, and Reflections. NIB* 4. Nashville, Tennessee: Abingdon Press, 1996.
McCann, J. Clinton, Jr. "The Shape and Shaping of the Psalter: Psalms in Their Literary Context." In *The Oxford Handbook of the Psalms*, edited by William P. Brown, 350–62. Oxford: Oxford University Press, 2014.
McDonald, James I.H. *Kerygma and Didache: The Articulation and Structure of the Earliest Christian Message.* Cambridge: Cambridge University Press, 1980.
McKnight, Edgar V. *What is Form Criticism?* Philadelphia, Pennsylvania: Fortress Press, 1969.
McLaughlin, John L. *The Marzēaḥ in the Prophetic Literature: References and Allusions in Light of the Extra-Biblical Evidence.* Leiden: Brill, 2001.
Mead, Margaret. *Culture and Commitment: A Study of the Generation Gap.* Garden City, New York: Natural History Press, 1970.
Metso, Sarianna. "In Search of the *Sitz im Leben* of the *Community Rule.*" In *The Provo International Conference on the Dead Sea Scrolls: Technological Innovations, New Texts, and Reformulated Issues*, edited by Donald W. Parry and Eugene Ulrich, 306–15. Leiden: Brill, 1999.
Meyendorff, Paul. Introduction to *On the Divine Liturgy: St. Germanus of Constantinople*, 9–54. Translated by idem. Crestwood, New York: St. Vladimir's Seminary Press, 1984.
Miller, Patrick D. *They Cried to the Lord: The Form and Theology of Biblical Prayer.* Minneapolis, Minnesota: Fortress Press, 1994.
Mir, Mustansir. "The Qur'ān as Literature." *R&L* 20, no. 1 (1988): 49–64.
Mir, Mustansir. "The Sūra as a Unity: A Twentieth Century Development in Qur'ān Exegesis." In *Approaches to the Qur'ān*, edited by Gerald R. Hawting and Abdul-Kader A. Shareef, 211–24. New York: Routledge, 1993.
Moore, Carey A. Introduction to *Esther*, xvi–lxiv. Translated by idem. New York: Doubleday & Company Inc., 1971.
Morgan, Donn F. *Wisdom in the Old Testament Traditions.* Atlanta, Georgia: John Knox Press, 1981.
Moulton, Richard G. *The Literary Study of the Bible: An Account of the Leading Forms of Literature Represented in the Sacred Writings.* London: Isbister and Company Limited, 1896.
Mowinckel, Sigmund. "Psalm Criticism between 1900 and 1935 (Ugarit and Psalm Exegesis)." *VT* 5, fasc. 1 (1955): 13–33.
Mowinckel, Sigmund. *Psalmenstudien II: Das Thronbesteigungsfest Jahwäs und der Ursprung der Eschatologie.* Amsterdam: Verlag P. Schippers, 1961 [1922].
Mowinckel, Sigmund. *The Psalms in Israel's Worship* [*Offersang og Sangoffer*]. 2 vols. Translated by D.R. Ap-Thomas. Oxford: Blackwell, 1962 [1951].
Muilenburg, James. "Form Criticism and Beyond." *JBL* 88, no. 1 (1969): 1–18.
Müller, David Heinrich. *Die Propheten in ihrer ursprünglichen Form.* Vol. 1. Wien: Alfred Hölder, 1896.
Müller, Friedrich Max. *Einleitung in die vergleichende Religionswissenschaft.* Strassburg: Verlag von Karl J. Trübner, 1874.
Murphy, Catherine M. *Wealth in the Dead Sea Scrolls and in the Qumran Community.* Leiden: Brill, 2002.

Murphy, Roland E. *Wisdom Literature: Job, Proverbs, Ruth, Canticles, Ecclesiastes, and Esther. FOTL* 13. Grand Rapids, Michigan: Wm. B. Eerdmans Publishing Company, 1981.

Nagel, Tilman. *Der Koran: Einführung, Texte, Erläuterungen.* 4th ed. München: C.H. Beck, 2002.

Nasuti, Harry P. *Defining the Sacred Songs: Genre, Tradition and the Post-Critical Interpretation of the Psalms.* Sheffield, England: Sheffield Academic Press, 1999.

Neff, Robert W. "Saga." In *Saga, Legend, Tale, Novella, Fable: Narrative Forms in Old Testament Literature*, edited by George W. Coats, 17–32. Sheffield, England: JSOT Press, 1985.

Neuwirth, Angelika. "Einige Bemerkungen zum besonderen sprachlichen und literarischen Charakter des Koran." In *Deutscher Orientalistentag*, vol. 1, edited by Wolfgang Voigt, 736–39. Wiesbaden: Franz Steiner Verlag, 1977.

Neuwirth, Angelika. "Erzählen als kanonischer Prozeß: Die Mose-Erzählung im Wandel der koranischen Geschichte." In *Islamstudien ohne Ende: Festschrift für Werner Ende zum 65. Geburtstag*, edited by Rainer Brunner, Monika Gronke, Jens Peter Laut, and Ulrich Rebstock, 323–44. Würzburg: Ergon Verlag, 2002.

Neuwirth, Angelika. *Der Koran als Text der Spätantike.* 3rd ed. Berlin: Verlag der Weltreligionen, 2013 [2010].

Neuwirth, Angelika. "Meccan Texts – Medinan Additions? Politics and the Re-reading of Liturgical Communications." In *Words, Texts and Concepts Cruising the Mediterranean Sea*, edited by Rüdiger Arnzen and Jörn Thielmann, 71–93. Leuven: Peeters, 2004.

Neuwirth, Angelika. "Qurʾānic Literary Structure Revisited: Sūrat ar-Raḥmān between Mythic Account and Decodation of Myth." In *Story-Telling in the Framework of Non-fictional Arabic Literature*, edited by Stefan Leder, 388–420. Wiesbaden: Harrassowitz Verlag, 1998.

Neuwirth, Angelika. "Qurʾānic Readings of the Psalms." In *The Qurʾān in Context: Historical and Literary Investigations into the Qurʾānic Milieu*, edited by eadem, Nicolai Sinai, and Michael Marx, 733–78. Leiden: Brill, 2011.

Neuwirth, Angelika. "Qurʾānic Studies and Philology: Qurʾānic Textual Politics of Staging, Penetrating, and Finally Eclipsing Biblical Tradition." In *Qurʾānic Studies Today*, edited by eadem and Michael A. Sells, 178–206. New York: Routledge, 2016.

Neuwirth, Angelika. "Referentiality and Textuality in Sūrat al-Ḥijr: Some Observations on the Qurʾānic 'Canonical Process' and the Emergence of a Community." In *Literary Structures of Religious Meaning in the Qurʾān*, edited by Issa J. Boullata, 143–72. New York: Routledge, 2000.

Neuwirth, Angelika. *Scripture, Poetry and the Making of a Community: Reading the Qurʾān as a Literary Text.* Oxford: Oxford University Press, 2014.

Neuwirth, Angelika. "Structural, Linguistic, and Literary Features." In *The Cambridge Companion to the Qurʾān*, edited by Jane Dammen McAuliffe, 97–113. Cambridge: Cambridge University Press, 2006.

Neuwirth, Angelika. *Studien zur Komposition der mekkanischen Suren.* 2nd ed. Berlin: Walter de Gruyter, 2007 [1981].

Neuwirth, Angelika. "Symmetrie und Paarbildung in der koranischen Eschatologie: Philologisch-Stilistisches zu Sūrat ar-Raḥmān." In *Mélanges de l'Université Saint-Joseph* 50 (1984): 445–80.

Neuwirth, Angelika. "Two Views of History and Human Future: Qur'ānic and Biblical Renderings of Divine Promises." *JQS* 10, no. 1 (2008): 1–20.

Neuwirth, Angelika. "Vom Rezitationstext über die Liturgie zum Kanon: Zu Entstehung und Wiederauflösung der Surenkomposition im Verlauf der Entwicklung eines islamischen Kultus." In *The Qur'ān as Text*, edited by Stefan Wild, 69–105. Leiden: E.J. Brill, 1996.

Neuwirth, Angelika. "Zum neueren Stand der Koranforschung." In *Deutscher Orientalistentag*, edited by Fritz Steppat, 183–89. Wiesbaden: Franz Steiner Verlag, 1983.

Neuwirth, Angelika. "Zur Struktur der Yūsuf-Sūre." In *Studien aus Arabistik und Semitistik: Anton Spitaler zum 70. Geburtstag von seinen Schülern überreicht*, edited by Werner Diem and Stefan Wild, 123–52. Wiesbaden: Otto Harrassowitz, 1980.

Neuwirth, Angelika, and Karl Neuwirth. "Sūrat al-Fātiḥa – 'Eröffnung' des Text-Corpus Koran oder 'Introitus' der Gebetsliturgie?" In *Text, Methode und Grammatik: Wolfgang Richter zum 65. Geburtstag*, edited by Walter Gross, Hubert Irsigler, and Theodor Seidl, 331–57. St. Ottilien: EOS Verlag, 1991.

Neuwirth, Angelika, and Michael A. Sells. Introduction to *Qur'ānic Studies Today*, edited by eadem, 1–14. New York: Routledge, 2016.

The New Oxford Annotated Bible: New Revised Standard Version with the Apocrypha. 4th rev. ed. Edited by Michael D. Coogan. Oxford: Oxford University Press, 2010.

Niebuhr, Barthold Georg. *Römische Geschichte*. 3 vols. Berlin: Realschulbuchhandlung, 1811–32.

Nöldeke, Theodor. *Geschichte des Qorāns*. 2 vols. 2nd ed. Edited by Friedrich Schwally. Leipzig: Dieterich'sche Verlagsbuchhandlung, 1909–19 [1860].

Nöldeke, Theodor. *Neue Beiträge zur semitischen Sprachwissenschaft*. Strassburg: Verlag von Karl J. Trübner, 1910.

Nöldeke, Theodor, Friedrich Schwally, Gotthelf Bergsträßer, and Otto Pretzl. *The History of the Qur'ān*. Translated by Wolfgang H. Behn. Leiden: Brill, 2013.

Norden, Eduard. *Agnostos Theos: Untersuchungen zur Formengeschichte religiöser Rede*. Leipzig: Verlag B.G. Teubner, 1913.

Norris, H.T. "Qiṣaṣ Elements in the Qur'ān." In *Arabic Literature to the End of the Umayyad Period*, edited by A.F.L. Beeston, T.M. Johnstone, R.B. Serjeant, and G.R. Smith, 246–59. Cambridge: Cambridge University Press, 1983.

Noth, Albrecht. "Der Charakter der ersten großen Sammlungen von Nachrichten zur frühen Kalifenzeit." *Isl.* 47, no. 1 (1971): 168–99.

Noth, Albrecht. *Quellenkritische Studien zu Themen, Formen und Tendenzen frühislamischer Geschichtsüberlieferung*. Vol. 1: Themen und Formen. Bonn: Selbstverlag des Orientalischen Seminars der Universität Bonn, 1973.

Noth, Martin. *Developing Lines of Theological Thought in Germany*. Virginia: Union Theological Seminary, 1963.

Noth, Martin. *Überlieferungsgeschichte des Pentateuch*. Stuttgart: Verlag W. Kohlhammer, 1948.

Noth, Martin. *Überlieferungsgeschichtliche Studien: Die sammelnden und bearbeitenden Geschichtswerke im Alten Testament*. Halle: Max Niemeyer Verlag, 1943.

Null, Ashley. "Official Tudor Homilies." In *The Oxford Handbook of the Early Modern Sermon*, edited by Peter McCullough and Hugh Adlington, 348–65. Oxford: Oxford University Press, 2011.

Oden, Robert A., Jr. *The Bible without Theology: The Theological Tradition and Alternatives to It.* San Francisco, California: Harper & Row, 1987.
Overbeck, Franz. "Über die Anfänge der patristischen Literatur." *HZ* 48, no. 3 (1882): 417–72.
Özen, Alf. "Die Göttinger Wurzeln der 'Religionsgeschichtlichen Schule.'" In *Die "Religionsgeschichtliche Schule": Facetten eines theologischen Umbruchs*, edited by Gerd Lüdemann, 23–64. Frankfurt am Main: Peter Lang, 1996.
Özen, Alf. "*Die Religion in Geschichte und Gegenwart* als Beispiel für Hoch-Zeit und Niedergang der 'Religionsgeschichtlichen Schule' (*II. Teil: RGG²*)." In *Die "Religionsgeschichtliche Schule": Facetten eines theologischen Umbruchs*, edited by Gerd Lüdemann, 243–98. Frankfurt am Main: Peter Lang, 1996.
Paret, Rudi. *Der Koran: Kommentar und Konkordanz.* Stuttgart: Verlag W. Kohlhammer, 1971.
Paret, Rudi. "Der Koran als Geschichtsquelle." *Isl.* 37, nos. 1–3 (1961): 24–42.
Pascal, Roy. "The 'Sturm und Drang' Movement." *MLR* 47, no. 2 (1952): 129–51.
Pernot, Laurent. "The Rhetoric of Religion." In *New Chapters in the History of Rhetoric*, edited by idem, 327–46. Leiden: Brill, 2009.
Peters, Francis E. "The Quest of the Historical Muḥammad." *IJMES* 23, no. 3 (1991): 291–315.
Prémare, Alfred-Louis de. *Aux origines du Coran.* Paris: Téraèdre, 2004.
Prémare, Alfred-Louis de. *Joseph et Muḥammad: Le chapitre 12 du Coran.* Aix-en-Provence: Publications de l'Université de Provence, 1989.
Puglisi, Mario. *La Preghiera.* Torino: Fratelli Bocca, 1928.
al-Qur'ān al-karīm. Cairo: s.n., 1924.
The Qur'ān. Translated by Alan Jones. Cambridge: Gibb Memorial Trust, 2007.
The Qur'ān: Style and Contents. Edited by Andrew Rippin. Aldershot, Hampshire: Ashgate Variorum, 2001.
The Qur'ān: Translated, with a Critical Re-arrangement of the Sūrahs. 2 vols. Translated by Richard Bell. Edinburgh: T&T Clark, 1937.
The Qur'ān Seminar Commentary / Le Qur'ān Seminar: A Collaborative Study of 50 Qur'ānic Passages / Commentaire collaboratif de 50 passages coraniques. Edited by Mehdi Azaiez, Gabriel Said Reynolds, Tommaso Tesei, and Hamza M. Zafer. Berlin: Walter de Gruyter, 2016.
Qutbuddin, Tahera. "*Khuṭba:* The Evolution of Early Arabic Oration." In *Classical Arabic Humanities in Their Own Terms*, edited by Beatrice Gruendler, 176–273. Leiden: Brill, 2008.
Rad, Gerhard von. *Der Heilige Krieg im alten Israel.* 4th ed. Göttingen: Vandenhoeck & Ruprecht, 1965.
Rad, Gerhard von. *Weisheit in Israel.* Neukirchen: Neukirchener Verlag des Erziehungsvereins, 1970.
Rad, Gerhard von. *Wisdom in Israel.* Translated by James D. Martin. Nashville, Tennessee: Abingdon Press, 1972.
Radscheit, Matthias. "Word of God or Prophetic Speech? Reflections on the Qur'ānic *Qul*-statements." In *Encounters of Words and Texts: Intercultural Studies in Honor of Stefan Wild*, edited by Lutz Edzard and Christian Szyska, 33–42. Hildesheim: Georg Olms Verlag, 1997.
Rahman, Yusuf. "Ellipsis in the Qur'ān: A Study of Ibn Qutayba's *Ta'wīl Mushkil al-Qur'ān.*" In *Literary Structures of Religious Meaning in the Qur'ān*, edited by Issa J. Boullata, 277–91. New York: Routledge, 2000.

Räisänen, Heikki. *Marcion, Muḥammad and the Mahatma: Exegetical Perspectives on the Encounter of Cultures and Faiths.* London: SCM Press Ltd., 1997.

Ranke, Leopold von. *Geschichten der romanischen und germanischen Völker von 1494 bis 1514.* 3rd ed. Leipzig: Verlag von Duncker & Humblot, 1885.

al-Rāzī, Fakhr al-Dīn. *Tafsīr al-Fakhr al-Rāzī.* Vols. 26 and 28. Beirut: Dār al-Fikr, 1981.

Reimarus, Hermann Samuel. *Uebrige noch ungedruckte Werke des Wolfenbüttlischen Fragmentisten.* Berlin: s.n., 1787.

Rendtorff, Rolf. "Botenformel und Botenspruch." *ZAW* 74, no. 2 (1962): 165–77.

Repschinski, Boris. *The Controversy Stories in the Gospel of Matthew: Their Redaction, Form and Relevance for the Relationship between the Matthean Community and Formative Judaism.* Göttingen: Vandenhoeck & Ruprecht, 2000.

Reventlow, Henning Graf. *Epochen der Bibelauslegung.* Vol. 4. München: Verlag C.H. Beck, 2001.

Reventlow, Henning Graf. *History of Biblical Interpretation.* Vol. 4. Translated by Leo G. Perdue. Atlanta, Georgia: Society of Biblical Literature, 2010.

Reynolds, Gabriel Said. *The Emergence of Islam: Classical Traditions in Contemporary Perspective.* Minneapolis, Minnesota: Fortress Press, 2012.

Reynolds, Gabriel Said. "Introduction: The Golden Age of Qurʾānic Studies?" In *New Perspectives on the Qurʾān: The Qurʾān in Its Historical Context 2*, edited by idem, 1–21. New York: Routledge, 2011.

Reynolds, Gabriel Said. Introduction to *The Qurʾān Seminar Commentary / Le Qurʾān Seminar: A Collaborative Study of 50 Qurʾānic Passages / Commentaire collaboratif de 50 passages coraniques*, edited by idem, Mehdi Azaiez, Tommaso Tesei, Hamza M. Zafer, 1–12. Berlin: Walter de Gruyter, 2016.

Reynolds, Gabriel Said. "Le problème de la chronologie du Coran." *Arabica* 58 (2011): 477–502.

Reynolds, Gabriel Said. *The Qurʾān and Its Biblical Subtext.* New York: Routledge, 2010.

Reynolds, Gabriel Said. "Reading the Qurʾān as Homily: The Case of Sarah's Laughter." In *The Qurʾān in Context: Historical and Literary Investigations into the Qurʾānic Milieu*, edited by Angelika Neuwirth, Nicolai Sinai, and Michael Marx, 585–92. Leiden: Brill, 2011.

Richter, Gustav. *Der Sprachstil des Koran.* Leipzig: Otto Harrassowitz, 1940.

Richter, Wolfgang. *Exegese als Literaturwissenschaft: Entwurf einer alttestamentlichen Literaturtheorie und Methodologie.* Göttingen: Vandenhoeck & Ruprecht, 1971.

Ringe, Sharon H. *Luke.* Louisville, Kentucky: Westminster John Knox Press, 1995.

Rippin, Andrew L. Foreword to *Qurʾānic Studies: Sources and Methods of Scriptural Interpretation*, by John E. Wansbrough, ix–xix. Amherst, New York: Prometheus Books, 2004 [1977].

Rippin, Andrew L. Introduction to *Approaches to the History of the Interpretation of the Qurʾān*, edited by idem, 1–9. Oxford: Clarendon Press, 1988.

Rippin, Andrew L. "Literary Analysis of Qurʾān, Tafsīr, and Sīra: The Methodologies of John Wansbrough." In *Approaches to Islam in Religious Studies*, edited by Richard C. Martin, 151–63. Tucson, Arizona: The University of Arizona Press, 1985.

Rippin, Andrew L. "The Qurʾān as Literature: Perils, Pitfalls and Prospects." *BSMESB* 10, no. 1 (1983): 38–47.

Rippin, Andrew L. “The Qur'ānic *asbāb al-nuzūl* Material: An Analysis of Its Use and Development in Exegesis.” PhD diss., McGill University, 1981.
Rippin, Andrew L. “Reading the Qur'ān with Richard Bell.” *JAOS* 112, no. 4 (1992): 639–47.
Rippin, Andrew L. Review of *Studien zur Komposition der mekkanischen Suren*, by Angelika Neuwirth. *BSOAS* 45, no. 1 (1982): 149–50.
Rippin, Andrew L. “Studies in Qur'ānic Vocabulary: The Problem of the Dictionary.” In *New Perspectives on the Qur'ān: The Qur'ān in Its Historical Context 2*, edited by Gabriel Said Reynolds, 38–46. New York: Routledge, 2011.
Robinson, Neal. *Discovering the Qur'ān: A Contemporary Approach to a Veiled Text.* London: SCM Press Ltd., 1996.
Robinson, Neal. “Hands Outstretched: Towards a Re-reading of Sūrat al-Mā'ida.” *JQS* 3, no. 1 (2001): 1–19.
Rogerson, J.W. Review of *Exegese als Literaturwissenschaft: Entwurf einer alttestamentlichen Literaturtheorie und Methodologie*, by Wolfgang Richter. *JSS* 20, no. 1 (1975): 117–22.
Rollmann, Hans. “Theologie und Religionsgeschichte: Zeitgenössische Stimmen zur Diskussion um die religionsgeschichtliche Methode und die Einführung religionsgeschichtlicher Lehrstühle in den theologischen Fakultäten um die Jahrhundertwende.” *ZThK* 80, no. 1 (1983): 69–84.
Rollmann, Hans. “Zwei Briefe Hermann Gunkels an Adolf Jülicher zur religionsgeschichtlichen und formgeschichtlichen Methode.” *ZThK* 78, no. 3 (1981): 276–88.
Rubin, Uri. “Abū Lahab and Sūra CXI.” *BSOAS* 42, no. 1 (1979): 13–28.
Rylaarsdam, J. Coert. Foreword to *Form Criticism of the Old Testament*, by Gene M. Tucker, iii–viii. Philadelphia, Pennsylvania: Fortress Press, 1971.
The Sailors' Prayer Book. London: John Snow, 1852.
Saleh, Walid A. “The Etymological Fallacy and Qur'ānic Studies: Muḥammad, Paradise, and Late Antiquity.” In *The Qur'ān in Context: Historical and Literary Investigations into the Qur'ānic Milieu*, edited by Angelika Neuwirth, Nicolai Sinai, and Michael Marx, 649–98. Leiden: Brill, 2011.
Saleh, Walid A. “The Psalms in the Qur'ān and in the Islamic Religious Imagination.” In *The Oxford Handbook of the Psalms*, edited by William P. Brown, 281–96. Oxford: Oxford University Press, 2014.
Sapir, Edward. *Time Perspective in Aboriginal American Culture: A Study in Method.* Ottawa: Government Printing Bureau, 1916.
Schacht, Joseph. “A Reevaluation of Islamic Traditions.” *JRAS* 2 (1949): 143–54.
Scott, William C. *The Oral Nature of the Homeric Simile.* Leiden: E.J. Brill, 1974.
Segovia, Carlos A. *The Quranic Noah and the Making of the Islamic Prophet: A Study of Intertextuality and Religious Identity Formation in Late Antiquity.* Berlin: Walter de Gruyter, 2015.
Segre, Cesare. *Avviamento all'analisi del testo letterario.* Torino: Giulio Einaudi, 1985.
Segre, Cesare. *Introduction to the Analysis of the Literary Text.* Translated by John Meddemmen. Bloomington: Indiana University Press, 1988.
Seidensticker, Tilman. “Sources for the History of Pre-Islamic Religion.” In *The Qur'ān in Context: Historical and Literary Investigations into the Qur'ānic Milieu*, edited by Angelika Neuwirth, Nicolai Sinai, and Michael Marx, 293–321. Leiden: Brill, 2011.
Seidl, Theodor. “Die literaturwissenschaftliche Methode in der alttestamentlichen Exegese, Erträge – Erfahrungen – Projekte: Ein Überblick.” *MThZ* 40, no. 1 (1989): 27–37.

Sells, Michael. "A Literary Approach to the Hymnic Sūras of the Qur'ān: Spirit, Gender, and Aural Intertextuality." In *Literary Structures of Religious Meaning in the Qur'ān*, edited by Issa J. Boullata, 3–25. New York: Routledge, 2000.

Seybold, Klaus. *Die Psalmen: Eine Einführung*. Stuttgart: Verlag W. Kohlhammer, 1986.

Shahîd, Irfan. "*Fawātiḥ al-Suwar:* The Mysterious Letters of the Qur'ān." In *Literary Structures of Religious Meaning in the Qur'ān*, edited by Issa J. Boullata, 125–39. New York: Routledge, 2000.

Shakespeare, William. *As You Like It*. Edited by Cynthia Marshall. Cambridge: Cambridge University Press, 2004.

Shepherd, Charles E. *Theological Interpretation and Isaiah 53: A Critical Comparison of Bernhard Duhm, Brevard Childs, and Alec Motyer*. London: Bloomsbury T&T Clark, 2014.

Sherif, Faruq. *A Guide to the Contents of the Qur'ān*. London: Ithaca Press, 1985.

Sherlock, Thomas. *The Trial of the Witnesses of the Resurrection of Jesus*. Hartford, Connecticut: Lincoln & Gleason, 1804 [1729].

Sidersky, David. *Les origines des légendes musulmanes dans le Coran et dans les vies des prophètes*. Paris: Librairie orientaliste Paul Geuthner, 1933.

Sinai, Nicolai. *Fortschreibung und Auslegung: Studien zur frühen Koraninterpretation*. Wiesbaden: Harrassowitz Verlag, 2009.

Sinai, Nicolai. "The Qur'ān as Process." In *The Qur'ān in Context: Historical and Literary Investigations into the Qur'ānic Milieu*, edited by idem, Angelika Neuwirth, and Michael Marx, 407–39. Leiden: Brill, 2011.

Sinai, Nicolai, and Angelika Neuwirth. Introduction to *The Qur'ān in Context: Historical and Literary Investigations into the Qur'ānic Milieu*, edited by eadem and Michael Marx, 1–24. Leiden: Brill, 2011.

Sister, Moses. "Metaphern und Vergleiche im Koran." *MSOS* 34 (1931): 104–54.

Smith, Sidney. *Isaiah Chapters XL-LV: Literary Criticism and History*. London: Oxford University Press, 1944.

Smith, William Robertson. *Lectures on the Religion of the Semites: The Fundamental Institutions*. 3rd ed. New York: The Macmillan Company, 1927.

Soulen, Richard N. *Handbook of Biblical Criticism*. 2nd rev. ed. Atlanta, Georgia: John Knox Press, 1981.

Sparks, Kenton L. "Genre Criticism." In *Methods for Exodus*, edited by Thomas B. Dozeman, 55–94. Cambridge: Cambridge University Press, 2010.

Speyer, Heinrich. *Die biblischen Erzählungen im Qoran*. Darmstadt: Wissenschaftliche Buchgesellschaft, 1961.

Spies, Otto. Foreword to *Der Sprachstil des Koran*, by Gustav Richter, v–vii. Leipzig: Otto Harrassowitz, 1940.

Steck, Odil Hannes. *Exegese des Alten Testaments: Leitfaden der Methodik*. 12th rev. ed. Neukirchen: Neukirchener Verlag, 1989.

Stewart, Devin J. "Divine Epithets and the *Dibacchius: Clausulae* and Qur'ānic Rhythm." *JQS* 15, no. 2 (2013): 22–64.

Stewart, Devin J. "The Mysterious Letters and Other Formal Features of the Qur'ān in Light of Greek and Babylonian Oracular Texts." In *New Perspectives on the Qur'ān: The Qur'ān in Its Historical Context 2*, edited by Gabriel Said Reynolds, 323–48. New York: Routledge, 2011.

Stewart, Devin J. "Reflections on the State of the Art in Western Qur'ānic Studies." In *Islam and Its Past: Jahiliyya, Late Antiquity, and the Qur'ān*, edited by Carol Bakhos and Michael Cook, 4–68. Oxford: Oxford University Press, 2017.

Stewart, Devin J. "Understanding the Qur'ān in English: Notes on Translation, Form, and Prophetic Typology." In *Diversity in Language: Contrastive Studies in English and Arabic Theoretical and Applied Linguistics*, edited by Zeinab Ibrahim, Nagwa Kassabgy, and Sabiha Aydelott, 31–48. Cairo: The American University of Cairo Press, 2000.

Stewart, Devin J. "Wansbrough, Bultmann, and the Theory of Variant Traditions in the Qur'ān." In *Qur'ānic Studies Today*, edited by Angelika Neuwirth and Michael A. Sells, 17–51. New York: Routledge, 2016.

Stuart, Douglas. *Old Testament Exegesis.* 2nd rev. ed. Philadelphia, Pennsylvania: The Westminster Press, 1980.

Sweeney, Marvin A. "Form and Eschatology in the Book of the Twelve Prophets." In *The Book of the Twelve and the New Form Criticism*, edited by Mark J. Boda, Michael H. Floyd, and Colin M. Toffelmire, 137–61. Atlanta, Georgia: SBL Press, 2015.

Sweeney, Marvin A. *Isaiah 1–39 with an Introduction to Prophetic Literature. FOTL* 16. Grand Rapids, Michigan: Wm. B. Eerdmans Publishing Company, 1996.

Sweeney, Marvin A. "The Prophets and the Prophetic Books, Prophetic Circles and Traditions – New Trends, Including Religio-psychological Aspects." In *Hebrew Bible / Old Testament: The History of Its Interpretation*, vol. 3, pt. 2, edited by Magne Sæbø, 500–30. Göttingen: Vandenhoeck & Ruprecht, 2015.

al-Ṭabarī, Muḥammad b. Jarīr. *Tafsīr al-Ṭabarī: Jāmiʿ al-bayān ʿan taʾwīl al-Qurʾān.* Vol. 1. 2nd ed. Edited by Maḥmūd Muḥammad Shākir and Aḥmad Muḥammad Shākir. Cairo: Maktabat Ibn Taymiyya, s.a.

Taft, Robert F. *The Great Entrance: A History of the Transfer of Gifts and Other Pre-anaphoral Rites of the Liturgy of St. John Chrysostom. OCA* 200. Roma: Pont. Institutum Studiorum Orientalium, 1975.

Taft, Robert F. *A History of the Liturgy of St. John Chrysostom.* Vol. 5: The Precommunion Rites. *OCA* 261. Roma: Pontificio Istituto Orientale, 2000.

The Targum to the Five Megilloth. Edited by Bernard Grossfeld. New York: Hermon Press, 1973.

Tenney, Merrill C. *New Testament Survey.* Revised by Walter M. Dunnett. Grand Rapids, Michigan: Wm. B. Eerdmans Publishing Company, 1985.

Terrien, Samuel. *The Psalms: Strophic Structure and Theological Commentary.* Grand Rapids, Michigan: Wm. B. Eerdmans Publishing Company, 2003.

Thackston, Wheeler M. *An Introduction to Koranic and Classical Arabic.* Bethesda, Maryland: Ibex Publishers, 2000.

Thomson, Clive. "Bakhtin's 'Theory' of Genre." *STCL* 9, no. 1 (1984): 29–40.

Travis, Stephen H. "Form Criticism." In *New Testament Interpretation: Essays on Principles and Methods*, edited by I. Howard Marshall, 153–64. Grand Rapids, Michigan: Wm. B. Eerdmans Publishing Company, 1977.

Tucker, Gene M. *Form Criticism of the Old Testament.* Philadelphia, Pennsylvania: Fortress Press, 1971.

Tucker, Jeffrey T. *Example Stories: Perspectives on Four Parables in the Gospel of Luke.* Sheffield, England: Sheffield Academic Press, 1998.

Underhill, Evelyn. *Worship.* New York: Harper & Brothers Publishers, 1957 [1936].

Van de Sandt, Huub, and David Flusser. *The Didache: Its Jewish Sources and Its Place in Early Judaism and Christianity.* Minneapolis, Minnesota: Fortress Press, 2002.
Van der Lugt, Pieter. *Cantos and Strophes in Biblical Hebrew Poetry with Special Reference to the First Book of the Psalter.* Vol. 1. Leiden: Brill, 2006.
Van Grol, Harm W.M. "Psalm, Psalter, and Prayer." In *Prayer from Tobit to Qumran*, edited by Renate Egger-Wenzel and Jeremy Corley, 41–70. Berlin: Walter de Gruyter, 2004.
Vermes, Geza. "Bible and Midrash: Early Old Testament Exegesis." In *The Cambridge History of the Bible*, edited by Peter R. Ackroyd, 199–231. Vol. 1. Cambridge: Cambridge University Press, 1970.
Vivante, Paolo. *The Epithets in Homer: A Study in Poetic Values.* New Haven, Connecticut: Yale University Press, 1982.
Voltaire. *Œuvres de Voltaire.* Vol. 15. Edited by M. Beuchot. Paris: Chez Lefèvre, 1829.
Wagtendonk, Kees. *Fasting in the Koran.* Leiden: E.J. Brill, 1968.
Wansbrough, John E. *Qurʾānic Studies: Sources and Methods of Scriptural Interpretation.* Amherst, New York: Prometheus Books, 2004 [1977].
Watt, W. Montgomery. *Early Islam: Collected Articles.* Edinburgh: Edinburgh University Press, 1990.
Watters, William R. *Formula Criticism and the Poetry of the Old Testament.* Berlin: Walter de Gruyter, 1976.
Weidinger, Karl. *Die Haustafeln: Ein Stück urchristlicher Paränese.* Leipzig: J.C. Hinrichs'sche Buchhandlung, 1928.
Weil, Gustav. *Historisch-kritische Einleitung in den Koran.* 2nd rev. ed. Bielefeld: Verlag von Velhagen & Klasing, 1878.
Welch, Alford T. "Allāh and Other Supernatural Beings: The Emergence of the Qurʾānic Doctrine of Tawḥīd." In *Studies in Qurʾān and Tafsīr*, edited by idem, 733–58. Chico, California: American Academy of Religion, 1979.
Welch, Alford T. "Formulaic Features of the Punishment-Stories." In *Literary Structures of Religious Meaning in the Qurʾān*, edited by Issa J. Boullata, 77–116. New York: Routledge, 2000.
Weren, Wim. *Windows on Jesus: Methods in Gospel Exegesis* [*Vensters op Jezus: Methoden in de uitleg van de evangeliën*]. Translated by John Bowden. Harrisburg, Pennsylvania: Trinity Press International, 1999.
Wesselhoeft, Kirsten M. Yoder. "Making Muslim Minds: Question and Answer as a Genre of Moral Reasoning in an Urban French Mosque." *JAAR* 78, no. 3 (2010): 790–823.
Westermann, Claus. *Basic Forms of Prophetic Speech.* Translated by Hugh Clayton White. Philadelphia, Pennsylvania: The Westminster Press, 1967.
Westermann, Claus. *Grundformen prophetischer Rede.* München: Chr. Kaiser Verlag, 1960.
Westermann, Claus. Introduction to *Ausgewählte Psalmen*, 11–24. Translated and commented on by idem. Göttingen: Vandenhoeck & Ruprecht, 1984.
Westermann, Claus. *Das Loben Gottes in den Psalmen.* 2nd rev. ed. Göttingen: Vandenhoeck & Ruprecht, 1961.
Westermann, Claus. *Praise and Lament in the Psalms.* Translated by Keith R. Crim and Richard N. Soulen. Atlanta, Georgia: John Knox Press, 1981.
Westermann, Claus. *The Promises to the Fathers: Studies on the Patriarchal Narratives.* Translated by David E. Green. Philadelphia, Pennsylvania: Fortress Press, 1980.

Westermann, Claus. *The Psalms: Structure, Content, and Message.* Translated by Ralph D. Gehrke. Minneapolis, Minnesota: Augsburg Publishing House, 1980.

Westermann, Claus. *Der Psalter.* Stuttgart: Calwer Verlag, 1967.

Westermann, Claus. *Die Verheißungen an die Väter: Studien zur Vätergeschichte.* Göttingen: Vandenhoeck & Ruprecht, 1976.

Westermann, Claus. *What Does the Old Testament Say about God?* Edited by Friedemann W. Golka. Atlanta: John Knox Press, 1979.

White, Hayden V. "Introduction: On History and Historicisms." In *From History to Sociology: The Transition in German Historical Thinking*, by Carlo Antoni, xv–xxviii. Detroit, Michigan: Wayne State University Press, 1959.

White, Monica. *Military Saints in Byzantium and Rus, 900–1200.* Cambridge: Cambridge University Press, 2013.

Whybray, Roger N. *The Intellectual Tradition in the Old Testament.* Berlin: Walter de Gruyter, 1974.

Whybray, Roger N. *The Making of the Pentateuch: A Methodological Study.* Sheffield, England: JSOT Press, 1987.

Wilson, Gerald Henry. *The Editing of the Hebrew Psalter.* Chico, California: Scholars Press, 1985.

Wilson, Lindsay. *Joseph, Wise and Otherwise: The Intersection of Wisdom and Covenant in Genesis 37–50.* Eugene, Oregon: Wipf & Stock Publishers, 2004.

Wilson, Walter T. *The Mysteries of Righteousness: The Literary Composition and Genre of the Sentences of Pseudo-Phocylides.* Tübingen: Verlag von J.C.B. Mohr (Paul Siebeck), 1994.

Wolff, Hans Walter. *Amos' geistige Heimat.* Neukirchen: Neukirchener Verlag, 1964.

Wolterstorff, Nicholas. *Divine Discourse.* Cambridge: Cambridge University Press, 1995.

Woolston, Thomas. *A Discourse on the Miracles of Our Saviour.* 2nd ed. London: s.n., 1727.

Woolston, Thomas. *A Free-Gift to the Clergy.* London: s.n., 1722.

Wulff, David M. *Psychology of Religion.* New York: John Wiley & Sons, 1991.

al-Zamakhsharī. *al-Kashshāf.* Vol. 1. Edited by W. Nassau Lees. Calcutta: W. Nassau Lees, 1856.

al-Zarkashī, Badr al-Dīn. *al-Burhān fī ʿulūm al-Qurʾān.* Vol. 2. Beirut: Dār al-Kutub al-ʿIlmiyya, 1988.

Zimmermann, Ruben. *Puzzling the Parables of Jesus: Methods and Interpretation.* Minneapolis, Minnesota: Fortress Press, 2015.

Subject Index

Anacrusis 120
Anecdotal Formula 177
Annunciation 219, 221
Aphorism 159, 176, 180 f.

Blessing Formula 142, 168, 220 f.
Bu'd Formula 208, 216

Canon Criticism 17–22
Cantilena 84
Catchword 94, 103, 105
Commission Formula 183 f., 203, 207 f., 230
Community Formation 30, 34, 269
Community Rule 228, 232–234, 269
Composition Criticism 16
Contextual Prayer 32, 54, 61, 81
Controversy Dialogue 211, 217
Conveyance Formula 33, 152, 168, 170
Cult-functional Method 13 f., 49

Debate Formula 201, 209, 211, 214, 217, 229, 238
Deictic Formula 33, 145, 172
Dialogic Formula 140, 164, 166, 177
Didactic Formula 125 f., 138 f., 145, 152, 162
Divine Imperative 230 f.
Doxological Formulae 32, 81, 93 f., 101
Doxology 51, 80, 88, 93, 95 f., 101, 111, 122, 141 f.

Emissarial Formula 230
Episode Divider 191, 216
Epistolary Formula 53
Eschatological Formula 29, 123
Eschatological Victory 117
Eschatological War 264
Eschatology 23, 29, 94, 123, 148, 167, 212, 229
Exempla 182, 192, 209, 225, 273
Expository Formula 138, 161, 168

Form Criticism 8–17, 20–24, 26, 32, 82 f., 129, 272 f., 276, 278–280
Formula Criticism 17
Formula for Admonition 131
Formula for Exhortation 132
Formula of Incomparability 103
Formula of Legitimation 188, 230
Formula of Liturgical Praise 32, 94
Functional Criticism 15, 56 f.

Genre Criticism 1, 3, 5, 10 f., 13 f., 16 f., 19, 22–26, 35, 272, 275, 278, 280
Genre History 23 f., 26, 272–280

Hagiography 7 f., 29, 221, 272 f.
Historical Aesthetics 3 f., 11 f., 25, 28 f., 35, 277
Historical Criticism 2–6, 10 f., 27, 119, 272, 274–276
History of Interpretation 7
History of Literature 5, 11, 13, 25 f., 278
History of Religion 2 f., 5, 11, 20, 83, 272
Household Code Formula 155

Imperative Formulae 129, 231
Imperative Hymn 98 f., 120
Inclusio 170, 208
Interrogative Formula 187
Interrogatory Framework 126
Introitus 49–54

Kadhdhabat Formula 190 f.
Katēchēsis 131, 161, 192
Kērygma 131, 192

Lament Formula 73
Literary Criticism 4 f., 7, 10 f., 14–18, 23
Liturgical Forms
– Hymn to Creation 32, 102–105, 108
– Hymn to the Creator of Humanity 105 f.
– Hymn to the Creator of the World 106–108
– Hymn to God 32, 92, 99–102, 121
– Hymn to the God of Salvation 110–114
– Hymn to the God of Salvation History 108–110
– Hymn to Victory 32, 115–118

– Litany of Lament 23, 33, 118, 125–129
– Litany of Praise 33, 118–125, 129
Liturgical Imperative 86, 91, 94, 97
Liturgical Instructions 41, 95, 97
Liturgy Formulary 32, 85–96, 101 f., 107, 122, 129
Localization 62, 65, 85, 111 f., 208, 230
Logia 9–11, 30, 130

Messenger Formula 188, 230
Messenger Speech 131, 228–230, 232
Meta-prayer 48 f.
Motif Criticism 32, 34, 60, 94, 102, 106, 108, 110, 112, 117, 124 f., 127, 129, 183, 201, 204, 212, 216, 218

Narrative Criticism 193
Narrative Forms
– Anecdote 193 f.
– Controversy Story 33, 178, 192, 200 f., 208
– Episode 33, 41, 62, 64, 66, 175 f., 182–191, 205, 207–225
– Example Story 33, 176, 180, 201 f., 225
– Historical Story 184, 206 f.
– Legend 20, 33 f., 175 f., 182, 184 f., 192 f., 204, 207–209
– Parable 21, 29, 33, 176, 191 f., 195 f., 199, 202, 225, 270
– Paradigm 33, 177 f., 180 f., 192, 196–200, 203, 225, 257
– Report 33, 175 f., 182, 184, 188, 202 f., 206
– Saga 33 f., 41, 62, 64, 66, 137, 175 f., 183, 185, 190 f., 193, 209, 211–225
– Similitude 33, 149, 176–180, 194 f.
– Summary Report 190, 203–207, 225
Narrative Formulary 55, 157, 177–191, 200, 205, 219, 222
Narrative Framework 186, 205

Oath 23, 28, 52–54, 73
Oath Formula 49, 52
Oral Formulary 116, 181, 190 f., 199, 244

Parable Formula 180
Paraenetic Catalogue 133, 152, 208 f.
Paraenetic Formula 132
Paraenetic Framework 209
Parallelism 124
Performative Marker 32, 97
Praise Formulae 76–78, 81, 93–96, 100, 102, 111
Prayer Forms
– Complaint Prayer 32, 71–73, 222
– Conversational Prayer 32, 54–61, 71
– Imprecatory Prayer 32, 74–76
– Penitential Prayer 32, 67–71
– Petitionary Prayer 47, 61–67, 71, 73, 211
– Praise Prayer 32, 76–81
– Rhetorical Prayer 32, 81 f.
Prayer Formulary 15, 32, 36–44, 47, 49, 65, 76, 81, 85, 111, 202, 211, 251
Prayer Protocol 246, 253
Prayer Setting
– Corporate Prayer 32, 39, 44–54, 64, 81, 85, 238
– Domestic Prayer 32, 44–47
– Private Prayer 32, 39, 44–47, 65, 68–70, 80–82, 86
Predication
– Divine Predication 76, 86, 94, 105, 107
– Divine Self-predication 229
– Dynamic Predication 92, 121
– Essential Predication 39, 91, 93
– Relative Predication 87, 91, 93
Proclamation Formulary 143, 227–232, 234, 252
Prose Prayer 14 f., 46, 55, 65
Protocol Formulae 97–100
Protocol Hymn 97 f.
Psalm Criticism 1, 13–15, 19, 21 f., 24 f., 34 f., 44–46, 84, 98 f., 104, 115, 274 f.

Reception Criticism 6–8
Redaction Criticism 16, 20
Refrain 64, 85, 99, 101, 103, 108 f., 112, 114, 116, 118 f., 121–125, 169, 182, 190, 210, 212 f., 216, 223
Regulatory Forms
– Rules of Authority 241–244
– Rules of Exclusion 236–241
– Rules of Inclusion 233–236
– Rules of Matrimony 260–262, 269

- Rules of Order 250–253
- Rules of Property 256–260
- Rules of Propriety 253–256
- Rules of Punishment 263, 269
- Rules of Purity 244–247
- Rules of Ritual 247–250, 269
- Rules of War 264–269
Repurposing 51, 53, 95
Response Formula 119
Ritual Protocol 54, 97
Ritual Text 173

Salvation History 108, 110, 192, 272 f.
Schemata 34, 195
Schematic Formulation 190, 208, 212 f., 216
Sermon Formulae 141, 143, 168, 174
Simile 149, 176
Simile Marker 178
Similitude Formulae 178–180
Single Response Prayer 32, 54, 61–63, 67
Sitz im Leben 4, 12–16, 21, 26, 28, 32, 35, 44–54, 97 f., 104, 116, 119, 129, 144 f., 191–193, 232, 271, 277, 279
Soteriology 124
Source Criticism 10, 17, 275
Speech-act 66, 97
Stylized Formulation 132 f., 184, 186, 213, 221
Substitution Formulae 40, 132, 181, 183, 185, 190, 198, 214, 223
Sumbolon 53 f.
Summons 95–99, 103, 106, 110–112, 114, 116, 120, 152

Tafsīr 6–8, 11, 26, 28, 50, 175, 179, 270, 277
Tendency Criticism 9, 279
Textual Criticism 16, 22
Theonym 51 f., 101 f., 114, 244 f., 276, 278
Topoi 66, 207 f.
Tradition Criticism 276
Transition Formula 183 f., 190, 200
Typology 60

Unrecorded Prayer 49, 54, 63

Vocative Formulae 34, 37, 86, 122, 131–135, 137, 143–145, 184, 195, 208, 227–232, 251, 269

Wisdom Forms
- Admonition 33, 131 f., 146–151, 174, 226, 270
- Code 133–135, 154 f., 174
- Conversation 137, 157 f.
- Exhortation 132, 151 f., 174, 226, 270
- Instruction 163–168
- Lecture 145, 158–160, 174
- Lesson 138, 145, 161–163
- Oracle 125 f., 135 f., 155 f.
- Paraenesis 132 f., 152 f.
- Sermon 19, 30 f., 33, 82, 129–132, 141, 143–145, 168–174, 192
Wisdom Formulary 33, 131–144, 174
Woe Formula 125 f., 135 f., 155 f.

www.ingramcontent.com/pod-product-compliance
Lightning Source LLC
Chambersburg PA
CBHW030608230426
43661CB00053B/1892